The Author as Character

Being

The true Hiſtory of the Play of *Pericles*, as it was
lately preſented by the worthy and an-
cient Poet *John Gower*.

John   *Gower.*

AT LONDON.
Printed by T.P. *for* Nat:Butter
1 6 0 8.

John Gower as the poet-narrator of the Pericles story (From the title page of George
Wilkins, *The Painfull Aduentures of Pericles, Prince of Tyre*, 1608).

The Author as Character

Representing Historical Writers in Western Literature

Edited by
Paul Franssen
and Ton Hoenselaars

Madison • Teaneck
Fairleigh Dickinson University Press
London: Associated University Presses

Associated University Presses
440 Forsgate Drive
Cranbury, NJ 08512

Associated University Presses
16 Barter Street
London WC1A 2AH, England

Associated University Presses
P.O. Box 338, Port Credit
Mississauga, Ontario
Canada L5G 4L8

The paper used in this publication meets the requirements
of the American National Standard for Permanence of Paper
for Printed Library Materials Z39.48-1984.

Library of Congress Cataloging-in-Publication Data

The author as character : representing historical writers in western
    literature / edited by Paul Franssen and Ton Hoenselaars.
        p.   cm.
    Includes bibliographical references and index.
    ISBN 0-8386-3786-8 (alk. paper)
    1. Literature, Modern—History and criticism.   2. Authors in
literature.   I. Franssen, Paul, 1955–   .   II. Hoenselaars, Ton,
1956–   .
PN56.5.A84A88   1999
809'.933528—dc21   98-33962
                                                                          CIP

*This book is dedicated
to the memory of*

**Anthony Burgess
1917–1993**

Contents

8   CONTENTS

Acknowledgments

Preparing this volume has been a pleasure with the liberal support of a number of people. Ieme van der Poel, Hans Hoenselaars, David Rijser, Linda Chown, Marijke Keitz, Harald Hendrix, and Erik Kooper have been most generous with their suggestions and advice.

Several people have read drafts of the manuscript or parts of it. Charles K. Haga read several early chapters with a critical eye, and Gene M. Moore wielded his red pen with generosity. Kristine Steenbergh read the entire manuscript, and helped to prepare the index; her incisive but also witty comments in the margin have prevented many an error. Responsibility for any remaining textual errors is ours alone.

We are grateful to Cordon Art (Baarn, The Netherlands) for permission to reproduce M. C. Escher's "Drawing Hands," and to Princeton University Library for permission to show F. Scott Fitzgerald in drag.

It may not be customary to acknowledge one's contributors and to thank them for their efforts. However, nothing much would have come of our original idea without their unflinching confidence at all stages of the project. We regret that Amy van Marken did not live to see the completion of the volume, but we comfort ourselves with the thought that she would have liked the final result.

Introduction. The Author as Character: Defining a Genre

PAUL FRANSSEN and TON HOENSELAARS

Novels, short stories, and movies about real-life, historical authors are currently very popular. Usually it is the great canonical writers who have become subjects in the works of their successors, but there are exceptions; some lesser writers have also received this tribute if their lives were or could be made to appear romantic. Anthony Burgess has on various occasions evoked the characters of Shakespeare, John Keats, and Christopher Marlowe, whereas Robin Chapman has more modestly given a new lease of life to a less famous Elizabethan dramatist, Thomas Kyd.[1] In Chapman's detective-like novel *Christopherus,* Kyd survives his ordeal of interrogation and imprisonment considerably longer than did the historical Kyd.[2] Peter Ackroyd has painted a full-length portrait of *Chatterton* (1988), the eighteenth-century poet and forger, and included vignettes of a number of English authors and artists in his *English Music* (1992).[3] Yet it is usually the great and famous whose lives are portrayed again and again. Lord Byron is the protagonist of a fictional biography by Sigrid Combüchen;[4] Alfred Lord Tennyson's male bonding with A.H.H. has been deconstructed in a serious story by A. S. Byatt, and Lynne Truss has poked elaborate fun at Tennyson and the sexual mores of an entire group of Victorians, including Charles Dodgson (better known as Lewis Carroll).[5]

The prevalence of real historical authors in recent fiction might suggest that this is somehow a postmodern phenomenon. In a paradox that is further explored by Aleid Fokkema in her contribution to this volume, the very postmodernism that proclaimed the death of the author and the demise of character delights in resurrecting historical authors as characters. This device offers a lively, economical way of not only raising but actually embodying such postmodern concerns as representation, the (im)possibility of historical knowledge, the share of the author in the genesis of a text, and intertextuality. The genre of the author as character may speak to

11

our postmodern world and help articulate the issues that concern us more than previous generations, but it is by no means restricted to recent times. The need for an author to come to terms with his illustrious predecessors is perennial; consequently, through the ages, older authors have often been resurrected in a variety of forms, from epic to lyric poetry, from prose narrative to drama.

A very early instance may well be the blind bard of the Phaeacians, Demodocus, in the eighth book of Homer's *Odyssey*.[6] Plato deployed two real-life dramatists in his *Symposium,* Agathon and Aristophanes, and was evidently aiming at fiction rather than a documentary account.[7] Aristophanes, of course, had introduced Socrates as a character in *The Clouds,* Euripides and Agathon in *Thesmorphoriazusae,* and Euripides and Aeschylus in *The Frogs.* The Roman poet Virgil's ghost haunts medieval literature, lending an aura of *auctoritas* to the post-classical poet.

Renaissance literature did not limit itself to the poet of the *Aeneid* and the *Eclogues,* even though it retained a preference for classical authors as characters. Plato himself is a speaker in Thomas Elyot's polemical dialogue *Of the Knowledge which Maketh a Wise Man* (1533).[8] Blind Homer came to serve as a choric figure in Thomas Heywood's three plays *The Golden Age* (1611), *The Silver Age* (1613), and *The Brazen Age* (1613), ironically introducing the theater audience to staged scenes from Greek history and myth that Homer, as he himself acknowledges, could not see.[9] The same Ben Jonson who attributed to Shakespeare his "small Latine, and lesse Greeke" mobilized Horace as his poetic model in the War of the Theaters, the quarrel over literary quality that raged in London at the turn of the sixteenth century. Jonson's *Poetaster* is also peopled by Propertius, Virgil, and Ovid. For Shakespeare, a single Roman author as character sufficed, in *Julius Caesar,* where Cinna the poet is mistaken for Cinna the conspirator and subsequently is assassinated. This case of bardicide, resulting from a confusion of the poet with the politician, continues to be reinterpreted with each new generation of critics, and has produced challenging criticism in recent years.[10]

A native canonical poet as Chorus figure may be found in Shakespeare's *Pericles,* which is narrated by the British poet Gower:

> To sing a song that old was sung,
> From ashes ancient Gower is come,
> Assuming man's infirmities,
> To glad your ear, and please your eyes.[11]

In 1608, George Wilkins tried to capitalize on the play's popularity with his novel *The Painful Adventures of Pericles Prince of Tyre.* The title page of the novel (see frontispiece) was not to carry the title, but a woodcut of John Gower with the words: "Being The true History of the Play of *Pericles,* as it was lately presented by the worthy and ancient Poet *John Gower.*"[12] To English audiences, Gower was not the only exemplary native poet. In Ben Jonson's 1616 masque *The Golden Age Restored,* one of the conditions for the return to earth of Astraea is that she be accompanied by poets. These include Geoffrey Chaucer, John Gower, John Lydgate, and Edmund Spenser, who duly appear as characters.[13]

The early modern period was particularly aware of the possibilities offered by the author as character, whether classical, medieval, or contemporary. Thus, Louise Labé mingled her own voice with that of Sappho, albeit in part via Ovid's *Heroides.* Sappho was popular, indeed, with early modern poets, though not always for her poetry: in John Lyly's *Sapho and Phao,* no reference is made to the poetic skills of this unrequited lover.[14] Another notable Renaissance instance of the author as character is that of Niccolò Machiavelli, who, in his discussion of the proper dialect for Italian vernacular literature, himself entered into "A Dialogue on Language" with Dante.[15]

The form adopted by Machiavelli—the dialogue of the dead—was to flourish especially in the eighteenth century. Numerous authors practiced the genre, modeling themselves largely on the work of Lucian of Samosata, whose satirical intent (Menippus was a frequent speaker) appealed to the age. Eighteenth-century practitioners—including Lord Littleton, Bernard le Bovier de Fontenelle, François de Salignac de la Mothe-Fénelon, Sir Fleetwood Sheppard, William King, Matthew Prior, and Elizabeth Montagu—in their dialogues revived authors ranging from Plutarch, Michel de Montaigne, and Sir Thomas More to Joseph Addison, Samuel Johnson, James Boswell, Samuel Richardson, and Henry Fielding.[16] The dialogue of the dead had a long tradition before it flourished in the eighteenth century, and it has been practiced ever since. The most prolific author in the genre during the romantic period was Sir Walter Savage Landor. Six of the ten volumes that make up his complete works consist of dialogues of the dead, or "Imaginary Conversations," as he himself termed them. International authors who make their appearance as characters in Landor's work include not only Lucian himself, but also Plato, Epictetus, Seneca, Dante, Boccaccio, Petrarch, Edmund Spenser, Sir Philip Sidney, Jean de la Fontaine, François de la Rochefoucauld, Jean-Jacques Rousseau, and Robert Southey. Interestingly, Landor also takes part in the dialogues, thus creating a curious tension between the modesty of his allegation, "I claim no place in the world of letters" and the immodesty of his character's claim:

> I have since written what no tide
> Shall ever wash away, what men
> Unborn shall read o'er ocean wide.[17]

The dialogue of the dead continues to flourish as a genre. In recent years, imaginary conversations between Samuel Johnson and G. K. Chesterton and between Antonin Artaud and Alain Robbe-Grillet have achieved printed status in scholarly journals.[18] Roger Scruton's *Xanthippic Dialogues* (1993) features Plato and Aristotle in conversation with marginalized members of the opposite sex: Socrates' wife Xanthippe and Plato's mother Perictione.[19]

Toward the end of the eighteenth century, a sharp rise may be witnessed in French stage plays featuring authors as characters. As Eric H. Kadler has shown in the only full-length study of the author as character, the period between 1784 and 1834 proved extremely fertile.[20] Between the mid-seventeenth century and the year 1784, only seven original plays with dramatizations of literary figures were recorded. Up to that time, French audiences had been able to enjoy an anonymous comedy like *Boileau, ou la Clémence de Colbert* (1664), or plays on Molière, including *L'Abjuration du magistrat* (1670) by his enemy Le Boulanger de Chalussay, Carlo Goldoni's *Il Molière* (1751), and Pietro Chiari's *Molière marito geloso* (1759). To the early period in France also belong Count Marsollier's *Beaumarchais à Madrid* (1774), performed with Beaumarchais himself present in the audience, as well as the 1782 French translation of Goethe's early play, *Clavigo,* also featuring the author of *The Marriage of Figaro.* Between 1784 and 1834, however, nearly two hundred plays were added to the list (Kadler, 2).

Thanks to the work of Kadler, one is in a position to recognize a pattern, a degree of canon formation. Molière was to remain the most popular author to serve as a stage character, perhaps because he had been a playwright himself. Twenty plays during this period took him as the principal character, while Voltaire inspired fourteen and Jean-Jacques Rousseau only seven by dramatists who themselves seem to have no other claim to fame. Two hundred plays in France were devoted to French writers, but only twelve dealt with foreigners like Cervantes (1794), Sterne (1800), Fielding

(1800 and 1823), Shakespeare (1804), Milton (1804), Sir Walter
Scott (1827), and Lord Byron (1834). However fictional the author
as character may be, a certain degree of audience acquaintance
with the subject seems a prerequisite for the dramatist. The discrepancy in the figures for natives and foreigners may also be patriotic. Whatever the reason, in this period at least, the author as
character does not appear to have traveled well between different
national literatures.

In the nineteenth century, the *vie romancée,* or fictional biography, came into its own, frequently taking the lives of historical
authors as its subject. Full-length novels of fulsome bardolatry
were produced on Shakespeare's life, some of them far removed
from what is known of the real dramatist, by otherwise obscure
authors such as John Boyd Thacher, Robert F. Williams, Emma
Severn, Captain Henry Curling, and Nathan Drake.[21] In his short
story, "A Lodging for the Night," Robert Louis Stevenson depicts
a fictitious François Villon as scrounging for his next meal, thus
perpetuating a literary tradition which, as Jelle Koopmans illustrates in his contribution to the present volume, dates from the
late Middle Ages.[22] In Holland, Arthur van Schendel followed suit
with *Shakespeare* (1910) and *Verlaine* (1927).[23] The *vie romancée*
became immensely popular, and it is still being practiced in works
such as Ursula Bloom's *The Romance of Charles Dickens,* Joan
Walker's Sheridan novel *Marriage of Harlequin,* Irving Stone's
Sailor on Horseback (about Jack London), Kay McKemy's *Samuel
Pepys of the Navy,* and Virginia Westervelt's novel, *Pearl Buck.*[24]

A variant on the *vie romancée* is the *vie imaginaire* developed
by the versatile French medievalist and poet, Marcel Schwob. Historical fact is almost completely abandoned in the *vie imaginaire.*[25]
Historiography, Schwob argued, leaves one in doubt about the individual. The individual as presented in history, he argued, is always
related to general events, and the writer or reader ought to be
granted the license to imagine, on the basis of the facts and shreds
of evidence, what may well have been true even if it was never
recorded by historians.[26] Schwob's *Vies imaginaires* (first published in Paris in 1896) make up a most peculiar collection, including the imaginary lives of the poets Lucretius and Petronius, of
Dante's rather obscure and frustrated contemporary, Paolo Uccello (born in Sienna on the same day as the poet of the *Divine
Comedy*), and of the playwright Cyril Tourneur, long assumed to
have been the author of that Jacobean orgy of sex and violence
entitled *The Revenger's Tragedy* (1607).[27] Schwob's dauntless allegation that "Cyril Tourneur was born of a union between an un-

known God and a prostitute" in 1929 led the prominent
Shakespearean scholar Allardyce Nicoll to note that "This maca-
bre conception, frankly fantastic as it may be, perhaps conceals
within its fantasy more than a fragment of truth."[28]

The *vie romancée* reached its apogee in the twentieth century
with such monumental works as Thomas Mann's *The Beloved Returns* (1939) about Charlotte Buff Kestner's meeting with her erst-
while lover, now the established genius known as Goethe.[29] No less
monumental is Hermann Broch's *The Death of Virgil*, over which
hangs not only the shadow of the classical author, but also that
of Dante, who had himself deployed Virgil as a character.[30] The
possibility of juxtaposing a twentieth-century Virgil with a late medieval one was irresistible, so that we have included here a study
of Broch's novel, by Jattie Enklaar, as well as one of Dante's poem
by Chris Kleinhenz. Other great biographical novels that deserve
mention here are Hella Haasse's *In a Dark Wood Wandering,* about
the medieval French poet and politician Charles d'Orléans, discussed in our volume by Martijn Rus;[31] and Robert Graves's *Wife
to Mr. Milton.*[32]

Despite the immense popularity of the *vie romancée*—perhaps
even more where composers are characters—the genre never had
a monopoly. Ezra Pound chose the poetic monologue to establish
his affinity with Propertius.[33] It was drama in particular, though,
that formed an alternative, often popular outlet for representations
of writers from the past. In the mid-nineteenth century, George
Sand chose to represent the national French playwright Molière
in dramatic form, as Rudolf Besier was to do with the Brownings
in 1930.[34] One is tempted to attribute the continuing popularity of
Savinien Cyrano de Bergerac (1619–55) to his appearance as the
protagonist of Edmond Rostand's *Cyrano de Bergerac* (1897). Anthony Burgess, the twentieth-century creator of the author as character par excellence, readapted and retranslated this play for the
American stage.[35] Meanwhile, Cyrano de Bergerac has come to
acquire generic status, to the detriment of his original biography
and his status as a fictional character. In the 1987 movie, *Roxanne,*
the hero has lost his name and become a modern-day American,
whose only resemblance to the original Frenchman would seem to
be a frustratingly big nose and some writing talent.[36]

Movies featuring authors as characters usually attempt to re-
create as much of the historical setting as possible; this form might
be seen as a worthy twentieth-century successor to the *vie romancée*. Recent movies featuring historical authors include Philip
Kaufman's *Henry & June* (1990) about the passionate love life of

Anaïs Nin and Henry Miller, and Christopher Hampton's *Carrington* (1995), depicting the eponymous heroine's unconventional affair with the eccentric Victorian author, Lytton Strachey. Carlo Levi was portrayed by director Francesco Rosi in *Christ Stopped at Eboli* (1979), while the same year saw Vanessa Redgrave as Agatha Christie in Michael Apted's *Agatha*. And there were more: such diverse authors as Gertrude Stein, Sean O'Casey, Janet Frame, Lord Byron, Walt Whitman, Colette, F. Scott Fitzgerald, Marcel Proust, Molière, de Sade, Lewis Carroll, Hans Christian Andersen, Jack Kerouac, George Sand, Yukio Mishima, Marcel Pagnol, Oscar Wilde, Joe Orton, D. H. Lawrence, C. S. Lewis, and Stevie Smith have all been portrayed in movies since the Second World War.[37] In line with the host of novels about the Brontës, more than one motion picture was devoted to them.[38]

The most intriguing type of author-as-character representation may be found in movies featuring living authors acting out fictional versions of themselves. Alan Metter's farcical movie, *Back to School* (1986), for instance, features Kurt Vonnegut Jr. as Kurt Vonnegut Jr. whose autobiographical writings—as a college professor suggests—cannot possibly be reliable, given the discrepancy between these autobiographical writings and his well-known fiction.

Whereas the motion picture tends to follow the *vie romancée* in preserving a large degree of historical verisimilitude, authors as characters can also be found in the far more stylized form of opera. The most popular musical drama of this kind is no doubt Richard Wagner's *Die Meistersinger von Nürnberg* (1868), featuring the medieval German poet and playwright Hans Sachs as a main soloist. As a popular hero during the romantic period, Sachs had already appeared in E.T.A. Hoffmann's historical novella, *Meister Martin der Küfner und seine Gesellen* (1820) and in a play by the Austrian dramatist, Johann Ludwig Deinhardstein (1827). Wagner was certainly familiar with these literary sources, and also with Gustav Albert Lortzing's 1840 opera, *Hans Sachs*.[39] François Villon also becomes an operatic character in A. A. Noelte's *François Villon* (1919), and Kardos G. György's *Villon és a többiek* (1978).[40] More recently, Lord Byron has been made to sing by Virgil Thomson (1986).[41]

In the twentieth century, the supremacy of the *vie romancée* has been challenged by modernist and postmodernist fiction. As we shall see, the very legitimacy of representation, including that of historical writers, has been called into question. This latest wave in the author-as-character ocean, threatening to wash away the genre altogether, suggests that it is high time to appreciate the importance of this genre.

The author as character is not a recent phenomenon, but we certainly seem to be living in its heyday. Ever since Shakespeare and Goethe were turned into fictional protagonists by Oscar Wilde and Thomas Mann, respectively, the lives of the poets have become an almost commonplace subject for fiction. One can hardly find a major (dead) writer in any language who has not been revived in fiction at some point or other. Although, until recently, much work in this genre was relatively marginal in terms of quality, in recent decades celebrated authors like Jorge Luis Borges,[42] J. M. Coetzee,[43] and A. S. Byatt have spent their imaginative energies on their no-less-famous predecessors in the field of writing. At the same time, the author-as-character tradition continues to ignore the artificial, though ever so tenacious, divide between so-called serious and popular literature. The father of Portuguese poetry, Camões, has been revived in verse by countless socially deprived authors, many of them virtually nameless oral poets in northeastern Brazil.

The obsession of international novelists, poets, dramatists, and movie directors with the adventures of their literary forebears may at first seem strange. On the whole, the lives of soldiers, politicians, adventurers, discoverers, spies, social reformers, serial killers, womanizers, or mystics would seem to make better stories than the lives of people whose main professional activity is to sit at a desk all day, or night, writing. However, it is the adventures of the mind, not of the body, that attract modern writers to this topic. In many cases, the presentation of the author as character is accompanied by an element of self-reflection: pondering the life and works of often illustrious predecessors, the modern author tends to reflect on the genesis of literary works in general and his or her own in particular.

One main purpose in preparing this volume has been to call attention to a genre that has so far received more attention from creative writers than it has from the critics.[44] More difficult than identifying new cases of authors as characters in their own medium of expression continues to be the attempt to locate this genre in the field of literary production.

The phenomenon of the author as character should be situated at the crossroads between the historical novel, biography, and the *Künstlerroman*. It comprises conspicuously fictional forms, such as novels, short stories, plays, movies, dialogues, and dramatic monologues, featuring real-life authors, often, though not always, from the past. The most reliable way to define our field is by studying how it differs from neighboring areas. Yet, as Aleid Fokkema illustrates in her contribution to this volume, it is impossible to circumscribe the genre in a kind of *cordon sanitaire;* some spillover from one field to another is inevitable. This indeterminacy may well constitute one of the most promising areas of investigation. We shall briefly consider the position of the genre of the author as character vis-à-vis the neighboring genres of the biography, the *vie romancée*, and the *Künstlerroman*.

The genre of the author as character is not scholarly biography, since it supplements or even replaces the documented facts of the author-character's life with fictional speculation. Indeed, this border is difficult to police, as many would-be serious biographies do, in fact, read between the lines of the documents to create their own, ultimately subjective, reality. The most reliable criterion would seem to be to what extent the work is openly presented to the world as fictional and to what extent as documentary.

It is less easy to draw a borderline with the *vie romancée,* the less responsible but more imaginative sister of biography; compared to the author-as-character genre, this category is both too broad and too narrow. On the one hand, the *vie romancée* covers only part of the field: novels and, possibly, plays and movies that take the life of a specific historical character as their subject. This leaves out of account, however, a large number of relevant forms, such as imaginary dialogues between writers who may never have met, or works in which a historical author makes only a brief appearance; or in which the adventures ascribed to that author have little or no relation with the documented facts of that author's life; or in which speculations about or investigations into the life of an historical author constitute (part of) the plot, making him or her only a character at one remove, so to speak. All these possibilities are excluded from the *vie romancée,* although they may reveal much about the status and reception of a historical author in a given period, and about the poetics of the modern author appropriating his predecessors. In fact, as we have demonstrated in our historical survey, the genre of the author as character is not restricted to a single specific form. Like satire, it may adopt any number of guises, although it may prefer some to others. The *vie romancée* is definitely the favorite form of one historical period, but it is not the only one. At the same time, the category of the *vie romancée* is far more inclusive than the author-as-character genre, as it may deal with all sorts of historical figures (ranging from mass murderers to American presidents), and not merely with literary people with whom a modern author might be expected to feel an obvious professional affinity. The *vie romancée* has this distinction in common with the historical novel, of which it is arguably a subgenre. As a genre, the author as character differs from other historical fiction in that the modern author is engaged in a dialogue with a more or less illustrious predecessor. Almost inevitably, therefore, the genesis of a literary work becomes one of its main themes, and some degree of self-projection on the part of the modern author seems inevitable.

The final neighboring category from which the genre of the author as character can be distinguished is that of the *Künstlerroman*.[45] The *Künstlerroman* also deals with an artist, often literary, in fictionalized form; however, in cases such as Goethe's *Wilhelm Meister* novels, Joyce's *A Portrait of the Artist as a Young Man,* or D. H. Lawrence's *Sons and Lovers,* we are dealing with a mode of veiled autobiography. By contrast, the genre of the author as character is at most an oblique autobiography, in the sense that the later author may project some of his own experiences onto the author-character, but this type of projection is always counterbalanced by a modicum of historical verisimilitude. Part of the interest in the genre of the author as character lies precisely in this tension between the autobiographical impulse and the recognition of the other as other—for instance, through historical perspective or even through outright rebellion against the historical author. The search for identification has to be balanced with the urge to establish difference and, perhaps, originality.

After mapping a number of tentative borders, a huge, differentiated field remains as a subject for investigation. We have thus collected a broad range of contributions on the author as character by scholars working in a number of major Western literatures. Our choice of topics has been guided by several considerations. We have included work on a representative selection of literature in terms of historical period, geography, and gender. We also have privileged works that were available in English and works by canonical authors, yet without excluding altogether some of the less famed writers.

We are well aware that completeness is beyond the scope of our present volume; but, in the course of our preparations we have come to realize that, because of its immense range, few have undertaken this kind of research in any systematic way. Our hope is to provide an experimental typology of the phenomenon of the author as character, one that may serve as a practical theoretical framework for further investigation. Our typology will take the shape of a survey of some parameters that may prove useful in understanding what ought by now to be recognized as a major literary genre, if only because of its vast heritage and worldwide scope.

In seeking to classify the multiple uses of the author as character, a number of interlocking criteria should be taken into account, the first of which is the relative importance of the author-character within the work.[46] A second criterion is the ontological status ascribed to the author-character in a particular work of literature. Further, we need to ascertain to which extent the author-character's life is embedded in historical documentation. Also, to what extent are the subject-author's own texts used as material that can be deployed to fill in gaps in his life? The final criterion is the attitude displayed by the later author toward his author-character. In the following pages we discuss each of these interlocking criteria in succession.

In many cases, the earlier author will be the protagonist of the story or novel, which then often becomes a fictionalized biography, or *vie romancée*. Alternatively, the subject-author may be one of several main characters, like Virgil in Dante's *Divine Comedy* or Horace, Ovid, Virgil, and Propertius in Ben Jonson's *Poetaster*. Even a world-famous author may be only a minor character: Shakespeare has a mere walk-on part in Anthony Burgess's last novel, *A Dead Man in Deptford,* written about the life and death of Christopher Marlowe. In George Sand's play, *Le Roi attend,* a pantheon of poets—including Plautus, Terence, Aeschylus, Sophocles, Euripides, Shakespeare, Voltaire, Rousseau, Marivaux, and Beaumarchais—liven up the dream of Molière. In Thomas Mann's *Lotte in Weimar (The Beloved Returns)*, Goethe features as a character only in the seventh chapter, and an even briefer appearance is granted him in Susan Sontag's *The Volcano Lover.*[47]

Beyond the possibility of the walk-on part, there is yet another: a subject-author's very status as a character may be so marginal that he or she walks through a book like a shadow who only "exists" in the fantasies, thoughts, or reveries of the protagonist or other characters. Thus, in Virginia Woolf's novel *Orlando,* Marlowe is a minor character, and Shakespeare scarcely remembered at all by the poet-narrator Nicholas Greene. But the subordinate status of Shakespeare is offset by the promise of future renown. As the reader gathers from Greene's account to Orlando:

> [Greene] could remember, he said, a night at the Cork Tavern in Fleet Street when Kit Marlowe was there and some others. Kit was in high

feather, rather drunk, which he easily became, and in a mood to say silly things. He could see him now, brandishing his glass at the company and hiccoughing out, "Stap my vitals, Bill" (this was to Shakespeare), "there's a great wave coming and you're on the top of it," by which he meant, Greene explained, that they were trembling on the verge of a great age in English literature, and that Shakespeare was to be a poet of some importance. Happily for himself, he was killed two nights later in a drunken brawl, and so did not live to see how this prediction turned out.[48]

Just as Marlowe and Shakespeare are presented by Woolf as representative of the literary scene of Orlando's early modern existence, so Alexander Pope, Joseph Addison, and Jonathan Swift feature as the character cameos that, stereotypically perhaps, adorn his/her eighteenth-century phase.

In the present volume, Frederick M. Keener shows how Dr. Samuel Johnson and Oliver Goldsmith, brought to life in a dialogue of the dead as tangible ghosts, invoke the less tangible spirit of Alexander Pope in their discussion. Lois Feuer addresses the issue of the limits of what might still be regarded as a character in greater detail, focusing on the presence of Shakespeare in Joyce's *Ulysses*. Feuer argues that Shakespeare really should be seen as a crucial character in Joyce's masterpiece, even though the playwright is as intangible as the Ghost of Hamlet's father. The fleeting Shakespeare in *Ulysses* represents a borderline case.

This issue leads to another parameter—namely, that of the ontological status ascribed to the author-character. The "shadowy" characters, who only exist in the imagination of the "real" characters, obviously lend themselves to speculation about the reliability of any attempt to analyze and describe a real person, whether this is done on the basis of biographical data or on the basis of his or her (literary) works. The main character may be a literary scholar, whose object of investigation, the author-character, proves elusive in a futile quest for certainty and hard evidence in a world that yields only competing discourses. This type of anxiety has all the makings of a postmodern concern. Aleid Fokkema discusses this motif in Julian Barnes's novel *Flaubert's Parrot* in the light of postmodern ideas on indeterminacy. A much earlier example is Oscar Wilde's pioneering study of the limits of representation and interpretation, *The Portrait of Mr. W. H.*[49] In Wilde's tale of an open-ended quest for the true story behind the genesis of Shakespeare's sonnets, a succession of gifted amateur scholars attempt to reconstruct Shakespeare's love life as a key to the sonnets. Their attempts to find conclusive proof founder in the face of unreliable, even fraudulent evidence. In the end, all that remains is a series of self-projections by readers who see their own images reflected in the sonnets, the last, fallible reader being Wilde himself.

There are also works in which the author-character is tangible enough, but where the author casts doubt on the status of his own representation by various means. In Anthony Burgess's *Nothing Like the Sun,* for example, the point of view is that of a drunken lecturer who obviously is unreliable, not least because in his drunken stupor he projects himself onto his ostensible subject, Shakespeare, and allows his narrative to drift into incoherence.[50] Peter Ackroyd's biography of Dickens uses a mixture of serious biography and speculative dialogues of the dead to obtain a comparable effect of undermining the factual correctness of his narrative.

Yet, historically speaking, the vast majority of author-characters are supposed to be taken as authoritative figures whose ontological status is assured within the framework of the fiction, even if this is a self-conscious fantasy rather than a biographical reconstruction. Paradoxically, it is perhaps in the most palpable fictions, when great authors rise again as ghosts to applaud or criticize the artistic or political views of their literary successors, that they have the most authority, in the sense that the views ascribed to them actually are meant to be taken as their own, not mere self-serving constructions by those successors who have raised their spirits. As Chris Kleinhenz points out, for Dante, Virgil is not a mere figment of his imagination but a historical reality, even though the Mantuan poet is a character. When George Sand's Molière has a vision of the ghosts of Shakespeare, Sophocles, Aeschylus, Euripides, Voltaire, Rousseau, and Beaumarchais, who stimulate his revolutionary feeling, we may not take the vision seriously; yet the political ideas attributed to the ghosts cannot be so easily dismissed—at least, not within the framework of the play.[51]

The issue of ontological status is of course related to, though not identical to, the degree to which the subject-authors are embedded in their (documented) historical context.[52] At one extreme stands the *vie romancée,* which is little more than a scholarly biography with imaginative touches added. At the other extreme, we have stories, novels, poems, in which the historical context is totally disregarded, and little remains of the historical author beyond the name and one or two of his or her most salient characteristics. In Ovid's conception of Sappho, discussed in our volume by Phyllis R. Brown, the poet's lesbianism and, to some extent also, her ability as a woman to write moving poetry, are obscured. The heroes of the Brazilian *folhetos de cordeiro* that form the subject of Ria

Lemaire's contribution seem completely unrelated to the historical Camões, except for his name which they borrow. Yet, Lemaire argues, they may be a healthy corrective to the Camões of the Portuguese establishment, who, in spite of his embedding in history, is no more than a construct—and a construct with a somewhat doubtful political charge, at that. Alternatively, a blatant disregard of historical accuracy may also be a deliberate strategy to cast doubt on all historical narratives as mere constructs, as in Stephen Marlowe's Cervantes novel discussed by Harm den Boer.

Apart from historical documentation, we find that the lives of subject-authors are frequently reconstructed on the basis of their own written works. This practice may range from fairly plausible inferences, if the works in question are clearly autobiographical, to the wholly unwarranted projection of the plots of putatively objective genres onto the life of the subject-author, as when a dramatist's play is treated as a record, in a somewhat displaced form, of what actually happened to him in his own life. This is otherwise known as the biographical fallacy. As a serious exercise, this phenomenon had its heyday with the advent of biographical criticism. It seems to have survived the demise of this school, however, in the form of fiction, providing an outlet for those critics who were exiled from mainstream scholarship with the advent of New Criticism. In the postmodern era, such equations of life and work are often the hallmark of low ontological status. Wilde's *Portrait of Mr. W. H.* also seems to be pivotal here: it began as a serious reconstruction of part of Shakespeare's life on the basis of the sonnets, but ended up calling into question the validity of all biographical criticism.

Politics are one possible dimension in an author's motivation for selecting an earlier author as his character. All art can be given a political charge, whether implicitly or explicitly, and one's reaction to that art may be constructed as a political act. Apart from politics in the narrow sense of the word, issues of gender, race, religion, sexual preference, or aesthetic theory may also attract an author to an illustrious predecessor. Broadly speaking, there are several possible reactions toward an earlier author: appropriation or confrontation, or both. These terms were introduced by Alan Sinfield in reference to intertextual practices such as rewriting existing masterpieces.[53] However, authors' lives, too, can be seen as texts with which later authors have similar relationships as with existing literary texts. In the case of appropriation, the later author presents himself, his views of life and art, and his own work as being in line with and thus having the authority of, the life, views, and works of the earlier writer. From a different perspective, one might say that the later author, in fact, presents a construction of his predecessor as being in line with his own work. In confrontation, the later author presents his own life, views, and works in opposition to those of the illustrious forebear, whose works and deeds are debunked. Or again, the earlier author is construed as sadly lacking in insight or integrity, or his life is "shown" to be inconsistent with the ideals he preached in his works. If we approach these attitudes along the lines suggested by Harold Bloom, confrontation is a direct way of coping with anxiety of influence.[54] Appropriation is a subtler form of the same strategy, in which an author neutralizes his predecessor by rewriting him in his own image. From a Freudian perspective, we have Oedipal rebellion versus acquiescence in the superior power of the father-figure.

Insofar as the contributions in this volume can be seen as typical, there is a historical development in attitudes toward the subject-authors. Most earlier biographical fictions are near-hagiographies, in which the author is appropriated for some cause or other, or becomes a personal model for the latter-day writer. The authority of the great writer of the past becomes the mantle that may fall on the younger man's shoulders one day, or that has already done so, as Chris Kleinhenz suggests in his contribution on Dante, and Matthew Steggle in his on Jonson. In extreme cases of appropriation, the great author might rise as a ghost from the past to defend his modern adept's position against his literary enemies, or to show him the way to glory or political correctness—Gretchen Smith's contribution on George Sand describes a case where Sand appropriates Molière and, through him, those great spirits from the past, including Shakespeare, that (in Sand's fiction) appear to Molière in his dream vision.

Such writing seems to have gone out of fashion, as have other genres of praise, to be replaced by more antagonistic forms in which the Bloomian cum Oedipal rebellion is less disguised. The authority of the long-deceased author has become the battleground for literary wars over issues of politics, gender, sexual preference, and race. Examples discussed in this volume include Anthony Burgess's deconstruction of Kipling's Shakespeare in order to repudiate the Edwardian's views of aesthetics and colonialism; A. S. Byatt's protest on behalf of all silenced women against Tennyson's appropriation of his sister's fiancé, A.H.H.; and Tennessee Williams's unsympathetic representation of F. Scott Fitzgerald and Hemingway as closet homosexuals, which, as Peter L. Hays argues, may be not unrelated to his own openness about being gay.

After delimiting the field of the author as character in literature—setting it off against such neighboring genres as the biography, the *vie romancée,* and the *Künstlerroman,* and defining a number of parameters that may prove serviceable in categorizing the veritable host of author-characters—one could creatively branch out again and suggest additional areas of study in the field of comparative research. As already stated, our interest in the author as character was to a large extent due to the fact that a particular literary work introduced a literary artist within its confines, not just a fictional artist but a predecessor to the author who had literally made a name in the field of literature.

Literature is not the only field that has produced artists as characters. Real-life painters, sculptors, and composers have also been represented in fiction, and the portrayal of these characters may provide a useful foil to the author as character. Are the same mechanisms of appropriation, self-projection, and anxiety of influence at work when the later author and his/her subject work in different artistic fields? It could be profitable indeed to study the painter as character in *Lust for Life* (1934) and *The Agony and the Ecstasy* (1961), both novels by the twentieth-century master of the fictional biography, Irving Stone, and dealing with the lives of Vincent van Gogh and Michelangelo, respectively, alongside his Jack London novel.[55] A rewarding comparison might also be made between the author as character and the representation of the Swiss-born painter Henry Fuseli (1742–1825) in Frances Sherwood's 1993 novel, *Vindication,* which also features artist-poet William Blake, Mary Wollstonecraft, and William Godwin.[56] No less worthwhile would be a comparison between the eponymous painters in Michael Kernan's *The Lost Diaries of Frans Hals* (1995), and Cocky van Bokhoven's *Johannes Vermeer* (1996).[57] It is intriguing that both the Kernan novel and the Bokhoven novella are presented in the diary mode. Clearly, the painter's brush has been exchanged for the pen as a means of communication between artist and audience. Here, the choice of literary mode inevitably raises questions about the identity of "the artist." The question may be glaringly obvious; nevertheless, it remains tantalizingly unanswerable. Does the reader communicate with the eponymous historical painter who is also talented as a literary artist, or with the modern author writing to transgress into the visual arts?[58]

Of the nonliterary artists as characters, no doubt the composers lead the field.[59] Wolfgang Amadeus Mozart is easily the most popular.[60] Anthony Burgess's *On Mozart*—also published as *Mozart and the Wolf Gang*—is not just an extraordinarily rich and eccentric source of composers as characters, but also deftly aligns the genre with that of the author as character.[61] Among other things, Burgess's Mozart lampoon includes a Prologue in Heaven, featuring Beethoven, Mendelssohn, Prokoviev, Sir Arthur Bliss, and Wagner, which is followed by an extravagant, timeless play which accommodates not only Mozart himself but also Berlioz, Rossini, Gluck, Salieri, Gershwin, and Schoenberg. The absurd Mozart playlet elicits a sharp response from author-as-character Henry James as soon as the curtain has fallen. In an allusion to the American novelist's dual experience of his friend, neighbor, and fellow poet Robert Browning—whom he considered "great" but "odd"[62]—Burgess has Henry James pronounce what is easily the most condemnatory statement about the artist, including the author, as character:

> Totally preposterous. The travesty of the life of a great artist. Apart from the ineptitude of the execution, it is inadmissible to consider that the artist's personality possesses any pertinence to the artist's work. This is a heresy permeating the modern world. I met Robert Browning. He looked like a decaying stockbroker long steeped in philistinism. Where was the poet of *The Ring and the Book? (On Mozart,* 87)

Lorenzo da Ponte, Mozart's great librettist, rightly assumes that James's discontent springs from the fact that "Mozart's life is not worth presenting, since he neglected life for art" (*On Mozart,* 90), but James takes it one step further:

> It is the shape that the artist imposes on life that is, in a sense, the thing that life aspires to. The sweat, the intrigues, the teeth knocked out, the sexual diseases, the tears and occasional exaltations—we do not wish to know these things. (*On Mozart,* 91)

Is Henry James, using the *pluralis majestatis,* speaking for himself or on behalf of a wide variety of readers? His reaction looks forward to the new critical approach that discouraged all biographical speculation—precisely the sort of attitude that, Burgess may have felt, was in the way of a proper appreciation of his own works in the field. Here, Henry James is at least as much the critic as character as the author as character. If fictional James's remark on sexual diseases may have some bearing on the predicament of the historical Henry James, it certainly has resonances with respect to Burgess's best-known work in the genre of the author as character, *Nothing Like the Sun,* in which Shakespeare is depicted as suffering from syphilis. The fictional James is allowed to have his say, as a representative *avant la lettre* of the critical establishment that will not take Burgess's work seriously, but this is no more than a strategy of containment. Ultimately, Burgess wins the day: the reluctant author has been made into a reluctant fictional author, who is at the real author's command. James's protest seems a mere rearguard action that will not keep authors from fictionalizing their predecessors, nor readers from enjoying their works.

Neglect of the genre of the author as character may be due to its hybrid nature, but it may also have something to do with a lingering suspicion among critics of anything that smacks of the biographical fallacy. Nonetheless, particularly in its most recent manifestations, the phenomenon confronts the reader and the critic with a number of relevant questions concerning the ontological status of a character, about the hazards of biography, and about the author's own limitations, biases, and tendencies to project his own concerns on the world around him. In addition, the genre shows one author trying to engage in a dialogue with a predecessor in the light of his or her own era, experience, or ideology: in other words, engaging in a kind of deliberate intertextuality. Epistemological questions and the ubiquity of intertextuality are among the key issues of the postmodern world. For this reason alone, there seems to be room for critical attention to works in this genre, as well as to those (usually older) ones in which such issues are consciously or unconsciously muted rather than foregrounded as problematic. It is hardly surprising that so many modern books, plays, and movies feature earlier authors whose certainties we may question, deconstruct, or contemplate with nostalgic envy: contemporary authors have instinctively recognized the challenges posed by this discursive field. It is the academic critics who, so far, have lagged behind.

NOTES

1. See, respectively, Anthony Burgess, *Nothing Like the Sun: A Story of Shakespeare's Love-life* (1964; repr. London: Vintage, 1992); *ABBA* (London: Faber and Faber, 1977); and *A Dead Man in Deptford* (London: Hutchinson, 1993).

2. *Christopherus or Tom Kyd's Revenge* (1993; repr. London: Mandarin, 1994).

3. Peter Ackroyd, *Chatterton* (London: Sphere, 1988), and *English Music* (London: Hamilton, 1992). Ackroyd was not the first author to find creative inspiration in the life and works of the Bristol-born poet; Alfred de Vigny devoted a play to him in 1835. See Alfred de Vigny, *Chatterton: Drame en trois actes,* in *Œuvres complètes,* 2 vols. (Paris: Éditions Gallimard, 1950), 1: 757–851. On

Vigny's play, see Georges Lamoine, "Thomas Chatterton dans l'oeuvre de Vigny et dans l'histoire," *Dix-huitième siècle* 3 (1971): 317–30; Barry V. Daniels, "An Exemplary French Romantic Production: Alfred de Vigny's *Chatterton*," *Theatre Survey: The American Journal of Theatre History* 16 (1975): 65–88; Carol Wootton, "The Deaths of Goethe's Werther and De Vigny's Chatterton," *Revue de Littérature Comparée* 50 (1976): 295–303; Jean Jourdheuil, "Les Enjeux de Chatterton," *Europe* 589 (1978): 108–14; and Robin Buss, *Vigny: "Chatterton,"* Critical Guides to French Texts, 34 (London: Grant & Cutler, 1984).

4. Sigrid Combüchen, *Byron: A Novel* (1988; repr. London: Heinemann, 1991).

5. Lynne Truss, *Tennyson's Gift* (London: Hamish Hamilton, 1996). For a review, see Keith Miller, "Freshwater Frolics," in *TLS,* 19 July 1996, 21. On the complex relationship between A. S. Byatt and Tennyson, see Christien Franken's contribution to this volume.

6. Homer, *The Odyssey,* Book 8, in particular, lines 43–73. Compare lines 471–98 for Odysseus's generous praise of the Bard. See *Homer: The Odyssey. A New Verse Translation by Albert Cook* (New York: Norton, 1967), 99–100. It is difficult to determine whether Demodocus is a fictionalized historical figure or a fictional character.

7. See also David Rijser, "Dichtung und Wahrheit: Agathon, Aristophanes en poetica in Plato's *Symposium,*" *Lampas: Tijdschrift voor Nederlandse classici* 29:5 (1996): 481–502.

8. On Thomas Elyot, see Robert Haynes's contribution in the present volume.

9. *The Dramatic Works of Thomas Heywood,* ed. R. H. Shepherd, 6 vols. (1874; repr. New York: Russell & Russell, 1964), 3:1–256.

10. For some recent views, see Thomas Pughe, "'What should the wars do with these jigging fools?': The Poets in Shakespeare's *Julius Caesar,*" *English Studies* 69:4 (1988): 313–22; Alan Sinfield, "Theaters of War: Caesar and the Vandals," in his *Faultlines: Cultural Materialism and the Politics of Dissident Reading* (Oxford: Clarendon Press, 1992), 1–28; and Gary Taylor, "Bardicide," in *Shakespeare and Cultural Traditions: The Selected Proceedings of the International Shakespeare Association World Congress, Tokyo, 1991,* ed. Tetsuo Kishi, Roger Pringle, and Stanley Wells (Newark: University of Delaware Press, 1994), 333–49.

11. William Shakespeare, *Pericles,* ed. F. D. Hoeniger, The Arden Shakespeare (London: Methuen, 1963), 1–4.

12. On Shakespeare's representation of Gower, see also, F. David Hoeniger, "Gower and Shakespeare in *Pericles,*" *Shakespeare Quarterly* 33:4 (1982): 461–79; Richard Hillman, "Shakespeare's Gower and Gower's Shakespeare: The Larger Debt of *Pericles,*" *Shakespeare Quarterly* 36:3 (1985): 427–37; Stephen Dickey, "Language and Role in *Pericles,*" *English Literary Renaissance* 16:3 (1986): 550–56; and Neville Davies, "Old Gower's Voyage to Byzantium," *KM 80: A Birthday Album for Kenneth Muir* (Liverpool: Liverpool University Press, n.d. [1987]), 34–35.

13. *Court Masques: Jacobean and Caroline Entertainments, 1605–1640,* ed. David Lindley, The World's Classics (Oxford and New York: Oxford University Press, 1995), 102–8.

14. John Lyly, *Sapho and Phao* (1584), in *The Complete Works of John Lyly,* ed. R. Warwick Bond, 3 vols. (Oxford: Clarendon Press, 1902), 2:361–416.

15. "A Dialogue on Language," in *The Literary Works of Machiavelli: "Mandragola," "Clizia," "A Dialogue on Language," "Belfagor." With Selections from the Private Correspondence,* ed. and trans. by J. R. Hale (1961; repr. Westport,

CT: Greenwood Press, 1979), 173–90. See Peter Wunderli, "'Machiavelli linguista,'" *Vox Romanica* 44 (1985): 33–58; and Ignazio Baldelli, "Il dialogo sulla lingua del Machiavelli e Dante," *L'Alighieri* 10:2 (1969): 5–11.

16. Frederick M. Keener's study of the English dialogues of the dead remains the standard work on the subject and a model for future research. See Keener, *English Dialogues of the Dead: A Critical History, an Anthology, and a Check List* (New York and London: Columbia University Press, 1973). See also his contribution in this volume.

17. See Landor, *Imaginary Conversations and Poems: A Selection,* ed. Havelock Ellis (London: J.M. Dent & Sons, 1933), vii.

18. See L. J. Filewood, "An Imaginary Conversation between Samuel Johnson and Gilbert Chesterton," *Chesterton Review* 5 (1978–79): 87–103; and Anu Aneja, "An Imaginary Conversation between Antonin Artaud and Alain Robbe-Grillet," *Neohelicon* 15:1 (1988): 255–62.

19. *Xanthippic Dialogues. Comprising "Xanthippe's Republic"; "Perictione's Parmenides"; and "Xanthippe's Laws"; together with a version, probably spurious, of "Phryne's Symposium,"* ed. Roger Scruton (London: Sinclair-Stevenson, 1993). Scruton's project is a variation on the theme developed by Christine Brückner as early as 1983, when she produced her biographical speeches by women who had largely remained unheard. Her collection of sketches, entitled *Wenn du geredet hättest, Desdemona* ["If you had spoken, Desdemona"], features Donna Laura speaking of Petrarch, and Christiane von Goethe talking about her husband Johann Wolfgang. See *Wenn du geredet hättest, Desdemona. Ungehaltene Reden ungehaltener Frauen. Mit Zeichnungen von Horst Janssen* (1983; repr. Frankfurt am Main and Berlin: Verlag Ullstein, 1986).

20. Eric H. Kadler, *Literary Figures in French Drama (1784–1834),* International Archives of the History of Ideas 26 (The Hague: Martinus Nijhoff, 1969).

21. Thacher, *Charlecote: or, The Trial of William Shakespeare* (New York, 1895); Williams, *Shakspeare and his Friends* (London, 1838); and *The Youth of Shakespeare* (Paris, 1839); Severn, *Anne Hathaway: or Shakespeare in Love* (London, 1845); Curling, *Shakespere, The Poet, The Lover: A Romance* (London, 1848); Drake, *Noontide Leisure: Including A Tale of the Days of William Shakespeare* (London, 1824). This list is not exhaustive.

22. Stevenson, "A Place for the Night," in *The Stories of Robert Louis Stevenson* (London: Victor Gollancz, 1928), 239–62.

23. Van Schendel, *Shakespeare* (Amsterdam: Versluys, 1910); and *Verlaine: Het leven van een dichter* (Amsterdam: Meulenhoff, 1927).

24. Bloom, *The Romance of Charles Dickens* (London: Hale, 1960); Walker, *Marriage of Harlequin: A Biographical Novel of the Important Years in the Life of Richard Brinsley Sheridan* (Toronto: McClelland and Stewart, 1962); Stone, *Jack London: Sailor on Horseback* (Toronto: New American Library of Canada, 1969); McKemy, *Samuel Pepys of the Navy* (New York: F. Warner, 1970); and Westervelt, *Pearl Buck: A Biographical Novel* (New York: Elsevier/Nelson Books, 1979).

25. See also Robert Ziegler, "'À chaudes larmes': Creativity and Loss in Marcel Schwob's *Vies imaginaires,*" *Dalhousie French Studies* 33 (1995): 71–82.

26. For a discussion of these views, see Schwob, "*Le Roi au masque d'or,*" "*Vies imaginaires,*" "*La Croisade des enfants,*" introduced by Hubert Juin (Paris: 10/18, 1979), 171–79.

27. Monique Jutrin, "Paolo Uccello ou une 'vie imaginaire' de Marcel Schwob," *Neohelicon* 14:1 (1987): 209–20.

28. *"Le Roi au masque d'or," "Vies imaginaires," "La Croisade des enfants,"* 258. See also, *The Works of Cyril Tourneur,* ed. Allardyce Nicoll (1929; repr. New York: Russell & Russell, 1963), 1.

29. Mann, *Lotte in Weimar* (Stockholm: Bermann-Fisher AB, 1939); trans. as *The Beloved Returns* by H. T. Lowe-Porter (Berkeley and Los Angeles: University of California Press, 1990). On the representation of Goethe in Mann's novel, see Gamin Bartle's "Displacing Goethe: Tribute and Exorcism in Thomas Mann's *The Beloved Returns*" in this volume.

30. Broch, *Der Tod des Vergil* (1945), in *Gesammelte Werke,* 10 vols. (Zürich: Rhein-Verlag, 1958), vol. 3; translated by Jean Starr Untermeyer as *The Death of Virgil* (London: Routledge, 1946). Broch's novel was to be one of the major sources of inspiration for Bernard-Henri Lévy's novel, *Les derniers jours de Charles Baudelaire* (Paris: Bernard Grasset, 1988).

31. Hella S. Haasse, *Het woud der verwachting* (1949). The Dutch version of this historical novel had an immediate appeal; within ten years it inspired Karel Eykman to produce his play, *François Villon,* staged in 1961. The novel appeared in English as *In a Dark Wood Wandering,* trans. Edith Kaplan, Kalman Kaplan and Anita Miller (London: Arrow Books, 1989).

32. Robert Graves, *Wife to Mr. Milton* (London and Paris: The Albatros, 1947). See also, Bridget Marie Engelmeyer, "Graves' Milton Redivivus: Another View," *Milton Quarterly* 14 (1980): 101.

33. Ezra Pound, "Homage to Sextus Propertius," in *Personae: The Collected Shorter Poems of Ezra Pound* (New York: New Directions, 1971). Compare Martine de Vos's contribution to this volume.

34. Sand, *Le Roi attend* and *Molière,* in *Théâtre complet de George Sand* (Paris, 1877), vol. 1; and Rudolf Besier, *The Barretts of Wimpole Street* (1930), in *Sixteen Famous British Plays,* compiled by Bennett A. Cerf and Van H. Cartmell (New York: Modern Library, 1942). Compare the contributions to this volume by Gretchen E. Smith and Rosella Mamoli Zorzi, respectively. More recent drama featuring historical authors includes Per Olov Enquist's caustic portrayal of his famous compatriot August Strindberg in *The Night of the Tribades* (1975); Tom Stoppard's pairing of James Joyce with Lenin in his early play *Travesties* (1975); and Peter Whelan's gathering of Kyd, Marlowe, and Shakespeare in a highly unusual constellation in *The School of Night* (1992). As a deft variation on Georg Büchner's political tragedy *Dantons Tod* ("Danton's Death"), Chilean-born playwright Gaston Salvatore wrote a feverish death-bed play entitled *Büchners Tod* (1972). In *Not about Heroes* (1983), war poets Siegfried Sassoon and Wilfred Owen have been revived by the playwright Stephen MacDonald to recite their poetry to each other and to discuss matters literary as well as political. In the United States, Tennessee Williams has portrayed F. Scott Fitzgerald and Ernest Hemingway in *Clothes for a Summer Hotel* (1980), a play discussed by Peter Hays in his contribution to this volume. Emily Dickinson featured as the sole stage character in *The Belle of Amherst* by William Luce (1976), and, together with Margaret Fuller, she counsels diarist Alice James, the great American novelist's sister, in Susan Sontag's stage play, *Alice in Bed* (1993).

35. *"Cyrano de Bergerac," by Edmond Rostand,* trans. and adapted to the modern stage by Anthony Burgess (New York: Knopf, 1978). For a discussion of the character and his predecessor, see J. A. Kilker, "Cyrano without Rostand: An Appraisal," *Canadian Modern Language Review/La Revue Canadienne des Langues Vivantes* 21:3 (1965): 21–25.

36. On the fate of Cyrano de Bergerac on the movie screen, see Don Kunz, "American Cinematic Adaptations of Cyrano de Bergerac," *Literature Film Quarterly* 16:3 (1988): 160–66; and Keith Reader, "Le phénomène Cyrano: Perceptions of French Cinema in Britain," *Franco-British Studies* 15 (1993): 3–9.

37. See, respectively: Jill Godmilow, *Waiting for the Moon* (1987); Jack Cardiff, *Young Cassidy* (1965); Jane Campion, *An Angel at My Table* (1990); David Macdonald, *Bad Lord Byron* (1951); John Kent Harrison, *Beautiful Dreamers* (1992); Danny Huston, *Becoming Colette* (1992); Henry King, *Beloved Infidel* (1959); Percy Adlon, *Celeste* (1981); Ariane Mnouchkine, *Molière* (1977); Cy Endfield, *De Sade* (1969); Gavin Miller, *Dreamchild* (1985); Charles Vidor, *Hans Christian Andersen* (1952); John Byrum, *Heart Beat* (1980); James Lapine, *Impromptu* (1991); Paul Schrader, *Mishima* (1985); Yves Robert, *My Father's Glory* (1990); Gregory Ratoff, *Oscar Wilde* (1960); Stephen Frears, *Prick Up Your Ears* (1987); Christopher Miles, *Priest of Love* (1981); Norman Stone, *Shadowlands* (1985), as well as Richard Attenborough's 1993 remake; and Robert Enders, *Stevie* (1978).

38. For Brontë movies, see Curtis Bernhardt, *Devotion* (1946); André Téchiné, *The Brontë Sisters* (1979); and Delbert Mann, *Brontë* (1983). Fictional works about the sisters include Elsie Thornton Cook, *They Lived: A Brontë Novel* (London: Murray, 1935); Kathryn Jean MacFarlane, *Divide the Desolation* (New York: Simon & Schuster, 1936); Elisabeth Kyle, *Girl with a Pen* (London: Evans, 1963); Philippa Stone, *The Captive Dove* (London: Robert Hale, 1968); and Jane Amster, *Dream Keepers: The Young Brontës. A Psycho-Biographical Novella* (New York: William-Frederick Press, 1973). This list is not exhaustive. In their *Brontë Bibliography* (London: Ian Hodgkins, 1978), G. Anthony Yablon and John R. Turner list no fewer than 29 relevant titles, in drama and fiction, from the 1930s on.

39. See Peter Wapnewski, "The Operas as Literary Works," in *Wagner Handbook,* ed. Ulrich Müller and Peter Wapnewski, trans. John Deathridge (Cambridge, MA: Harvard University Press, 1992), 3–95 (75). Interestingly, Wolfram von Eschenbach, whose poetry provided a source for Wagner's *Lohengrin, Tristan und Isolde,* and *Parsifal,* features as a character in the composer's own *Tannhäuser.*

40. For the checkered career and afterlife of François Villon, see Jelle Koopmans's contribution to the present volume.

41. On Virgil Thomson's *Lord Byron,* see, for example, Samuel Lipman, "'Lord Byron' Undone," *Grand Street* 5:3 (1986): 180–93.

42. Borges's short story about Shakespeare is "Everything and Nothing," in his *Dreamtigers* (1964; repr. London: Souvenir Press, 1973), 46–47. Cervantes ruminates on his character Don Quixote in *The Book of Sand,* trans. Alastair Reid (Harmondsworth: Penguin, 1979), 157. The latter also contains a dramatic monologue entitled "Browning Resolves to Be a Poet" (142–45). See also, Maria-Esther Vazquez, "'La memoria de Shakespeare': El ultimo juego de Borges," *Revista Iberoamericana* 56:151 (1990): 479–87.

43. J. M. Coetzee's *Foe* (London: Penguin, 1987) features Daniel Defoe, while his *The Master of Petersburg* (New York: Penguin, 1994) is about Fyodor Dostoevsky. For *Foe,* see also, Aleid Fokkema's contribution to this volume.

44. Exceptions cover only part of the field, such as the aforementioned studies of literary figures in French drama by Eric H. Kadler, of the eighteenth-century genre of the dialogue of the dead by Frederick M. Keener, or Maurice J. O'Sullivan's "Shakespeare's Other Lives," *Shakespeare Quarterly* 38:2 (1987): 133–53.

45. See Maurice Beebe, *Ivory Towers: The Artist as Hero in Fiction from Goethe to Joyce* (New York: New York University Press, 1964).

46. We are aware that the notion of "character" is a hazardous one in a post-modern climate. Indeed, "character" in the traditional, liberal-humanist tradition has ceased to exist. Our sole criterion for referring to any textual phenomenon as a character, and in particular as an author as character, is the occurrence in the source text of a name which, in the annals of world literature, corresponds to that of a *real-life* author.

47. On Mann's *Lotte in Weimar,* see Gamin Bartle's contribution in this volume. For Susan Sontag, see a.o. Gisela Brude-Firnau, "Zur Intertextualität von Susan Sontags *The Volcano Lover* und Goethes *Italienische Reise,*" in *Analogon Rationis: Festschrift für Gerwin Marahrens zum 65. Geburtstag,* ed. Marianne Henn and Christoph Lorey (Edmonton, AB: Author, 1994), 181–92; and Stacey Olster, "Remakes, Outtakes, and Updates in Susan Sontag's *The Volcano Lover,*" *Modern Fiction Studies* 41:1 (1995): 117–39.

48. Woolf, *Orlando: A Biography* (London: Hogarth, 1928), chap. 2.

49. See Wilde, *The Portrait of Mr. W. H.* (1889), in *The Works of Oscar Wilde,* ed. G. F. Maine (London: Collins, 1948; repr. 1961), 1089–1112; Andreas Höfele, "Portraits of Mr. W. S.: Shakespeare als Rätsel in Iris Murdochs *The Black Prince* und Anthony Burgess' *Enderby's Dark Lady,*" *Deutsche Shakespeare Gesellschaft West Jahrbuch* 1985 (Bochum: Verlag Ferdinand Kamp, 1985): 117–31; and Paul Franssen, "Portraits of Mr. W. S.: The Myth of Sweet Master Shakespeare in Asimov, Wilde, and Burgess," in *Reclamations of Shakespeare,* ed. A. J. Hoenselaars (Amsterdam and Atlanta: Rodopi, 1994), 139–50.

50. See, for example, John J. Stinson, "*Nothing Like the Sun:* The Faces in Bella Cohen's Mirror," *Journal of Modern Literature* 5 (1976): 131–47.

51. Sand, *Le Roi attend: prologue* (Théâtre de la République—9 April 1848), in *Théâtre complet* (Paris, 1876), 1:125–42. See also, the contribution by Gretchen Smith in this volume. On posthumous stage appearances by Shakespeare in general, usually as a regal ghost whose word is not to be doubted, see Michael Dobson, *The Making of the National Poet: Shakespeare, Adaptation and Authorship, 1660–1769* (Oxford: Clarendon Press, 1992).

52. For Irving Stone, himself a prolific practitioner of the biographical novel, the "truth" of historical fiction seems to depend largely on the quality of the scholarly research: "How can the question, 'How much of this is true?' be answered? Only by insisting that the biographical novel must be as complete in its documentation as the most scholarly history and biography, and as honest in its interpretation." See Irving Stone, John O'Hara, and MacKinlay Kantor, *Three Views of the Novel* (Washington: Library of Congress, 1957), 4.

53. See Sinfield, "Making Space: Appropriation and Confrontation in Recent British Plays," in *The Shakespeare Myth,* ed. Graham Holderness (Manchester: Manchester University Press, 1988), 128–44.

54. Compare Bloom, *The Anxiety of Influence: A Theory of Poetry* (New York: Oxford University Press, 1973).

55. Stone, *Lust for Life* (London: The Bodley Head, 1934), and *The Agony and the Ecstasy: A Biographical Novel of Michelangelo* (1961; repr. London: Collins, 1970). Both novels have been reprinted and translated many times.

56. Sherwood, *Vindication* (New York: Farrar, Straus & Giroux, 1993).

57. Kernan's *The Lost Diaries of Frans Hals* (New York: St. Martin's Press, 1995), featuring Frans Hals, Judith Leyster, and René Descartes; and Cocky van Bokhoven, *Johannes Vermeer* (Breda: Uitgeverij De Geus, 1996).

58. Like the author as character, the painter as character is not limited to a single literary genre. Robert Browning presented the painters Fra Filippo Lippi

(1406–69) and Andrea del Sarto (1486–1531) in the dramatic monologue. Equally, Michelangelo is not only a character in the Irving Stone novel; he is also a daunting presence, together with Raphael Sanzio, in Friedrich Hebbel's two-act play *Michel Angelo* (1850). In their joint play, *Goya's Last Portrait* (1989), John Berger and Nella Bielski successfully present the most famous nineteenth-century Spanish painter. The stage, with its appeal to man's ocular sense, has proved a most suitable site for the fictionalization of the painter and his art. Arguably the clearest example is Austrian-born painter/playwright Oskar Kokoshka's fifth and last play, *Comenius* (1972). In this pseudo-historical drama, the eponymous Czech reformer meets his Dutch contemporary, Rembrandt van Rijn, at Amsterdam. The plot is fictional, but it does include the painting of *The Night Watch*, making nearly impossible demands on the pictorial skills of any theater company that might consider staging it. See Kokoschka, *Comenius*, in *Das Schriftliche Werk*, 4 vols. (Hamburg: Christians, 1973), vol. 1, *Dichtungen und Dramen*. For an in-depth analysis of the play, see the standard work on the subject by Henry I. Schvey, *Oskar Kokoschka: The Painter as Playwright* (Detroit: Wayne State University Press, 1982), 116–33.

59. Robert Browning revived Baldassaro Galuppi (1706–85) in "A Toccata of Galuppi's," and Georg Joseph Vogler (1749–1814) in "Abt Vogler (*After He Has Been Extemporizing Upon the Musical Instrument of His Invention*)." In the field of music, the *vie romancée* has proved a most popular genre. As early as 1859, Herbert Rau wrote a historical novel on Ludwig van Beethoven. Since then, Franz Werfel has revived Giuseppe Verdi (1924); Patrick de Rosbo has turned Antonio Vivaldi into a writer of memoires (1986); while Samuel Chotzinoff has revisited Beethoven in his novel, *Eroica* (1930). The field seems to lend itself to further subdivisions, such as the composer's youth: while Felix Huch concentrated on young Beethoven (1927), F. N. Monjo was concerned with W. A. Mozart as a boy of fourteen (*Letters to Horseface*, 1975), and Martin Stade with young J. S. Bach (1985). Love tends to be a key word, too; Hermann Richter's novels on Robert Schumann, Johannes Brahms, and Joseph Haydn explicitly carry the word "love" in their titles (*Von ewiger Liebe: Ein Schumann-Brahms-Roman*, 1929, and *Die Jahreszeiten der Liebe: ein Haydn-Roman*, 1931), as does Viktor Trautzl's Franz Schubert fiction (*Franz Schuberts letzte Liebe*, 1928). Maria Matray was fascinated by the love life of George Sand, devoting one novel to her affair with composer Frederic Chopin (*Die Liebenden: George Sand und Frederic Chopin*, 1977, written together with Answald Krüger), another to her involvement with the French poet and dramatist Alfred de Musset (*Ein Spiel mit der Liebe: George Sand und Alfred de Musset*, 1990). Beethoven keeps attracting attention, in novels by Joachim Kupsch (*Die Mühsal eines Tages*, 1975), Vernon A. Chamberlain (1977), and Dieter Kühn (1990).

60. An early exercise in the genre was Eduard Mörike's *Mozart auf Reise nach Prag* (1855). Early, too, was Alexander Pushkin's short verse play *Mozart and Salieri* (1831). It served as the model for the libretto of Rimsky-Korsakov's opera *Mozart and Salieri*, and was a source of inspiration for Peter Shaffer's *Amadeus* (1980), which, in turn, formed the basis of Milos Forman's highly successful 1984 movie with the same title. Recent novels on Mozart include David Weiss's *Sacred and Profane* (1968) and Michel Alibert's *Sacré Mozart* (1995).

61. Burgess, *On Mozart: A Paean for Wolfgang. Being a celestial colloquy, an opera libretto, a bewildered rumination, a Stendhalian transcription, and a heartfelt homage upon the bicentenary of the death of Wolfgang Amadeus Mozart* (New York: Ticknor & Fields, 1991).

62. Leon Edel, *The Life of Henry James* (1953–72; repr. in two vols., Harmondsworth: Penguin, 1977), 1:848. Among other things, Edel quotes James as saying that Browning was "no more like to Paracelsus than I to Hercules" (1: 537). The discrepancy is also captured in a confession of James's to his sister Alice: "evidently there are two Brownings—an esoteric and an exoteric. The former never peeps out in society, and the latter has not a ray of suggestion of *Men and Women*" (1: 537). It is worth noting that James also experienced such disappointment with other artists, like Lord Tennyson (Edel, 1: 572–75).

The Author as Character

The Author:
Postmodernism's Stock Character

ALEID FOKKEMA

There are brief and complex descriptions of postmodernism in literature. A catch phrase to sum it all up might run as follows: the author is dead, character is dead, this is the end of the story. Obviously, a more cautious definition can be much longer and will, inevitably, contain objections, restrictions, and counterexamples. The first is offered by postmodernism's detractors, the second by its advocates who do not see the end of story, but rather a shift toward a new paradigm of narrative. Is there, in that new paradigm, any room for those cherished, humanized, and humanist figures, authors and characters? For a while, in the 1970s, when the first attempts were made to define postmodernism, this seemed indeed impossible, as postmodernism was all about fragmentation, anti-representation, and the breakdown of narrative.[1] Now, however, we cannot be so sure.

It is true that Roland Barthes's proclamation of the death of the author became the war cry of postmodernism. However, arguing against the idea of the author as agent, as source of a text, is not an exclusively postmodern phenomenon at all. The idea is also close to Eliot's poetics of impersonality, or the New Critics' emphasis on the text itself as the source of meaning.[2] Barthes's major target in his famous essay, "The Death of the Author" (1968), was not really the author but a practice of reading that construes a single or unified meaning by means of the authority of the author, and that practice has indeed changed (at least in the universities) and moved beyond the point of no return.[3] The act of reading, however, involves presuming an author a priori, even when this author is elusive, institutional, divine, or dehumanized, a text generator dressed up with all the postmodern trappings. As Linda Hutcheon argues, "[the] *position* of discursive authority still lives on, because it is encoded in the enunciative act itself."[4] Thus, what occurs in postmodernism is not the abolishment of the author but a relocation and reconsideration of his (its) function.

Instead of single and unique authorship, we appear to have an encoded subject position situated in discourse. With this substitution, however, the humanist predecessor cannot altogether be reasoned away; he sticks on as a residue that resists being swallowed up. The idea of the author as a mere discursive subject is rather deficient and lacks explanatory power. Authors of postmodern fiction will not disown their creations when summoned to accept a literary prize, and in criticism, too, the concept of a "personal" author lingers on. Is an author's gender ever actually irrelevant to the gender critic? If the author is therefore at once personal and impersonal, both gendered and sexless, both scriptor and a system where various discursive and historical formations meet, then a theory of authorship threatens to collapse from sheer weight. The challenge set is to prevent this. Therefore, what is at stake now in postmodernism is not the "death" of the author but how the discursive author can be reconciled with a personal author in clear terms that salvage, if not enrich, thinking on the subject. What this entails for postmodern fictions, including biographical fictions and fictional biographies, shall be argued below. As for criticism, it is worth pointing out that the emphasis in poststructuralist or New Historicist criticism may have been on the linguistic or sociocultural processes that intersect in a given work, but that the (tacit) assumption has always been that the reason why such processes play any role in the production of meaning is that someone, and not just an institution, bothered to put that work together, to *write* it, in the first place. Or, as Seán Burke argues, those recent developments in criticism "suggest the restoration of a working concept of authorship if only to provide a point of access to historical, cultural and colonial contexts."[5] And so, postmodernism may, in its final stages, return to resurrecting a workable and theoretically sound author concept—a destiny to be fulfilled in pages other than these.

What, then, of character? True, realistic character has been replaced by a type that flaunts in various degrees its embedding in textuality. The same issues of origin and control that affect thinking about the author turn up again, and discourses, language, and simply history are shown to intersect in "character." But is this the end of conventional, representational character? Think of Susan Barton, the lost voice in J. M. Coetzee's *Foe* (1985), the woman whose narrative was allegedly appropriated by Daniel Defoe and turned into his bestselling *Robinson Crusoe*.[6] Susan Barton is, by all means, a bookish character indeed. She has a totally anachronistic awareness of language and power that is perfectly in tune with contemporary postmodern concerns. But is she, therefore, unrepresentational? Obviously, her part has been muted by Defoe. She may not be "alive" in the "leaping-from-the-page" sense, but is she dead? We read her thoughts, we read her emotions; she even shows growth, or development, as her changing relation to the character "Friday" may witness. It is better to qualify the observation that "character" has come to an end by considering the possibility that perhaps the conventions of mimesis have changed.[7]

And so, the end is a beginning. Postmodernism is not about the end of the story but, rather, about the story of story. Curiously, one of those stories that pervades this movement is the one that figures an author. The prevalence of this theme is fascinating, even when not counting the numerous appearances of the writing self, the writer doubling as character.[8] Where, in earlier literary movements, a character is only occasionally based on the biography of a real author, without any serious impact on that movement's general aspect, real-world authors appear abundantly as characters in postmodern fiction. They are the flesh and bones, so to speak, of postmodernism, embodying its major themes: concern with writing, origin and loss, the question of representation.

It is no great exaggeration to say that postmodernism's stock character is an author. I will argue this case by discussing three different variations on the motif. Here, the postmodern crisis of representation will be the binding idea.[9] This will lead, first, to a discussion of how the limitations of representation can be circumnavigated and how irrational, extralinguistic knowledge can be acquired. As a sample text I shall use not a fiction about a real author but a case of a postmodern biography that incorporates fiction, namely Peter Ackroyd's *Dickens*. Then I will move on to the more familiar idea that there is no knowledge except in language, that the representation of that knowledge leads, in an infinite regress, to other representations but never to the (mistaken concept of) referential knowledge. A large number of postmodern novels might have illustrated this case (some are, indeed, the subject of other essays in this volume); but I shall limit my discussion to *Flaubert's Parrot* by Julian Barnes. Finally, I shall illustrate postmodernism's obsession with the idea that representation is never disinterested, with a discussion of a short story by Angela Carter, entitled "Black Venus." This section will branch out into a brief discussion of similar postmodern works.

A NOVEL IN DISGUISE: POSTMODERN BIOGRAPHY

Readers may now be skeptical of the writer who supremely and autonomously originates a text, but they still appear to thirst for biographical knowledge. As, in retrospect, the last decades of the twentieth century might well be characterized as the age of biography rather than of postmodernism, that thirst may easily be quenched with the numerous "Lives" that continue to appear. The real fan, however, is not so much interested in new facts or in reading that Jane Austen jilted two lovers rather than one, but in understanding why she wrote, and how. Perhaps readers actually are thirsty for a biographical replica of their favorite novelist's fiction, as a lost work that is recovered from a dusty attic. So it is demanded from the biographer that he or she be a novelist. A conflict of interests may be the result: how can the objectivity of factual evidence be protected from the accusation of fantasy?[10] Reviewers do not take kindly to a biographer's novelistic tendencies. Penelope Fitzgerald, herself a writer of fictions and biographies (such as *The Blue Flower* of 1995, a novel on the life of the German poet, Novalis), takes Morton N. Cohen to task for "ungainly speculations," citing the following passage from his biography of Lewis Carroll as an example:

> Alice might have impetuously piped up: "I'm going to marry Mr. Dodgson." And if Charles were present, perhaps taking it as a teasing remark, or not, he might have picked up the thread and replied: "Well said, and why not!" That might have much to do with the case. Young females can bat their eyes, shake their heads, toss their locks about, feign innocence, and make outrageous suggestions—all with intent to shock and call attention to themselves. And the three clever Liddell sisters were probably expert in these arts.[11]

This is unacceptable, Fitzgerald suggests, not because of Cohen's projective imagination but because this fictional, imaginative excursion is muffled, swathed in tentative mights and perhaps, in order to produce the scholarly text, the authorized version. A reverse effect ensues; the probable becomes a laughable improbable, and the whole exercise fails, because the paradigm of scholarship is that fact always prevails over fiction. Fiction in biography, though desired, is at best an indulgence, at worst mere aberration.

The postmodern biographer refuses to play that game. He or she will question the value of factual evidence and overcome the conflict between truth and lies by treating both as versions of what can no longer be recovered. The British postmodern novelist and biographer Peter Ackroyd has integrated this conflict in his work, making visible the opposition between the two tasks. The major theme of his fictional writing is the idea of recurrence, both in support of a mystic, romantic notion of a spiritual continuity, and manifesting a more postmodern fascination with the circulation of language and the principle of intertextuality.[12] Fragments from other writers reverberate in his fiction, and the authors he alludes to in his novels most frequently are Charles Dickens, William Blake, Oscar Wilde, T.S. Eliot, as well as Thomas Chatterton, that impostor, camp romantic or "marvelous boy" whose work has not succeeded in entering the canon and whose residual phrases in Ackroyd's work are therefore easy to miss. The interesting thing is that Ackroyd has also written biographies on three of these authors. His works on Eliot (1984), Dickens (1990), and Blake (1995) are seriously researched biographies that have the status of standard texts. In addition, the other two authors have been the subject of his novels *The Last Testament of Oscar Wilde* (1983) and *Chatterton* (1987). Ackroyd's oeuvre is centered on writers' lives and writers' words that make up a web of cross-references.

What caused a minor shock when his biography on Dickens appeared, is the set piece where all five authors make an appearance and actually have a fictional conversation with each other on the nature of art. (Blake does not make his appearance but is mentioned in passing, and "Chatterton" prophetically says that "he will be joining [the group] shortly"[13]). Each character acts his part faithfully. As a result the conversation is an anachronistic jungle of observations on plagiarism, truth, falsehood, mimesis, religion, and inspiration. As the third of eight so-called interludes scattered throughout the biography, it is called, characteristically, "A true conversation between imagined selves." The conversation is true in the sense that it is a patchwork of phrases, the words that survived the writer and that stand in his stead. The words are what we know, Ackroyd seems to say, but when we want to know what motivates them, to what secret passions and fears they are related, we enter a different domain: abandoning knowledge, we make a leap with the imagination. Therefore his fictional conversation is "true," or no less true than the stricter parts of this biography, and just as factual as the events of the other interludes, where Dickens meets the characters from his own novels and, in turn, meets his author/biographer in a typical postmodern topos that allows for yet another ontological clash (McHale, 213). No wonder the biographer himself arranges for an interview, subject of one interlude, in which he admits to cheating and treating Dickens like a character in one of this Victorian's own novels (*Dickens*, 894 and 896). Yet this should not be taken to imply that Ackroyd played a simple postmodern hoax; rather it indicates that Ackroyd is serious about fully admitting the conflict of fact and fiction as an integral part of (biographical) writing. There is no fact without fiction, or, the author *has* to become a character.

The eight numbered interludes do not figure on the contents page where thirty-five chapters, the notes, the epilogue, and the like are faithfully listed. Instead, the interludes pop up irregularly, at unexpected places in the text. They have, therefore, no "official" status in the main text, but they are not bracketed by any disclaimers either. It is as if fiction has crept in, unaccountably, pasting a haze over the transparency of facts. On the one hand, the ontological certainties of the representational biography are undermined, at the expense of conventional mimesis; but, on the other, an imaginative power is restored. The postmodern paradox is that the ideology of "knowing" through representation is shattered, to be replaced with a paradigm of representing the unrepresentable, as Jean François Lyotard has argued.[14] Lyotard's postmodernism is, in this respect, a form of romanticism. As I have mentioned, Ackroyd, too, is essentially a romantic writer: not at peace with an epistemological impasse, he fills with a leap of the imagination the gap between the irrecoverable subject or referent (Dickens) and its representation or sign (the biography).[15] Substituting the "author" Dickens with the "character" of a writer called Dickens, a character like any of the other characters from books written by an author called Dickens, the biography may then turn into one of those novels; it may work for you and me, thirsty readers, as a posthumous Dickens. There is one difference, though, between the character "Dickens" and the characters in his novels: he remains the writer, and the postmodern concern with his character is properly one with writing. The interludes dwell on the issue of representation, to the point of self-reflexivity, on the origins and effects of writing, and on the autonomy of the author, forcing us to wonder whether Dickens (and, by implication, any author) possesses language or is possessed by it.

Such, then, is the postmodern biography: a game of "art and lies" (as Jeanette Winterson jokes). It is also an attempt to draw the author out (in more than one sense) by upsetting the conventional limitations of scholarly, factual representation. Ackroyd's *Dickens* exemplifies the postmodern aporia of representing the unrepresentable. As an official biography, it may not fall strictly within the boundaries of a discussion of authors as characters in fiction. But postmodernism cares little for such boundaries anyway, and it is, of course, no more than the flip side of the coin of a continuum of postmodern fictions about, or around, an author. The problem of authorship lies at the core of the issue of representation which, in various guises, recurs in postmodern texts, so that the story of an author might even be designated as postmodernism's "Urtext" were it not that the mere notion of "Ur" is inimical to postmodernism.

THE WRITER'S LIFE: A NOVEL

The profound disbelief in conventional representation could be frustrating when matched by a desire to represent; but it is not, because that frustration is reversed to become, creatively, the subject of writing. In *Flaubert's Parrot,* Julian Barnes takes an oppositional course to Ackroyd's *Dickens,* resolutely denying his favorite author even a fictional "life." His Flaubert simply cannot be recovered; but that impossibility to summon up the "presence" of Flaubert then becomes the subject of an entertaining and surprisingly knowledgeable novel. An apparent report of the painstaking efforts of a Flaubert amateur, the middle-aged physician Geoffrey Braithwaite, to gather the facts of Flaubert's life, the book contains, among other things, three different "chronologies" of the kind sometimes found in an introduction to a great author's work: dates with an outline of important events, a type of shorthand biographies. One of these is entirely positive. Another gives the same dates but dwells exclusively on the failures of Flaubert's life; and the last quotes passages from letters by Flaubert written on those dates that bear on neither the first nor the second. Clearly each "biography" is not a sign that transparently refers to the referent, Flaubert, but an artifact, at best an interpretation of his life, with certain vested interests: to celebrate his greatness, to create an image of the *poète maudit* and *méconnu,* and, most significantly, to present samples from his writing as the best key to his life. *Flaubert's Parrot* is about attempting to write about a writer one admires—Flaubert is to Barnes what Dickens, or Blake, is to Peter Ackroyd—in different ways, serious and nonsensical, without ever getting any closer to this subject than one can by reading his novels or letters. Thus, at crucial moments Flaubert is quoted and he speaks, literally, for himself, and that language is both the only key to the writer as subject and the final barrier that withholds his

presence, in particular as the quotes in the texts proleptically en-
visage the postmodern dilemma, as in the following:

> Words came easily to Flaubert; but he also saw the underlying inade-
> quacy of the Word. Remember his sad definition from *Madame Bovary:*
> "Language is like a cracked kettle on which we beat out tunes for bears
> to dance to, while all the time we long to move the stars to pity."[16]

Through the powerful and versatile trope of the parrot, Barnes
investigates language, origin, and authenticity. Braithwaite, the
would-be biographer, is happy to find in Rouen a relic that, he feels,
brings him closer to the writer he admires, a stuffed parrot once
borrowed by Flaubert when he wrote *Un cœur simple:* "I gazed
at the bird, and to my surprise felt ardently in touch with this writer
who disdainfully forbade posterity to take any personal interest in
him" (Barnes, 16). To his dismay, however, he discovers that there
is another such parrot in a rival museum, and by the end of the
novel the number of parrots claiming authenticity has increased to
fifty. The lack of authentic biographical truth that is embodied
by the parrot then metonymically extends to language in general,
leading Braithwaite to wonder whether "the writer [is] much more
than a sophisticated parrot?" (Barnes, 18). At best, it seems, the
biographer is quite literally no more than a writer's parrot, substituting the author's language for the unreliable "hard" data of unauthentic facts. When that author's language is parroted as well, the
result is a spiral of infinite regress.

Flaubert's Parrot records the different attempts to write Flaubert's life, including biographical fictions; but it withholds the illusion of reality. At one point, it "define[s] a net as a jocular
lexicographer once did: he called it a collection of holes tied together with string" (Barnes, 38). Flaubert, this elusive protagonist,
is such a collection of holes; but the novel Barnes wrote demonstrates that even out of frustrated representation a book, or perhaps strings of words and strands of text, can be accomplished.
Alternatively, the metaphor can be taken one step further: Flaubert, then, is a slippery fish, forever trapped in a language, his
own, that was his life. Like the Dickens of Ackroyd, he is first and
foremost a writer, and the novel is in true postmodern fashion
concerned with his *writing.*

THE RISE OF THE REPRESSED "OTHER"

Best known for her explorations of the cultural potential of myth
that resulted in the rich rewritings of a collection of fairy tales,

The Bloody Chamber, Angela Carter has also addressed the literary topos of the romantic poet in love. Choosing Charles Baudelaire's celebrated infatuation with his dark lady, the "weird
goddess, dusky as night" who has been identified as the (possibly)
Caribbean Jeanne Duval, Carter sets herself the task of imagining
the story of this woman.[17] This has the double effect of reversing
the subject-object relation that characterizes the male romantic
poet's stance and giving life, dignity even, to a woman whose biography, as the narrator drily remarks, has so far been obscure.
Baudelaire, the author, is a proper character in this short story,
not, as in the previous cases, the subject of admiration that cannot
be known but, rather, an obsessed and careless figure who can only
project his colonial fantasies on his objet trouvé, his Jeanne. This
leads to comic scenes, where the poet croons that he will take her
back to her "parrot forest" and she explodes, "No, not the bloody
parrot forest! Don't take me on the slaver's route to the West-
Indies, for godsake!" (Carter, *Black Venus,* 11). Subtly, Carter
shows that Jeanne is indeed no more, cannot be more than the
object of Baudelaire's speculative gaze until she is liberated from
him by his death. When his mistress, she is, in the biographical
vignette "in neither a state of innocence nor a state of grace" and
dutifully performs her tasks as the poet's exotic lover, undressing
where Baudelaire stays fully clothed (*Black Venus,* 9). The subject-
object relation, immortalized as one of doctor and patient in Luce
Irigaray's *Spéculum* (a work familiar to Carter), is emphasized by
the reference to Baudelaire's pink gloves that he will always keep
wearing and that "fitted as tenderly close as the rubber gloves that
gynecologists will wear."[18] She only awakens from her apathy once
the poet dies, as if only then the language of his poems can no
longer trap her. Characteristically, he has not only infected her,
according to Carter, with syphilis, but has also failed to provide for
her after his death. Miraculously, though, she survives, in Carter's
rewriting (which she contrasts, in accordance with the postmodern
convention, to a contemporary witness's account of her demise),
and returns to what Carter imagines is her home country, Martinique, in the company of a self-styled brother.[19] In Martinique she
regains full dignity, having "found herself" as a madam. Carter, a
Marxist but no moralist, has always been fond of the finer ironies
of life: where before Jeanne was a commodity and did not even
know her "own use value," she is now herself in control of the
commodity that is "woman" (*Black Venus,* 13).

"Black Venus" is more than an attempt to set the record straight.
A fiction that at different points crosses the border into the dis-

course of criticism, its ontological status is, as in so many postmodern works, undefinable. What this story has in common with other postmodern works, including the ones discussed here, is a commitment to *writing,* to the pragmatics of text in the broadest sense: how language shapes, models, and even captivates experience, not only that of the two fictional protagonists, Jeanne Duval and her lover, the poet Baudelaire, but also of readers. By cunningly giving at the end of the story a full quotation of "Sed non satiata," that poem can now be read only as an example of Baudelaire's gross misunderstanding and puerile mystification of his lover. This new reading is not innocent, nor in a state of grace, to refer to Carter's description of Jeanne; but neither was, this story implies, any earlier pre-lapsarian reading. The Foucauldian paradigm of the interdependence of power and language is reinforced by the colonial subtext: this is not merely about woman being muted by man but a colony kept dumb by the colonizer. Jeanne was "the pure child of colony" who, in Paris, gives up Creole to speak French, but that language of the other "made her dumb." As in Coetzee's *Foe,* where the slave Friday does not speak because, possibly, his tongue has been cut out, Jeanne experiences her alienation "as though her tongue had been cut out and another one sewn in that did not fit well" (*Black Venus,* 17–18).

This postcolonial development may appear to lead us away from what should be the central concern of this essay: the author as fictional character. But that is precisely the point. When power and language are at issue, the author who *fathers* texts must be displaced, decentered, marginalized, and debunked. In "Black Venus," Baudelaire is an author who wrote enchanting poetry but he was also syphilitic, abusive, self-possessed, imperialist, dirty, impotent, and a poor judge of the objets d'art that he professed to collect. Carter's story is typical of the concern with the relation between power and representation that has inspired most of the postmodern "author" fictions. In a few cases, this theme surfaces as a resurrection of the minor author who has been neglected because of the mechanisms of the canon; Peter Ackroyd's *Chatterton* is a case in point.[20] Mostly, however, a famous author is exposed as a manipulative scoundrel. In *Foe,* it is Daniel Defoe who is dismissive of the woman captive, Sue Barton. A schemer and manipulator, he mutes her side of the story and effectively appropriates it, rewriting Friday's part as well. The eponymous romantic poet in Sigrid Combüchen's *Byron: A Novel* (1988) is not shown from his best side either (and Shelley gets even worse treatment).[21] Through the different, contrasting perspectives of his contemporaries and some enthusiastic Byronites in the 1930s, a portrait is painted of a man obsessed with manipulation, abusive of women, indulging in an incestuous love affair, whose major life events return thinly disguised in his poems. It is interesting to note here that only male authors are subjected to this treatment (in fact, only a few female authors ever occur as characters, and then mostly in novels that do not question representation).[22] As if indeed the founding fathers of literature must be robbed of their phallic power. Perhaps this also explains why some authors recur again and again in postmodern fiction; authors who have towered over twentieth-century culture, casting an inescapable shadow. Henry James is a case in point. In Joan Aiken's *The Haunting of Lamb House*, he is a vulnerable, rather pompous figure who is only dimly aware of the reasons for his sister Alice's depression and is severely criticized by Edith Wharton for a (fictional) ghost story, written during James's abstruse "late phase."[23] Susan Sontag's play *Alice in Bed* also focuses on Henry James's misunderstanding of his sister's depression (in true postmodern, unfactual fashion, Emily Dickinson is far more understanding), and in *Henry James' Midnight Song*, a novel by Carol de Chellis Hill, he is a secret but avid consumer of trash novels.[24] In this novel he also meets Sigmund Freud, another founding father, whose case histories have often been praised for their literary qualities. Of all authors, Freud is most conspicuously the subject of pastiche, a topic worthy of another book: Freud is shown at work, as case histories are rewritten and invented, but he is exposed as a prejudiced manipulator who, because of his own biases, the discourses that influenced and constituted his thinking, falsely represents the case histories of his patients.[25]

The story of an author is told again and again in postmodern texts. That story is all about representation, querying its (im-)possibilities, its relation to knowledge, language, and power. But the author rarely turns into the poststructuralist topos of the 1980s: a reductive subject in language. The postmodern stock character, also known as the author, has a number of properties: he is, nearly exclusively, a man (Emily Dickinson and Edith Wharton, from the previous examples, are little else than figureheads, not portrayed for their writing). He is shaped by and concerned with his writing, to such an extent that this writing, involving both inspiration and the question of representation, becomes the theme of the narrative. Finally, he shows at least two faces as he occupies both a subject position in the system (or chaos) of writing and effectively pro-duces texts as a person, even when little else may be known about him.

NOTES TO "THE AUTHOR: POSTMODERNISM'S STOCK CHARACTER"

1. See Hans Bertens, *The Idea of the Postmodern: A History* (London: Routledge, 1995). An example of a study that celebrates the "end" of character in postmodernism is Thomas Docherty, *Reading Absent Character: Towards a Theory of Characterization in Fiction* (Oxford: Clarendon Press, 1983). In his chapter, "Authors: Dead and Posthumous," Brian McHale traces the tendency of certain postmodern authors to erase authorship. See his *Postmodernist Fiction* (New York: Methuen, 1992), 197–215.

2. Stanley Fish, "Biography and Intention," in *Contesting the Subject,* ed. William H. Epstein (West Lafayette: Purdue University Press, 1991), 13.

3. Barthes, "The Death of the Author," in *Image-Music-Text,* ed. and trans. Stephen Heath (London: Fontana, 1984), 79–124. For a discussion of this point, see also, Cheryl Walker, "Feminist Literary Criticism and the Author," in *Critical Inquiry* 16 (1990): 551–71.

4. Hutcheon, *A Poetics of Postmodernism* (New York: Routledge, 1988), 77.

5. Burke, "Introduction," in *Authorship: From Plato to the Postmodern: A Reader* (Edinburgh: Edinburgh University Press, 1995), xxvii.

6. Coetzee, *Foe* (1986; repr. Harmondsworth: Penguin, 1988).

7. For a full discussion of this subject, see my study, *Postmodern Characters: A Study of Characterization in British and American Postmodern Fiction,* Postmodern Studies, 4 (Amsterdam and Atlanta: Rodopi, 1991).

8. This appears to be the trademark of some postmodern authors: Gilbert Sorrentino, Martin Amis, and Iain Sinclair.

9. See also, Bertens, *Idea of the Postmodern,* 242.

10. In the words of Richard Holmes, "the inventing, shaping instinct of the storyteller struggles with the idea of a permanent, historical, and objective document." See his "Inventing the Truth," in *The Art of Literary Biography,* ed. John Batchelor (Oxford: Clarendon Press, 1995), 20.

11. Cohen, *Lewis Carroll: A Biography* (New York: Knopf, 1995), as quoted by Penelope Fitzgerald, in "In the Golden Afternoon: Psychological Adventures with Lewis Caroll," *Times Literary Supplement,* 17 November 1995, 3.

12. See my "Abandoning the Postmodern? The Case of Peter Ackroyd," in *British Postmodern Fiction,* ed. Theo D'haen and Hans Bertens (Amsterdam and Atlanta: Rodopi, 1993), 167–79.

13. Ackroyd, *Dickens* (London: Sinclair-Stevenson, 1990), 430.

14. Lyotard, "Answering the Question: What Is Postmodernism?" in *Innovation/Renovation: New Perspectives on the Humanities,* ed. Ihab and Sally Hassan (Madison: University of Wisconsin Press, 1983), 340.

15. See Patricia Waugh, *Practising Postmodernism Reading Modernism* (London: Edward Arnold, 1992), 32.

16. Barnes, *Flaubert's Parrot* (London: Jonathan Cape, 1984), 19.

17. The quotation is Carter's translation of the first line of "Sed non satiata" from Baudelaire's *Les Fleurs du mal.* See Carter, "Black Venus," in *Black Venus* (London: Chatto & Windus, 1985), 15 and 23.

18. Luce Irigaray, *Spéculum de l'autre femme* (Paris: Minuit, 1974); and Carter, *Black Venus,* 20.

19. At this point, other intertexts intersect in the production of meaning, namely Charlotte Brontë's *Jane Eyre* and Jean Rhys's rewriting of it as *Wide Sargasso Sea.*

20. Ackroyd, *Chatterton* (1987; repr. London: Abacus, 1988).

21. Combüchen, *Byron: A Novel* (1988), trans. Joan Tate (London: Heinemann, 1991).

22. See Christine Duhon, *Une année amoureuse de Virginia Woolf* (Paris: Olivier Orban, 1990); and Jamie Fuller, *The Diary of Emily Dickinson* (San Francisco: Mercury House, 1993).

23. Joan Aiken, *The Haunting of Lamb House* (London: Jonathan Cape, 1991).

24. Sontag, *Alice in Bed: A Play* (New York: Farrar, 1993); and Carol de Chellis Hill, *Henry James' Midnight Song* (1993; repr. New York: Norton, 1995). I would like to thank Liedeke Plate for drawing my attention to these two works.

25. On Sigmund Freud as a character, see Anita Loos, *Gentlemen Prefer Blondes* (New York: Boni Liveright, 1925), D. M. Thomas, *The White Hotel* (1981; repr. London: Penguin, 1985), and *Eating Pavlova* (London: Bloomsbury, 1994), Anthony Burgess, *The End of the World News* (New York: McGraw-Hill, 1983), Keith Oatley, *The Case of Emily V.* (London: Secker and Warburg, 1993), and Hélène Cixous, *Portrait of Dora,* trans. Sarah Burd, *Diacritics* 13:1 (1983): 2–32.

Virgil in Dante's *Divine Comedy*

CHRISTOPHER KLEINHENZ

In the *selva oscura* of the first canto of the *Divine Comedy,* Dante the Poet stages the meeting between his principal character—Dante the Pilgrim—and the shade of Virgil, the Roman poet. In that strange and unfamiliar landscape, one fraught with moral and allegorical significance, two literary characters meet, converse, and begin their journey through the otherworld. However, these characters have—and had—real, historical identities; thus each brings, for the Poet's imaginative use, a rich complex of cultural, literary, and historical elements. Ontological truth is the foundation of the *Divine Comedy*—"the fiction of the *Divine Comedy* is that it is not fiction," as Charles S. Singleton so aptly remarked: it is this basic premise that endows the poem with its extraordinary dramatic power, its moral validity, and ultimately its spiritual authority.[1] The dramatis personae of Dante's poem are not simply "characters" in a literary text, whose words and actions exist and have meaning only in that text; rather, they are all made integral parts of the eternal order of the universe—are placed in Hell, or in Purgatory, or in Paradise—according to their earthly life and actions. They are not abstract personifications, mere metaphors. They are the shades of real historical figures, seen, summed up, and judged in the afterlife—shades made "flesh and blood" again by the poet's special genius.[2]

Among the myriad characters in the *Divine Comedy,* the figure of Virgil is the most important, after that of Dante the Pilgrim. He is present through sixty-four of the one hundred cantos of the poem and is principally responsible for guiding Dante through the first two realms of the afterlife. This essay is concerned with Dante's use of the historical and legendary Virgil as a character in his great medieval eschatological epic and with his incorporation of Virgilian verse into its poetic fabric.[3]

52

When Virgil appears to Dante in the first canto of the *Inferno*, he introduces himself using precise information about his historical existence:[4]

> . . . *li parenti miei furon lombardi,*
> *mantoani per patrïa ambedui.*
>   *Nacqui sub Iulio, ancor che fosse tardi,*
> *e vissi a Roma sotto 'l buono Augusto*
> *nel tempo de li dèi falsi e bugiardi.*
>   *Poeta fui, e cantai di quel giusto*
> *figliuol d' Anchise che venne di Troia,*
> *poi che 'l superbo Ilïon fu combusto.*
>
> (1:68–75)

Both of my parents came from Lombardy, / and both claimed Mantua as native city. / And I was born, though late, *sub Julio*, / and lived in Rome under the good Augustus—/ the season of the false and lying gods. / I was a poet, and I sang the righteous / son of Anchises who had come from Troy / when flames destroyed the pride of Ilium.

These verses contain what, for Dante, were the most important facts about Virgil's life and, thus, the most compelling reasons for his selection as the Pilgrim's guide in this Christian epic. Virgil was born in 70 B.C. near Mantua and was thus "Italian." He associates himself with the Julio-Claudian line of emperors and was a pagan, although he died (in 19 B.C.) not many years before the coming of Christ. Most important, he was a poet who, in the *Aeneid*, recorded the founding of Rome and her subsequent imperial glory. Besides these matters of historical accuracy, Dante here presents a "medieval" Virgil who offers a moralizing commentary on the fall of "proud" Troy, as well as some understanding of the progress of history according to Providential design—from pagan to Christian Rome.

Dante's own character—the Pilgrim—immediately identifies the apparition before him:

> "Or se' tu quel Virgilio e quella fonte
> che spandi di parlar sì largo fiume?"
> rispuos' io lui con vergognosa fronte.
>   "O de li altri poeti onore e lume,
> vagliami 'l lungo studio e 'l grande amore

> *che m' ha fatto cercar lo tuo volume.*
> *Tu se' lo mio maestro e 'l mio autore,*
> *tu se' solo colui da cu' io tolsi*
> *lo bello stilo che m' ha fatto onore."*

(1:79–87)

"And are you then that Virgil, you the fountain / that freely pours so rich a stream of speech?" / I answered him with shame upon my brow. / "O light and honor of all other poets, / may my long study and the intense love / that made me search your volume serve me now. / You are my master and my author, you—/ the only one from whom my writing drew / the noble style for which I have been honored."

From these few verses we recognize the great admiration and respect the Pilgrim has for the historical Virgil, but this is not simply a passive acknowledgment of his worth. Indeed, we learn that Dante has been an active learner at his master's feet, and it is precisely this dynamic relationship that provides the basis for their dramatic interaction in the poem. Virgil's works were the standard texts in the schools of antiquity and the Middle Ages; he was a "curriculum author," and for centuries students received instruction from his works—they were all, so to speak, students of Virgil.[5] Here and elsewhere, Dante the Pilgrim acknowledges his literary and intellectual debt to Virgil, whose poetry served as a stylistic model and whose championing of the Roman empire shaped his own views on temporal power. Virgil is both teacher (*maestro*) and author (*autore*), and the latter term has many important etymological connotations: authority, creator, maker, producer. The ordering of these terms suggests a hierarchy: while the *maestro* conveys and explains a given tradition to others, the *autore* is the inventor and guarantor of that tradition. For Dante, Virgil subsumes these two identities and functions in his single person.

Virgil's remark that he lived in Rome "*nel tempo de li dèi falsi e bugiardi*" ("the season of the false and lying gods") also establishes the pattern for what could be termed his "personally pathetic situation"; that is, he often refers to the fact that he is not a Christian, that, despite his great virtues and worth as a poet, he is not among the blessed. This "tragedy" of Virgil is compounded by the proximity of his death (19 B.C.) to the advent of the Christian era and even more by the common perception in the Middle Ages that his Fourth Eclogue may be read as a prophecy of the coming of the Messiah.[6]

The initial scene of encounter between our two protagonists in *Inferno* 1 is laden with allegorical significance. The Pilgrim who has lost his way in the "*selva oscura*" ("dark wood") attempts to climb the sunlit mountain and meets opposition in the form of three beasts—the leopard, lion, and she-wolf. The dark wood suggests the gloom and confusion of morally corrupt human society, while the sun both illuminates the delectable mountain and leads "men straight along all roads" ("*che mena dritto altrui per ogne calle,*" 1:19). The beasts appear to embody specific vices or sinful dispositions (she-wolf = incontinence or avarice; leopard = fraud or lust; lion = violence or pride), and show themselves more or less pernicious according to the Pilgrim's own tendency to error. It is the she-wolf that eventually drives the Pilgrim back to the dark wood "*là dove 'l sol tace*" ("where the sun is speechless," 1:60). The wood, the sun, the beasts all then partake of that "doubleness" which is central to allegorical interpretation: they are both *res et signum,* the "thing" and the "sign"—they are what they are, and they also point beyond themselves to higher realities, higher truths. For this reason, Dante's Pilgrim has often been called an "Everyman." This, however, is incorrect, for while it is true that we as readers can identify at times with the figure of the Pilgrim, he is not a faceless figure without any personal history. Dante's journey through the other world is his, and his alone, one granted to him through the agency of Divine Grace; not, therefore, one in which the reader fully participates at every step of the way. Dante's journey is personal, but his poem has the broadest and deepest purpose: to provide positive guidance to the corrupt world: "to profit that world that lives badly" ("*in pro del mondo che mal vive,*" *Purg.* 32:103). Similarly, in the allegorical structure of the *Divine Comedy,* Virgil has often been identified as the personification of Human Reason, and while this is partially true, it would be wrong to view his character only in this reductive way. Virgil is, first and foremost, the Latin poet of the *Aeneid,* the *Georgics* and the *Eclogues,* whose shade resides in Limbo among the virtuous pagans. These particularizing historical features are essential for his interaction with Dante the Pilgrim and with the other characters of the *Comedy.*

In this first encounter scene, the stage is set for the dramatic action of the poem as a whole. Virgil informs Dante of their imminent journey together through Hell and Purgatory, and concludes by referring obliquely to Beatrice ("*anima . . . più di me degna,*" "a soul more worthy than I"), who will lead him to God. In Virgil's construction God becomes the "emperor" who will not let him enter His city ("*non vuol che 'n sua città per me si vegna*") because

he has "been rebellious to His law" ("*ribellante a la sua legge*").
Virgil concludes by exclaiming:

> *In tutte parti impera e quivi regge;*
> *quivi è la sua città e l' alto seggio:*
> *oh felice colui cu' ivi elegge!*

$$(1:127–29)$$

He governs everywhere, but rules from there; / there is His city, His
high capital: / oh happy those he chooses to be there!

We note the sadness that enters Virgil's words when he describes
his lack of grace, for which he cannot enter the celestial city. As
a Roman citizen, Virgil quite naturally would construe the universe
to be ordered as an empire—whose capital city is Eternal Rome,
"*quella Roma onde Cristo è romano*" ("the Rome in which Christ
is Roman," *Purg.* 32:102)—and the Supreme Power to be as the
emperor. Virgil's concluding exclamation, tinged with pathos, pre-
pares the ground for the problem that will dominate the second
canto: the necessity of "election," of being "chosen" to accede
to Paradise.

Virgil's lament raises questions in the Pilgrim's mind concerning
his own fitness for the journey he is about to undertake. He is not,
he declares, Aeneas; nor is he Paul ("*Io non Enëa, io non Paulo*
sono," 2:32), whose journeys—to the underworld and to the third
heaven, respectively—were ordained by God and had a major role
in Providential History. Aeneas founded Rome, which then became
the seat, first, of the empire and then of the Church; as the Chosen
Vessel ("*Vas d'elezïone*," 2:28), Paul strengthened the Christian
faith. The Pilgrim's crisis of self-doubt is very real and, for strate-
gic narrative reasons, must be raised—and resolved—early on.
Virgil encourages his charge, describing as best he can the operation of the three gracious ladies in Heaven—the Virgin Mary, Lucy,
Beatrice—and how, according to this "chain of grace," Beatrice
descended into Limbo to entrust him with this special mission.
Having received assurance that his journey is authorized by
Heaven, Dante regains the sense of election and determination he
had momentarily lost. And the Pilgrim does indeed become, in the
course of the *Comedy,* a "new Aeneas" and a "new Paul."[7]

At the end of the second canto, the Pilgrim declares his respect
for Virgil with the words "*tu duca, tu segnore e tu maestro*"
(2:140). These three terms describe the special hierarchical relationship that exists between the Pilgrim and Virgil, who in all cases

is the superior: he is the Pilgrim's guide (*duca*), protector (*seg-nore*), and teacher (*maestro*). In the course of the poem Virgil will also be a father, mother, and friend to the Pilgrim. Herein lies much of the dramatic power of the *Divine Comedy,* for the Poet is always adjusting and developing the dynamics of his characters in perfect keeping with the action of his narrative.

As the Pilgrim's guide, Virgil is also his protector. This proprietary attitude is manifested as early as the third canto, on the shore of the river Acheron when, in response to Charon the infernal boatman's challenge, he says:

> *Caron, non ti crucciare:*
> *vuolsi così colà dove si puote*
> *ciò che si vuole, e più non dimandare.*
>
> (3:94–96)

Charon, don't torment yourself: / our passage has been willed above, where One / can do what He has willed; and ask no more.

This formulaic phrase—which will be repeated either exactly (*Inf.* 5:23–24) or with modifications (*Inf.* 7:10–12) to counter other challenges—announces the divinely ordained nature of the Pilgrim's journey and, consequently, its specially privileged—and protected—status. Virgil succeeds admirably in his dealings with almost all the infernal guardians or monsters: Charon (canto 3), Minos (5), Cerberus (6), Plutus (7), Phlegyas (8), the Minotaur and Centaurs (12), Geryon (17), the giant Antaeus (31), among others. These triumphs establish the bond of trust and dependence that joins the Pilgrim to him.

However, Hell and its denizens being what they are, we should not be surprised to find that Virgil's stewardship is not without problems and failings. Indeed, there are two anxious moments in the *Inferno.* In cantos 8–9, at the gate of the City of Dis, hordes of rebellious angels, together with the three Furies, refuse the two wayfarers entrance, and Virgil unsuccessfully attempts to bargain a solution to the impasse.[8] The desperate situation is resolved only with the arrival of the Heavenly Messenger, who, Christ-like in appearance and action, subdues the devils' insurrection and opens the gates to the travelers. The allegorical interpretation most frequently given to this scene is that there are times in which Human Reason is insufficient in itself and Divine Grace must come to the rescue.

The second time Virgil fails as a guide occurs in cantos 21–22, where he is deceived by Malacoda, leader of the demons who torment the barrators. By means of an artfully constructed lie, Malacoda convinces Virgil of the existence of a bridge over the next infernal ditch, the *bolgia* containing the hypocrites, and offers his "trusty" devilish colleagues as guides. The Pilgrim is suspicious and would prefer that the two of them proceed by themselves. His instinctive response to the devils and their infernal antics proves correct, whereas Virgil's logical analysis of the proposition is wrong. Virgil is altogether too human and has failings: even "Reason" can be deceived by "Fraud." Indeed, Virgil appears to be unaware of this deceitful ruse until he is reminded by one of the hypocrites that the devil is "a liar and father of lies" ("*è bugiardo e padre di menzogna,*" 23:144). To escape the devils' clutches, Virgil must act instinctively—as a mother who rescues her child from a fire (23:38–42)—grabbing his protégé and sliding down the bank into the next ditch, "*portandosene me sovra 'l suo petto, / come suo figlio, non come compagno*" ("while bearing me with him upon his chest, / just like a son, and not like a companion," 23:50–51).[9] The bonds that join Virgil to Dante are many and reflect varying degrees of intimacy. Here, the description of Virgil as mother displays the strong affective bond that has been growing between the two travelers. Virgil usually calls Dante "son" ("*figlio*" [*Inf.* 7:115; *Purg.* 27:35, 128] or "*figliuol[o]*" [*Inf.* 3:21; 7:61; 8:67; 11:16; *Purg.* 1:112; 4:46; 8:88, et al.]), underscoring the closeness of the *magister-discipulus,* or father-son, relationship. Despite these momentary failings—which, of course, add immeasurably to the "realism" of the work—Virgil succeeds in protecting his charge from numerous dangers during their journey through Hell.[10] Virgil's solicitous attitude continues in Purgatory as well, although there the dynamics are of a very different nature.

In his role as teacher, Virgil must identify a variety of sinners and explain to the best of his ability the structure of Hell and its rationale. He is also called upon to describe, for example, the operation of Fortune (*Inf.* 7:70–96) and the "hydrology" of Hell (*Inf.* 14:94–120). Virgil's reputation in antiquity as a great sage follows him through the medieval period: Dante refers to him as "*quel savio gentil, che tutto seppe*" ("the gentle sage, aware of everything," *Inf.* 7:3). Moreover, following the standard etymological play on Virgil's name (Publius Vergilius *Maro*), the Poet describes him as the "*mar di tutto 'l senno*" ("sea of all good sense").[11]

Virgil condenses his lessons on sin into memorable, powerful verses in the grand style: of the prodigal and avaricious he says that "*mal dare e mal tener lo mondo pulcro / ho tolto loro*" ("ill giving and ill keeping have robbed both / of the fair world," 7:58–59); of the wrathful: *"Figlio, or vedi / l'anime di color cui vinse l'ira"* ("Son, now see / the souls of those whom anger has defeated," 7:115–16). In canto 11, Virgil gives a minute exposition of the divisions of Hell and particularly of the seventh, eighth, and ninth circles, in which are punished, respectively, violence, fraud, and treachery. The scheme followed is basically Aristotelian; so, to bolster his disquisition, Virgil frequently asks the Pilgrim to recall what Aristotle, the *"maestro di color che sanno"* ("master of the men who know," 4:131), said in his *Ethics* or *Physics* (*Inf.* 11:80, 101). The character Virgil's thorough knowledge of the philosophical categories of evil is perfectly in accord with his historical counterpart, but this knowledge does not prepare him for what he will discover in Purgatory. Indeed, once the two wayfarers escape the night of Hell and emerge on the shore of the mountain of Purgatory, Virgil finds himself a stranger in a strange land, one so totally Christian in its conception as to be impenetrable to the pagan mind.

Meanwhile, the disparity between the Pilgrim and his guide in terms of knowledge has virtually disappeared by the time they leave Hell—as Virgil notes, *"oramai / è da partir, ché tutto avem veduto"* ("it is time / for us to leave; we have seen everything," 34:68–69), implying that to see is to know. Thus, when they find themselves in Purgatory, they are more or less intellectual equals, and because of this their relationship, which began as a strict hierarchy and developed over the course of the *Inferno* into mutual trust and respect, must now assume a different cast. Dante will move from being, by and large, a passive observer to an active participant on the seven purgatorial terraces. Here the Pilgrim—as a Christian—has the distinct advantage. His knowledge will continue to grow, whereas Virgil's will forever remain fixed from lack of faith.

In the general absence of the *magister-discipulus* relationship that characterizes the *Inferno,* Virgil and the Pilgrim now operate more as friends and fellow travelers. As they move through the clear early morning air on Mount Purgatory, they see the stars and rising sun, but neither really knows anything about where he is going or how he should proceed. This problem is clearly manifested in the following exchange. A group of souls newly arrived in Purgatory ask: *"Se voi sapete, / mostratene la via di gire al monte"* ("Do show us, if you know, / the way by which we can ascend this slope," 2:59–60), to which Virgil responds: *"noi siam peregrin come voi siete"* ("we are strangers here, just as you are," 2:63). Virgil has to reconceptualize his role, given the change in ground rules and his complete ignorance of them. Readers of the *Comedy* find his ignorance an endearing trait, one that makes him appear even more human and, as such, a generally amiable traveling companion. In the journey from Hell to the Earthly Paradise, the Pilgrim's knowledge grows, while Virgil's anguish can only increase. The necessity of his departure and return to Limbo—forever—becomes more and more evident in the poem, and this inevitably increases the compassion of both the Pilgrim and Dante's readers. We understand the nature of the cruel "trick" being played on Virgil; we are caught up in his personal "tragedy." He is in a place he cannot comprehend on any more than a literal level—Purgatory is simply a mountain that must be scaled—and to which he will never return. His three days in the sun, far from his shadowy "home" in Limbo, are bittersweet, for they constantly remind him of what he has lost and through no fault of his own.[12]

Yet, there are also moments of triumph for Virgil in Purgatory, even though these same jubilant moments are tinged with sadness. In the sixth canto the two travelers meet Sordello who asks them about their provenance. Virgil begins "*Mantüa . . . ,*" and the shade of Sordello "who had been / so solitary, rose from his position, / saying: 'O Mantuan, I am Sordello, / from your own land!' And each embraced the other" ("*tutta in sé romita, / surse ver' lui del loco ove pria stava, / dicendo: 'O Mantoano, io son Sordello / de la tua terra!'; e l' un l' altro abbracciava,*" 6:72–75).[13] Their embrace, as a gesture of friendship based solely on their common civic heritage, motivates the fierce invective against the chaotic state of affairs in Italy—"*Ahi serva Italia*" ("Ah, abject Italy")—that occupies the second half of the canto. It is not until the next canto that Sordello discovers Virgil's identity, and this occasions a second embrace but not as equals, for Sordello, assuming an inferior position, addresses him as "*O gloria di Latin . . . per cui / mostrò ciò che potea la lingua nostra*" ("O glory of the Latins, you / through whom our tongue revealed its power," 7:16–17).[14] Virgil, however, discounts, as it were, this mundane praise by supplying the sad backdrop of his eternal exile in Limbo because of his lack of faith. In fact, Virgil describes his condition in such a way that he becomes a sort of negative *exemplum:*

> *Io son Virgilio; e per null' altro rio*
> *lo ciel perdei che per non aver fé.*
>
> . . .
>
> *Non per far, ma per non fare ho perduto*

a veder l' alto Sol che tu disiri
e che fu tardi per me conosciuto.

(7:7–8; 25–27)

I am Virgil, and I am deprived of Heaven / for no fault other than my
lack of faith. . . . Not for the having—but not having—done, / I lost the
sight that you desire, the Sun—/ that high Sun I was late in recognizing.

By their rhetorical alternation, these verses (and those that follow)
emphasize the involuntary nature of Virgil's shortcomings, and
thus increase the pathos of the scene.

Virgil's second triumph occurs in cantos 21–22 of the *Purgatory*
when the two travelers meet Statius, whose soul, now completely
purified, has just been released to ascend to Heaven. Statius (another classical Latin poet who plays a major role as a character in
Dante's poem) relates how he converted to Christianity and remained a "secret Christian" (*"chiuso cristian,"* 22:90) because of
the persecutions by the Emperor Domitian. Statius declares that
Virgil was his mentor both in poetry (his *Thebaid* followed the
great example of the *Aeneid*) and in religious matters (he became
a Christian because of the prophetic message contained in the
Fourth Eclogue):[15]

"Tu prima m' invïasti
verso Parnaso a ber ne le sue grotte,
e prima appresso Dio m' alluminasti.
   Facesti come quei che va di notte,
che porta il lume dietro e sé non giova,
ma dopo sé fa le persone dotte,
   quando dicesti: 'Secol si rinova;
torna giustizia e primo tempo umano,
e progenïe scende da ciel nova'.
   Per te poeta fui, per te cristiano."

(22:64–73)

"You were the first to send me / to drink within Parnassus' caves and
you, / the first who, after God, enlightened me. / You did as he who
goes by night and carries / the lamp behind him—he is of no help / to
his own self but teaches those who follow—/ when you declared: 'The
ages are renewed; / justice and man's first time on earth return; / from
Heaven a new progeny descends.' / Through you I was a poet and,
through you, / a Christian."

The image of Virgil as the one who carries the lamp to illuminate
the path for others, but not for himself, contributes to the growing
aura of pathos surrounding his figure in the *Comedy*.

In his last words in the poem, on the threshold of the Earthly
Paradise in *Purgatory* 27, Virgil recapitulates their journey and
declares the Pilgrim's *"arbitrio"* ("will") to be *"libero, dritto e
sano"* ("free, erect, and whole," 140). Virgil has done for the Pilgrim
all he can do. He has taken him as far as he can—to the Earthly
Paradise. Virgil's protégé is now ready to move and act completely
on his own. As a sign of this readiness, Virgil "crowns" and "mi-
ters" the Pilgrim: *"per ch' io te sovra te corono e mitrio"* ("therefore I crown and miter you over yourself," 142). This ritual act of
coronation and investiture concludes a series of such acts that
began with the baptismal ritual in the first canto of *Purgatory*
where Virgil, under Cato's direction, washed the infernal grime
from the Pilgrim's face.[16] Here the ritual is again a sort of baptism
that has a distinctly secular significance.[17]

Virgil will accompany the Pilgrim until the advent of Beatrice.
Then he suddenly disappears from the scene. Dante's sadness
knows no bounds:

> *volsimi a la sinistra col respitto*
> *col quale il fantolin corre a la mamma*
> *quando ha paura o quando elli è afflitto,*
> *per dicere a Virgilio: 'Men che dramma*
> *di sangue m' è rimaso che non tremi:*
> *conosco i segni de l' antica fiamma'.*
> *Ma Virgilio n' avea lasciati scemi*
> *di sé, Virgilio dolcissimo patre,*
> *Virgilio a cui per mia salute die'mi;*
> *né quantunque perdeo l' antica matre,*
> *valse a le guance nette di rugiada*
> *che, lagrimando, non tornasser atre.*

(30:43–54)

I turned around and to my left—just as / a little child, afraid or in
distress, / will hurry to his mother—anxiously, / to say to Virgil: 'I am
left with less / than one drop of blood that does not tremble: / I recognize the signs of the old flame.' / But Virgil had deprived us of himself,
Virgil, the gentlest father, Virgil, he / to whom I gave my self for my
salvation; / and even all our ancient mother lost / was not enough
to keep my cheeks, though washed / with dew, from darkening again
with tears.

Together with the tributes to Virgil offered by Sordello and Statius,
Dante the Poet does him perhaps the greatest honor by incorporating in this farewell scene two passages from Virgil's own works:
one verse—*"conosco i segni de l' antica fiamma"* (48)—is an exact

translation of Dido's words to her sister Anna in the fourth book of the *Aeneid:* "*agnosco veteris vestigia flammae*" (4:23); and the triple evocation of Virgil's name recalls that of Orpheus who calls out, three times, to Eurydice as she disappears, once more and forever, into Hades (*Georgics* 4:525–27).[18] But Dante's textual borrowings from Virgil are extensive, and one other such citation occurs in this canto in *Purgatory*. When the Mystical Procession, together with the empty chariot, stops opposite the Pilgrim, the angels call for the advent of Beatrice, using a variation on the words of the Gospel—*Benedictus qui venis!* ("Blessed are you who come")—and, amid the cloud of falling flowers, cry out the Virgilian verse "*Manibus, oh, date lilïa plenis!*" ("O, give lilies with full hands!"). The presence of this particular verse from the sixth book of the *Aeneid* in this new context is striking. There it referred to the sadness surrounding the premature death of Marcellus, here to the sublime and triumphant appearance of Beatrice on the chariot.[19] The homage paid to Virgil and his poetry through the use of this verse, sung by angels, is suffused with a double sadness: it first recalls the original context; it then foretells its own maker's imminent departure, or "death," in the poem.

Honor is paid to Virgil in a number of ways, one of which is Dante's deliberate choice to have Virgil deliver the discourse on love at the very center of the Purgatory, on the fourth terrace, halfway up the seven purgatorial terraces (canto 17, vv. 85–139) and, by extension, at the very center of the entire *Divine Comedy* (canto 51 of 100, the middle canto of the middle realm). There are no immediately obvious reasons why Virgil should be chosen for this singular honor, except that this is a way for Dante to pay him tribute for the "*lungo studio e grande amore*" ("long study and the intense love") which, as he says, "*m'ha fatto cercar lo tuo volume*" ("made me search your volume," *Inf.* 1:83–84). Although Virgil does quit the narrative, necessarily, he remains present always in the minds and hearts of Dante's readers.

Dante the Poet does not simply make Virgil a character in his work and incorporate a large number of the older poet's verses to his own ends, he also includes many of Virgil's characters in his poem. One very minor character in the *Aeneid*—Ripheus—assumes paradigmatic importance in the *Comedy*. Described by Virgil as "*justissimus unus / Qui fuit in Teucris, et servantissimus aequi*" (2:426–27: "foremost in justice among the Trojans, and most zealous for the right"), this Ripheus is elevated by Dante to the Heaven of Jupiter where he, together with other just rulers, forms part of the eye of the eagle:

> *Chi crederebbe giù nel mondo errante*
> *che Rifëo Troiano in questo tondo*
> *fosse la quinta de le luci sante?*
>
> (20:67–69)

Who in the erring world below would hold / that he who was the fifth among the lights / that formed the circle was the Trojan Ripheus?

Dante the Poet obviously is making a theological point here: mere mortals cannot presume to know how Divine Justice operates, cannot fathom the infinite mystery of God's plan, for even the blessed who sit in the presence of God do not know who all of the elect will be: "*ché noi, che Dio vedemo, / non conosciamo ancor tutti li eletti*" (20:134–35). On the basis of statements such as these some critics have argued for Virgil's eventual salvation, or at least that Dante viewed his salvation as a possibility, and the intensity and fervor with which they plead their case are extraordinary.[20] In my view, the basic problem with this hypothesis and line of argumentation is that it is beyond demonstration; no "evidence" can ever be adduced to prove it. Indeed, Virgil cannot be saved—is not saved—because the textual strategy and integrity of the *Divine Comedy* depend on his damnation.

Such is the extraordinary power of Dante's poetry. He makes us care for Virgil, has us worry about him in his eternal exile in Limbo, urges us to question the justice of God for condemning such a worthy man and poet. In short, he makes the figure of Virgil come alive for us. We would like to repeat the greeting of the souls in Limbo offered to Virgil when he returned to them at the beginning of the journey with Dante the Pilgrim in tow: "*Onorate l'altissimo poeta; / l'ombra sua torna, ch'era dipartita*" ("Pay honor to the estimable poet; / his shadow, which had left us, now returns," *Inf.* 4:80–81). Long vanished materially from this earthly scene, that most exalted poet returned, a spectral shade, to Dante in the fourteenth century and so still speaks to us today, thanks to the genius of the Florentine poet.

NOTES TO "VIRGIL IN DANTE'S *DIVINE COMEDY*"

I wish to acknowledge the invaluable contributions of my son, Michael Kleinhenz, *lettore attento e stilista per eccellenza*, toward the final version of this essay. Needless to say, what errors and infelicities remain are mine and mine alone.

1. See Charles S. Singleton, *Dante Studies 1: Commedia: Elements of Structure* (Cambridge, MA: Harvard University Press, 1954), 62.

2. In his philosophical treatise, the *Convivio* (the "Banquet"), Dante distinguishes between two kinds of allegory, one appropriate to poets and the other to theologians. In the former, the literal level of the text is simply a convenient cover, a pleasant fiction that conceals a more important allegorical meaning. In the latter, the literal level of the text is true, as it is in the Bible, and, at appropriate moments, may open up to higher allegorical, moral, and anagogical interpretations. See Dante Alighieri, *Convivio,* in *Opere minori,* Tomo I, parte II, ed. Cesare Vasoli and Domenico De Robertis (Milan: Ricciardi, 1988), II, i, 2–8. In his Letter to Cangrande della Scala, Dante discusses the polysemous nature of the *Comedy* and provides a guide to the interpretation of its allegory, that of the theologians. (The authorship of the Letter is very controversial, and we will not enter the debate in this essay.) For the text and English translation of the letter, see Paget Toynbee, *Dantis Alagherii Epistolae: The Letters of Dante,* 2nd ed. (Oxford: Clarendon Press, 1966), 160–211. On the literal level, the *Comedy* is about the state of various individuals in the next world; and on the allegorical level, it displays the operation of Divine Justice that either rewards or punishes individuals for their earthly actions accomplished through the exercise of free will.

3. The bibliography on the topic of Virgil and Dante is vast. Among the works most pertinent to this essay are the following: Edward Moore, *Studies in Dante, First Series: Scripture and Classical Authors in Dante,* new introductory matter edited by Colin Hardie (Oxford: Clarendon Press, 1896 [1969]); J. H. Whitfield, *Dante and Virgil* (Oxford: Basil Blackwell, 1949); Robert Hollander, *Il Virgilio dantesco: Tragedia nella* Commedia (Florence: Olschki, 1983) and *Studies in Dante* (Ravenna: Longo, 1980); *The Poetry of Allusion: Virgil and Ovid in Dante's* Commedia, ed. Rachel Jacoff and Jeffrey T. Schnapp (Stanford: Stanford University Press, 1991); Anthony K. Cassell, *Inferno I* (Philadelphia: University of Pennsylvania Press, 1989); and the entries in the *Enciclopedia dantesca,* 6 vols., 2nd ed. (Rome: Istituto della Enciclopedia Italiana, 1984), by Domenico Consoli ("Virgilio Marone, Publio," 5:1030–44), and Alessandro Ronconi ("Echi virgiliani nell'opera dantesca," 5:1044–49).

4. All passages from the *Comedy* follow the text established by Giorgio Petrocchi, *La commedia secondo l'antica vulgata,* 4 vols. (Milan: Mondadori, 1966–67). The translation is that of Allen Mandelbaum: *Inferno* (New York: Bantam Books, 1982); *Purgatorio* (New York: Bantam Books, 1984); *Paradiso* (New York: Bantam Books, 1986).

5. See Ernst Robert Curtius, *European Literature and the Latin Middle Ages,* trans. Willard R. Trask (New York: Harper & Row, 1963), 48–54. The Pilgrim is well acquainted with Virgil's *Aeneid;* indeed, Virgil notes that Dante knew it by heart: "*ben lo sai tu che la* [= 'l' *alta mia tragedia*'] *sai tutta quanta*" ("you know that well enough, who know the whole [of my high tragedy]," *Inf.* 20:114). The use of the word "volume" to refer to Virgil's great epic poem is important, for it establishes from the beginning the idea of the *Aeneid* as a sort of sacred text, analogous to the Bible. Careful in his lexical choices, Dante imbues certain words with a particularly powerful charge: for example, "volume" is used only to indicate the *Aeneid,* the Bible (God's Book) and the Universe (which is "God's Other Book"), thus establishing the analogous relationship among the referents. On this point, see Robert Hollander, *Allegory in Dante's* Commedia (Princeton: Princeton University Press, 1969), 78–79. The reference to Virgil as the spring that "freely pours so rich a stream of speech" suggests the poet's verbal eloquence and, according to some critics, his role in the ritual schematics of the *Comedy* as a baptismal figure.

6. See, for example, Domenico Comparetti, *Vergil in the Middle Ages,* trans. E.F.M. Benecke (1908; repr. Hamden, CT: Archon Books, 1966), 96–103; and Pierre Courcelle, "Les exégèses chrétiennes de la quatrième Églogue," *Revue des études anciennes* 59 (1957): 294–319.

7. Evidence for this double identity is provided in the greeting offered the Pilgrim by his ancestor Cacciaguida in the Heaven of Mars: "*O sanguis meus, o superinfusa / gratïa Deï, sicut tibi cui / bis unquam celi ianüa reclusa?*" ("O blood of mine—o the celestial grace / bestowed beyond all measure—unto whom / as unto you was Heaven's gate twice opened?" *Par.* 15:28–30). Here, the web of allusions links Dante both to Paul—the only other person to whom Heaven's gate was opened twice—and to Aeneas who, in the sixth book of the *Aeneid,* meets his father Anchises. In the Virgilian context, Anchises uses the phrase *sanguis meus* (v. 835) to address Julius Caesar. The text and translation of passages from Virgil follow the Loeb Classical Library, ed. and trans. H. Rushton Fairclough, *Virgil,* 2 vols. (Cambridge, MA: Harvard University Press, 1967).

8. Another aspect of Virgil that often escapes modern readers, far removed from the cultural context of the Middle Ages and from the decidedly more "popular" features of this matrix, concerns the legends about Virgil the sorcerer, the necromancer, the one who engages in the black arts and whose literary excellence is secondary to his awesome magical powers. Elements of that legacy may survive in Dante's poem (for example, in Virgil's admission [*Inf.* 9:22–27] that his shade had been summoned by the Thessalian witch Erichto to retrieve a soul from the deepest part of Hell) and may come into even sharper focus in the canto of the diviners (*Inf.* 20). There, Virgil tells the story of the founding of Mantua and "changes" the account he had given in the *Aeneid* (10:198–200), emphatically stating that no augury was involved in its establishment or naming: "*Mantüa l'appellar sanz'altra sorte*" (20:93). Perhaps Virgil protests too much. For this aspect of Virgil, see Comparetti, *Vergil in the Middle Ages,* and John Webster Spargo, *Virgil the Necromancer: Studies in Virgilian Legends* (Cambridge, MA: Harvard University Press, 1934).

9. The mother-son relationship is evoked once more, in *Purgatory* 30, and with a notable reversal: when Virgil disappears to return to Limbo, Dante experiences the son's need for his mother's care and protection: "*volsimi a la sinistra col respitto / col quale il fantolin corre a la mamma / quando ha paura o quando elli è afflitto*" ("I turned around and to my left—just as / a little child, afraid or in distress, / will hurry to his mother—anxiously," 43–45).

10. For example, Cerberus (canto 6), Filippo Argenti (8), and the Minotaur (12).

11. In his commentary on the poem, Grandgent notes the following: "The 'Sea of all wisdom' is of course Virgil. In a Virgil ms. of the 9th century we read: 'Maro dicitur a mare. Sicut enim mare abundat aqua, ita et ipsi affluebat sapientia plus ceteris poetis'" (note to v. 7 on p. 75). Dante Alighieri, *La Divina Commedia,* ed. C. H. Grandgent, rev. ed. Charles S. Singleton (Cambridge, MA: Harvard University Press, 1972).

12. It has been reported that the power of the departure scene in *Purgatorio* 30 was so strong that Ulrich Leo wept every time he came to that passage in his Dante course, and was unable to continue the lesson (see Robert Hollander, *Il Virgilio dantesco,* 125).

13. It is tempting to think that Dante the Poet had in mind the epitaph written for Virgil when he wrote these verses and that his Virgil would have completed the phrase thus: "*Mantua me genuit.*" Singleton notes that "the epitaph (written probably by one of his friends) is quoted by Suetonius (*Vita Virgili* XXXVI):

'Mantua me genuit, Calabri rapuere, tenet nunc Parthenope; cecini pascua rura duces.' ('Mantua gave me the light, Calabria slew me; Parthenope now holds me. I have sung shepherds, the countryside, and wars')." See Dante Alighieri, *The Divine Comedy, Purgatorio: 2. Commentary* (Princeton: Princeton University Press, 1973), 45.

14. The precise meaning of Sordello's words of praise is not clear and hinges on the interpretation of "lingua nostra": is Virgil being lauded for his excellence in Latin? Or is it his preeminence in the Romance languages in general—Sordello's Provençal being one of them, thus stressing the continuity of classical and medieval civilizations? Or is it that Virgil was the most excellent writer of *human* language—that is, of all time?

15. Statius also remarks (*Purg.* 22:34–54) that his (creative) reading and (mis-) understanding of a passage in Virgil's *Aeneid* (3:56–57)—"*Quid non mortalia pectora cogis, / auri sacra fames!*" ("To what dost thou not drive the hearts of men, O accursed hunger for gold!")—warned him against avarice, but pushed him to the opposite sin of prodigality! For a full discussion of this episode see, among others: R. A. Shoaf, "'Auri sacra fames' and the Age of Gold (*Purg.* XXII, 40–41 and 148–50)," *Dante Studies* 96 (1978): 195–99; H. D. Austin, "*Aurea Justitia:* A Note on *Purgatorio,* XXII, 40f," *Modern Language Notes* 48 (1933): 327–30; and Christopher Kleinhenz, "The Celebration of Poetry: A Reading of *Purgatory* XXII," *Dante Studies* 106 (1988): 21–41.

16. Virgil first appears as a "baptist" figure in the Pilgrim's first words to him in *Inferno* 1, as noted above. See Hollander, *Allegory in Dante's* Commedia, 261.

17. On this and related points, see Ernst H. Kantorowicz, *The King's Two Bodies: A Study in Medieval Political Theology* (Princeton: Princeton University Press, 1957), 491–94.

18. For "borrowings" from Virgil in the *Comedy,* see the work of Edward Moore (note 3 above) and Robert Hollander, "Le opere di Virgilio nella *Commedia* di Dante," in *Dante e la "bella scola" della poesia: Autorità e sfida poetica,* ed. Amilcare A. Iannucci (Ravenna: Longo, 1993), 247–343.

19. In our consideration of this particular verse, we must remember that, as the Virgilian Marcellus, Beatrice also died prematurely, and the sadness of that event, which Dante recounts in the *Vita Nuova,* has here been transformed to joy because of Christian hope.

20. See, for example, Mowbray Allan, "Does Dante Hope for Virgil's Salvation?" *Modern Language Notes* 104 (1989): 193–205; "Much Virtue in *Ma: Paradiso* XIX, 106, and St. Thomas's *Sed contra,*" *Dante Studies* 111 (1993): 195–211; and Nicolae Iliescu, "Will Virgil Be Saved?" *Mediaevalia* 12 (1989 for 1986): 93–114.

François Villon:
Character Within or Without His
Own Poetry?

JELLE KOOPMANS

The fifteenth-century French poet François Villon has long been considered one of the most important medieval writers. In his *Art poétique* (1674), Boileau was already calling him the first modern poet. Translations of Villon's poems exist in twenty-six languages. Famous actors, including Serge Reggiani and Klaus Kinski, have given their voices to Villon's poetry. Many composers have set his words to music, including Claude Debussy (*Trois ballades de François Villon,* 1910) and Ezra Pound (*Le Testament de François Villon,* 1926).

Not only his poetry but his biography as well, has continued to haunt the imagination of artists in later centuries. It is amazing to see to what extent this Parisian poet has been re-created in both narrative literature and numerous other genres.[1] Here, Villon is the sympathetic criminal, the poor student, and flamboyant rogue who has tragic love affairs with many, largely unknown women. Here, too, Villon is the genial trickster, endearing in a renardine way, since he always defies the established order. Many poets imitate Villon or have him appear in their poetry, and a great number of plays are devoted to the Villon legend, including Otis Skinner's *Villon the Vagabond* (which had its premiere in Chicago in 1895), Herbert Edward Palmer's *The Judgment of François Villon: A Pageant Episode Play in Five Acts* (published by Leonard and Virginia Woolf in 1927), and Karel E. Eykman's *François Villon* (an open-air play staged at Utrecht in 1961). Operas about Villon are not lacking either. There is A. A. Noelte's *François Villon* (1919) and the rock opera *Villon és a többiek* ("Villon and the others") by the Hungarian, Kardos G. György (1978). Villon is also the hero of several movies, like the magnificent *Beloved Rogue* (directed by Alan Crosland in 1927), André Zwoboda's *François Villon,* based on a scenario by Pierre Mac Orlan (1945), and, of course, Frank

Lloyd's *If I Were King* (1938; remade by Michael Curtiz in 1956 as *The Vagabond King*). The number of historical novels (which also includes most of the "serious" biographies of Villon) is enormous; the novel *Le roman de François Villon* by Francis Carco (1926) is dedicated to Pierre Champion, whose *Villon, sa vie et son temps* (1913) contains a wealth of material on the inheritors mentioned in Villon's *Testament*. John Erskine's *Brief Hour of François Villon* (1937) is still quite well known, as are the two novels Fritz Habeck devoted to the person whom he saw as a primitive rebel, namely *Der Scholar vom linken Galgen* (1941), and *François Villon oder die Legende eines Rebellen* (1969).

This is only the tip of the iceberg. Even without commentary, a catalogue of appropriations of *maître François* would be interminably long. For that reason it seems more appropriate, following a brief comment on the origins of the Villonian legend, to focus on the different types of characters for which Villon stood as a model. My main concern will be with a typology of projections, which also means that I shall have occasion to discuss the tensions between textual scholarship and pseudo-biography. Villon appears to be not just a poet—meaning, the writer of his poetry—but also a romanticized poet, a revolutionary rebel as well as a comfort for the poor. This is apparent not only in fictional, historical novels, but also in scholarly publications. We try to read a poet into his own text; our reading of the obscure, dense poetry of *maître François* is determined primarily by the person or character we want to see, or are used to seeing, behind it.

From Life to Legend: The Trickster

On Christmas eve 1456, Villon claimed to be writing his *Lais*. However, he used this date mainly to provide himself with an alibi, since, at that time, he and some of his criminal friends were busy robbing the *Collège de Navarre*. After a wandering life in the provinces (which, generally, means that we do not know where Villon was), by 1462, he was back in prison in Paris. There are myriad suggestions about and extrapolations of this wandering life, many stories based on this or that obscure line of the *Testament*. Between 1457 and 1462, Villon probably visited the court of Charles d'Orléans in Blois, and perhaps Thibaud d'Aussigny kept him in the prison of Meung-sur-Loire. He would have been released on the occasion of the royal entry of Louis XI. In 1462, Villon was sentenced to death because of an obscure battle in the study of the notary, François Ferrebouc, but his (possibly poetical) appeal was successful, and the parliament in Paris granted him three days to take leave of his friends before being banished from the city for ten years. Thus, between 5 and 8 January 1463, the poet François Villon, at the age of thirty-one, disappeared from history.

Villon's rich lyrical work about marginal life in late-fifteenth-century Paris (especially his *Ballad of the Hanged*) was to have a rich afterlife. Between the first printed edition of Villon's works (Paris: Pierre Levet, 1489) and the first critical edition by Clément Marot (Paris: Galiot du Pré, 1532), some thirty editions of his works were published. Marot has already noted that, in order "sufficiently to understand and explain the industry or intention of the bequests [Villon] makes in his *Testament,* it is necessary to have been a Parisian of his time and to have known the places, things and people of which he speaks, the memory whereof, as it shall more and more pass away, so much the less shall be comprehended the poet's intention."[2]

Nearly as important as the afterlife of his work is the fate of the poet himself in literature. Villon seems to have preluded that "personal" myth, when he noted in the *Testament,* "'Twill serve to keep my name in store, / As that of a good crack-brained wag" (*Testament,* lines 1882–83). A joyous *Testament* is, by nature, already a signal from the other side to the living.

From the late fifteenth century on, the name François Villon becomes synonymous with "trickster." He is often mentioned alongside Pierre Pathelin and other fictional, literary characters as if his mere name recalled the tricks he played on others. Although this side of Villon is only implicit in his poems, a fascination with his criminal life is to be found in nearly all sixteenth-century references to him.

Pseudo-biographical uses of Villon are also of an early date. Only a few days after his disappearance in January 1463, a friend of Villon wrote a *sermon joyeux,* a theatrical mock sermon, devoted to the poet's banishment. This carnivalesque homily on *saint Belin* ("saint Mutton") features the complete text of Villon's *Ballad of the Appeal;* it is possible that the ballad was composed as part of this homily. The general idea behind the sermon is straightforward: Villon is to be compared to the (Holy) lamb, but he was right to appeal his death sentence.[3] Within this dramatic monologue, the *Ballad of the Appeal* is interpreted as a reply:

> Garnier, how did you like my appeal?
> Did I wisely, or did I ill?
> Each beast looks to his own skin's weal.
>   (*Ballad of the Appeal,* lines 1–3)

The animalization in this sermon follows a technique frequently employed by the real or historical Villon. After killing the priest, Sermoise, in 1455, for example, he used the alias Michel Mouton. The theater often had to use all kinds of metaphors to avoid censorship. This joyous sermon is one of the most eloquent documents on the close relationship of criminal marginality and the theatrical culture of the late fifteenth century.

Some fifteen years after his disappearance, between 1474 and 1480, Villon was the object of a series of legends in *The Free Meals of Master Villon and His Companions.* The oldest texts we have are incunabula printed by Jean Trepperel and Denis Meslier in the early 1490s. In this collection of facetious tales, the central theme of which is ways to get free meals, Villon is the hero of the first series of astute tricks for hungry vagrants.[4] This funny booklet was to determine the image of Villon as a trickster, a joyous naughty thief, the sympathetic voice of the poor. It is the prelude to a rich, legendary afterlife of the Parisian poet, recorded in numerous sixteenth-century texts (Rabelais, Budé, Marot, Colletet) and is crucial in the formation of the Villonian legend we know today. In this context, it is also noteworthy that, in these early texts, Villon and his companions are depicted as hungry plebeians who gather around the Paris *palais de justice,* not in the students' *quartier latin* on the Left Bank, but on the isle of the *Cité.*

In his *Fourth Book,* Rabelais twice introduces Villon as a character. In chapter 67, King Edward V proudly shows that he keeps the French arms in the men's room. Villon observes that if the king had them depicted elsewhere, he would empty his bowels everywhere out of fear. This flagrant anachronism is a clear case of epic concentration. In chapter 13—where Villon has retired to Saint Maixent, Poitou, the place where Rabelais spent his youth—the old Villon and his fellow actors disguise themselves as devils in order to frighten brother Etienne Tappecoue. This passage clearly is inspired by the last of the *Free Meals* episodes (in which Villon plays no part). The brief appearance of Villon in *Pantagruel*'s Hell, where he pisses in the mustard of Xerxes, is equally to be explained on the basis of the popularity of his *Free Meals,* where Villon often uses scatological means to obtain comestibles.

If we consider the use of Villon's name in the sixteenth century, it soon becomes clear that either there is some kind of biographical knowledge about the poet that has been lost since then, or a newly shaped Villon, modeled after popular types like Howleglass and Rabelais's Panurge or after his own *Free Meals* legends, has supplanted the poet. By that time, the historical poet already had become a character and he would remain so, despite some structuralist nonbiographical readings of his work.

ROMANTIC VILLON: THE *POÈTE MAUDIT*

In the nineteenth century, it was the merit of Théophile Gautier in *Les Grotesques* to rediscover Villon as an ancestor of the *poètes maudits*. It was Gautier who set the tone for the study of Villon's works. Following his interpretation, the poetry would be considered autobiographical and highly subjective. With his interpretation, Gautier had a clear goal. François Villon had to be refashioned into a romantic poet, a poor *poète maudit* and a model for the radical youngsters whom Honoré de Balzac described so well in his *Illusions perdues*. Théodore de Banville wrote several ballads in "the Villon manner," and John Payne dedicated his translation of Villon's poetry to Banville. The notion of Villon as a model for the romantic poets was not at all inappropriate, especially because of the special role of the city of Paris in Villon's poetry. Here was a huge myth of fifteenth-century Paris ready to be revived in the manner of the rhetorician Pierre Gringore in Victor Hugo's *Notre Dame de Paris*. As the romantics constructed their Villon as a misunderstood poet of genius, they could hardly have guessed that even with the advent of modernity, this romantic vision of Villon would be enlarged rather than discarded.

At the beginning of the twentieth century, Villon became a model for the "moderns." The bibliographies of Sturm and Peckham reveal that the 1920s were particularly fond of Villon adaptations, legends, and biographies. The year 1923 saw the publication at Toulouse of Jean Alphonse Azals's play, *Villon: Comédie-héroï-comique*. A year later, Robert Gordon Anderson's *For Love of a Sinner* appeared, followed in 1926 by the premiere of Ezra Pound's Villon opera in the *Salle Pleyel* in Paris. In 1927, Leonard and Virginia Woolf published Herbert Palmer's *Judgment of François Villon: A Pageant Episode Play*. The reason for the apparent revival during the period of the historical modernity must be related to the alleged modernity of Villon's work, which, according to my research, seems to be mainly an extrapolation that originated in the sixteenth century. Blaise Cendrars even comments on the fact that the first modern poet, Villon, and the last one, Guillaume Apollinaire, are said to be sons of priests.[5]

VILLON POLITICIZED: REBEL WITHOUT A CAUSE?

In many ways, our century is politicized. It should not be surprising, then, to see that Villon, too, has become a victim of projection along these lines. In Fritz Habeck's *Scholar vom linken Galgen* (1941), Villon writes his *Testament:*

> "Long live the deformation," he wrote. "Long live the existence without limitations, and the liberty of the individual."
> Gone were all national thoughts, gone were all fraternal feelings.[6]

Twenty-eight years later, in 1969, Habeck restructured the character under the title *François Villon oder die Legende eines Rebellen.* It seems obvious that his refashioning was determined mainly by the events of May 1968: Villon became the patron saint of the student revolt of the *rive gauche.*

The image of Villon in Eastern Europe was determined in part by Bertolt Brecht, who took him as the original hero for *Baal* and who used several ballads by Villon in his *Threepenny Opera* (without naming his source: the Ammer translation). In the German Democratic Republic, we find some peculiar appropriations. Villon is an exile or a critic of the oppression of the police state.[7] In twentieth-century Hungary, he becomes synonymous with the proletarian rebel and, later, the oppressed people. Here, Villon is a sympathetic anarchist; sometimes the poet also serves as a pretext to speak of social tensions and, above all, the loss of illusions concerning Marxist promises. The sheer number of works devoted to Villon suggests that Villon-as-a-character has become an organic element in Magyar culture.[8] Thus, Villon's poverty, and his supposed opposition to power and hierarchy, may be considered major characteristics of his fictional use. The systematic exploitation of the Villon character in Eastern Europe, as well by Russian and Bohemian poets, is noteworthy, as is the return to poetry, to the lyrical genre, for these exploitations.

LOVERBOY VILLON

Another, more widespread use of Villon concerns his supposed love affairs. Nearly all the names of the women mentioned in the *Testament* have been used, in both serious biographies and historical novels, to produce love stories involving Villon. Many new names have also appeared.

Villon's ballad—to which Marot gave the title *Ballade pour Rob-ert d'Estouteville*—was translated by John Payne as *Ballad that Villon gave to a newly married gentleman to send to his lady, by him conquered at the sword's point.* Payne thus suggests an affair between Villon and d'Estouteville's wife, Ambroise de Loré, whose name may in fact be read in acrostic in this ballad. Also, in John Erskine's *Brief Hour of François Villon* (1937), the seventeen-year-old Villon has fallen in love with the older Ambroise, only to live ever after with the scar, not of his love but of his disappoint-ment. In the novel *Villon, den ganz Paris gekannt* by Johanna Hoffmann (1975), the poet even has an affair with Mary of Cleves, for which he is banned from the court of Charles d'Orléans in Blois. In the film *Beloved Rogue* (1927), Villon has conflicts with Louis XI and a romance with a melancholic lady at the court. In the opera *François Villon* by Albert Noelte, master Francis is stuck in an intrigue with three women and a friend. Villon finally commits suicide, thus drawing attention to the tragical side of his life. Has certain death become more tragic than banishment? It seems like a cruel joke to play on a poet whose work is already impregnated with the idea of death. In his *Brief Hour of François Villon,* Erskine follows Rabelais in imagining Villon in Saint-Maixent. Here, Villon quickly becomes a renowned teacher and notary, raising his daugh-ter, Jeanne, named after Joan of Arc. His real love, however, his love of a "brief hour," is one Louise de Grigny (for whom no textual evidence exists). For Fritz Habeck, in his *Scholar vom linken Galgen* (1941), Villon sees Paris merely as "a collection of women's legs." Habeck even imagines some kind of farce in which Villon and Denise are surprised by the returning husband: Villon saves himself by escaping through the chimney. All we really know about Denise we learn from the lines in *The Testament:* "When action 'gainst me Denise brought, / Saying I had miscalled her" (ll. 1234–35). The general tendency can be formulated as follows: either Villon knew the love of his life quite early (Catherine, Am-broise . . .) and can never, in his subsequent affairs, find her equal; or Villon, looking for some kind of absolute love, is disappointed by his affairs (with Marthe, Margot, Marion . . .).

These loves of Villon, however, are not restricted to fiction. He has been the subject of an important series of biographies, from Colletet in the sixteenth century to the recent bestseller by Jean Favier. A biography, it would appear, always needs a character. And the poetry of Villon, which needed a two-volume commentary in Louis Thuasne's 1923 edition, needs more in biography. That is why every small detail in the poems is exploited by biographers, as in *The Ballad of Villon to His Mistress* (*Testament,* 950–55): the acrostic MARTHE leads, with no serious biographical data, to a long series of speculations about the (love) relationship between Villon and Marthe, who supposedly was his mistress. This Marthe, in turn, is used to explain other lines where reference is made to an unidentified woman, possibly one of Villon's mistresses. This shows the general tendency: we have only the acrostic, for which there is no explanation, neither textual nor biographical. Subsequently, from our general knowledge of Villon (?), we invent a love relationship; we effect a biographical extrapolation from the text. Finally, we start to use this extrapolation of biographical data to explain other lines. A thorough investigation of the textual criticism on Villon yields numerous instances of such curious circular reasoning.

Unfortunately this is not the place to discuss in greater detail the vast range of intriguing instances, though one striking example is worth considering. It is to be found in a difficult, inadequately explained eight-line poem, or *huitain,* about a woman named Catherine de Vaucelles:

> De moy povre je vueil parler:
> J'en fuz battu comme à ru telles,
> Tout nu, ja ne le quiers celler.
> Qui me fist macher ces groselles,
> Fors Katherine de Vauselles?
> Noël le tiers ot, qui fut là,
> Mitaines à ces nopces telles.
> Bien (est) heureux qui riens n'y a!

Payne's translation follows the traditional erroneous interpretation:

> And even I, poor silly wight,
> Was beaten as linen that lies
> In washer's tubs for bats to smite;
> And who gat me this sour surprise
> But Vausel's Kate, the cockatrice?
> And Noël, too, his good share got
> Of cuffs at those festivities.
> Happy is he who knows them not.[9]

For reasons that are by no means clear, the tentative explanation of the obscure expression *faire manger des groseilles* as "beating someone up" is widely accepted. It leads to all kinds of speculation in textual criticism, but it also leads to many unfounded romantic

love stories in so-called biographies, even to far-fetched psychological extrapolations. Villon probably loved Catherine, the reasoning goes; she had him beaten up at the instigation of a lucky rival.
Because Catherine rejected Villon's love and because we know
that in his *Lais* he mentions a mistress who made him leave Paris,
this Catherine may well have been that woman; so he knew her
already in 1456, six years before his *Testament*. Then Villon, to
forget Catherine, fell in love with Marthe and started calling Catherine Rose (another unexplained name in the *Testament*) out of disappointment. It is all a construction, where textual extrapolations
become biography and are used in turn to feed biographical expla-
nations of other lines in the text. *Marthe* is only an acrostic, *Rose*
is not even a name but a simple noun, and the expression *faire
manger des groseilles* actually means "to transmit a venereal
disease."[10]

Villon's love life has been constructed largely by literary criticism. For Gaston Paris, Villon knew one serious love between his
vulgar affairs; for Auguste Longnon, this "real love" is Catherine
de Vaucelles; Pierre Champion, on the other hand, just as Jean
Dufournet does, sees two women who have tortured Villon's heart:
Catherine and Marthe.[11] Dufournet even suggests that the above-
mentioned Denise might be Catherine. We may also consider what
Jean Favier, a recent Villon biographer, has to say about Villon
and Catherine de Vaucelles:

> Villon doesn't deplore the carnal love that Catherine refused him. He
> deplores the enmity she gave him, which was only a trick. What he
> couldn't stand, was the memory of their closeness and the patience
> with which she listened to his long bedtime stories.[12]

Biographers, even if they are directors of French national archives,
want to sell books, and apparently a bad youth and several unhappy
love affairs, making up a tragical existence, sell.[13] It is thus noteworthy that the critical discourse on Villon's poetry often is concerned mainly with the biographical explanation of his poetry,
which implies that most critics see Villon as a character within his
own work; but it is interesting that this tendency dates from the
fifteenth century. A special feature of historical novels, however,
is to try, with a kind of posthumous irony, to describe Villon's
death as if his death penalty changed into banishment had to become a real death again. Then, of course, it is mainly Villon's own
poetry that lies at the bottom of it. Some critics, like Jean Dufournet, even explain Villon's *Testament* as a conscious self-fashioning
in which, paradoxically, François de Moncorbier (Villon's real
name) chose to combine the proverbial frankness of *François* with

the image of the villain *Villon*. Most criticism, however, fails to show such subtlety, and simply constructs a poet's life from his highly ambiguous poetry. It seems as though his poetry has no status of its own, but can be appreciated only within a fictional biography. A major problem with this kind of biographical exegesis remains that Villon can hardly have entertained close relations with all the personalities mentioned in his *Testament*. This, however, has not kept critics from assuming the most intimate relations between Villon and any person mentioned in his work—all of which creates a rich, superabundant biography consisting of conjecture and vague interpretations of difficult lines in Villon's *Testament*. However interesting this problem of biographical extrapolations may be, with the cultivated ambiguity of Villon's poetry and the huge number of names, Villon's verse is an easy construction kit. The pseudo-biographical Villon, the purely fictional character of the fifteenth-century *poète maudit,* is as much present in criticism as it is in creative literature.

From Marcel Schwob, who also wrote a *vie imaginaire* of one prostitute mentioned by Villon, and Pierre Champion, whose biography is based primarily on Schwob's archival work, to Jean Favier, whose biography is a rhapsody of existing biographies, Jean Dufournet, whose psychological approach has one wonder if he has not become Villon himself, and Gert Pinkernell, obsessed with the relations between Villon and Charles d'Orléans, Villon has become a character in his own work: *"L'écrivain est un monsieur,"* the subtext runs.[14] Clearly, we like to think of a writer as a person.

Legends about Villon and his poems have made up a totally fictional biography that was used afterward to explain his poems. This, the intermingling of biography and fiction, of legend and textual criticism, has, in modern critical practice, led to some hilarious mistakes, to many unfounded affirmations, and to manifest misunderstandings of Villon's texts. Many biographies read as novels, and they are, but many novels about François Villon are also well documented.

SOME FINAL REMARKS

The aim of this article has been to show to what extent the poet Villon has been used as a character, and by what kinds of contemporary projections that use was justified. Particular attention has been devoted to the first legendary uses of Villon in the fifteenth century, especially because the thematic cluster of the *free meals* and the Rabelaisian retirement to Saint Maixent have specific importance. Criticism of Villon scholarship in the nineteenth and twentieth centuries has been inevitable. I am aware that such criticism may seem gratuitous if not complemented by a more coherent or more convincing approach, a reading of the Villon text that eschews the pseudo-biographical fallacy. Such a reading is currently being prepared by my colleague, Paul Verhuyck, and myself.

Several questions remain. Is biography a natural misunderstanding? It may be a far-reaching question, but in the case of Villon, the point has to be made. Could one read the texts of Villon without having a "character" of Villon? It is almost certain that the Villon myth largely determines our reading of his work, as if the available biographical data did not suffice to explain his mostly obscure texts. But, as Blaise Cendrars objects to Francis Carco's *Roman de François Villon* (1926), "it isn't upon leaving a whorehouse that one writes a poem" ("Sous le signe," 59). On the other hand, it must be acknowledged that if we try to read Villon's *Testament* as a text, we find some *pièces d'anthologie* in his ballads; for the rest, we really do not understand the text. It is equally true that whenever critics have tried to study the "pure" and sole text of Villon—for example, from a structuralist point of view—their methodological introduction is often impressive. Nevertheless, the results of their analyses are poor. Here, the linguistic methods of Pierre Guiraud, who claims that Villon constructs a gigantic judiciary farce based on the puns contained in contemporary names, may be an important exception.[15]

Is there an author without a character? In the case of novel characters like Don Quixote, Madam Bovary, and Oblomow, the authors modestly seem to disappear behind their own protagonists. Even though the biography of the respective authors may be enlightening, the characters prove sufficient in themselves. In the lyrical genre, however, the problem has different parameters (the verse of Verlaine, Rimbaud, Maiakovsky and Ehrenbourg is a case in point). In the case of Villon's poetry, the problem is different, especially due to the historical divide of five centuries. Beyond Villon, of course, there is the enormous number of anonymous works of the Middle Ages. The curious tendency to ascribe them to well-known poets suggests that, just as we may prefer characters to authors, we may prefer authors to texts.

Notes to "François Villon: Character Within or Without His Own Poetry?"

1. See R. D. Peckham, *François Villon: A Bibliography* (New York: Garland, 1990); and R. Sturm, *François Villon: Bibliographie und Materialien, 1489–1989,*

2 vols. (Munich: K. G. Saur, 1990). The first volume by Sturm is a chronological bibliography, the second contains a short general history of the reception of Villon's works. Useful information is also to be found in *Villon hier et aujourd'hui*, ed. J. Dérens, J. Dufournet, and M. Freeman (Paris: Bibliothèque Historique de la Ville de Paris, 1993).

2. John Payne, trans., *The Poems of Master François Villon of Paris now first done into English Verse* (London: The Villon Society, 1892). This translation is used throughout.

3. Jelle Koopmans and Paul Verhuyck, *Sermon joyeux et truanderie (Villon—Nemo—Ulespiègle)* (Amsterdam and Atlanta: Rodopi, 1987).

4. *Le Recueil des repues franches de maistre François Villon et de ses compagnons*, ed. Jelle Koopmans and Paul Verhuyck (Geneva: Droz, 1995).

5. Cendrars, "Sous le signe de François Villon," *La Table ronde* 51 (1952): 47–69, esp. 67.

6. Habeck, *Der Scholar vom linken Galgen: Das Schicksal François Villons* (Berlin: P. Zsolnay, 1941), 273. The translation is my own.

7. E. DuBruck, "François Villon en Allemagne," in *Villon hier et aujourd'hui*, 231–47, esp. 234.

8. O. Süpek, "Villon en Hongrie," in *Villon hier et aujourd'hui*, 249–67, esp. 255–56.

9. The French text derives from *Villon: Poésies complètes*, ed. Claude Thiry (Paris: Livre de Poche 1991), 143. For Payne's translation, see page 48. Note that the translation *gat me this sour surprise*, for *me fist macher ces groselles*, is an interpretation, a reduction of the polysemy, a threat to the original meaning. On this issue, see also Jelle Koopmans, "Groseilles et Vaucelles," in *François Villon: The Drama of the Text*, ed. Mike Freeman and Jane Taylor (Amsterdam and Atlanta: Rodopi). Forthcoming.

10. For a further discussion, see my "Groseilles et Vaucelles," in *François Villon: The Drama of the Text*.

11. On this problem, see Jean Dufournet, *Recherches sur le Testament de Villon*, 2 vols. (Paris: SEDES, 1971), 1: 71–129.

12. J. Favier, *François Villon* (Paris: Marabout, 1982), 475. The English translation is my own.

13. Blaise Cendrars comments on Thuasne's introduction: "One sees that any supposition is permitted in order to romance Villon" ("Sous le signe," 68).

14. Schwob, *Les Vies imaginaires* (Paris: Charpentier & Fasquelle, 1896); Champion, *François Villon: sa vie et son temps* (Paris: Champion, 1913); and Pinkernell, *François Villon et Charles d'Orléans (1457 à 1461): d'après les* Poésies diverses *de Villon* (Heidelberg: Winter, 1992).

15. Guiraud, *Le Testament de François Villon ou le gai savoir de la Basoche* (Paris: Gallimard, 1970).

A Voice Restored:
Louise Labé's Impersonation of Sappho

Ever since the publication of her *Œuvres* in 1555, Louise Labé's name and poetic voice have been closely linked with the name, voice, and identity of the ancient Greek poet Sappho.[1] Labé's contemporaries called her the *"Sappho Lyonnaise,"* and Labé names and alludes to Sappho at several points in her writings. For example, in Labé's first elegy the persona specifies that Apollo has given her the lyre which was accustomed to sing about lesbian love and which would at the same time cry about hers:

> *Il m'a donné la lyre, qui les vers*
> *Souloit chanter de l'Amour Lesbienne:*
> *Et à ce coup pleurera de la mienne.*
>
> *(Œuvres complètes,* 107)

He gave me the lyre which was accustomed to sing about the woman from Lesbos's love: and with that touch it will weep about my love.[2]

Far less conspicuous than the association between Labé and Sappho is the idea of Sappho that Labé responds to and evokes in her writings, for Sappho has had and continues to have many different meanings and identities for different people. Not only poets and novelists, but also literary historians and biographers, have created fictitious "Sapphos." The poetic persona Labé creates derives in part from knowledge of the historical woman and poet Sappho and in part from the fictions of Sappho to which classical writers like Ovid contributed.[3]

In her *Fictions of Sappho,* Joan DeJean traces developments in the French literary and historical construct called "Sappho" from 1546 to 1937. She reveals that since about 1660, Sappho has more often been associated with unrequited heterosexual love than with homoeroticism. Although DeJean gives the French credit for having "made the fictionalization of Sappho into a national obsession," she adds that "nearly every element used through the centuries of Sapphic fiction-making can be found in embryonic form in commentaries in antiquity."[4] She concludes her introduction saying,

> For centuries, Sappho commentary has been torn between two radically opposed visions: on the one hand, Sappho as the abandoned woman, the essence of unmediated female suffering and pain; and, on the other, Sappho as detached and wry commentator on "the vanity and impermanence" of *human—not* essentially female—passion.
>
> (*Fictions of Sappho,* 28)

These visions, for simplicity's sake, can be credited to Ovid in the fifteenth letter of the *Heroides,* and Catullus in "*Ille mi par esse*" ("To me he seems godlike"). Although Ovid certainly did not invent the story of Sappho's suicide after her falling in love with the boatman Phaon, his version of the story, available in French translation throughout the sixteenth century, "succeeded in capturing the collective literary imagination of the age that prepared the way for French neoclassicism" (*Fictions of Sappho,* 42). Similarly, Catullus's "*Ille mi par esse*" transforms Sappho's poem, "To me he seems to match the gods," which expresses female sexual desire kindled by seeing another woman talking with a man, into a poem in which a male speaker's desire for a woman is intensified by the competition implicit in her conversation with another man. DeJean argues that "Catullus then reclaims for male poet-lovers the control over the gaze that positions the scene of desire" (*Fictions of Sappho,* 35). Catullus's poem, by naming Lesbia as the object of his desire, simultaneously adds to the fame and legends associated with the historical woman-poet Sappho.

François Rigolot suggests that most readers have read Louise Labé's "Amour Lesbienne" as more closely related to Catullus's poetic expressions of love for Lesbia, or Ovid's poetic re-creation of Sappho in *Heroides,* than to the historical poet Sappho herself. Nevertheless, as Rigolot and DeJean point out, Labé's publication of her work occurred during the very decade when two of Sappho's poems were published and translated into Latin and French, and when Marc-Antoine de Muret, in his edition of Catullus, articulated the relationship between Catullus's "To me he seems godlike" and Sappho's "To me he seems to match the gods." Rigolot goes further to suggest that a Greek ode praising Labé and linking her to Sappho may have been written by Henri Estienne, the scholar who had included two of Sappho's poems in his edition of Anacreon published in 1554.[5] The Greek ode is as follows:

The songs of sweet-voiced Sappho which the power
Of all-consuming time destroyed,
Louise Labé, having been reared in the gentle lap
Of the Paphian [Aphrodite] and Loves, restored.
If anyone wonders at how strange it is and says,
"Whence comes this new poetess?"
Let him know that the unfortunate [poetess] has a beloved
Phaon, vigorous and inflexible;
Struck by his flight, she being wretched began to adopt
A shrill song to the chords of her lyre,
Through these poems, a vehement passion penetrates
The love of arrogant young boys.

If, indeed, Estienne admired Labé's poetry and credited her with
the restoration of Sappho's odes, then it seems likely that Labé's
knowledge of the historical poet Sappho was enriched by her association with Estienne, who later was to publish more of Sappho's
poetry and fragments in an edition of Greek lyrics (1566). An examination of Labé's elegies in the two very different contexts—
the Renaissance image of Sappho rediscovered in the sixteenth
century and the legendary Sappho appropriated by poets like Ovid
and Catullus[6]—reveals Labé impersonating and imitating the historical Sappho in ways which serve to reverse, at least briefly, the
sixteenth-century trend of making women silent and powerless,
and the trend that runs from the ancient world to the modern, in
which male writers "displace the female subject from the position
of control."[7]

    The difficulties of reconstructing Sappho as Labé might have
envisaged her result not only from Sappho's near erasure from
literary history but also from our ignorance of Labé's own biography, especially her education. Most critics express their confidence that Labé read Latin but not Greek. If that is so, she must
have read Sappho in translation, in Latin or French, although the
Latin source is the more likely, since the first published French
translation was not to appear until 1556, a year after Labé published her own works. In addition to knowing the two recently
recovered Sapphic odes, Labé is likely to have been aware that
Greek and Latin meters were named after Sappho. In *Débat de
folie et d'amour,* Apollo's inclusion of Sappho in a list of the best
ancient poets and philosophers suggests that Labé must have been
aware of the high esteem Sappho's poetry had earned in ancient
Greece. It is no less likely, however, that Labé's knowledge of
Sappho to a large extent derived from the Catullan and Ovidian
appropriations of Sappho, especially since Labé's poetry includes

numerous other signs of borrowings from Catullus and Ovid. Furthermore, the Greek ode praising Labé and naming her as the restorer of Sappho's song also names Phaon, the fictional boatman whose power over Sappho was perpetuated by Ovid's *Heroides*. Labé's second elegy in particular, epistolary in form, is powerfully evocative of Ovid's *Heroides*. Although Labé never names Sappho in the second elegy, she seems to be adopting first a character and voice like those of Ovid's grieving, abandoned women brought to life in the *Heroides*, and then, more specifically, the voice of the simultaneously fictional and historical "author"-character Sappho.[8] Yet, whereas Ovid silenced Sappho in the fifteenth verse letter of the *Heroides*, Labé was to restore her voice and her poetic powers in her second elegy.

A closer look at Labé's second elegy reveals several parallels to Ovid's *Heroides*. As in each of the first fifteen *Heroides*, the situation is that of a woman writing to a man who has abandoned her. Consistently the man is mobile, traveling by water, and the abandoned woman stationary, on land. Ovid's women, however, vary from the chastely married Penelope, who we know ultimately will be reunited with Odysseus, to the naively innocent Phyllis, who relinquished both her kingdom and her virginity to Demophoon only to have her trust betrayed. Ovid's situations vary from that of Laodamia—newly married to Protesilaus, who will die the moment he sets foot on Trojan soil—to that of Medea, cast aside by Jason when the opportunity of marriage to Creon's daughter presents itself. Some of the women reveal themselves to be helpless as well as hopeless, while others respond to their circumstances with cunning or rage. Harold Isbell points out that a source of irony in the *Heroides*

> is to be found in the fact that every lover is writing out of a desire for union with the beloved, a union which it is hoped will result in stability and permanence. While this is the stated desire of the writer, it is the reader's universal experience that nothing in this life can be static. The irony arises with the reader's realization that the only stability free of change is to be found in the death of either one or the other or both parties. While love causes one to desire the unchanging fulfilment of love, it is only in death that anything can be said to be free of change.[9]

A further irony resides in Ovid's simultaneous empowerment of women by giving them voices and transforming them from minor characters in epic to central characters in lyric, and disempowerment of women through the depiction of their inability to perceive themselves as autonomous individuals. Typically, the al-

ternatives seem to be either reunion with the loved one or death.
Even Penelope closes with the reminder:

> *Certe ego, quae fueram te discedente puella,*
> *protinus ut venias, facta videbor anus.*

> Just remember, I was a young girl when you left;
> if you came at once you would find an old woman.[10]

Age and time have more control over who she is than she does
herself, although Penelope exercises more control over her situation than do most of the women, albeit through patient faith and
waiting.

Louise Labé's "Elegy 2," while sharing many characteristics
with Ovid's *Heroides*, introduces changes that associate her persona more with the broader Renaissance image or conception of
Sappho than with legend's and Ovid's Sappho, and with the poet
of the *Amores, Heroides,* and *Metamorphoses* more than with the
women in Ovid's poetry. The Sappho of Ovid's *Heroides* differs
from Ovid's other women letter writers, inasmuch as Sappho is
historical whereas the other women are fictional. By Ovid's time,
however, the legend of Sappho's unrequited love for Phaon had
attached itself to the historical figure. Ovid embroiders on this
legend, having his Sappho specify that nothing—not even the girls
of Lesbos—can now give her any joy:

> *non oculis grata est Atthis, ut ante, meis,*
> *atque aliae centum, quas non sine crimine amavi;*
> *inprobe, multarum quod fuit, anus habes.*
> (*Heroides,* XV.18–20; Loeb, 182)

> Atthis no longer brings joy to my eyes as
>   she did once. Nor do I find pleasure
> in the hundred others I have loved in shame.
> Yours is now the love these maids once had.
> (*Heroides,* 134)

Ovid's Sappho acknowledges, then undercuts, the greatness of her
lyric artistry:

> *iam canitur toto nomen in orbe meum.*
> *nec plus Alcaeus, consors patriaeque lyraeque,*
> *laudis habet, quamvis ille sonet.*
> (*Heroides,* XV.28–30; Loeb, 182)

> my name is known all over the earth.
> Alcaeus himself has no richer fame: he
>   who shares not only my gift for song

but also my homeland, though he sings a song
        of more dignity than my lyrics.

(Heroides, 134)

Therefore, it is even more significant, when, toward the end of the
poem, she describes the death of her art:

> *nunc vellem facunda forem! dolor artibus obstat,*
>   *ingeniumque meis substitit omne malis.*
> *non mihi respondent veteres in carmina vires;*
>   *plectra dolore tacent, muta dolore lyra est.*

(Heroides, XV.195–98; Loeb, 194)

I wish that eloquence were mine now, but grief
        kills my art and woe stops my genius.
The gift of song I enjoyed will not answer
        my call; lyre and plectrum are silent.

(Heroides, 140)

Ovid's poetry intensifies the poignancy of her destruction, first
as a poet and subsequently as a woman, as a result of Phaon's
abandoning her.

Labé's second elegy plays with many of the same themes and
images, while naming neither the speaker nor the male loved one.
Like Sappho, the persona of Labé's elegy has earned wide fame,
not only in France but in Spain and Germany as well:

> *Non seulement en France suis flatee,*
> *Et beaucoup plus, que ne veus, exaltee.*
> *La terre aussi que Calpe et Pyrenee*
> *Avec la mer tiennent environnee,*
> *Du large Rhin les roulantes areines,*
> *Le beau païs auquel or'te promeines,*
> *Ont entendu (tu me l'as fait à croire)*
> *Que gens d'esprit me donnent quelque gloire.*

(61–68)

Not only in France am I flattered, but celebrated much more, which I
do not desire. The land which Gibraltar and the Pyrenees hold encircled
with the sea, the rolling sands of the broad Rhine, the beautiful country
where you formerly rambled, have also heard tell (according to your
own account) that intelligent folk confer glory on me.

Labé's persona also threatens suicide if her lover does not return
to her. Both speakers cite inscriptions that will be engraved to

commemorate their deaths. Yet these parallels intensify significant differences. For example, Sappho's inscription in Ovid's *Heroides* focuses on the return of her lyre to Phoebus, emphasizing simultaneously her loss of poetic voice and power and Ovid's skill as a poet:

> *Grata lyram posui tibi, Phoebe, poetria Sappho:*
> *Convenit illa mihi, convenit illa tibi.*
>
> (*Heroides,* XV.183–84; Loeb, 192)

The grateful poet Sappho gives you, Phoebus, the lyre that is appropriate to us both.

Ovid plays with the idea of Phoebus being honored and grateful when a great poet honors him and a poet being honored and grateful when Phoebus inspires him. The balance of the two *convenit* clauses is introduced not only by the names of Phoebus and Sappho in the first line of the inscription, but also by the double meaning of *gratus,* as "grateful" and "deserving thanks." In a very real sense, Ovid has appropriated Sappho's voice and used it for his own purposes: her voice is an extension of his fame and honor as a poet. Meanwhile, he has taken from love poetry the ironic convention of lovers singing about their inability to sing, and literally silenced her.

Knowledge of the inscription described in Ovid's poem gives new resonance to Labé's account of her persona's poetic beginnings in the first elegy. Labé invents a myth in which her persona describes Apollo's gift to her, Sappho's lyre, with which she will sing simultaneously of her own love and Sappho's. In this way, Labé aligns herself and her persona with the early modern image of Sappho, the Sappho who was famous for her poetry, and with Ovid himself, who gained fame for his love poetry, rather than the character of Sappho in the fifteenth letter of the *Heroides.* While Ovid perpetuates a myth that contributes to his poetic glory while silencing Sappho, Labé creates a myth that valorizes her poetry through association with Sappho, Apollo, and, obliquely, even Ovid.

Ovid plays similar games with the opening of Sappho's letter to Phaon, in which Sappho points out that Phaon may be confused to see her writing in elegiacs, since she is famed for her sapphics. She explains:

Flendus amor meus est—elegiae flebile carmen;
non facit ad lacrimas barbitos ulla meas.

(*Heroides*, XV.7–8; Loeb, 180)

But I weep and tears fit well the elegy—
a lyre cannot bear the weight of tears.

(*Heroides*, 133)

Love prevents her from writing in the mode that made her famous. Moreover, as the letter continues, Howard Jacobsen argues, the blatant artistry self-consciously and heavy-handedly draws attention to itself in ways reminding the reader of the historical Sappho's style and Ovid's style in the *Amores*, convincing the reader that "If Phaon has deprived Sappho of her poetic skills, so too he has rendered her incapable of loving and being loved by others. . . . He has destroyed her both as lover and as poet."[11] Love prevents Ovid (he tells us) from writing in the epic mode (though his *Metamorphoses* is in hexameters); writing his *Amores* and *Heroides* in elegiacs brought Ovid fame.

Labé's second elegy is full of weeping and tears, as befits an elegy. However, instead of singing about the inability to sing, Labé's persona continually emphasizes the power of her words as lament, prayer, and poem. In line 8, Labé's speaker explicitly refers to her letter-poem as lament ("*en vain mon desir se lamente*"— my desire laments in vain). Whereas, in Ovid's poem, the lament quality contributes to Sappho's loss of autonomy and power as a woman and a poet, Labé taps into a source of female power with her lament. In her *Dangerous Voices: Women's Laments and Greek Literature*, Gail Holst-Warhaft explores lament as a woman's art potentially posing such a threat to society that from the sixth century B.C. "the more advanced city-states" developed legislation to control "extravagant" mourning by women.[12] Critics agree that Ovid's *Heroides* builds on the tradition of women's lament that survives in the ancient Greek epic and tragedy, notably Sophocles' *Antigone*, as well as in Catullus's *Ariadne*.[13] When Ovid builds on the lament tradition, however, he participates in the disempowerment of women. Labé, on the other hand, recovers the lament as a woman's art and appropriates its power.

Labé's persona is even more explicit about the power of her prayers: she cannot believe that the man she loves can be held back from returning by sickness, or because he has lost his way: the gods would have to be more cruel than tigers not to heed her prayers:

> [. . .] *car tant suis coutumiere*
> *De faire aus Dieus pour ta santé priere,*
> *Que plus cruels que tigres ils seroient,*
> *Quant maladie ils te prochasseroient.*
> (*Œuvres complètes*, 34–37)

[. . .] because I am in the habit of praying so much to the gods for your well-being that they would be more cruel than tigers if they allowed any harm to draw near you.

She goes on to say that even though her lover may deserve suffering, God will restrain his wrath on account of her prayers:

> *Bien que ta fole et volage inconstance*
> *Meriteroit avoir quelque soufrance,*
> *Telle est ma foy, qu'elle pourra sufire*
> *A te garder d'avoir mal et martire.*
> *Celui qui tient au haut Ciel son Empire*
> *Ne me sauroit, ce me semble, sesdire:*
> *Mais quant mes pleurs et larmes entendroit*
> *Pour toy prians, son ire il retiendroit.*
> (*Œuvres complètes*, 37–44)

Your crazy and fickle vacillations ought to result in some suffering. However, such is my faith, that it will be able to do enough to shield you from evil and martyrdom. He who holds his empire in the heavens above would not be capable of telling me otherwise, it seems to me: when he heard my weeping and tears, praying for you, he would restrain his wrath.

His inconstancy contrasts sharply with her faith and loyalty, with the result that he deserves to be punished; nevertheless, her power of language through prayer and lament is adequate to protect him.

Labé's persona next turns to her considerable powers as a woman and a poet. No new lover could possibly be as widely respected as she is for her beauty, virtue, grace, and fluency in speech:

> [. . .] *say je bien que t'amie nouvelle*
> *A peine aura le renom d'estre telle,*
> *Soit en beauté, vertu, grace et faconde.*
> (*Œuvres complètes*, 55–57)

[. . .] I know very well that your new friend will scarcely have the fame of being such [as I am], be it in beauty, virtue, charm, or eloquence.

In lines reminiscent of the first of the letter in *Heroides,* she stresses her attractiveness to other men. Like Penelope, she has many suitors:

> *Maints grans Signeurs à mon amour pretendent,*
> *Et à me plaire et servir prets se rendent,*
> *Joutes et jeus, maintes belles devises*
> *En ma faveur sont par eus entreprises.*
>
> (*Œuvres complètes,* 75–78)

Many great lords lay claims to my love, and are ever ready to serve and please me, [and] tournaments and games, and many fine devices have been attempted by them to honor me.

Perhaps most important, however, in setting Labé's persona apart from Ovid's Sappho, but in company with the poet Ovid and the historical Sappho, is the inscription with which she closes the elegy. Labé's inscription appropriates the convention of poetry immortalizing its writers. Labé's persona will not even be silenced by death. The words of her inscription, like Labé's, Ovid's, and Sappho's poetry, will continue to speak throughout time.[14]

Labé's inscription simultaneously reflects the persona's emotional disturbance resulting from unreciprocated love and the poet's rhetorical skills which immortalize the female persona's passion and power. The elegy closes:

> *PAR TOY, AMI, TANT, VESQUI ENFLAMMEE*
> *QU'EN LANGUISSANT PAR FEU SUIS CONSUMEE,*
> *QUI COUVE ENCOR SOUS MA CENDRE EMBRAZEE*
> *SI NE LE RENS DE TES PLEURS APAIZEE.*

By you, friend, so much, I lived enflamed
That languishing I am consumed by fire,
Which still smolders beneath my burning cinders
[To be] quenched by nothing but your tears.

The careful, rhetorical quality of these lines—especially the syllepsis of *le* in the final line, agreeing grammatically with *feu,* while *apaizee* agrees with the feminine *cendre*[15]—combines with the traditional imagery of burning love to emphasize the phoenix-like grandeur and immortality of her love and her poetry. Only the lover's tears could extinguish the flame of her passion. Whereas Ovid's Sappho will take the proverbial Leucadian leap, presumably extinguishing flame and pain in the waves far from her homeland,

Labé's persona may die of love (indeed, she says she is dying of love a thousand times a day as she writes), but the finite verb of the inscription is the past historic of *vivre*, meaning "to live." Furthermore the intransitive verb *couve*, or "smolder," may bring with it some of its transitive sense, of "to hatch," or "to brood." This female poet is not so easily silenced and put to death as is Ovid's Sappho. Like a phoenix, Labé's persona bursts back to life after she has been consumed by the fire of love.

While Sappho frequently appears as a character in poetry, Louise Labé creates a poetic persona that not only draws on the Renaissance conception of Sappho as a woman and poet, but also on the fictions passed to her by poets like Catullus and Ovid. In contrast to these male poetic appropriations of Sappho, which tend to obscure the power of her female voice, Labé restores Sappho's voice, its gender and its sexual inclination, speaking with her as another woman experiencing passionate desire. Besides, through her impersonation of Sappho, Labé's persona demonstrates more generally that grief need not silence and destroy women. As the Greek ode says of Labé:

> Struck by his flight, she being wretched began to adopt
> a shrill song to the chords of her lyre,
> Through these poems, a vehement passion penetrates
> the love of arrogant young boys.
>
> (trans. George Hardin Brown)

Thus, Labé's persona in the second elegy converts her wretchedness to poetic artistry, as Sappho had done in her lyrics. Since nothing but the tears of her beloved could possibly extinguish the fires of her love, her passion will smolder and burst into new life, as Sappho's does through the sixteenth-century recovery of her poems and fragments. Although both Labé and Sappho have tended to be marginalized by literary history, their interlinked voices have survived. Perhaps their passion still has the power to penetrate "the love of arrogant young boys."

NOTES TO "A VOICE RESTORED: LOUISE LABÉ'S IMPERSONATION OF SAPPHO"

1. As François Rigolot points out, the combination of the mid-sixteenth-century discovery and publication of Sappho's fragment 31 ("To me he seems to match the gods"), and Labé's evocation of lesbian love in her first elegy, contributed to her association with Sappho during her own time and since. "Préface" to

Louise Labé: Œuvres complètes—Sonnets, Élégies, Débat de folie et d'amour,
ed. François Rigolot (Paris: GF Flammarion, 1986), 20 (all references to Louise
Labé's works will be to this edition); and "Louise Labé et la redécouverte de
Sappho," *Nouvelle revue du seizième siècle* 1 (1983): 21.

2. Unless stated otherwise, the English translations are my own.

3. Catullus's famous poem 51 ("*Ille mi par esse*"), a free translation of
Sappho's poem with the genders reversed, would have been well known to
sixteenth-century poets, as would the fifteenth verse letter in Ovid's *Heroides,*
purporting to be from Sappho to Phaon.

4. Joan DeJean, *Fictions of Sappho: 1546–1937* (Chicago: University of Chicago Press, 1989), 16.

5. "Louise Labé et la redécouverte de Sappho," 21–23. Rigolot includes the
Greek text of this ode as well as a French translation in his edition *Œuvres
complètes.* The English translation quoted below was made specially for this
article by George Hardin Brown.

6. DeJean remarks in her introduction, "I no longer see [Sappho's] history as
a progression toward greater knowledge. It now seems to me that the first erudites
who worked to recover Sappho—notably Henri Estienne . . . —knew more about
Sappho than any other pre-nineteenth-century scholars" (22).

7. See *Fictions of Sappho,* 44. In her chapter "Loss and Legitimation: Labé's
Elegiac Voice," Deborah Lesko Baker discusses ways in which "the Sapphic
allusion" in this elegy "does not erase the Petrarchan presence, but works subtly
to challenge its exclusivity" through a "rhetorically ambivalent strategy of modesty and boldness, or independence and traditionalism, in their curious juxtaposition of authorial voices." See *The Subject of Desire: Petrarchan Poetics and the
Female Voice in Louise Labé* (West Lafayette, IN: Purdue University Press,
1996), 94.

8. Another important source for Labé's grieving, abandoned woman is Boccaccio's *The Elegy of Lady Fiammetta,* available in a translation by Mariangela
Causa-Steindler and Thomas Mauch (Chicago: University of Chicago Press,
1990). Boccaccio's elegy is in prose, is much longer than either Ovid's or Labé's
elegies, and depicts Fiammetta as a tiresome, selfish, foolish woman.

9. *Ovid: "Heroides,"* trans. Harold Isbell (New York: Penguin, 1990), xi–xii.
Subsequent translations of Ovid's *Heroides* will be from this edition.

10. Ovid, *"Heroides" and "Amores,"* Loeb Classical Library (1963), *Heroides,*
I.115–16; Loeb, 18.

11. Howard Jacobson, *Ovid's "Heroides"* (Princeton: Princeton University
Press, 1974), 289–91.

12. Gail Holst-Warhaft, *Dangerous Voices: Women's Laments and Greek Literature* (London and New York: Routledge, 1992), 3.

13. Jacobson points out that "it is Euripides who must be considered the distant
ancestor of the *Heroides,* not merely because he so effectively and influentially
utilized women's speeches, but also because in the *Heroides* Ovid—whether consciously or not—inherited many of the intellectual and moral attitudes that were
Euripides'" (*Ovid's "Heroides,"* 7).

14. The survival of such a minuscule portion of Sappho's writings is made all
the more poignant by Antipater of Thessaloniki's poem:

> These women Mt. Helicon and the Macedonian rock of Pieria
>   raised—with godlike tongues for songs:
> Praxilla, Moero, the voice of Anyte (the female Homer),
>   Sappho, the ornament of the fair-tressed Lesbians,

> Erinna, Telesilla of wide fame, and you, Korinna,
>   singing of the impetuous Child of Athena,
> Nossis of womanly tongue, and sweet-sounding Myrtis—
>   all of them composers of pages that will last for all time.
> Great Heaven created nine Muses, but Earth
>   bore these nine, as everlasting delight for mortals.

Antipater's poem suggests a very different tradition from that of Catullus and Ovid, a tradition more in line with Labé's impersonation of Sappho. The translation is by Jane McIntosh Snyder, who uses this poem as the epigraph to *The Woman and the Lyre: Women Writers in Classical Greece and Rome* (Carbondale: Southern Illinois Press, 1989).

   15. See Rigolot's note in *Œuvres complètes,* 114.

Plato as Protagonist in Sir Thomas Elyot's *Of the Knowledge which Maketh a Wise Man*

ROBERT HAYNES

By the early 1530s, King Henry the Eighth had broken with the "Bishop of Rome," and the king was in no mood to tolerate dissent or criticism of his decision to establish himself as the head of the English church. Those Englishmen in a position to advise the king faced a dangerous dilemma. On one side lay the alternative of avoiding provocation either by resorting to a safe silence or by indulging the king's vanity through flattery. On the other side, there was the prospect of attempting to provide Henry with prudent and judicious advice—a risky prospect under the circumstances. As he pondered the need for political reform in England, Thomas Elyot fully recognized the need for a certain subtlety in the presentation of his thoughts. In 1533, Elyot published two dialogues dealing with the proper relation of the humanist to the monarch. One of these dialogues, *Pasquil the Playne,* involves a conversation between three characters: a flatterer, an advocate of safe silence, and a talking statue (Pasquil) who argues for the active involvement of educated men in politics.[1]

In his other dialogue from this year, *Of the Knowledge which Maketh a Wise Man,* Elyot again uses a dramatic format to introduce a certain distance between himself as author and the views of his speaking characters. This distancing effect enables Elyot both to comment and to dissociate himself from his comments, a technique perfected by Plato, one of Elyot's favorite classical authors. In fact, one particularly notable feature of this dialogue is Elyot's explicit assignment of it to the genre of Platonic dialogue. And not only does the second edition of the work bear the subtitle "A Disputacyon Platonike," but the dialogue's principal speaker is Plato himself, who has just returned from his narrow escape from Dionysius of Syracuse.[2] Elyot's making the famous ancient philosopher his main speaker places this character's views at a certain

fictitious distance from contemporary Tudor politics, enabling
Elyot to employ both the character Plato and the Platonic dialogue
itself as mechanisms for promulgating Elyot's own views. The setting of Elyot's colloquy, of course, is Greece, and the dialogue
occurs during a journey, apparently between the coast, where Plato
has just landed, and an unnamed town. If, as is most likely, Elyot
intended this setting to suggest the journey between the Peiraeus
and Athens, the dialogue echoes the opening of Plato's *Republic,*
where Socrates describes an earlier journey to the Peiraeus. The
theme of dialogue during journey also reminds us of Plato's *Laws,*
which conversation occurs as the three aged interlocutors make
their way toward a shrine on Crete.

The other character in Elyot's dialogue is Aristippus, like Plato
a historical character, who functions as antagonist in order to bring
out Plato's views on hedonism, the personal philosophy of Aristippus. Aristippus, who had been with Plato at the court of Dionysius,
is able to contribute his own perspective about Plato's behavior in
Sicily. Despite the disparity of Aristippus's and Plato's views, the
deference of the hedonist philosopher to his more austere friend
helps with the characterization of both. If anything, Aristippus
seems more tolerant than Plato. Plato's conviction about the validity of his own views contrasts dramatically with Aristippus's relative uncertainty and apparent tractability. If both characters were
as unbending as Plato, no dialogue would be possible, but this
essential difference in character enables the dialogue to move forward with a certain energy and dramatic liveliness informed by
Plato's oft-voiced disapprobation of Aristippus's love of pleasure
and by the latter's bemused admiration of Plato's aversion to personal compromise. Thus, the dialogue's dramaturgy combines with
its representation of two opposed schools of thought a formal dis-
junction between the world of this literary work and the world of
Elyot and his contemporaries.

Yet the subject that preoccupies "Plato" here is one of the principal political problems of the first half of the sixteenth century. This
problem was substantially treated both by Sir Thomas More in the
Utopia and by Thomas Starkey in the *Dialogue between Pole and
Lupset,* but Elyot's treatment of it is especially interesting because
he published his dialogue in English at a time when Henry the
Eighth was resolving to extend and consolidate his personal power
at whatever cost was necessary.[3] If it is true that books published
by the royal printer Thomas Berthelet at this time were singled out
for endorsement by the government, Elyot's dialogue is a valuable
indication of the extent to which indirect dissent was still possible.[4]

Like More and Starkey, Elyot was concerned with contributing what he could to the "common weal." He also realized that getting involved in politics could be dangerous; but as a Christian philosopher, he recognized that the involvement of good men in government was necessary to offset both the effect of the greedy and selfish flatterers who flock to the courts of the powerful and the other temptations that beset all monarchs. Thus, Elyot resolved to take the risks involved in the publication of his own views of what constituted good counsel and proper kingship, and, although his medium of communication involved indirection and authorial self-distancing, we shall see that the relevance of the dialogue *Of the Knowledge which Maketh a Wise Man* to contemporary politics was immediate, and that Elyot's personal risk was great indeed.

During the years leading up to Henry's final break with Rome, a strong mutual influence extended between the humanist writers. In the *Utopia,* More praised his friend Cuthbert Tunstal and gave his fictional character Hythloday some characteristics that would have been recognized as resembling those of Erasmus. With the inclusion of the various letters and poems that were added to the text, it is easy to see the enthusiasm with which these humanists celebrated their communication. Thomas Starkey assigned the dramatic roles in his long dialogue to two friends who were distinguished humanists, and we can assume that the theories set forth by these characters would not have been entirely alien to their historical counterparts—or else the literary connection could not have been an act of friendship. Elyot's humanist connections were also strong. He considered More a friend, and having himself served Henry the Eighth in a diplomatic role, he must have been on close terms with other members of humanistic circles.[5] Whether Elyot ever met Erasmus is doubtful, but the latter was a strong influence on Elyot, whom one recent critic has called Erasmus's "most notable English disciple."[6]

Elyot's political writings, however, following More's *Utopia* by a decade and a half, should be seen as incorporating an awareness of changes that occurred in England during that interval. It is also necessary to remember that Elyot addressed his writings to an English audience, whereas More, though deeply concerned with reform in England, wrote his *Utopia* in Latin for the pleasure and profit of humanists everywhere. As in Erasmus's *The Praise of Folly,* play and imaginative satire inform the essence of More's book. As Thomas Elyot readied himself to contribute his own views of how the state should be improved, he had before him the problem of whether Thomas More had achieved anything of political consequence either in publishing *Utopia* or in entering the king's service. Another serious question concerns whether More's views in 1530–31 were the same as they had been before the fall of Cardinal Wolsey and the increased friction between King Henry and Rome over the royal divorce. Surely matters had changed sufficiently to explain Elyot's departures from what may have been More's views. It is quite possible that More himself had lost interest in radical speculation about political reform. Yet, the connections between Elyot and the other humanists have a special significance when we turn to a particular theme this work shares with *Utopia* and with Starkey's *Dialogue,* a theme derived principally from the classical works of Plato and Cicero: the rejection of tyranny. This theme is also central to Elyot's dialogue *Of the Knowledge which Maketh a Wise Man.*

Although Plato's powerful critique of tyranny in the *Republic* was familiar to the English humanists, it was the description of his Sicilian adventures in the pages of Diogenes Laertius that established the Athenian philosopher as an active participant in the perilous politics of the real world—or, more explicitly, of a tyrant's court.[7] No dialogist of the period drew more heavily on Laertius than did Thomas Elyot. In composing a dialogue between the philosophers Plato and Aristippus, Elyot employed the Laertian lives of both historical characters. One of the more positive things that can be said about Diogenes Laertius is that, whoever he may have been, he had an affinity for stories in which tyrants suffer setbacks, and Elyot's recourse to the *Lives of the Philosophers* in his dialogue *Of the Knowledge which Maketh a Wise Man* includes an allusion (voiced by "Plato") to the Eleatic Zeno's heroic defiance of one tyrant.[8] Elyot's use of this source will be further discussed below; it will suffice here to point out that Laertius did furnish subsequent readers with the background of Plato's difficulties with Dionysius, the tyrant of Syracuse.[9]

In accordance with the anti-tyrannical philosophy of Plato, Elyot, an avowed devotee of monarchy, reflected at length on the forces that could transform a ruler from a good king into a tyrant. Despite his frequently reiterated belief that the properly ordered "publike weal" must be governed by a monarch, Elyot does perceive a clear distinction between the king and the tyrant, a distinction identical to that established by Plato between *basileus* and *tyrannos.*[10] The king governs according to virtue, whereas the tyrant is ruled by pleasure and pride. Elyot's concern in *The Boke Named the Governour* with the correct education of noble counselors for the king had suggested that he saw the counselor's role as the best medium for preventing the metamorphosis of king into tyrant.[11] In the later work, *Of the Knowledge which Maketh a Wise Man,* Elyot represents a situation in which Plato defends his own unsuccessful effort to transform the tyrant Dionysius of Syracuse into a king. Where *The Boke Named the Governour* places a positive emphasis on monarchy, only incidentally alluding to tyranny as the inevitable consequence of the failure of kingly virtue, the dialogue *Of the Knowledge which Maketh a Wise Man* focuses on the philosophical imperative facing the counselor himself—an imperative embodied in the very nature of Elyot's book. The "Proheme" reveals that he was aware that publishing his book involved some personal risk, as he says:

> Some wyll maliciously diuine or coniecte that I wryte to the intent to rebuke some perticuler persone couaytinge to brynge my warkes and afterward me into the indignation of some man in auctorytie. Thus vnthankfully is my benefyte receyued / my good wyll consumed, and all my labours deuoured. Such is of some menne the nature serpentine, that lappyng swete mylke they conuerte hit forthe with in to poyson, to distroy hym of whose liberalitie they late had receyued it.[12]

In comparing his work to "swete mylke," Elyot is arguing that this dialogue is intended to be both pleasant and salubrious. We should not, then, assume that in employing the story of Dionysius's unfortunate treatment of Plato, Elyot wishes to represent that he has no further hope for King Henry.[13] Negative examples may well constitute positive counsel, as in the case of the Old Testament story of the prophet Nathan's parable that made King David see the scurrility of his own behavior in murdering Uriah the Hittite in order to get Uriah's wife.[14] In using the story of Dionysius and Plato, in fact, Elyot was simply elaborating a theme More had brought up in the *Utopia,* where Hythloday uses the same example as support for his own policy of political noninvolvement.[15] Thus the dialogue *Of the Knowledge which Maketh a Wise Man* should not be taken as Elyot's abdication of the role of counselor to Henry. Whereas actually he was outside the royal service, he still sought to influence the king through his publications.

In the "Proheme" to the dialogue *Of the Knowledge which Maketh a Wise Man,* Elyot, to some extent following the obligatory custom of flattery, expresses gratitude to Henry for his gracious reception of Elyot's *Governour* and goes on to praise Henry's sensitivity and tolerance. He then approvingly cites a story in which the emperor Marcus Aurelius hired "a playne & rude persone / whiche alwaye spake in the rebuke of all men" because, as the

emperor said, "princis vices were sooner espied by other men than
by them selfes: and . . . there was moche more difficultie in re-
membring them of their vice or lack, than in extolling and com-
mendynge their vertues."[16] As Edwin Johnston Howard points out,
"Despite Elyot's disclaimers this narrative can be interpreted only
as Elyot's justification of his criticism of the king" (*Of the Knowledge,* xxvii).

As the "Proheme" shows, Elyot still hoped that his writing could
be beneficial to the king. We must remember that at this time More,
Fisher, and the Carthusians were still alive. In fact, at this time,
More engaged in a vigorous, but almost surprisingly civilized, controversy with Christopher St. German during which More called
attention to St. German's lack of mastery of the dialogue form.
Thus, in reading Elyot's dialogue *Of the Knowledge which Maketh
a Wise Man,* it must be kept in mind that, despite some disturbing
developments in England, there remained some hope for general
reconciliation—or, at least, moderation—and Henry the Eighth remained the critical figure. Even after the executions of Sir Thomas
More and Bishop John Fisher, Reginald Pole expressed a desperate
hope for Henry's return to orthodoxy; so there is no need to wonder whether Elyot had hoped in brighter days for some measure
of royal enlightenment.

If, then, Elyot intended his "disputacyon Platonike" to provide
a negative example of autocracy in the tyrannical Dionysius, whose
ill treatment of the noble philosopher Plato ensured his own perpetual infamy, what are we to make of the dialogue's preoccupation
with knowledge, a concern whose centrality is emphasized in the
work's title? The dialogue is explicitly about that knowledge which
makes a wise man, and the two interlocutors begin their conversation holding very different opinions about wisdom. Aristippus and
Plato agree that they both have a high regard for pleasure, but in
the former case the pleasure is physical, whereas for Plato what is
desirable is the pleasure of the virtuous intellect, the engagement
in the pursuit of truth and knowledge. For Aristippus, wisdom lies
in hedonism, and it was his counsel that the tyrant Dionysius had
found agreeable. In *Of the Knowledge,* we see a dialogue between
counselors, just as Elyot had produced in *Pasquil the Playne;* but
here the less effective counselor is Plato, and the example of Plato's
adherence to virtue in Dionysius's court establishes a paradigm
Elyot must have chosen to solace the virtuous but ineffectual humanists who aspired to repair the regime of Henry the Eighth.
Thomas More, Thomas Starkey, and Elyot all suffered disappoint-
ments as reformers, and the example of Plato may have been of

some comfort to them as they witnessed Henry's progress away from the role of enlightened and benevolent monarch. Whereas, in 1533, Elyot still hoped to supply effective counsel to the king, his choice of this classical precedent includes tacit acknowledgment of the evident possibility of a failure like that of Plato. His assignment to Plato of a conviction of the rightness of his effort in Sicily shows Elyot's own conviction that his duty lay in making the same effort Plato made, whatever the consequences. This conviction is a consequence of knowledge, the specific knowledge that commits the good man to action in behalf of the "publike weal."

It is in the fifth chapter of Elyot's dialogue, after extended discussion in earlier chapters of the nature of knowledge and the providential nature of human suffering, that Plato, explaining his general plan of exposition, arrives at the principal conclusion made in the work. Reverting to his account of his experience at Dionysius's court, Plato argues that the mere possession of knowledge is not sufficient:

> Wherefore all though wisedome be knowlege, yet by knowledge onely none may be called a wise man, but operation of that whiche is in knowledge called wysedome / expressynge the wysedome, maketh the vser or exercisar thereof to be iustly named a wyse man.
>
> (*Of the Knowledge*, 196–97)

Aristippus enthusiastically agrees with Plato's conclusion but wonders why Plato has made this particular point. Plato recapitulates the entire previous discussion, making it clear that all has served to justify his conduct in the court of Dionysius. Concluding his summary, Plato adds:

> Nowe Aristippus reuoluyng all this in thy mynde / whiche in a short Epilogation I haue endeuoured my selfe to reduce vnto thy remembrance, Consyder well bothe me and kynge Dionise / as we were at that tyme, whan we were togither. Thou knowest well that from the tyme that I was .xx. yeres old, I alway continued disciple of Socrates, vntyll that he dyed. Who (as thou knowist) the answere of god determyned to be of al mortall men the wysest.
>
> (*Of the Knowledge*, 197)

Here, Elyot establishes an implicit analogy between Plato's use of Socrates as example, on the one hand, and, on the other, his own use of Plato as example. Plato, it will be remembered, has his character Socrates claim to be the only true statesman.[17] Plato, of course, made his revered teacher a character in dialogue just as

Elyot is here making Plato such a character. If Socrates was the wisest of men, then his knowledge must have been that which Elyot's dialogue seeks to set forth. Plato continues:

> And that whiche I lerned of hym was wysedome: whiche as he euer affirmed was included in these two wordes, Knowe thy selfe. And by that doctrine (as thou mayste remembre) he abated the presumption of dyuers, whiche supposed them selfe to be excellent wyse men. Also reuoked many that were dissolute and resolued into vice, and made them to ensue vertue. And by his exaumple of lyuynge he prouoked men to contemne fortune, and to haue onely vertue in reuerence. And also therby, laste of all, whan he was iniustely condemned to deth, he constantly and ioyfully susteyned to haue the mortall body dissolued / that the soule mought be at reste and haue her immortal rewarde. Whiche example giuen of hym was the corroboration of al his doctrine / and no lasse part of lerning vnto his scolers, but rather moch more than his often disputations or lessons.
>
> *(Of the Knowledge,* 201–2)

The recognition of the ultimate value of providing an example accords perfectly with Elyot's own commitment to involvement. Socrates' "exaumple of lyuynge," argues Plato, along with his example of dying, was a better form of teaching than his actual words had been. It was the dialogue perfected by Plato that promulgated both the Socratic example and the Socratic words. Therefore, Elyot, recognizing the danger of providing philosophic counsel to an increasingly self-willed autocrat, indicates his own conviction that it is better to act according to reasoned principle than to guide one's actions by the likelihood of official approbation or reward.

As Plato and Aristippus approach the town (presumably Athens), Plato at some length reiterates his conviction that his words to Dionysius had not only been appropriate but were necessary, given both his own character and his desire to be a proper example of a wise man. As he says:

> if I shuld haue holden my peace, as well my commynge to kynge Dionise had ben frustrate and vayne, and his gentylle desyre had ben vnsatisfied, as also by my silence beinge thought (as raison was that I shulde be) to be subdued eyther with fere or affection: I shuld seme to condemne min owne doctrine, wherfore I shuld be demid vnworthi that good opinion, that kyng Dionise had of me.
>
> *(Of the Knowledge,* 228–29)

Aristippus, who had diligently flattered Dionysius, hastily replies, "Wel Plato in such experience of wysdome I wyl not folow the."

Here, Elyot may have had in mind those of his contemporaries who avoided the danger involved in giving good counsel to the king, yet he seems to hold out hope that the good example of the wise man can even move the hedonistic flatterer closer to wisdom. As the two philosophers part after their long conversation, the tone of their final exchange is gracious.

Whereas Aristippus has not been totally convinced by Plato's arguments, his views have changed to some extent, and Plato's final comment shows confidence that reason can yet prevail in the mind of the affable hedonist. In the course of the conversation, Plato has frequently expressed contempt for his companion's devotion to pleasure; but the dialogue is generally characterized by an atmosphere of philosophical benevolence and cooperation. After all, both men are disciples of Socrates, and both seek the truth. Their discussion is a pattern of the value of dialogue itself. If Plato was unsuccessful in changing the ways of the tyrant Dionysius, at least his arguments have had some effect on a flatterer, and his main argument has aimed at demonstrating that the philosopher is morally obliged to apply his knowledge in the world of affairs. Thomas Elyot thus argues his own case for activism, emphasizing the value of establishing an example even in situations such as those of Socrates and Plato where immediate success was not likely. Elyot's use of classical sources, principally Diogenes Laertius and the Platonic letters, gives his work a certain distance from contemporary issues; but careful consideration of the implicit analogy between Elyot and Plato—like that discussed earlier with the plain-speaking philosopher hired by Marcus Aurelius—raises the question of who was intended to be the Tudor equivalent of Dionysius of Syracuse.

Another consideration remains with respect to Elyot's use of his sources. In Diogenes Laertius, with whose *Lives* Elyot assumes his readers to be familiar, it is clear that Plato's Sicilian misadventure occurred when the philosopher visited the court of Dionysius I.[18] Plato later returned to Sicily, where he experienced no more success with Dionysius II than he had with the tyrant's father, although this time he at least evaded the ordeal of being sold as a slave. Elyot makes no reference to Plato's second and third visits to Sicily and no distinction between Plato's relations with Dionysius I and Dionysius II, an omission made the more striking by the fact that the Dionysius addressed in the Platonic letters, from which Elyot borrowed extensively, is the second one. Is Elyot's point that Plato, after his initial difficulties with Sicilian tyranny, will return to Syracuse to try again? This work's emphasis on putting knowledge into operation, along with its implicit analogy between Plato and Elyot himself, surely suggests that the English humanist is here reaffirming his intention to continue participating in the risky business of counseling kings.

In his 1946 edition of Elyot's dialogue, Edwin Johnston Howard suggested that the conflict between Dionysius and Plato in this work represents the contemporary conflict between Henry the Eighth and Sir Thomas More.[19] Forty years after Howard's suggestion, Alistair Fox argued that the respective circumstances of More and Plato were not sufficiently alike to justify such an interpretation, and that, in fact, Elyot himself was a likelier analogue to Plato.[20] Although such arguments must, to some extent, remain conjectural, the reality of the humanist predicament in the early 1530s is clear. It seems less noteworthy whether Elyot linked Plato to himself or to More than that both men were facing crises of conscience and of moral responsibility. The problem was not of one man but of an entire class of individuals, including Reginald Pole, Cuthbert Tunstal, and Thomas Starkey, all of whom faced hard decisions because of Henry's policy. As Elyot himself pointed out in his "Proheme" to the dialogue,

> For there be Gnathos in Spayne as wel as in Grece, Pasquilles in Englande as welle as in Rome, Dionises in Germanye as welle as in Sicile, Harpocrates in France as wel as in Aegipt, Aristippus in Scotlande as well as in Cyrena, Platos be fewe, and them I doubt where to fynde. And if men wyll seke for them in Englande / whiche I sette in other places, I can nat lette them.[21]

Although the individual circumstances of the men just named are various and complex, the decisions of each bear out Elyot's assertion of the scarcity of Platos. Pole, at a safe distance, defied Henry the Eighth and became a cardinal. Tunstal, within easy grasp of the king's form of justice, went along, after some initial opposition, with the Henrician program. Thomas Starkey, although one scholar has discovered evidence of his private disapproval of the king's reforms, frantically sought to dissociate himself from Pole after the latter attacked Henry in 1536, and he seems to have retained some measure of royal favor for a number of years.[22] Elyot himself, as has often been noted, was forced to disavow his own friendship with Thomas More; thus it may be that he himself should be excluded from the small number of Platos. Although the parallels between Elyot's dialogue *Of the Knowledge which Maketh a Wise Man* and Starkey's dialogue between Pole and Lupset are numerous, and the common concern with tyranny appears to have posed distinct perils for both thinkers, it was after all only Thomas More among the king's counselors who refused to compromise when confronted by the truth of brute force. Elyot's Plato approvingly cites the Laertian example of Zeno of Elea, the philosopher who, when brought before a tyrant and ordered to betray members of the opposition, bit off his own tongue and spat it at the tyrant.[23] Elyot himself, however, perhaps because of his often expressed love of order, was unable either to emulate Zeno's example or that of Thomas More.

In defense of the humanists who yielded to the pressure of Henrician reform, it must be said that their choice was not only between Henry and the Pope but also between England and England's enemies. Although Elyot's Plato refused to compromise himself at the court of Dionysius, Elyot himself was in a somewhat different situation in England. In view of the well-known corruption of the Roman church, Henry's rejection of papal authority must have made some sense to reform-minded Englishmen. The social conditions documented in the *Utopia* and in Starkey's *Dialogue* certainly derived to some extent from unenlightened Church policy. The problem was an old one, as Chaucer and Langland attest; but the advent of classical ideas brought a new readiness to resolve old problems—especially those problems which seemed to result from mere ignorance. Through his friend Thomas Cromwell—to whom Reginald Pole attributed an enthusiasm for the theories of Machiavelli—Elyot retained, at least in the early 1530s, some hope of bringing positive influence to bear upon Henry the Eighth.[24] Later, the necessity of collaboration must have been softened by the fact that the course of events kept Elyot in a position to be of possible benefit to his country. In any case, his Platonic paradigm's argument that the knowledge which makes a man wise is applied knowledge seems to have brought about a different approach for Elyot than for the Plato of Elyot's dialogue. In view of the difference between the responses of More and Elyot to Henry's policy, Elyot must have regarded his heroic friend much as Cicero regarded the younger Cato, of whom Cicero once wrote:

> our friend Cato is not more to you than to me: but still with the best of intentions and unimpeachable honesty at times he does harm to the country: for the opinions he delivers would be more in place in Plato's Republic than among the dregs of humanity collected by Romulus.[25]

Elyot's Platonic dialogue, then, proposes a paradigm for good counsel which Elyot himself was unable fully to emulate. As his experience of actual politics matured, he must have reflected on the passage in the *Utopia* where Morus tells Hythloday that the counselor must play a role appropriate to his circumstances. As it happened, it was More who followed Plato's paradigm, while Elyot followed the advice of Morus.

NOTES TO "PLATO AS PROTAGONIST IN SIR THOMAS ELYOT'S *OF THE KNOWLEDGE WHICH MAKETH A WISE MAN*"

1. For the text of *Pasquil the Playne,* see *Four Political Treatises by Sir Thomas Elyot,* ed. Lillian Gottesman (Gainesville: University of Florida Press, 1967).

2. Frederick W. Conrad has told me in conversation that he believes that the subtitle "A Disputacyon Platonike" was probably not added by Elyot himself. The point does not seem critical here, however, in view of Plato's presence as principal character in the dialogue. All references to and quotations from Elyot's *Of the Knowledge which Maketh a Wise Man* come from the edition by Edwin Johnston Howard (Oxford, OH: Anchor Press, 1946).

3. St. Thomas More, *Utopia,* vol. 4 of *The Complete Works of St. Thomas More,* ed. Edward Surtz, S.J., and J. H. Hexter (New Haven: Yale University Press, 1965), and Thomas Starkey, *A Dialogue between Reginald Pole and Thomas Lupset,* ed. Thomas F. Mayer (London: Royal Historical Society, 1989).

4. The Yale editors of More's *Debellation of Salem and Bizance* assert that Christopher St. German, who was writing at the same time as Elyot, must have had royal authority behind him because Berthelet printed his works. See St. Thomas More, *The Debellation of Salem and Bizance,* vol. 10 of *The Complete Works of St. Thomas More,* ed. John Guy et al. (New Haven: Yale University Press, 1986), xxi and note.

5. For background on Elyot, see Frederick W. Conrad, "A Preservative against Tyranny: The Political Theology of Sir Thomas Elyot," unpublished Ph.D. dissertation, Johns Hopkins University (1988), and "The Problem of Counsel Reconsidered: The Case of Sir Thomas Elyot," in *Political Thought and the Tudor Commonwealth,* ed. Paul A. Fideler and T. F. Mayer (London: Routledge, 1992), 75–107; Pearl Hogrefe, *The Life and Times of Sir Thomas Elyot, Englishman* (Ames: Iowa State University Press, 1967); Stanford E. Lehmberg, *Sir Thomas Elyot, Tudor Humanist* (Austin: University of Texas Press, 1960); and John M. Major, *Sir Thomas Elyot and Renaissance Humanism* (Lincoln: University of Nebraska Press, 1964).

6. Alistair Fox, in *Reassessing the Henrician Age: Humanism, Politics, and Reform 1500–1550,* ed. Alistair Fox and John Guy (Oxford: Blackwell, 1986), 53.

7. Diogenes Laertius, *Plato,* in *Lives of Eminent Philosophers,* trans. R. D. Hicks, Loeb Classical Library, 2 vols. (1925; repr. Cambridge, MA: Harvard University Press, 1991), 1: 276–373; and *Aristippus,* 1: 194–233.

8. Diogenes Laertius, *Zeno of Elea,* in *Lives of Eminent Philosophers,* vol. 2, ix.25ff.

9. Elyot also admired Xenophon, one of whose dialogues (*Hiero*) is about another Syracusan tyrant. See Leo Strauss, *On Tyranny [Hiero]* (Ithaca: Cornell University Press, 1963).

10. A valuable discussion of this distinction is that by A. Andrewes, *The Greek Tyrants* (1956; repr. New York: Harper, 1963), who explains: "For Plato the terms are not at all equivalent: king and tyrant are at opposite poles, the philosopher-king the best and happiest of all men, the tyrant the worst and most miserable. . . . This is a real and basic change from the attitude of Herodotus, who died about the year that Plato was born" (28).

11. *The Boke Named the Gouernour,* ed. Henry Herbert Stephen Croft, 2 vols. (London, 1880). Diogenes Laertius, it may be noted, cites the Athenian Solon, a great hater of tyranny, as opposing the performance of tragedies (*Lives of the Eminent Philosophers,* 1: 59–60).

12. Sir Thomas Elyot, *Of the Knowledge which Maketh a Wise Man,* 4–5.

13. Pearl Hogrefe, in *The Life and Times of Sir Thomas Elyot, Englishman,* cites a letter that Elyot wrote to Thomas Cromwell, apparently about this dialogue, and comments: "The letter adds to the evidence that Elyot was making every effort to influence Henry VIII" (383n15).

14. In his *Pro Ecclesiasticae Unitatis Defensione,* Reginald Pole, reproaching Henry the Eighth for executing More and Fisher, was to compare himself to Nathan the Prophet confronting a guilty King David. Cited in Martin Haile [= Marie Hallé], *A Life of Reginald Pole,* 2nd ed. (London: Pitman, 1911), 56–57.

15. St. Thomas More, *Utopia,* 87.

16. Sir Thomas Elyot, *Of the Knowledge which Maketh a Wise Man,* 8.

17. Plato, *Gorgias,* trans. W. D. Woodhead, in *The Collected Dialogues of Plato,* ed. Edith Hamilton and Huntington Cairns (New York: Pantheon Books, 1961), 302.

18. Diogenes Laertius, *Lives of the Eminent Philosophers,* 1:293.

19. Sir Thomas Elyot, *Of the Knowledge which Maketh a Wise Man,* xxv ff.

20. Alistair Fox, "Sir Thomas Elyot and the Humanist Dilemma," *Reassessing the Henrician Age,* 64ff.

21. Sir Thomas Elyot, *Of the Knowledge which Maketh a Wise Man,* 9.

22. Thomas F. Mayer, *Thomas Starkey and the Commonweal: Humanist Politics and Religion in the Reign of Henry VIII* (Cambridge: Cambridge University Press, 1989). Chapter 3 deals particularly with Starkey's *Dialogue between Reginald Pole and Thomas Lupset* and with what Mayer sees as Starkey's conciliar leanings.

23. Diogenes Laertius, *Zeno of Elea,* in *Lives of Eminent Philosophers,* vol. 2, ix.25ff.

24. For Elyot's friendship with Thomas Cromwell, see *The Letters of Sir Thomas Elyot,* ed. K. J. Wilson (Chapel Hill: University of North Carolina Press, 1976), 15. For Pole's account of Cromwell's favorable view of Machiavelli, see Martin Haile, *A Life of Reginald Pole,* 56–57.

25. Marcus Tullius Cicero, *Letters to Atticus,* trans. E. O. Winstedt, Loeb Classical Library, 3 vols. (London: Heinemann, 1912), 2:1.

The Bard, the Bible, and the Desert Island

PAUL FRANSSEN

Over the past two centuries, there has hardly been an author, certainly in the English-speaking world, who has commanded greater reverence than Shakespeare. Cultural prestige can hardly be divorced from politics: it is well known that Shakespeare often has been invoked as the figurehead of British cultural and political hegemony. Usually, however, such appropriations are linked to the plays, particularly to *The Tempest*.[1] Another form of appropriation that has received scant attention is that of his life: not so much in serious scholarly biographies, although these, too, may have their share, but in stories, novels, and plays freely embroidering on the known biographical data.[2] Such fictions, too, often invoke the Bard in the name of a wide variety of causes, political or otherwise. For instance, various authors have presented him as an exponent of emerging British colonialism.[3]

There is only one text in the English language that carries comparable prestige to the works of Shakespeare: the Bible, in particular in its most renowned version, the King James Bible, otherwise known as the Authorized Version, of 1611. Indeed, this is often mentioned in one breath with the works of Shakespeare in the context of British or Anglophone cultural hegemony.[4] It is sometimes asserted that the two most translated books in the world are the works of Shakespeare and the Bible,[5] and in the renowned BBC radio program *Desert Island Discs,* these are presented as absolutely indispensable equipment for someone who is to spend a year on a desert island.[6] The American critic Louis Marder gives them pride of place in a hypothetical interstellar cultural exchange:

> On this planet the reputation of Shakespeare is secure. When life is discovered elsewhere in the universe and some interplanetary traveler brings to this new world the fruits of our terrestrial culture, who can imagine anything but that among the first books carried to the curious strangers will be a Bible and the works of William Shakespeare.[7]

This passage has been discussed by Michael Dobson as a latter-day example of "hailing the Bard . . . as the legitimizing spirit of

106

Anglophone empire-building" (230). The American program of space exploration is seen as a logical sequel to British colonial expansion, which, as Dobson points out, had been underpinned by Bardic authority from the eighteenth century on.

In view of the persistent juxtaposition of these two Anglophone cultural icons, the King James Bible and the works of Shakespeare, it is hardly surprising that they also feature together in a number of fictions of Shakespeare's life, in the form of the fantasy of the Bard as a co-translator of the Authorized Version. The originator of this motif seems to have been Rudyard Kipling. In his story "Proofs of Holy Writ," Kipling imagines Shakespeare in the process of revising parts of the Authorized Version with the help of Ben Jonson.[8] In view of the political implications of both Shakespeare's works and the King James Bible, it is tempting to read Kipling's juxtaposition of these central texts in the light of his well-known role as the age's chief literary spokesman for British imperialism. Although Kipling's story makes no overt references to British colonial aspirations, the hegemonistic implications of Shakespeare's translation work become clearer if this story is read in conjunction with Kipling's poem, "The Coiner."[9]

Kipling's subtle appropriation of Shakespeare did not go unchallenged. Anthony Burgess's story "Will and Testament," which consciously echoes Kipling's motif of the Bard as Bible translator, reads like a deconstruction of Kipling's views on a range of issues, such as the nature of poetic inspiration and the function of art within society.[10] Moreover, read in the context of Burgess's other works on Shakespeare, "Will and Testament" becomes a focal point for Burgess's views on the political dimensions of cultural products, in particular in a (post)colonial perspective, which are totally different from Kipling's. Burgess's comic novel *Enderby's Dark Lady,* in which "Will and Testament" was incorporated, deals with the possibility of alternative, even subversive readings of Shakespeare. Finally, his fictional Shakespeare-biography *Nothing Like the Sun* reveals Burgess's underlying philosophy on the need to confront the (cultural, racial) Other, in life as in art.[11]

In Kipling's "Proofs of Holy Writ," we see Shakespeare collaborating with Ben Jonson on the revision of some chapters of Isaiah. The work has been entrusted to Shakespeare, much to Jonson's chagrin, by Miles Smith, one of the translators appointed by the king. As we watch the two men struggling with the text until they finally produce the definitive wording that we know from the Authorized Version, we become aware of the differences between them. Jonson is truculent and full of self-conceit. He cannot help lecturing Shakespeare about the need for didacticism, the unities, and the use of original plots. He rails at colleagues as well as the common mob that does not understand him. It is clear that he regards himself as a highbrow author, unlike Shakespeare; predictably, he is somewhat crestfallen when the latter shows him the Bible translations that have been entrusted to him.

Shakespeare, by contrast, is all sweetness and tolerance. He shows remarkable patience in the face of Jonson's tactlessness, and generously offers him a chance to collaborate on the Bible text. When Jonson asks why it is that he, Shakespeare, is the only colleague he can get along with, Shakespeare replies that it takes two to fight, and he always believes in keeping up his dignity in front of the groundlings. After all, they have an important mission, the "betterment of this present age—and the next, maybe," in the face of which personal antagonism must give way. When they set about their work, wondering who but God will ever know they did it, Jonson contributes the Latin learning, Shakespeare the poetic inspiration. By cooperating they together produce the definitive wording of two passages from Isaiah, chapter 60.[12]

There can be little doubt that Kipling fashioned Shakespeare in accordance with his own self-image. David H. Stewart has argued that this Shakespeare resembles his maker in his preference for shortness of expression and for oral composition. Kipling also projects his own belief in his "Daemon," a divine afflatus that gives him poetic inspiration, on Shakespeare.[13] And this is only the tip of the iceberg. It is quite clear that Miles Smith has intuitively made the correct choice in commissioning Shakespeare with the task of improving the English text of Isaiah; and from Jonson's complaints it becomes clear that Shakespeare is the more popular author. This, too, fits well into Kipling's conception of his own status as a writer: like Shakespeare, or rather, like *his* Shakespeare, Kipling was a middle-brow author, who felt excluded from the intelligentsia, but had a fairly broad popularity among the ordinary readership.[14] Like his Shakespeare, he saw his task as a civilizing one, believing that solidarity among the elite (the sahibs) was necessary to carry out that task. Nor did he expect any thanks for his troubles from any living person; the completion of the task had to be its own reward. Only, with Kipling that task was associated mainly with British imperial aspirations, most famously laid down in "The White Man's Burden," which also speaks of the thankless task of civilizing the masses, be it that these masses are those of foreign races (*Works*, 323–24).

If Kipling's conception of Shakespeare's role as an early colonial propagandist emerges only obliquely in this story, in as yet unfocused notions of the "betterment of this present age—and the next, maybe," there are clearer signs elsewhere in Kipling's works that he associated Shakespeare with British imperialism. His main contribution to Shakespeare studies consists of an article on that most colonial of the Bard's plays, *The Tempest,* which fascinated him.[15] During a visit to Bermuda in 1894, Kipling had noticed that the topographical details of the island actually matched Shakespeare's description of Prospero's island. In an article entitled "Shakespeare and *The Tempest,*" he laid down his observations.[16] Kipling suggests that Shakespeare must have had excellent knowledge of and a lively interest in the burgeoning colonial expansion, perhaps derived from some sailor's story overheard in a tavern (Carrington, 265).

Kipling recast his theory of Shakespeare's second-hand knowledge of Bermuda in imaginative form in his poem "The Coiner." The speaker is a former sailor who has returned to England, together with a few comrades, after being shipwrecked near the Bermudas. They make a living by telling the story of their maritime adventures to whoever wants to listen and pay for it. To add interest, they embellish their tale with fantastic lies of a "Magical Island," of "Mermaids and Devils and Sprites, / And Voices that howl in the cedars o'nights" (ll. 9–10). The speaker remembers one evening in particular when they made a lot of money out of some "poor players" in Southwark. Ironically, the sailor thinks he got the better of the one (unnamed) player who paid their meal, because they started to tell him outright lies: ". . . seeing him greedy for marvels, at last / From plain salted truth to flat leasing we passed" (ll. 23–24). The player, however, was quite satisfied and rewarded his informants generously, and gave them a word of advice:

> . . . "Never match coins with a Coiner by trade,
> Or he'll turn your lead pieces to metal as rare
> As shall fill him this globe, and leave something to spare."
> (ll. 26–28)

The sailor's limited vision does not allow him to grasp the full meaning of these words, so he and his comrades just drink to the health of that "Coiner."

Unlike the sailor, the reader is expected to understand the hints and puns ("globe") hidden in his account: the unknown naive benefactor was no less than the Bard himself, who has here received, in the sailors' mixture of lies and facts, the kernel of the plot of *The Tempest*. In this oblique portrayal of Shakespeare, we again recognize the generosity and tolerance of the Bible translator: although, in the sailors' estimation, he belongs to a company of "*poor players*," he is willing to pay them "a crown or five shillings" each for their pack of lies, in addition to the price of their meal. Again, he is like Kipling, in that his art transmutes the "lead" of the low-life experience of adventurers and sailors into gold; moreover, he is fascinated by tales of the unknown, the stuff that the dreams of empire are to be made on. This, then, is the other side of the coiner who, in Kipling's vision, also translated the Bible.

One wonders if it is really a coincidence that Kipling followed the title "The Coiner" by the date "*Circa* 1611," which is, of course, the year in which the Authorized Version was published. This might be a sign that for Kipling the two activities he attributes to Shakespeare were complementary: both literary enterprises form part of the ideological backdrop to the imperial project. Conversely, in "Proofs of Holy Writ," Kipling seems to allude to his (earlier) poem when he makes Shakespeare speak of his only two plays that, he claims, are not derived from a traditional plot:

> My *Love's Labour* (how I came to write it, I know not) is nearest to lawful issue. My *Tempest* (how I came to write *that,* I know) is, in some part, my own.

Just how Shakespeare came to write *The Tempest,* the Kipling aficionado would have realized, Kipling had reconstructed in "The Coiner."

This allusion seems to indicate that Kipling's two visions of Shakespeare, as a Bible translator and as the muse of empire, are by no means separate but part of a unified conception. Although there is no explicit mention of colonies anywhere in "Proofs of Holy Writ," or of the Bible in "The Coiner," it seems that Kipling's Shakespeare, at the eve of the expansion of the British empire, is shouldering the White Man's Burden, by equipping the future empire builders with the two texts they will need to take with them to desert islands (or not-so-deserted islands—a Caliban or two to be civilized would do no harm).

Anthony Burgess undoubtedly was familiar with Kipling's story when he wrote his own "Will and Testament."[17] In fact, Burgess stands Kipling's preconceptions on their heads so consistently that his story can be read as a deconstruction of Kipling's. Burgess's

Shakespeare is not a patient empire builder or visionary, but rather an unhappy man caught in an unenviable position, at the midlife crisis age of forty-six. Instead of the work being entrusted to him directly by the proper authorities, here it is Jonson who generously passes some of the psalms on to his friend. Burgess's point may well be that literary quality is not always recognized during one's lifetime, although he also provides motivation for this change in the plot: due to an ill-advised display of his wit in the presence of the king, Shakespeare currently is out of favor.

The direct occasion for Shakespeare's revision of the psalm in question, Psalm 46, undermines Kipling's premise that great art arises from self-negation. For Burgess's Shakespeare, the revision of the psalm is the ultimate act of self-assertion. When he comes home to his bigoted puritanical family in Stratford, with the galley proofs entrusted to him by Jonson in his saddle bags, he finds that they have found out about the Sonnets, published a year before, and this has brought their dislike of his sinful profession to the boiling point. Stung by their narrow-mindedness and religious fervor, he seizes on the psalms to assert the dignity of his profession. Unlike his family, he claims, those in authority do know the importance of a poet's profession, as may be shown by the fact that he has been entrusted with the task of correcting and improving the proofs of the psalms for a new Bible translation authorized by the king himself. This is only a half-truth, of course, as Jonson's mediating role is totally ignored; but it serves its purpose, of annoying if not altogether convincing his relatives.

Shakespeare's injured sense of his own worth is not yet allayed, so he goes on to revise the text right before his wife and family, to demonstrate his power over words and his ability to leave the stamp of his personality on the psalms. Particularly ingenious in Burgess's story is the way Shakespeare even hides his name in the text of the psalm. As he is forty-six years of age, he chooses Psalm 46; he counts to the forty-sixth word, replaces it by "shake"; then he starts at the end, counts forty-six words backwards (leaving out of account the cadential *"selah"*), and changes that word into "speare." The surprising thing is, that the evidence shoring up this highly unlikely scenario is in itself authentic: in Psalm 46 AV, the forty-sixth word really is "shake," the forty-sixth word from the end (not counting *"selah"*) being "spear."[18]

Although Burgess's Shakespeare revises the psalm for wholly selfish ends, out of defiance and sinful pride, he does not thereby lose our sympathy. Unlike Kipling's self-confident sahib, he is not a superman that can lead nations; rather, in his everyday struggle

with political realities, an unhappy marriage, and uncomprehend-
ing neighbors, he is a modern antihero whom we cannot begrudge
his one moment of triumph. The difference between Burgess's
Shakespeare and Kipling's is quite telling for the changing concep-
tions of the role of the artist after the world wars. Gradually, the
confidence that great art is the result of the willpower of a superior
intellectual being was lost. Kipling, writing this story in 1934, was
already a sort of Victorian/Edwardian fossil. For Burgess, art is
the result of suffering between the hammer of what is and the anvil
of what should be. He projects that vision on the supreme artist,
Shakespeare, whose drive for self-realization, impeded by his surroundings, finds an outlet in this act of creativity.

"Will and Testament" in itself does not contain any references
to Shakespeare's supposed role as a prophet of empire. Yet *Enderby's Dark Lady,* the novel in which "Will and Testament" was
incorporated as the opening story, does deal with the Bard from a
postcolonial perspective. The supposed author of this story, Burgess's alter ego Enderby, has been invited to Indiana to write the
script of an American musical based on Shakespeare's life. Enderby tries hard to preserve as much authenticity as possible, in the
face of philistinism, commercial pressures, and the egos of the star
actors. He is, however, sorely tempted to compromise by the
charms of April Elgar, the black American actress who is to play
the lead role of the Dark Lady. She entreats Enderby to increase
her part in Shakespeare's life story, unwittingly forcing him to
choose between loyalty to the Bard and his love for her.

Although April's attempts to hijack the Shakespeare show and
turn it into an advertisement for her talents are no less selfish
than, say, the monetary motives of the director, her influence on
Enderby's writing also has its emancipatory aspects. He turns her
voice into that of black America. As the Dark Lady, April sings:

> The white man's knavery
> Sold me in slavery
> To an unsavoury
> Household.

She concludes her lament with a desire to get her own back:

> I slaved like the slave I was,
> Ripe for the grave I was,
> But I was brave, I was
> Ready
> For my master's remorse and my

> Freedom of course and my
> Monetary source
> Safe and steady.
> Now see me here in London,
> Ready for revenge.
>
> *(Enderby's Dark Lady,* 82)

The situation of this Dark Lady obviously is a projection of April's
own ambiguous feelings as a black star in a white society: if Enderby's verse, inspired by her, is unauthentic in relation to Shakespeare's Dark Lady, it does speak some truth about April. In an
idea for a scene that keeps playing through Enderby's head, the
Dark Lady lectures the Queen on questions of power and race:

> Madam, queen you may be, but it is of a blanched and bleached king-
> dom unblessed by the sun, a nearly quondam queendom, leprous, de-
> cayed, weakly tyrannical. Know you not where the future lies? Look
> westward, sister / from this derelict / island, a blister / soon to be
> pricked. I speak for the future, madam, Cleopatran New Rome, I speak
> of black power, / that's what we'll get; / although I lack power, / I'll get
> it yet.
>
> (101)

Like Kipling, Burgess is aware of the political dimensions of cultural forces, whether it be the Bible or the (other) works of Shakespeare. For him, however, Shakespeare can be a liberating, even
revolutionary force as well as a reactionary, hegemonistic one. As
Shakespeare can turn the Bible against his bigoted and reactionary
relatives by stamping it with his own name, so the American Dark
Lady can hijack Shakespeare's works and even his life and give
them an emancipatory twist. This undermines Kipling's notion that
Shakespeare's works, like the Bible, automatically have a civilizing
(that is, Westernizing) effect; instead, for Burgess, all meaning has
to be produced, so that Shakespeare can be appropriated by anti-
colonial, anti-white, and anti-establishment discourses. Whether
we like it or not, a new culture is produced by a cross-fertilization
of the old and the new, not by fruitless attempts to preserve the
old, such as Enderby's.

However, for a full understanding of Burgess's conception of
Shakespeare's role in the postcolonial debate, it is necessary to
investigate his earlier work on the Bard. The frustrated Shakespeare of Enderby's story is a comic variant of the one in Burgess's
novel, *Nothing Like the Sun.* Although this is not a reaction against
Kipling in particular, it does touch on the relations between Shake-

speare and the British empire, on more than one level. The narrative of Shakespeare's life is presented within the framework of a farewell lecture by a British teacher, called Mr. Burgess, to his Oriental students. Moreover, in this lecturer's fantasy, he is himself of Shakespeare's blood, come to the East so that the line that has died out in the West may carry on there (234). This seems to be another typical Burgess pun: the lecturer is called Burgess, like the author, who also taught Shakespeare in the Orient.[19] This suggests that the lecturer is Burgess's alter ego. Burgess's real name, however, was Wilson, or Will's Son, so his name gave him some right to regard himself as a descendant of Shakespeare. Thus, Shakespeare, his works as well as his blood, is transplanted to the empire, to blossom there.[20]

Lest this, too, seem like a one-sided exercise in cultural imperialism, it should be pointed out that, within Burgess's fantasy, the empire is only getting back from Britain what it had given in the first place. In the lecturer's imaginative account of Shakespeare's life, the Dark Lady is identified as a Malay woman, with whom Shakespeare has a passionate love affair. She bestows an ambiguous gift on him: she infects him with syphilis. This ostensible curse is a blessing in disguise as it enhances his genius.[21] In particular, it opens his eyes to the reality of evil in this world, an insight that enables him to write the great tragedies. Thus, in Burgess's vision, Shakespeare's genius is the result of his interaction, in the most intimate way imaginable, with the Other. In his syphilitic delirium, he equates sexual intercourse with his Dark Lady with the descent of the muse (229).

Needless to say, both the miscegenation and the cultural cross-fertilization resulting from it would have offended Kipling; yet these seem to lie at the heart of Burgess's conception of Western culture in this novel and elsewhere. In his article on Burgess's *MF*, Geoffrey Aggeler has argued that incest is an important motif in Burgess's fiction.[22] In particular, it symbolizes Western culture's inwardness, its refusal to meet the Other. Aggeler's paradigm is helpful in analyzing *Nothing Like the Sun*, in which Shakespeare oscillates between incestuous and homosexual tendencies, on the one hand, and his basically healthy desire for the unknown, expressed in his lust for black beauties, on the other. Part of the reason for the failure of his relationship with his fair-haired wife Anne is her "Arden pallor" and "carrotiness" (29), which remind him of his domineering fair-haired mother Mary Arden (23). This nearly incestuous marriage only reinforces his desire to confront the Other, embodied in the Dark Lady. His interaction with her, sinful as it may be, is a measure of his greatness and his success as an artist. By contrast, Enderby's comic inability to make love to *his* Dark Lady (he masturbates thinking of her but fails to rise to the occasion when she offers herself to him, 120), symbolizes his failure to achieve the full confrontation with the Other that is a prerequisite for truly great art.

In the stories by Kipling and Burgess, read within their contexts, the *topos* of Shakespeare translating the Bible becomes the site of an ideological struggle over such issues as the nature of literary inspiration, the construction of the meaning of a literary text, and the political dimensions of cultural products, in particular in a (post)colonial context. By appropriating a wholly imaginary episode in Shakespeare's life, the two authors attempt to throw Shakespeare's cultural weight behind their radically different political points of view.

In addition, Burgess's story enacts its theme of the subversive potential of any text, sacred or nonsacred, by simultaneously deconstructing and subverting Kipling's story. Ultimately, Burgess's emphasis on the multiplicity of meanings latent in the text of Shakespeare's life foregrounds his own appropriation of Shakespeare: for, if his fictional Shakespeare could take a sacred text and turn it to his own advantage, even stamping it with his signature (Shakespeare), Burgess has hardly done less by Shakespeare, in *Nothing Like the Sun:* he has forced the life of his predecessor into a pattern of his own devising, and left his signature on it to lay claim to it (Wilson–Will's Son). Clearly, this is not an inconsistency on Burgess's part but a deliberate pointer at the inevitability of appropriating any given text, particularly that most irresistible one of Shakespeare's life.

NOTES TO "THE BARD, THE BIBLE, AND THE DESERT ISLAND"

1. Terence Hawkes, *That Shakespeherian Rag: Essays on a Critical Process* (London and New York: Methuen, 1986), chap. 3 passim, in particular pp. 67–68.

2. Compare Samuel Schoenbaum, *Shakespeare's Lives* (Oxford: Oxford University Press, 1970), passim.

3. E.g. Clemence Dane [pseudonym Winifred Ashton], *Will Shakespeare: An Invention in Four Acts* (New York: Macmillan, 1922); and, from an Irish nationalist perspective, Norreys Connell [alias Conal O'Riordan], *Shakespeare's End,* in *Shakespeare's End and Other Irish Plays* (Adelphi: Stephen Swift, 1912). An American equivalent is Denton J. Snider, *Shakespeariad: A Dramatic Epos* (St. Louis: Sigma Publishing, 1916).

4. John Drakakis, "Theatre, Ideology, and Institution: Shakespeare and the Roadsweepers," in *The Shakespeare Myth,* ed. Graham Holderness (Manchester: Manchester University Press, 1988), 24–41. Stephen Greenblatt, while also bringing the two texts together in the context of colonial expansion, seems more willing to differentiate between them. See his *Shakespearean Negotiations: The Circulation of Social Energy in Renaissance England* (Oxford: Clarendon Press, 1988), 161–63.

5. William Haggard notes that "within the brief space of twelve years, 1611–23, first appeared the two outstanding books which have most moved mankind. They have been converted into more languages and dialects than any other book" ("Preamble" to E. Hamilton Gruner, *With Golden Quill: A Cavalcade, Depicting Shakespeare's Life and Times* [Stratford: Shakespeare Press, 1936], p. ix). The suggestion seems to be that the Authorized Version rather than its Hebrew and Greek originals was the great work of art that served as the basis for all these translations!

6. Malcolm Evans, *Signifying Nothing: Truth's True Contents in Shakespeare's Text* (New York: Harvester Wheatsheaf, 1986), 86.

7. Louis Marder, *His Exits and his Entrances: The Story of Shakespeare's Reputation* (Philadelphia: J. B. Lippincott, 1963), 362; quoted by Michael Dobson, *The Making of the National Poet: Shakespeare, Adaptation and Authorship, 1660–1769* (Oxford: Clarendon Press, 1992), 230.

8. Rudyard Kipling, "Proofs of Holy Writ" (1934), in *The Collected Works of Rudyard Kipling,* XXIII, *Uncollected Prose* (New York: Garden City, 1941; repr. New York: AMS Press, 1970), 663–78.

9. *The Works of Rudyard Kipling* (Ware: Wordsworth Editions, 1994), 778–79.

10. "Will and Testament" was read as a plenary lecture at a conference on Shakespeare in 1976; see *Shakespeare: Pattern of Excelling Nature,* ed. David Bevington and Jay L. Halio (Newark: University of Delaware Press, 1978), 46–65. Later it was published as part of a novel, supposed to be one of the two stories on Shakespeare written by the titular hero, the poet Enderby. See Anthony Burgess, *Enderby's Dark Lady: Or No End to Enderby* (New York: McGraw-Hill, 1984), 9–34.

11. Anthony Burgess, *Nothing Like the Sun: A Story of Shakespeare's Love-Life* (1964; repr. London: Vintage, 1988).

12. David H. Stewart, "Kipling's Portrait of the Artist," in *English Literature in Transition* 31 (1988): 265–83, has pointed out that there are, in fact, some "minor (and audacious) alterations. [Shakespeare] prefers monosyllabic 'on' for 'upon' and 'cloke' for 'cover'" (274). Surprisingly, Stewart then goes on to hold this against Kipling's Shakespeare as a sign of his "presum[ption] to know more about composition than the scholars who created the King James Version" (276). In terms of the story, however, this is a reversal of the chronology; the arrogance lies with the scholars, who tamper with Shakespeare's poetic text, thereby diluting the conciseness that, as Stewart himself points out, was Kipling's own preference (274).

13. See John Bayley, "Introduction" to *Mrs Bathurst and Other Stories,* ed. Lisa Lewis (Oxford: Oxford University Press, 1991), xii; and 305n.

14. David H. Stewart asserts that "The intelligentsia repudiated him [Kipling] after 1900" (op. cit., 277). Oscar Wilde said about Kipling that he was "our best authority on the second-rate." Quoted in Charles Carrington, *Rudyard Kipling: His Life and Work* (1955; repr. Harmondsworth: Penguin, 1986), 401–2.

15. See Angus Wilson, *The Strange Ride of Rudyard Kipling: His Life and Works* (New York: Viking, 1977), 168; and Carrington, 265.

16. "Shakespeare and *The Tempest*," originally a letter to the *Spectator* of 1898. It was reprinted in *The Collected Works of Rudyard Kipling*, XXIII, *Uncollected Prose*, 401–5.

17. For Burgess's familiarity with Kipling's story, see his Shakespeare biography, *Shakespeare* (New York: Knopf, 1970), 233–34. Maurice J. O'Sullivan suggests a connection between the two stories, but does not elaborate. See his "Shakespeare's Other Lives," *Shakespeare Quarterly* 38 (1987): 150n.

18. For a full discussion of the merits of this theory, see my "Half a Miracle: A Response to William Harmon," *Connotations* 3:2 (1993–94): 118–22.

19. See his "Genesis and Headache," in *Afterwords: Novelists on their Novels*, ed. Thomas McCormack (New York: Harper & Row, 1969), 34.

20. On this pun in general, though not specifically in this passage, see Samuel Coale, *Anthony Burgess* (New York: Ungar, 1981), 161. Burgess himself complains that the first reviewers overlooked his "personal monograms sewn into the fabric of the work." See "Genesis and Headache," 43.

21. In "Genesis and Headache," Burgess states: "Since long before reading Thomas Mann's novel *Doctor Faustus,* I had been pondering on the relationship between genius and disease" (30).

22. "Incest and the Artist: *MF*," in *Critical Essays on Anthony Burgess*, ed. Geoffrey Aggeler (Boston: Hall, 1986), 172–85.

Horace the Second, or, Ben Jonson, Thomas Dekker, and the Battle for Augustan Rome

MATTHEW STEGGLE

During the last years of the sixteenth century and the early years of the seventeenth, the London theater scene witnessed an extended fight over acting styles and dramatic writing, a fight now generally known as the War of the Theaters. In the plays that were written as part of this conflict, we find a polemical use of the author-as-character motif. Ben Jonson's *Poetaster* (1601) and Thomas Dekker's *Satiromastix* (1601) present two rival interpretations of Horace, as part of a wider argument about the relationship between classical literature and contemporary professional drama. In his *Poetaster,* Jonson opted for an imperial Roman setting, offering a literary standard in the shape of Virgil and Horace, as well as representations of the detractors of his own time. In the "Apologetical Dialogue" at the end of the play—suppressed "by authority" after one performance but included in the 1616 Folio edition of Jonson's works to date—"The author" says the setting is:

> Augustus Caesar's times,
> When wit and arts were at their height in Rome,
> To show that Virgil, Horace, and the rest
> Of those great master spirits did not want
> Detractors then, or practisers against them.[1]

Dekker approached the battle from a different angle. In his *Satiromastix* he featured a dehistoricized, defamiliarized Horace at a Norman court, his words a patchwork of Jonsonian echoes. At the end of the play, Dekker's "Horace" is exposed as a fraud, a nasty ex-bricklayer and itinerant actor trying to "usurp" the role of distinguished Roman poet and critic. Particularly in the reference to the bricklaying profession, one recognizes a jibe at the expense of Ben Jonson himself, an attack that is part of a larger network of criticism of Jonson in the play. In *Poetaster* and *Satiromastix*, the War of the Theaters really takes on the appearance of a battle for

118

Horace and his Rome. And, surprisingly, it is Horace—not one of the classical comedians such as Plautus, Terence, Menander, or Aristophanes—who is the object of contention in this argument over classical precedents and professional English drama. To appreciate this construction, a first requirement is to examine the profile of Horace during the early modern period. Horace was central to the debate over drama, for four reasons: his personal associations; his role as a translator; the assumed moral value of his writings; and the association of Horace, via the *Ars poetica,* with the genre of drama.

Up until now, critical attention to the Renaissance reception of Horace in general, and Ben Jonson's use of him in particular, has tended to focus on Horace as a personal model. In this context, Joanna Martindale has discussed the importance of Horace's personal integrity and his easy relationship with Augustus, while Robert B. Pierce examines Jonson's efforts to reproduce the versatility and discrimination of the Horatian voice.[2] Jonson's use of Horace must also, I suggest, be seen in the context of the Augustan's wider literary affinities; nonetheless, it remains important that Horace was seen as a personal model.[3]

Second, there is Horace's reputation as a translator. Roger Ascham, arguably the most famous tutor to Queen Elizabeth the First, is one of the authors to bestow praise on Horace for his skills in this field. As Ascham puts it in *The Scholemaster* (1570):

> Euen as *Virgill* and *Horace* deserue most worthie prayse, that they, spying the vnperfitnes in *Ennius* and *Plautus,* by trew Imitation of *Homer* and *Euripides* brought Poetrie to the same perfitnes in *Latin* as it was in *Greke,* euen so those that by the same way would benefite their tong and contrey deserue rather thankes than disprayse in that behalfe.[4]

According to Ascham, then, Horace did for the drama what Virgil did for the epic: make respectable a certain vernacular tradition (Plautus) by adopting a classical model (Euripides). This also explains why Horace is so attractive a model for practitioners of *imitatio* in general, and for Jonson in particular.[5]

Third, Horace offers a classical example of a didactic or morally improving writer. In this respect Sir Philip Sidney, like Ascham, pairs him with Virgil. As he puts it in his *Defence of Poetry* (1583):

> who is it that euer was a scholler that doth not carry away some verses of *Virgill, Horace,* or *Cato,* which in his youth he learned, and euen to his old age serue him for howrely [= hourly] lessons?[6]

Later, Jonson himself, in his *Discoveries,* was to praise Horace as "the best master, both of vertue and wisdome."[7]

Finally, there is Horace's *Ars poetica.* Ascham alluded to it as an excellent yardstick for modern drama, and Thomas Lodge quoted from it at length in his *Defence of Poetry* (Smith, 1: 74). George Webbe went so far as to summarize parts of it toward the conclusion of his *Discourse of English Poetrie* (1586).[8] The importance of Horace's *Ars poetica*—as read and interpreted during the Renaissance—is its emphasis on the morally improving nature of drama, including comedy, combining "utile" and "dulce," the useful and the delightful. A measure of its popularity are the two contemporary translations into English. The first was by Thomas Drant, and Jonson provided his own translation in 1604, in the wake of the War of the Theaters.[9]

English Renaissance Horace, then, straddles the fields of politics, poetic translation, virtuous satire, and virtuous comedy (via the *Ars poetica*). Moreover, he is presented as a way of accessing the world of Augustan Rome where "wit and arts were at their height." His connections with Augustus and Virgil in particular are crucial. He gains stature and importance from his context, and Jonson's *Poetaster* is eager to present Horace as part of the larger Augustan picture.

POETASTER

As early as *Every Man Out of his Humour* (1599), Ben Jonson's "Comical Satire" had been claiming moral utility, innovation on the basis of classical precedent, and a familiar—indeed, over-familiar—relationship with the great.[10] Horace was Jonson's natural role model. But the question that arises with regard to *Poetaster* is to what extent Jonson's Horace is a character in his own right, rather than a mere incarnation of this myth. Is Horace here, as Dekker suggested, just one of Jonson's "suites of names" for himself (*Satiromastix,* 1.2.310)? These questions are to be asked not merely about Horace, but about Jonson's entire version of Augustan Rome, because Jonson's treatment of Horace is programmatic of his treatment of the entire classical heritage.[11] Jonson is laying claim not just to Horace but to all of classical literature.

The first stage of this argument is to show that the imagery in *Poetaster* attempts to present the play as a classical text. This process begins as early as the Induction by Envy, where the play goes into terrible contortions in its effort to appear classically aloof rather than topical and engaged. In the Induction, Envy reads the forthcoming play as relative to the "present state" (Induction, l. 34), and is condemned for doing so: but this reading is, as we have seen, precisely what the character named Author says he wants in the "Apologetical Dialogue." Furthermore, it is an awkward paradox that Envy should find her allies in "players" and "poet-apes," against a play itself performed by players (Induction, l. 35). As for "poet-apes," the deliberate echo of this word apparently coined by Sidney in his *Defence of Poetry* (*OED, sv* "poet-ape"), suggests that the *Defence of Poetry* may well be one of the most important poetics texts underlying *Poetaster*'s critical assumptions.

On the one hand, therefore, there is the world of performance containing Envy's allies; on the other hand, there is this play, figured as a text, threatened in every "word or accent" by the "glosses" of Envy (Induction, ll. 48 and 40). "Glosses" and "accent" both apply in their technical senses of the *apparatus criticus* of a classical text. In its eagerness to avoid the genre of mere performance, *Poetaster* is disguising itself as a classical edition. It even goes so far as to introduce marginal glosses of its own sources, and in this the printed edition reflects the patterns of imagery in the text. Furthermore, like much of the content of Envy's Induction, imagery specifically of classical textual exegesis turns up in the play itself: Lupus is a "ridiculous commenter" on the text of Horace's emblem (5.3.74).

Thus, in Envy's Induction, Jonson is simultaneously creating two distinct sets of imagery to describe comedy: a cluster of literary, classicizing imagery for his own work, and a second for his rivals which serves to demonize them according to the standards of Elizabethan dramatic criticism. Horace is part of a wider framework of textual strategies even before he makes his appearance in the play.

Horace is even absent from the first two acts, which deal mainly with the other poets of the time: Ovid, Gallus, Propertius, and Tibullus. Jonson's version of the poetic community of Augustan Rome takes its cues largely from Suetonius, and the works of the poets involved. Jonson does, however, telescope dates to allow Tibullus (who died in 19 B.C.) to be alive at the time of the banishment of Ovid (8 A.D.), and he removes the internal divisions within the literary circles of classical Rome to present the Augustan poetic world as a single unified community with an internal hierarchy and (as is shown in act 5) a quasi-judicial authority. The authors Gallus, Propertius, and Tibullus provide the background to Horace, Ovid, and Virgil. The light in which Horace is shown does much to make sense of the presentation of Ovid and Virgil, so I will consider the three in turn.

Horace's first four scenes (his first five in the Folio version, which inserts as 3.5 a translation of Horace's debate with the lawyer Trebatius) are all dramatized adaptations of Horace's own *Satires.* Thus, in his first scenes Horace simply acts out some of his best-known work, and he appears to make little specific reference to Jonson. In the scene with Trebatius, however, the lapses from direct translation forge thematic links between the play, its Inductions, and its "Apologetical Dialogue." One example is Horace's statement that he offers "sharp yet modest rhymes / That spare men's persons and but tax their crimes" (3.5.133–34). These famous lines, taken from Martial, reemerge in the mouth of the character known as Author in the "Apologetical Dialogue" (l. 72): the Author and Horace are made to utter the same phrase, as if they were doubles. Conversely, Horace's talk of Envy in the scene with Trebatius, where Envy is alleged to have "teeth unsound" (3.5.122), looks back to the evocation of the latter character with "rusty teeth" in the Induction (l. 47).

Trebatius awards Horace the freedom to satirize, a freedom worded more solemnly in Jonson's translation than the original actually warrants. This liberty of personal reference given to Horace justifies, in turn, Jonson's treatment of Crispinus and Demetrius in *Poetaster,* thin disguises for his enemies John Marston and Thomas Dekker. Crispinus and Demetrius bear little resemblance to their shadowy Horatian originals and are most interestingly contemporary in the way they inhabit a demi-monde of seedy professional playhouses specific in its Elizabethan reference and with no Roman prototype.

Poetaster, however, uses the image of the River Tiber as an axis along which this bad drama is divided from a virtuous type of drama associated with Horace and Jonson. As Captain Tucca, the swaggerer, complains to Histrio, the plays nowadays are not bawdy enough for the tastes of himself and his prostitute:

TUCCA: . . . they say you ha' nothing but humours, revels and satires that gird and fart at the time, you slave.
HISTRIO: No, I assure you, captain, not we. They are on the other side of Tiber. We have as much ribaldry in our plays as can be, as you would wish, captain. All the sinners, i' the suburbs come and applaud our action daily.

TUCCA: I hear you'll bring me o' the stage there: you'll play me, they
          say. I shall be presented by a sort of copper-laced scoundrels
          of you. Life of Pluto! And you stage me, stinkard, your man-
          sions shall sweat for't, your tabernacles, varlets, your
          Globes, and your Triumphs!
HISTRIO: Not we by Phoebus, Captain.

                                                      (3.4.194–204)

Histrio's side of the Tiber represents the South Bank of London,
as is clear from the naming of the Globe here, and the fact that it
is the base of Dekker and Marston. Jonson demonizes this theater
according to the standards of the Elizabethan critics, claiming that
it offers bawdiness on stage, and bawds in the audience: "a horse
fair for hores," in Stephen Gosson's phrase.[12] Meanwhile, the other,
North-Bank drama (corresponding to the Blackfriars private play-
house where *Poetaster* is being acted) is given a moral, reprehen-
sive function. As Tucca complained earlier: "An honest decayed
commander cannot skelder, cheat, nor be seen in a bawdy house,
but he shall be straight in one of their wormwood comedies"
(1.2.49–52). Tucca is unconsciously echoing Horace's *Satires*
(I:4.1–5), in which Greek Old Comedy (also praised by the Author
in the "Apologetical Dialogue," ll. 173–74) is admired for exposing
individuals' immorality. The drama Tucca dislikes has classical
warrant, the drama he likes does not. Thus, all the undesirable
characteristics of drama are being concentrated south of the Tiber,
whereas "good" drama is situated to the north. The representation
of living people on stage, however, is made part of "good" drama,
which incidentally defends *Poetaster*'s practice of doing just that.
    Tucca's reference to "humours, revels and satires" (3.4.194) half-
way alludes to the titles of Jonson's recent "comicall satires,"
Every Man Out of his Humour (1599) and *Cynthia's Revels* (1600).
Cross-reference blends this reference with Horace's own reputation, since Lupus and Tucca later taunt Horace:

LUPUS: I'll tickle you, satyr.
TUCCA: [to HORACE] He will, Humours, he will. He will squeeze you,
          poet puck-fist.

                                                      (5.3.31–34)

Later in the scene, Demetrius criticizes Horace for his translations
and his "*satirical humours*" (5.3.299). These insults promiscuously
mix several different traits. Some are applicable to Horace and
emphatically not to Jonson, such as the detail of Horace's small
"puck-fist" stature, derived from the Suetonian *Life*. Some are ap-

plicable to both: both Horace and Jonson were satirists and translators. But, in attributing to Horace a characteristic of writing
"humours," Jonson clearly is being autobiographical more than
biographical. One might say this is a Jonson-inflected version of a
Suetonian/Horatian Horace, constructed with reference to a debate about the poetics of drama.

Horace is further defined by his relations with Ovid, writing his
Medea for the "common players" and expelled forcefully from the
idealized poetic Rome of the play. Why is this necessary? Critics
have tried to pin the blame on the 1590s fashion for pseudo-Ovidian
erotic poetry and the epyllion, or they have examined the connection between Ovid and Marlowe. But *Poetaster* is a play about
theater; perhaps the answer is to be found, instead, in Ovid's connection with the theater.[13] After all, "a horse fair for hores" is
specifically Gosson's comment on the immorality of the theatrical
venue as presented in Ovid's version of the Rape of the Sabine
Women.

Sidney and Lodge, and others writing against Gosson's attacks,
were embarrassed by Ovid. Sidney, in the entire *Defence,* mentions
him only once, and then very briefly. Even the pugnacious Lodge
abandons Ovid: "Shall on[e] man's follye destroye a vniuersall
commodity?" he pleads (1:75). Ovid, whose poetry itself is treated
with respect in *Poetaster* (1.1), is disgraced for his role in a lewd
and blasphemous banquet, organized with the assistance of players, an event belonging to the realm of performance, not text, and
it is this that excludes him from taking his place alongside Horace
and Virgil in Jonson's idealized poetic community.

In complete contrast to Ovid's frivolity and theatricality, there
is Virgil. He does not appear until act 5, and from then on he
dominates the action, with more weighty speeches than any other
character in that act. Although the focus would seem to be on
Virgil, part of the purpose of introducing this stage character is to
define Horace, too, as the juxtaposition of these two great writers
recalls the Horace/Virgil relationship that one finds in Elizabethan
poetics. Horace represents a way to get at Virgil, whose work
Jonson represents as the acme of textuality. His "sacred lines"
(5.3.161) on their own command utter respect; they are complete
of themselves and will last forever. Caesar himself falls silent when
Virgil recites, and guarantees Virgil's work the "hallowed circum-
stance" for its reception (5.3.163). In the final act of Jonson's *Poetaster,* Virgil reads a passage chosen at random by opening his book:
the thematic relevance of the "chosen" passage on Rumour has
rather overshadowed appreciation of the fact that this is a wry

anticipation of the post-classical custom of Virgil's Lots, or the *sortes virgilianae.* Jonson's Virgil, like his Horace and his Ovid, is to be read relative to Renaissance biographical criticism. At the end of the play, Horace and Virgil are explicitly presented as symbolic guardians of the classical heritage. They prescribe, in medical fashion, a selective diet of literature to the luckless Crispinus: Cato and Terence are approved of, but "Shun Plautus and old Ennius: they are meats / Too harsh for a weak stomach" (5.3.530–31). Again, this reproduces the views of the Elizabethan poetics writers about the literary affinities of Horace and Virgil. Sidney, as we have seen, bracketed Horace, Virgil, and Cato together as providers of "howrely lessons" in virtue. Ascham described Horace and Virgil as reformers of the stylistic barbarities of Ennius and Plautus in particular. For these writers, and for *Poetaster,* moral purity and literary excellence are conveniently indistinguishable.

The issue, therefore, is considerably wider than simply using Horace as a personal model. *Poetaster* lays claim not just to Horace, but to the entire literary heritage of Augustan Rome, which it then seeks to prescribe to others. In its characters, in the physical format of the printed version, and in its use of translation, it seeks to redefinc the category of drama and make itself into a literary artcfact.

SATIROMASTIX, OR THE UNTRUSSING
OF THE HUMOROUS POET

In Thomas Dekker's *Satiromastix,* "Horace" finds himself at the Norman court of William II, suffering the type of moral purgation he himself had been administering in *Poetaster.* "Horace"—or Horace/Jonson—is constructed specifically as an anti-Horace, everything the classical Horace was not. *Satiromastix,* in its printed incarnation, opens with a flurry of Latin: an epigraph on the title page, two more under the dramatis personae, and an address "To the World" armed with no less than six Latin phrases.[14] Of these nine quotations, two are from Martial, three from Horace, and one from Virgil. In his prefatory material, Dekker is, by familiar quotation, claiming these authors for himself, and out-Jonsoning Jonson. By contrast, the play itself eschews—indeed, mocks—such classical reference; it also mocks Jonsonian ideas of textuality.

The preface explicitly distinguishes the classical "true *Venusian Horace*" ("To the World," 54–55) from "Horace the second," author of "*Euery man in's Hvmour,*" and "our new *Horace*" ("To the World," ll. 8, 28, 45). Thus, *Satiromastix* poses a different author-as-character problem, how to subvert a previous use of the author-as-character motif. Especially when Jonson has the name of one of the most prominent and revered poets in the classical world, while the characters representing Marston and Dekker labor under the aliases of poets known only for being famously bad, namely Crispinus and Demetrius.

Dekker's approach is to use the Norman setting to separate "Horace" from his Augustan context, from Virgil and Augustus: from all the things that give him his strength and his importance in the eyes of the poetics writers. He also steadily increases the pressure of circumstantial detail that separates "Horace" from Horace. Taking material Jonson gives him and altering the context until the original meaning becomes ridiculous, Dekker does to the character-names what he will go on to do to Jonson's own words.

Horace's first appearance in the play presents a version of Jonson compiled from details Jonson has already arrogated to himself. He is presented as surrounded by books, working by candlelight (cf. *Poetaster*, "Apologetical Dialogue," ll. 199–200). Also like *Poetaster*'s Horace, he is first seen composing an ode "*sitting in a study behinde a Curtaine, a candle by him burning, bookes lying confusedly.*" He rehearses it in soliloquy:

> To thee whose fore-head swels with Roses,
> Whose most haunted bower,
> Gives life and s[c]ent to euery flower:
> Whose most adored name incloses,
> Things abstruse, deep and diuine,
> Whose yellow tresses shine,
> Bright as *Eoan* fire.
> O me thy Priest inspire.
> For I to thee and thine immortall name,
> In—in—in golden tunes,
> For I to thee and thine immortall name—
> In—sacred raptures flowing, flowing, swimming, swimming:
> In sacred raptures swimming,
> Immortall name, game, dame, tame, lame, lame, lame,
> Pux ha't, shame, proclaime, oh—
> In Sacred raptures flowing, will proclaime, not—
> O me thy Priest inspyre!
> For I to thee and thine immortall name,
> In flowing numbers fild with spright and flame,
> Good, good, in flowing numbers fild with spright and flame.

                                                              (1.2.1–20)

The ode is made up (as Cyrus Hoy painstakingly shows) of a cento of Jonson echoes, but what makes it ludicrous is the way its composition is presented.[15] This, in fact, is a textbook example of deconstruction in the strict sense of the word—depriving a text of its monolithic power and unity by exposing the structures that construct it, in particular the rhyme words it chooses to repress, forget, and reject.

A Derridean "logocentrism"—the attribution of an almost divine stability to the relationship between signifier and signified—is perceived throughout as one of Horace's flaws. The ode, which at later recitations (45–60) seems so spontaneous, is, in fact, a self-conscious act of writing. This is typical of Dekker's strategy in *Satiromastix*'s satirical subplot: Jonsonian language, not just from *Poetaster*'s Horace, but also from Crites/Criticus of *Cynthia's Revels* and Asper in *Every Man Out,* is discredited by being spoken in farcical situations.

What are all these meticulous echoes of Jonson leading up to? The significance of all these direct verbal borrowings is revealed when Crispinus and Demetrius enter, in Crispinus's first major speech:

> *Horrace, Horrace,*
> To stand within the shot of galling tongues,
> Proues not your guilt, for could we write on paper,
> Made of these turning leaues of heauen, the cloudes,
> Or speake with Angels tongues: yet wise men know,
> That some would shake the head, tho Saints should sing,
> Some snakes must hisse, because they're borne with stings.
> (1.2.204–10)

This is an argument about inherent good and evil, whose most prominent appearance in the literature of this period will occur in *Paradise Regained*.[16] There, Satan's persuasions are no less evil for being couched in biblical quotations, for words themselves do not carry an absolute value or power. The particularly Scriptural application of this idea, reflected here in Crispinus's imagery of angels and saints, is especially appropriate as it is precisely a quasi-Scriptural ideal of inviolable text—with the "sacred lines" of Virgil as the highest example—that we have seen to govern Jonson's thinking in *Poetaster*.

Horace's profligate oaths are another example of the uselessness of mere language. His "dam me" is the most powerful form of speech available, and the most dreadful oath one can make: one can, after all, be damned only once. But, says Dekker, Horace/

Jonson is using and overusing this oath in a sort of linguistic infla-
tion and not convincing anyone at all. It is a point made fun of in
almost every subsequent Horace scene. Furthermore, the philosophical objection seamlessly joins to personal insult: his excessive
swearing is linked to a personal allegation of Catholicism against
Jonson, and to suggestions of informing.[17] So, the logocentrism of
Jonson is attacked.

Second, "Horace" is stripped of his context—the associations
that made him valuable to the Renaissance. In the court of William
Rufus, the set of like-minded intellectuals is shrunk from Tibullus,
Gallus and the rest down to just Asinius Bubo. Horace can hardly
be said to have the Emperor's ear—King William has never heard
of him: "*Horrace,* what's he sir *Vaughan? . . .* I neither know that
Horrace, nor mine anger" (2.1.115, 122). Virgil has disappeared
without trace apart from Dekker's allusion to him in the address
"To the World." As for Maecenas, his name is used in the play
merely as a synonym for a patron.

Third, Horace's reputation as the mildest of satirists is in contrast to the viciousness of "Horace's" satirical intent; he wishes
to use his satires to hurt in the manner of a 1590s railer, and not
to correct, as Sidney had praised the real Horace for doing. As
"Horace" puts it in the concluding lines to the second scene of the
play: "No, they haue choakt me with mine owne disgrace, / Which
(fooles) ile spit againe euen in your face" (1.2.403–4). The climactic
moment in the unmasking of the Jonsonian Horace is the presentation of two portraits: one of "true *Venusian Horace,*" the other of
the Horace/Jonson. The difference is plain for all to see:

> *Horace* lou'd Poets well, and gaue Coxcombes to none but fooles; but
> thou lou'st none, neither Wisemen nor fooles, but thy selfe: *Horace*
> was a goodly Corpulent Gentleman, and not so leane a hollow-cheekt
> Scrag as thou art. (5.2.259–63)

Here, the praise of the real Horace is mild rather than adulatory.
No raptures about the divinity of poetry, merely a favorable account of Horace's friendliness. The Augustan world is not accorded any central importance to the affairs of today, for, as Sir
Vaughan tells Asinius Bubo, there is no point having pretensions
to reading Latin poetry until one has managed to master the vernacular: "you shall not carry Lattin Poets about you, till you can
write and read English at most" (5.2.274–76).

Similarly, the remedies proposed reflect a different scale of values from *Poetaster.* Treatment takes the form, not of a Lucianic

purge followed by a reading list, but of a reform of manners, a code of good conduct when attending the theater. Even the reform is related to performances, and not to classical texts.

Conclusion

Jonson's *Poetaster* and Dekker's *Satiromastix* use authors as characters in a remarkable way. Unfussed by all the possible paradoxes and impossibilities of writers within writings, the two Horaces are embroiled instead in other major theoretical issues. Beyond the personal feud, we witness an argument about the nature of professional Elizabethan drama. Jonson is laying out a manifesto for drama as literature, as a text worthy of the respect accorded the classics. His "Apologetical Dialogue," with its inset poems, marginal glosses, and classical name-dropping, exemplifies this. In contrast, Tucca's "Epilogus" to Dekker's *Satiromastix* stresses the performed nature of the occasion, the cold weather, the dramatic company's responsibility to the "two penny Tenants" watching ("Epilogus," 31–32). Text, for Dekker, is something plastic, relativistic, subordinate to the occasion and context in which it occurs. And, if it was Jonson's view that created the Folio editions of the dramatists—starting with his own—and indirectly launched the academic study of English drama as text, then it is Dekker's that now seems the less anachronistic. In the middle of this contest over the future of English drama, Horace has a crucial role.

Notes to "Horace the Second, or, Ben Jonson, Thomas Dekker, and the Battle for Augustan Rome"

1. Ben Jonson, *Poetaster,* ed. Tom Cain, The Revels Plays (Manchester and New York: Manchester University Press, 1995), "Apologetical Dialogue," 88–92.

2. Joanna Martindale, "The Best Master of Virtue and Wisdom: The Horace of Ben Jonson and His Heirs," in *Horace Made New: Horatian Influences on British Writing from the Renaissance to the Twentieth Century,* ed. Charles Martindale and David Hopkins (Cambridge: Cambridge University Press, 1993), 50–85. Robert B. Pierce, "Ben Jonson's Horace and Horace's Ben Jonson," *Studies in Philology* 71:1 (1981): 20–31.

3. Readings of how Jonson uses Horace more generally as a personal model can be found in Richard Helgerson, *Self-Crowned Laureates: Spenser, Jonson, Milton and the Literary System* (Berkeley and Los Angeles: University of California Press, 1983), 101–35.

4. Roger Ascham, "'Of Imitation': *The Scholemaster* (Book II). 1570," in *Elizabethan Critical Essays,* ed. with an introduction by G. Gregory Smith, 2 vols. (1904; repr. London: Oxford University Press, 1959), 1:1–45 (33–34).

5. For an excellent reading of the way Horace conditioned the Renaissance approach to drama, see B. R. Smith, *Ancient Scripts and Modern Experience on the English Stage, 1500–1700* (Princeton: Princeton University Press, 1988).

6. Sir Philip Sidney, *An Apology for Poetry,* in *Elizabethan Critical Essays,* ed. G. Gregory Smith, 1: 148–207 (183).

7. *Ben Jonson,* ed. C. H. Herford, Percy and Evelyn Simpson, 11 vols. (Oxford: Clarendon Press, 1925–1952), 8: 642, line 2592.

8. William Webbe, *A Discourse of English Poetrie (1586),* in *Elizabethan Critical Essays,* ed. G. Gregory Smith, 1: 226–302 (290–98).

9. See *Ben Jonson,* ed. C. H. Herford, Percy and Evelyn Simpson, 11: 110.

10. The abortive alternative ending of *Every Man Out of His Humour,* which personated Queen Elizabeth on stage, is discussed by Helen Ostovich in "So Sudden and Strange a Cure: A Rudimentary Masque in *Every Man Out of his Humour,*" in *English Literary Renaissance* 22 (1992): 315–32.

11. See G. E. Rowe, *Distinguishing Jonson* (Lincoln: Nebraska University Press, 1988); and Robert C. Evans, *Jonson and the Contexts of his Time* (Lewisburg PA: Bucknell University Press, 1994) for perceptive and innovative readings of the War.

12. Stephen Gosson, *School of Abuse* (London, 1579), ed. Edward Arber (London, 1868), 22. See also A. F. Kinney's work on Gosson in *Markets of Bawdrie: The Dramatic Criticism of Stephen Gosson,* Salzburg Studies in English Literature (Salzburg: Institut für Englische Sprache und Literatur, 1974).

13. *Poetaster,* ed. Tom Cain, Introduction, 19–23.

14. For *Satiromastix,* see *The Dramatic Works of Thomas Dekker,* ed. Fredson Bowers, 4 vols. (Cambridge: Cambridge University Press, 1953–1961), 1 (1953): 307–89.

15. Cyrus Hoy, *Introductions, Notes and Commentaries to Texts in "The Dramatic Works of Thomas Dekker,"* 4 vols. (Cambridge: Cambridge University Press, 1980), 1: 207–8.

16. Stanley Fish, "Things and Actions Indifferent: The Temptation of Plot in *Paradise Regained,*" in *Milton Studies* 17 (Pittsburgh: Pittsburgh University Press, 1983), 163–86.

17. See respectively 4.2.89–91 (where Tucca says "Nay I smell what breath is to come from thee, thy answer is that there's no faith to be helde with Heritickes and Infidels, and therfore thou swear'st anie thing"); and 2.1.116–21 (where the Welshman Sir Rees ap Vaughan addresses the king about Horace as follows: "tis a Poet, we call them Bardes in our Countrie, singes ballads and rymes, and I was mightie sealous, that his Inke, which is blacke and full of gall, had brought my name to your maiestie, and so lifted vp your hye and princely coller").

Encores: The Dialogue of the Dead Within English Literature

FREDERICK M. KEENER

One of the most conspicuous features of high and relatively high culture in eighteenth-century England is the expectation that writers and readers be learned about certain writings of earlier times. In "An Essay on Criticism," Pope counsels, "Be *Homer*'s Works your *Study,* and *Delight, /* Read them by Day, and meditate by Night."[1] To find the best commentator on Homer, Pope's poem adds, a reader need not look beyond Virgil (line 129). Pope's comments represent the high end of eighteenth-century culture. Not quite so high is the enterprise of *The Spectator,* cultivating its readers by, among other things, insisting that the acquisition of literary-critical ability should be a concern of not only the publishing critic, and that the formation of good literary taste profits from study of the best critics, including ancient ones.[2] Samuel Johnson echoes Pope on Homer when he praises Addison as follows, advising the would-be writer and mediating between Pope's high claims and Addison's high-middle ones: "Whoever wishes to attain an English style, familiar but not coarse, and elegant but not ostentatious, must give his days and nights to the volumes of Addison."[3]

In much eighteenth-century writing, the authors present themselves, relatively distinctly and distinctively, as not alone but accompanied by dead writers in some manner alive and returning for encores in the works of the living. When Pope writes against the dunces, the writer is not just Pope. There would be no "Dunciad" without its powerful echoes—the contributions—of Milton, Virgil, and other poetic predecessors, including Dryden: Pope's collaborators with implicit speaking parts. Johnson displays the same impulse in "The Vanity of Human Wishes," an imitation of Juvenal, when he exclaims, "Once more, *Democritus,* arise on Earth."[4] In some manner, the rest of the poem is spoken not only by Johnson, but also by Democritus and Juvenal.

In England, eighteenth-century higher culture sharply distinguished itself from that of preceding eras. Johnson asserts, "The new versification, as it was called, may be considered as owing its establishment to Dryden; from whose time it is apparent that English poetry has had no tendency to relapse to its former savageness."[5] But, as we have seen, that sense of superiority went together with the acknowledgment of debts to certain great predecessors, English and otherwise.

"Mac Flecknoe" is an influential example. In it, Dryden has Richard Flecknoe praise Thomas Shadwell by relating him to Ben Jonson (spelled as *Johnson*), inversely:

> Nor let false friends seduce thy mind to fame,
> By arrogating *Johnson*'s Hostile name.
> Let Father *Fleckno* fire thy mind with praise,
> And Uncle *Ogleby* thy envy raise.
> Thou art my blood, where *Johnson* has no part;
> What share have we in Nature or in Art?
> Where did his wit on learning fix a brand,
> And rail at Arts he did not understand?
> Where made he love in Prince *Nicander*'s vein,
> Or swept the dust in *Psyche*'s humble strain?
> Where sold he Bargains, Whip-stitch, kiss my Arse,
> Promis'd a Play and dwindled to a Farce?
> When did his Muse from *Fletcher* scenes purloin,
> As thou whole *Eth'ridg* dost transfuse to thine?
> But so transfus'd as Oyl on Waters flow,
> His always floats above, thine sinks below.
> This is thy Province, this thy wondrous way,
> New Humours to invent for each new Play:
> This is that boasted Byas of thy mind,
> By which one way, to dullness, 'tis inclin'd.[6]

Dryden's implication in these and the following lines is that he himself is Jonson *redivivus* by being in the tradition of Jonson.

Something curious occurs in Dryden's poem, however. While aligning himself with Jonson, Dryden permits Flecknoe to speak as if in the tradition himself, to excoriate Shadwell for not being so. That is, Dryden permits Flecknoe to exhibit an informed, judicious appreciation of Jonson, and of what in Shadwell falls short of that. Flecknoe, as the monarch of "*Non-sense*," should be incapable of such assessment, but even the verse Flecknoe speaks here is not unworthy of Jonson.[7] A Flecknoe who speaks so is to that extent Jonsonian himself, hence, very different from what he says Shadwell represents, and is Drydenian to the extent that Dryden wants to show his descent from Jonson, his own membership in the tribe of Ben.

These considerations have a certain effect on the poem's satire. If Flecknoe can speak thus, either the satire is beginning to misfire, so far as he is concerned, or Flecknoe is portrayed as evil rather than dull, because the merit of what he says and how he says it indicates that he knows better than to praise Shadwell. Of course, he is promoting Shadwell to the throne of nonsense. To preserve the point, Dryden might better have somehow introduced someone more qualified to say what he attributes to Flecknoe, perhaps Dryden himself. Or perhaps the point finally is that Flecknoe has become chastened as his reign ends.

The example also goes beyond the recommendation that dead authors be studied and indicates that they be imitated in some manner, though apparently not merely repeated. Consistently or not, it was standard in allusive writing of the eighteenth century, when presenting oneself *in propria persona,* to some extent to speak *in propriis personis,* to echo those with whom one aligns oneself. The comparatively learned eighteenth-century author became himself, or herself, by becoming a certain combination of revered predecessors.

To speak for Jonson, if Jonson needs to be spoken for, who more capable than Jonson? In his play *Poetaster,* Jonson had introduced Horace and other ancient poetic worthies to speak for themselves. "Mac Flecknoe" sustains Jonson's voice, for example by disparaging the playwright Thomas Dekker as Jonson had in *Poetaster.*

To this extent, English writing, especially of the late-seventeenth and eighteenth centuries, is generally equivalent in very significant ways to a peculiar, marginal genre that, appropriately, became much less marginal then, indeed may be said to have flourished: the dialogue of the dead. As distinguished from narratives and most other accounts of the afterlife, this dramatic but nontheatrical genre was invented by Lucian in the second century, resurfaced in the Renaissance within the *Colloquia* of Erasmus and elsewhere, and came to prominence in France among the works of Boileau, Fontenelle, and Fénelon. Such typically short, frequently satirical dialogues, usually between historical or mythological personages, are relatively prominent in eighteenth-century English literature. The finest English examples are the four produced by Matthew Prior, among them splendid confrontations between Thomas More and the Vicar of Bray, and between Montaigne and Locke. It is a series no reader should neglect.

Although they were known to Alexander Pope, Prior's dialogues were not published until 1907; but many others appeared publicly in the eighteenth century and later, most prominently in a collection written by George, Lord Lyttelton and Elizabeth Montagu (1760, augmented 1765). Samuel Johnson was no partisan of the genre, as practiced by Lyttelton or in general, but himself regularly became a character in it after his death in 1784, not least because in what is called his *Lives of the English Poets* (1779–81), where he disparaged Lyttelton's dialogues, he had forthrightly championed certain standards in literature and other things which had become contested toward the end of his life. What Cato the Elder had been in earlier dialogues of the dead, the undyingly outspoken censor on moral and cultural manners, Johnson became in numerous dialogues after his time. The publication of Boswell's *Life of Johnson* in 1791 added fuel, attracting special attention to the peculiarities of Johnson's personality.

As my book *English Dialogues of the Dead*, from which the substance of this and the two preceding paragraphs derives, seeks to show, there remains considerable vitality in many of the English dialogues of the dead—for example, in the nineteenth-century dialogues in which Johnson levels his glare at Wordsworth, or at "The Rime of the Ancient Mariner" in conversation with Coleridge, or at Browning: "Yes, Sir, Browning could read men. The pity is, men cannot read Browning."[8]

One anonymous dialogue only mentioned in my book features Johnson as a character and has a certain historical and theoretical significance regarding the use of historical people as literary characters: *A Dialogue between Dr. Johnson and Dr. Goldsmith, in the Shades, Relative to the Former's Strictures on the English Poets, Particularly Pope, Milton, and Gray* (London, 1785). The dialogue is relatively unusual because in verse, appropriately, because the topics are poetry and more particularly Goldsmith's dismay at the appraisals of certain writers in Johnson's *Lives of the English Poets.*

Both Johnson and Goldsmith were accomplished poets themselves, and this raises a theoretical issue. There usually is no point in introducing historical figures into a work of fiction unless they are distinctly themselves (as Johnson may well be said to be in that comment on Browning) or, for satirical ends, distinctly inferior to themselves. To introduce historical personages well known for their poetry into a work in verse is to complicate the point, since, on the face of the matter, they ought to speak as, or distinctly not as, they did as poets. Johnson does neither here; Goldsmith, and Johnson, speak more or less as Goldsmith's verse does, at least in a generic way, but the matter is complicated by the almost constant presence in the text of a poet who is not a character in the dialogue,

Pope. The issue is further complicated by the fact that, historically, this dialogue's sentiments and style mark it as reflecting cultural changes after Pope's time.

The dialogue begins with an aside by Goldsmith, dead since 1774, as he perceives Johnson's approach: Goldsmith will "gently chid[e]" Johnson for the severity of his criticism. They meet with pleasantries, then from Goldsmith an abrupt, indeed heavy, change:

> JOHNSON's presence can amend the day.
> *If thou be'st he,* but oh! how chang'd from him
> Whose noontide lustre might the sun's bedim;
> Whose moral writings such effulgence shed,
> But ah, why quit the heart, to judge the head?
>
> $(6-7)$[9]

The passage begins to reveal the theoretical significance of the dialogue when it signals with italics an allusion to *Paradise Lost,* to the passage in which Satan, beginning to collect himself after being hurled onto Hell's fiery lake, exclaims, to his fallen comrade, Beëlzebub:

> If thou beest hee; but O how fall'n! how chang'd
> From him, who in the happy Realms of Light
> Cloth'd with transcendent brightness didst outshine
> Myriads though bright.[10]

Evidently, the eighteenth-century dialogue is a dialogue of not only the poets named in the title.

The passage begins to substantiate what is historically significant about this dialogue because it evidently seeks to bring poets who preceded the later eighteenth century, in telling respects an "Age of Sensibility,"[11] into that era without much loss of authority, in reaction to the candid reflections on some of them evident in Johnson's *Lives,* as compared with his earlier, less outspoken, especially moral writings, notably in his periodical *The Rambler.*

In the dialogue, as soon as Johnson begins to reply and seek to justify himself, he brings in another poet, implicitly:

> I only judg'd the head to mend the heart;
> Taste to restore, and from each wand'ring part
> Collectively to raise the beauteous *whole,*
> Inform'd with sense, *of ev'ry art the soul;*

That future bards might from the model draw,
And burn to reach perfection's brightest law.

(7)

The italicized words are quoted from Pope's "Epistle IV: To Richard Boyle, Earl of Burlington": "Still follow Sense, of ev'ry Art the Soul, / Parts answ'ring parts shall slide into a whole" (3:2, 65–66), lines in which quintessential Pope distills himself especially from "An Essay on Criticism," notably its couplet which, with the same rhyme-words, begins to compare "Art" to a human soul: "In some fair Body thus th' informing Soul, / With Spirits feeds, with Vigour fills the whole" (1, 76–77). The passage in the dialogue indeed vibrates with instances of Popean diction, scarcely a major word in it not prominently his, like *sense, taste, restore,* and *beauteous;* also certain words in combination, *head* and *heart* ("An Essay on Criticism," 1, 732). More generally, the passage reflects Pope's dismay in "An Essay on Criticism" (1, 263–64) and elsewhere that critics neglect the whole of a text in favor of its parts.

What is more, Johnson's remarks immediately prompt Goldsmith to defend Pope, "But why view POPE with microscopic eye?" (7)— but this is virtually Pope defending very typical Pope. There is "Why has not Man a microscopic eye?" in "An Essay on Man" (3:1, Epistle I, 193), in the context of the importance of seeing the whole of things, and of course there are the lines which "The Dunciad" puts in the mouth of Richard Bentley, and which repeat the topics of soul and body and the whole of things and the rhyme of "soul/whole":

The critic Eye, that microscope of Wit,
Sees hairs and pores, examines bit by bit:
How parts relate to parts, or they to whole,
The body's harmony, the beaming soul,
Are things which Kuster, Burman, Wasse shall see,
When Man's whole frame is obvious to a *Flea*.

(5, Book IV, 233–38)

There is no need to describe all the stages of the dialogue's development, which is clumsy in several respects. Johnson eventually accedes to Goldsmith's accusations of unkind severity, even admits to having envied some of those he criticized. More fundamentally, the dialogue presents problems because it depicts Johnson as having been much more critical of certain poets than he actually was—"Sensibility" is thin-skinned—and the dialogue makes no acknowledgment of the fact that Goldsmith and Johnson, in life, knew each other well.

To its credit, however, the dialogue permits Johnson to make a definite if disruptive difference in the outcome. Goldsmith's praise of Pope's oeuvre remains selective, very complimentary to the translation of Homer—also "Eloisa to Abelard," "Windsor-Forest," "An Essay on Man," and "An Essay on Criticism"—and remains substantially Popean in diction. Goldsmith's selectivity gives Johnson grounds to object,

> POPE himself, with all his pow'rful parts,
> Oft shot, perhaps, the most invenom'd darts;
> Made poverty disgrace, and ev'ry strain,
> Tho' sung for bread, thro' him, was sung in vain.
>
> (18)

To speak bluntly: Goldsmith, here the champion of the feeling heart, ultimately has to concede that Pope did write satire, including the "Dunciad" which is especially the topic here, but first Johnson's objection simply scatters Goldsmith's forces, or thoughts.

Goldsmith immediately digresses, adducing Johnson's alleged mistreatment of Milton, Addison, Gray, and others and praising Pope further, notably his "Messiah"—then praising Milton again—then, after Johnson's recantatory admission, broadening the subject to include the importance of satire. If critics are too severe,

> Satire no more her deadly sting shall dart,
> And wound the villain through his spotted heart.
> O Liberty! chief blessing from above,
> Divinely sent us on the wings of love;
> Thy presence makes each heavenly gift more dear.
>
> (29)

Johnson gets to say no more, and, except for a link between satire and patriotic defense of "Liberty," Goldsmith concludes the dialogue mainly by changing the subject. The celebration of liberty with which Goldsmith ends the dialogue has not been addressed in it to this point, is not a topic likely to silence Johnson given his impatience with liberty as a general, political rallying cry, and appears to be a desperate measure on Goldsmith's part, as if he had lost sight of the common ground on which he and Johnson had been conversing from the start, especially the topic of Pope.[12]

Implicitly, however, a little further along, Goldsmith's fervid peroration renews some contact with this ground, returning to Pope

implicitly, at least to Pope as modified somewhat by late-eighteenth-century taste. That taste is most evident as the climactic
passage begins with repetition of the couplet on liberty, repetition
(except that "chief blessing" becomes "sweet blessing") for a soar-
ing, sublime effect. Such incantatory repetition within a text is as
definitely non-Popean as it is definitely a feature of writing under
the aegis of "Sensibility."[13] The "from above" has a tinge of the
anti-sublime, bathos, in that the lines when repeated are "from
above" themselves, but the rest may be said to be Pope's poetry
as a late-eighteenth-century writer might have rewritten it, here
did rewrite it.

The paean to liberty continues:

> Extend thy influence from shore to shore,
> Till nations wond'ring thy soft name adore.
> Where impious monarchs rule with iron sway,
> O shew thy power, and shed a brighter day!
> Through frozen climes, and Afric's burning skies,
> Bid RUSSELLs, SIDNEYs, in succession rise,
> And point to trembling wretches public wrong,
> While some bold poets lift the free-born song;
> While truth, and harmony, and joy, and peace
> Descend from Heaven and bid all discord cease;
> That all mankind may taste the living spring,
> Whence flow those sweets the muse would gladly sing.
>
> (30)

On the next page, Goldsmith draws the dialogue to a close as he
notices Pope approaching and predicts harmonious friendship
among Pope, Johnson, and himself.

As I have indicated, however, here, Pope had joined Goldsmith
and Johnson almost from the beginning of the dialogue. They had
been speaking with him, as it were, nearly all the time. Consistent
with that claim, Goldsmith's peroration certainly draws on Pope,
especially from the equivalent part of "Windsor-Forest"—

> Oh stretch thy Reign, fair *Peace!* from Shore to Shore,
> Till Conquest cease, and Slav'ry be no more . . .
>
> (1, 407–8)

—and, among the final lines of Pope's poem, the reference to

> the green Forests and the flow'ry Plains
> Where Peace descending bids her Olives spring,
> And scatters Blessings from her Dove-like Wing.
>
> (1, 428–30)

—and, "Let Discord cease" (1, 327), and once again additional Popean expressions, from "Windsor-Forest" and elsewhere.

As readers may have noted earlier, the entire dialogue is not as Popean as the parts; even the whole of any such part is not. The verse of the dialogue is not pointed with a maximum of cognitive sense, as Pope's verse typically is; it is more reader-friendly in the manner of Goldsmith rather than Pope or Johnson—if "reader-friendly" means fewer intellectual demands. Swift had ironically complained that Pope "can in one couplet fix / More sense than I can do in six."[14] The verse Goldsmith actually wrote has much in common with Pope's but is nevertheless not particularly Popean in this and other respects.

Thus, the main speaker in this dialogue is a historical figure who is not directly presented as speaking in it, Pope, contending especially with historically later speakers representing standards of morality and taste somewhat different from his own. Moreover, the representation of Pope by the dialogue's author stands as extremely knowledgeable and genuine in its appreciation of Pope's poetry, even intensely so, despite the filter of the dialogue-writer's less rigorous, historically later style. For the reader who already appreciates Pope's writing, the odd, probably unintentional effect of this unequal combination is to induce a yearning to reread Pope rather than the dialogue. The dialogue effaces itself by taking to an extreme the desire of eighteenth-century writers that the dead speak up for them.

Notes to "Encores: The Dialogue of the Dead Within English Literature"

1. Citations of Pope employ the Twickenham Edition of *The Poems of Alexander Pope,* ed. John Butt et al., 11 vols. (London and New Haven: Methuen, 1939–1969), 1, lines 124–25.

2. *The Spectator,* ed. Donald F. Bond, 5 vols. (Oxford: Clarendon Press, 1965), 3: 530 (No. 409).

3. "Addison," *Lives of the English Poets,* ed. George Birkbeck Hill, 3 vols. (1905; repr. New York: Octagon, 1967), 2: 150.

4. *The Poems of Samuel Johnson,* ed. David Nichol Smith and Edward L. McAdam, 2nd ed. (Oxford: Clarendon Press, 1974), 117 (line 49).

5. "Dryden," *Lives of the English Poets,* 1: 421.

6. *The Works of John Dryden,* vol. 2, ed. H. T. Swedenberg, Jr. (Berkeley: University of California Press, 1972), 58–59, lines 171–90.

7. Ibid, 54 (line 6).

8. *English Dialogues of the Dead: A Critical History, an Anthology, and a Check List* (New York and London: Columbia University Press, 1973). Given there, page 135, the quotation is from a dialogue of 1889 by William Watson.

9. Parenthetical citations are by page; the lines are not numbered.

10. John Milton, *Complete Poems and Major Prose,* ed. Merritt Y. Hughes (New York: Odyssey Press, 1957), 213 (Book I, lines 84–87). As a footnote by Hughes indicates, Milton's "how chang'd / From him" itself particularly echoes a phrase from the *Aeneid,* II, 275–76.

11. Northrop Frye, "Toward Defining an Age of Sensibility" (1956), repr. in *Eighteenth-Century English Literature: Modern Essays in Criticism,* ed. James L. Clifford (New York: Oxford University Press, 1959), 311–18.

12. *Boswell's Life of Johnson,* ed. George Birkbeck Hill, rev. L. F. Powell, 6 vols. (1934; repr. Oxford: Clarendon Press, 1971), 2: 60.

13. Frye, 314.

14. Frye, 314, alludes to these lines as defining a norm opposed to that of "Sensibility." I quote the lines—from, aptly here, "Verses on the Death of Dr Swift, D.S.P.D"—as given in Jonathan Swift, *The Complete Poems,* ed. Pat Rogers (New Haven and London: Yale University Press, 1983), 486 (lines 49–50).

Aurore Dupin Dudevant and Jean-Baptiste Poquelin: George Sand Reconstructs Molière

GRETCHEN ELIZABETH SMITH

La grande force et la seule vraie, c'est le talent.

The great strength and the only true one is talent.
                                        —George Sand[1]

Though celebrated predominantly for her novels, George Sand also wrote twenty-one plays which received Paris premieres, twenty of them between April 1848 and November 1872.[2] In *George Sand's Theatre Career,* Gay Manifold writes that "Revolutionary changes in Sand's personal and professional life coincided with the 1848 Revolution," and she proceeds to link the political event of the Revolution with the culmination of the novelist's notorious love affair with Chopin and the inception of her career as a serious playwright (Manifold, 35). For Sand, then, the year 1848 marked both an end and a beginning: she found her art reborn in a new medium (one in which she had only dabbled until that time), and with a new political purpose and energy. By the end of 1851, the Revolution was an acknowledged failure, and Sand's drama lost its sharp political edge.

   In the three years between the beginning of the Revolution and its dismal conclusion, however, Sand had five new plays produced. Two of those plays, opening in April 1848 and in May 1851, centered on the historical and literary figure of Molière, the great French neoclassical playwright. In the plays, entitled *Le Roi attend* and *Molière* respectively, Sand revisioned the playwright for the people of France, loading political agendas onto the shoulders of her appropriated hero. It is in this act of negotiating the real-life person of Jean-Baptiste Poquelin into Molière, the "people's playwright," that Sand finds a spiritual father to help guide her project of attracting and educating "a 'people's audience' in anticipation of creating a 'people's theatre'" (Manifold, 35).

By the time of the Revolution of 1848 and the beginning of the Second Empire, scholars and critics such as Désiré Nisard and Saint-Marc Girardin were already rewriting Molière's biography for political purposes[3]: the reclamation of Molière as modern property became one of the pet projects of the nineteenth century in French literary criticism, based on "a unanimous desire to integrate him into the national patrimony" (Albanese, 239). It was Sand, however, who painted Molière as a modern hero of the people and who brought this figure to the public stages of Paris in her two plays. In part, the plays helped set the tone for the century's deification of Molière: he became the Artist, the Sad Clown, the Genius. Sand believed that the theater was a political conduit to the masses and that the 1848 Revolution was a turning point in the fortunes of the French people. Therefore, she deliberately selected "Molière" (rather than Jean-Baptiste Poquelin) as the link between the glory of France's history and the needs (as she perceived them) of modern audiences. These two plays, then, offer unique opportunities to examine the ways in which Sand's political ideals and dramaturgy influence each other, as well as the early reinterpretation (and thus institutionalization) of a national figure, Molière, by another of the most controversial figures of French literature, George Sand.

At first glance, Molière seems an odd choice to become Sand's folk hero of the Revolution. His work was the product of the baroque patronage theater. True, the playwright wrote for a public theater in which all classes were welcomed and entertained. True, his comedy parodied the aristocracy as well as the bourgeois and servant classes. But Molière's company was the Troupe du Roi.[4] Between 1658 and 1673, the actors survived not only because of their popularity with Parisian audiences but through annual subsidies from Louis XIV and royal performances, for which the company was well paid. Molière considered Louis not only his patron but his friend and sponsor. Louis gave the troupe its theater, the Palais Royal, which it shared with the Italian comedians.[5] The king was godfather to Molière's child. And, while Molière infuriated many people (Sand would say that the 1664 censorship of *Tartuffe* was only one example of the work of Molière's *ennemis*[6]), it was the king's influence (as well as Molière's talent) that kept the Troupe du Roi performing and solvent.

Thus, Molière himself hardly seems the material for a hero of the people. Albanese's article points to the general disinterest in Molière's biography in the early nineteenth century. Sand, however, belonged to those who nevertheless continued in their esteem of Molière. She felt the need to emphasize his profound merits: *"Si Molière ne provoquait que le rire, il y a longtemps qu'il serait oublié, et il faudrait, aujourd'hui déjà, l'exhumer comme une curiosité littéraire passée de mode"* ("If it was only laughter that Molière provoked, he would have been forgotten long ago, and it would be necessary today to exhume him like an unfashionable literary curiosity").[7] Sand may be exaggerating a bit. During the latter part of the century, building on the work of early writers such as Nisard, Girardin, and Sand, critics draw the character of "Molière" out of his work, translating the voice of the playwright in his plays to stand for a world vision of ethics, morals, and manners that include uniquely "French" qualities. Yet, whereas later writers use Molière to promote "the famous shopkeeper's morality," Sand approaches her subject with a sense of vitality and freshness.[8]

Sand began her reclamation of the character of Molière with the short play, *Le Roi attend*. She had already published pamphlets and journal articles attacking the self-interest of the bourgeoisie and aristocracy (Manifold, 36–37). In her early playwrighting, Sand focused her dramaturgy in two areas: the genre of folk plays and "the idea that man's natural state is in a social context," a slight corruption of Rousseau's philosophies (Manifold, 35–36). The folk plays celebrated the life of the French countryside and the character of the French people living there. At the same time, Sand turned her pen to what she believed to be the Republic's best interests: the consideration of man as an active force within the society of men.

Le Roi attend premiered at the Théâtre de la République on 6 April 1848, two months after the Revolution.[9] The evening's bill included Pierre Corneille's *Horace*, Molière's *Le Malade imaginaire*, and "new and old patriotic songs."[10] Sand's play opened the evening. The Théâtre de la République was the renamed Comédie Française, and its usual audiences were drawn from the upper middle class.[11] Manifold calls *Le Roi attend* Sand's "beau geste" for the Revolution (Manifold, 37). On the night of 6 April, the theater was filled with "the people," possibly because admission was free. "The people," as Sand called them, included primarily workers of the lower classes.

The one-act play has eleven French scenes, which appear to proceed in real time; however, there is a curious, theatrical twist (discussed below). Besides Molière, played by the actor Samson, Sand's characters included the "Muse de la République" (played by the great tragic actress Rachel [= Elizabeth Félix, b.1821]), actors of Molière's troupe, Molière's maid La Forêt (played by leading actress Augustine Brohan), and the spiritual manifestations

of Sophocles, Æschylus, Euripides, Shakespeare, Voltaire, and
Beaumarchais. As *Le Roi attend* opens, Molière is writing the final
scene of a play to be performed that fictional night; Sand borrows
the theatrical convention of Molière's *L'Impromptu de Versailles,*
showing the Troupe du Roi unprepared for imminent royal performance. In Sand's text, the playwright is just completing the final
script, while the actors have not yet arrived nor rehearsed. Louis
XIV is due at the theater in one hour to see the finished piece.
Molière seems unconcerned: *"Le roi aura de l'indulgence"* ("The
king will be lenient,"*Le Roi attend,* 126). His maid, La Forêt, takes
a less sanguine view of the indulgences of kings: *"Les rois n'en ont
point pour ce qui regarde leurs amusements"* ("Kings don't have
any leniency about their entertainment," *Le Roi attend,* 126). The
first part of *Le Roi attend* closely emulates Molière's self-conscious
rehearsal play; in fact, La Forêt remarks on this: *"Ah! monsieur,
nous voici comme le jour de* l'Impromptu de Versailles" ("Ah! Sir,
here we are as on the day of *l'Impromptu de Versailles," Le Roi
attend,* 127). In scenes 3 through 8, actors and *"nécessaires"* enter
to tell Molière that the king has come and waits for him to begin;
the king, waiting offstage, has departed by the end of the eighth
scene (*Le Roi attend,* 131).

Molière, abandoned by king, courtiers, and actors, muses on his
career. He despairs:

> *Ah! maudite soit l'heure où j'acceptai les commandements d'un roi, le
> renom d'auteur et la livrée de comédien! . . . Assurément, quand je
> considère ma vie, il ne me semble point que j'aie encouru le reproche
> d'hypocrisie, ce vice à la mode qui jouit, en repos, d'une impunité
> souveraine.*
>
> (*Le Roi attend,* 133)

> Ah! cursed be the hour when I accepted the commands of a king, the
> fame of an author, and the livery of an actor! . . . Surely, when I look
> at my life, it doesn't seem to me that I have incurred the reproach of
> hypocrisy, that fashionable vice which quietly enjoys a sovereign
> impunity.

Finally, he sleeps—and dreams. Sand's stage directions read:

> *Un nuage l'enveloppe lentement; un choeur de musique chante derri-
> ère le nuage. Quand le nuage se dissipe, on voit debout, autour de
> Molière endormi, les ombres des poëtes antiques et modernes: Plaute,
> Térence, Eschyles [sic], Sophocle, Euripide, Shakspeare, Voltaire,*

Rousseau, Marivaux, Sedaine, Beaumarchais, etc. La Muse du théâtre est au milieu d'eux.

(Le Roi attend, 135)

A cloud slowly envelops him; a choir sings behind the cloud. When the cloud lifts, one sees standing, around the sleeping Molière, the shades of poets Classical and modern: Plautus, Terence, Æschylus, Sophocles, Euripides, Shakespeare, Voltaire, Rousseau, Marivaux, Sedaine, Beaumarchais, etc. The Muse of the theater is in their midst.

The Muse and the shades of the poets present Molière with the entwined history of art and politics, and point to his place in that history. The Muse greets Molière thus:

Dors, o poëte chéri! que ton âme généreuse et pure goûte les bienfaits du repos, en attendant le jour où, sur cette scène illustrée par tes oeuvres, tu t'endormiras une dernière fois pour te réveiller dans le sein des dieux.

(Le Roi attend, 135)

Sleep, darling poet! May your generous and pure soul taste the blessings of rest, in anticipation of the day when, on this stage made illustrious by your works, you go to sleep one last time in order to awake in the bosom of the gods.

While Molière apparently continues "sleeping," the playwrights of the past address him, offering wisdom and advice in order to support Molière's "drooping spirit" (*Le Roi attend,* 136), as the Muse puts it.[12] This parade of shadows visually connects the tragedians of antiquity and Athenian democracy with the European playwrights of democratic modernity. The Muse calls forth Shakespeare, *"grand tragique et grand philosophe de la renaissance . . . . Voltaire, précurseur d'une grande révolution; Beaumarchais, puissant levier d'une lutte mémorable"* ("great tragedian and great philosopher of the Renaissance. . . . Voltaire, harbinger of a great revolution; Beaumarchais, powerful lever of a memorable struggle," *Le Roi attend,* 137–38). At the end of the dream, the Muse states, *"Il est passé, le temps de la vengeance! La raison humaine a triomphé, l'obstacle est détruit, le chemin est libre"* ("The time of vengeance is past! Human reason has triumphed, the obstacle has been destroyed, the road is free," *Le Roi attend,* 139).

In the final scene, Sand's dramaturgical twist has Molière awakening—in 1848! Through the medium of the dream, both the playwright and his maid have been transported into the present. Further, Molière discovers that his waiting audience is not Louis XIV, absolute ruler of seventeenth-century France, but "the people! the sovereign people!" (*Le Roi attend*, 141). He approaches the apron of the stage and, breaking the fourth-wall convention which has held until this moment, addresses the actual audience before him. On opening night, Molière's words and salute were met with "tremendous applause" (Manifold, 38). When La Forêt corrects Molière's address of the audience as *"Messieurs"* (*"Il faut dire citoyens, à cette heure"* "Nowadays, one must say 'citizens,'" *Le Roi attend*, 142]), immediately the playwright connects the new revolutionary France of 1848 with historical republics:

> *Sommes-nous donc à Rome ou à Sparte? . . . Mais non, je sens que nous sommes mieux encore à Paris. Citoyens, le Théâtre de la République est heureux de vous ouvrir ses portes toutes grandes, et il vous invite à y entrer souvent.*
>
> (*Le Roi attend*, 142)

> Are we then in Rome or Sparta? . . . No, I feel that we are better still in Paris. Citizens, the Théâtre de la République is happy to open its doors wide to you, and invites you to enter here often.

Molière, hesitating to address the audience for fear they will not comprehend his old-fashioned language, is again reassured by La Forêt: *"Tous les hommes sont semblables par les paroles, et ce n'est que les actions qui les découvrent différents; vous voyez que je vous sais par coeur"* ("All men are alike in their speech, and it is only by their actions that you discover the difference; you see that I know you through and through," *Le Roi attend*, 141–42). True to her politics, Sand ends the play by having her hero declare that the proletariat audience is welcome in that bourgeois theater, where it can discover its own great literary past which will be, from now on, intimately joined to the history of democracy. More, Sand's dramaturgy looks forward to the future of the French people under their new government. Sand, thrilled with the reception not only of her play but of the entire evening, wrote of the premiere:

> Never have our great artists found a public more sympathetic and more intelligent, not one orange peel in the loges, no conversation during Corneille's verses or Molière's prose. . . . The people are more delicate and more gentlemanly than all the gentlemen and dandies of yesterday.
>
> (Manifold, 37)

Sand became involved in the Revolution eagerly and early. She had hurried to Paris from Nohant in 1848, once she heard the news; on arrival, she immediately became active:

> She arranged that her friends should be made Commissaires of the Republic at Châteauroux and La Châtre. At Bourge, she brought about the dismissal of her former lover, Michel, who, said she, was betraying the democracy from dread of demagogy. She succeeded . . . in having Maurice [her son] appointed Mayor of Nohant. Through her influence Pauline Viardot was accorded the honour of being asked to compose a "new *Marseillaise* to words by Dupont." . . . She herself was given a permit which entitled her to see all the members of the Provisional Government whenever she wanted to do so. . . . *She became the muse of the Revolution.*[13]

She also served as Information Minister, writing pamphlets entitled "Bulletins to the People," which were directed at both the lower and upper classes; in addition, she wrote theatrical tracts for the "left-wing journal *La Cause du Peuple*" (Manifold, 36–37). In *George Sand and Idealism,* Naomi Schor discusses Sand's participation in the Fête de la Fraternité on 21 April 1848, only two weeks after *Le Roi attend* opened: "Sand was, as the historical record shows, a privileged though unofficial female participant in the otherwise all male group that governed France between the fall of Louis-Philippe [in February 1848] and the bloody June days that marked the end of the initial phase of the Revolution."[14] Schor quotes from Sand's letters to her son Maurice describing the festival, which she claims brought together "'one million souls . . . the entire population'" (Schor, 135). Sand's vantage point on 21 April was the top of the Arc de Triomphe (Schor, 136).

Le Roi attend clearly is another form of Sand's propaganda for the Revolution's cause. Why would Sand turn to this medium?— The very public nature of dramatic performance, the accessibility of the theater to the masses. Sand's commitment to "the idea that man's natural state is in a social context" led her in this direction. Manifold notes that Jules Michelet, a writer and lecturer in 1848, proposed "national revolutionary heroes for subject matter in a new people's theatre" (Manifold, 36). Undoubtedly, Sand was aware of Michelet's statements; and *Le Roi attend* fits within this pronouncement about heroes. Sand reconstitutes the seventeenth-century playwright as a modern people's poet, connecting him visually and figuratively with the workers' audience of 6 April 1848, as well as demonstrating that he and his work are part of this new society. This marks Sand's movement away from the conventions of romanticism. Her dramaturgy encompassed her interest in this location of man in society, the folk play, "ensemble and strong psychological development," and the new style of realism just coming into flower on the French stage (Manifold, 35). In addition, Sand had the twin agendas of bringing "the people" into theaters and thereby educating them; she positions *Le Roi attend* as a clear opening gambit in this action.

Sand revisioned Molière so that the audience would recover their own heritage. The playwright becomes a conduit; he goes to sleep under the tyranny of royal patronage and wakes to a new world, one where he finds himself in a symbiotic relationship with *le peuple*. His plays, along with those of Racine, Corneille, Shakespeare, and Beaumarchais, are the property of the modern French audience: Sand's renegotiation of Molière positions him as a sort of frame into which the audience may look to see both their newly glorious past and their unstained, shining future. By virtue of this figurative leap across two centuries, courtesy of Sand's pen, the playwright brings his character, his canon, and those of his fellow playwrights into the modern age, now reclaimed for all French people. Previously, Molière and his plays were tainted by their connection to royal patronage; Sand baptizes them anew with her dramaturgy. Thus, it is no mistake when the Muse, portrayed by France's leading actress, declares, *"Le chemin est libre"*: we can hear Sand's own voice in these words.

Sand opens her preface to the published version of her plays by stating, *"Quand nous avons abordé le théâtre, le matérialisme l'avait envahi. À la suite des événements politiques, les maîtres s'en étaient un peu retirés"* ("When we first turned to theater, materialism had taken hold of it. Following the political events, the master playwrights had withdrawn a little," in "Préface," 1). The arrangement of the bill of 6 April 1848 points to Sand's agenda: her one-act play centers Molière in his new, modern persona as a sort of master of ceremonies. Further, Molière becomes the doorway through which the audience is invited into the rest of the evening's performance. The juxtaposition of the plays by Corneille and Molière with *patriotic* songs (which, though unnamed, are undoubtedly from both the 1789 and 1848 revolutions) repositioned France's greatest literary era (now freed by Sand from its initial connection to tyranny) within the context of the workers' agendas. In the structure of the entire performance night, it is as if the theater itself makes both past and present, France's great literary heritage and workers' revolution, welcome at once in this previously bourgeois space.

There is great optimism in *Le Roi attend,* as there was in the first flush of revolutionary fervor. Although Sand uses the stage devices of the time—the music, the spectacle of the shadows appearing in a cloud accompanied by the allegorical Muse (perhaps a self-inspired character)—the drive of the piece derives from the appearance of the poets and from Molière's subsequent "awakening" to the exciting possibilities of his new public. As the Molière character says, doors previously closed to the workers are now flung open, and he adds *"Nous avons de bonnes choses à vous servir, et nous savons qu'elles vous seront agréables, étant offertes du mieux que nous pourrons"* ("We have good things to offer you, and we know that they will please you, since we offer them as best we can," *Le Roi attend,* 142). Sand, in the persona of the Muse, announces the triumph of human reason.

Fortunately, Sand got *Le Roi attend* produced in April; in June 1848, the theaters closed down for a month due to outbreaks of fighting in working-class districts.[15] In March, the provisional government eliminated state censorship of plays but retained the strict licensing system that maintained the caste levels of Parisian theaters. By 1850, the laws of censorship had been reestablished; licensing had been strengthened, and a new manager was imposed on the Théâtre de la République by the government.

Between *Le Roi attend* of 1848, and *Molière* (produced three years later in 1851), George Sand continued writing plays. *François le Champi,* produced in 1849, shows the development of Sand's interest in the realistic style in both staging and story; two years later, her drama, *Claudie,* was a rustic folk play (Manifold, 50), previously produced at Nohant and brought to the Parisian theater of Porte Saint-Martin, a theater seating 1,500 and known a decade earlier for doing "new and daring dramas" (Manifold, 53). *Claudie,* too, demonstrated Sand's innovative ideas about staging and story in the new realistic style: the use of ensemble acting; the depth of character; the connection of folk rituals of the French countryside with specific actions of the fictional plot; the interest in all authentic details of costume, setting, and properties.

By the time Sand became interested in writing *Molière* in 1851, her dramaturgy had changed, even if her agenda remained (somewhat) the same. Pierre Bocage, Sand's director, was the one to suggest she work on a serious biography of the playwright:

he offered the . . . proposal that she write the real historical drama of *Molière* rather than merely the suggestion of Molière in the character of Marielle [first written in 1850, but never produced]. He wants "frankness, valor, greatness . . . and what charms me is the alliance of the two names: Molière and George Sand." (Manifold, 74)

This time, the play is a five-act drama. The two principal characters are Molière and his wife, Armande Béjart.

Once Sand began writing the biographical play, she found herself caught up in it, despite her earlier reservations: "To Sand the most interesting things about famous people are the details of their intimate lives, what is least known about them. She prefers a version of Molière's life which deals with his spirit and heart rather than the exterior life of noble deeds" (Manifold, 75). As she states in the dedication written for opening night, 10 May 1851:

> De là cette pièce de Molière, où je n'ai cherché à représenter que la vie intime, et où rien ne m'a intéressé que les combats intérieurs et les chagrins secrets.
>
> (Dedication to *Molière*, 310).

Hence, this play *Molière,* in which I sought to represent only his private life, and in which nothing interested me except for the inner struggle and the secret sorrows.

She wanted to deconstruct the "facts" known about Molière and focus instead on a psychological portrait, to write *Molière* in the new style of realism and thus distance it from the theater's conventional interest in *"l'homme extérieur"* (or "outer man").

In writing the biography of her hero, Sand acknowledged the difficulty of the task. As today, the known facts of Molière's life were few and unequal: we know much about the theater manager, director, actor, and playwright but little about the person. Molière and his troupe left behind them financial records and playtexts, audience memoirs and reviews, cast lists and property lists, but no personal information beyond the bare facts of marriages, births, hirings, dismissals, and deaths. In fact, Molière's life is still being uncovered, through documents and verification brought to light by contemporary biographers.[16] Many questions remain to be answered. In essence, most of the "facts" we have relate to the character of "Molière," the well-known, easily recognized leader of the Troupe du Roi rather than to the man behind the mask, Jean-Baptiste Poquelin, who remains almost entirely invisible.

Poquelin is elusive. Unlike his fellow dramatists, Molière was content to speak through his drama, rather than by involving himself in the extensive pamphlet wars or other public forums favored by various writers. He did, however, attach dedications and prefaces to his printed works (especially in the *livrets* which accompanied the *comédies-ballets*), but these pieces are disarmingly straightforward yet somehow impossible to grasp. On the other hand, Poquelin left no artifacts behind that might connect him to the young man who, in the early 1640s, had not yet become attracted to theater.

Sand "discovers" Molière in her biographical drama. As we have seen, those who were revisioning Molière in the nineteenth century emphasized "the relationship between genius and moral goodness" in Molière, based, most notably, on the critics' didactic readings of the plays (Albanese, 241). Sand herself, in her dedication to Alexandre Dumas, extols *"la mémoire de l'homme de bien et de génie qui fut Molière"* ("the memory of the man of goodness and genius who was Molière," *Théâtre complet,* vol. 1, 312).

It is to this *"maître des maîtres"* ("Préface" to *Molière,* 315) that Sand is drawn, and it is through his relationship with his wife that Sand explains him. This is in keeping with her continuing interest in realism: *Molière* is psychological drama, giving the audience a "backstage view" of a genius who is also a husband and a man. By giving greater weight to Armande's character, whom Sand claimed to be "a new type for the theatre," the playwright finds new ways to approach her subject.[17] She refutes parts of the legends about Molière and his wife:

Non, Molière ne fut pas l'amant de la mère de sa femme, cela est désormais acquis à l'histoire par des preuves certaines.—Non, rien ne prouve qu'il ait été même l'amant de la soeur de sa femme, de Madeleine Béjart.—Non, rien ne prouve qu'il fût l'amant de mademoiselle Duparc ou de mademoiselle Debrie.—Non, rien ne prouve que sa femme, Armande Béjart, lui ait été infidèle par les sens, tandis que tout prouve qu'elle lui a été infidèle par le coeur.—Non, Molière ne fut pas le courtisan lâche, mais l'ami fidèle de Louis XIV et de Condé.— Non, Amphitryon n'est pas et ne peut pas avoir été la réhabilitation de l'adultère du roi. ("Préface" to *Molière,* 315)

No, Molière was *not* the lover of the mother of his wife, that is now generally accepted as history on the basis of definite proof.—No, there is no proof whatsoever that he was even the lover of his wife's sister, Madeleine Béjart.—No, there is no proof that he was the lover of Mademoiselle Duparc or of Mademoiselle Debrie. No, there is no proof that his wife, Armande Béjart, was unfaithful to him in actual fact, while everything proves that she was unfaithful to him in her heart.— No, Molière was *not* a weak courtier, but the faithful friend of Louis XIV and of Condé.—*Amphitryon* is not and *cannot* have been an attempt to rehabilitate the adultery of the king.

It is not enough, however, for Sand to point out what is unproven about the Molière legend; she must add that these "facts," accepted by many, do not fit the character she sees in the plays:

> *Non, le mépris de Molière pour la calomnie n'est pas une preuve de sa culpabilité, mais de son innocence.—Non, Molière ne fut ni insolent, ni servile, ni ridicule, ni vindicatif: il fut homme de bien autant qu'homme de génie: son coeur fut le plus ardent, le plus tendre, le plus pur, le plus fidèle coeur de son époque.*

("Préface" to *Molière*, 315)

> No, Molière's contempt for slander is not proof of his guilt, but of his innocence.—No, Molière was neither insolent, nor servile, nor ridiculous, nor vindictive: he was a man of goodness as well as a man of genius: his heart was the most passionate, the most tender, the purest, the truest heart of his age.

Sand's advice: read his plays. Then realize that a man cannot be a genius every moment, that he is still simply a man ("Préface" to *Molière*, 317).

Sand has come a long way from *Le Roi attend*. In that one-act play, Molière was a figurehead who, through Sand's recovery, brought France's glory back to the people; he was little more than a device that served Sand's socialist purposes. *Le Malade imaginaire*, as part of the celebratory bill, represented Molière's canon.

Here, in *Molière*, the playwright stands for his canon. The action of the play traces the events from Molière's declaration of love for Armande to his death on the stage of the Palais Royal, approximately twelve years later (dates are never explicitly stated and Sand clearly assumed that her audience would be familiar with the Molière legend and chronology). The only Molière plays mentioned, as in *Le Roi attend*, include *Tartuffe*, *Le Misanthrope*, and *Le Malade imaginaire*. *Molière* presents the playwright's slow decline, not only from illness but from marital unhappiness: in Sand's version, Armande is not unfaithful, but she is drawn as "intelligent and ambitious, proud, flirtatious only by design, mocking, vain, dry, ungrateful. . . . Armande inspires Molière, and she destroys him" (Manifold, 75). She is a complex character; in act 2, scene 4, while looking at herself in the mirror, she says of Molière, *"je l'aime bien, et je goûte un grand plaisir à le faire enrager!"* ("I love him well, and I much enjoy making him angry," *Molière*, 364). Ten scenes later, in a trick worthy of the playwright's own dramaturgy, Molière, hiding in his "cabinet," overhears Armande's declaration of love—the irony of the trick is that Armande has staged her "spontaneous" speech for Molière's benefit: Sand's stage directions are definite.

This play, too, takes advantage of the age's theatrical possibilities: there are four carefully described settings, including Versailles and the stage of the Palais Royal immediately after a performance of *Le Malade imaginaire*. Characters appear in costumes for court masques and Molière's plays, as well as "street clothes." Sand was certainly taking advantage of the audience's interest in authenticity by giving them five acts of this historical period, including Louis XIV "*déguisé en Égyptien*" (*Molière*, 381), the Prince de la Condé (with whom Armande was rumored to have committed adultery), and actors from the Troupe du Roi. We even meet the young daughter of Molière and Armande. In addition, Sand offered spectacle throughout, although it is curiously disengaged from Molière; the first act is set in the country, and the actors of Molière's troupe arrive onstage in carriages drawn by horses, with dogs leashed. The final act opens at the Palais Royal, while the stagehands, musicians, and candle-snuffers visibly go about their post-performance business behind the action. The performances incorporated music, pieces by Lully adapted by Gounod (Manifold, 76).

Molière was performed at the Gaîté, a boulevard theater founded in 1760 best known as a house for melodrama (Hemmings, 167). The play had only twelve performances, closing on 24 May (Manifold, 77). It seems that neither the audiences of the Gaîté nor the critics knew what to make of it; the worst disappointment came from those Sand wanted to reach, "the people":

> The public of the boulevards, which I wished to instruct and treat well, the public at ten sous . . . for whom I've sacrificed the high-paying public of the Théâtre Français, took no notice of my devotion. They like murders and poisonings better than literature with style and heart.[18]

In her preface, Sand satirically lists the many contradictory comments she received from critics. To us, *Molière* seems terribly dated, weighted as it is with less-than-subtle psychological examination and that curious blend of melodrama and dramaturgical realism that marks it as a mid-nineteenth-century play. But, in 1851, Sand showed great daring by ignoring most of the excessive spectacle of melodrama that drugged mass audiences. Her attempt to draw the (for the period) delicate nuances of her hero's life, to set the man side by side with the genius, defied convention. For the second time, in a different way, she renegotiated Molière for Parisian audiences. Sand rejected the "fact" that Armande had cuck-olded Molière in explicit act, while retaining the opinion that she had been unfaithful to him in thought and feeling; thus, Molière was to be reconsidered with pity and understanding, rather than with mockery and laughter: the Sad Clown. In this way, Molière, in the eyes of the audience, began to become a man whose suffering was turned to a purpose, writing the human experience into his plays for the benefit of his audience. Again, Sand sought to enter-tain *and* educate, and again she chose Molière as her material. The optimism of the 1848 Revolution had turned to bitterness: within the year, Louis-Napoleon would stage a coup d'état and a year later declare himself Napoleon III, the new emperor.

For me, *Le Roi attend* is more interesting as a performance piece. The didactic nature of the piece is swallowed up by its theatricality and optimism; there is tremendous force in the writing that demon-strates Sand's fervor for the events of 1848. Despite its brevity, the sweep of literary history introduced by the play and the agendas for drama it demands are handled with deftness by the playwright. *Molière,* on the other hand, seems more of a reclama-tion piece, not only (and perhaps least!) for its hero but for the crushed ideals of the Revolution and for Sand as the muse of the people; this reclamation goes sour.

Born Aurore Dupin and married into the Dudevant name, our female author took "George Sand" as a pen name and public per-sona in 1832. Maurois's biography shows the change simply: one letter, to Emile Regnault, is signed Aurore Dudevant, while the next noted by Maurois is by George Sand (Maurois, 156, 161). The name "George Sand" signaled her independence, much like the men's clothes she found so comfortable. It was also a name for a new persona unconnected to those of her past, a way of distancing her family from her unorthodox and notorious new life. Her upper-class mother-in-law refused to allow the Dudevant name to appear on the title page of a published novel. Jean-Baptiste Poquelin took the stage name "Molière" sometime in the 1640s when he deserted his middle-class family and their expectations and joined an acting troupe; in the period it was usually considered polite to distance one's respectable relatives from the stage's notoriety, and to ac-knowledge oneself an outcast from regular folk. "Molière," as well as "George Sand," served both these purposes.

In *Le Roi attend,* Sand sought a hero for the people's theater she envisioned growing out of but also supporting the politics of February 1848. Three years later, she was drawn to the story of a playwright struggling to balance his human existence and his great gift, and wrote *Molière.* This time her agenda was less overtly political but still revolved around her interest in man's location within his society; it is, however, decidedly less optimistic a vision. If Sand still looked to Molière as a spiritual father for France's literary history, she presents him killed in the final act by wife and enemies. The play's final event is Molière lowering himself into a chair, surrounded by his actors, his maid, his wife, and Condé and giving the final, poignant line, *"Mon Dieu! qu'un homme souffre avant de pouvoir mourir!"* ("My God! How much a man must suffer before he is allowed to die," *Molière,* 454): this is a rather different Molière from the figure at the end of *Le Roi attend,* Sand's vigorous theatrical spirit welcoming *"le peuple"* to the theater, a place of reclamation and rejuvenation.

By the end of the nineteenth century, Molière had become a cottage industry for France, in the same way Shakespeare had for England and English-speaking people. He was "the epitome of France's cultural heritage" (Albanese, 245). Sand was instrumental in beginning this reclamation and in bringing Molière back to his public; despite the failure of the immediate politics, Sand was in step with the sentiments of her fellow critics and writers in selecting Molière for revisioning. That her drama brought Molière forcefully, immediately, and actively to audiences in living form separated her from these others: rather than cater to a literary or educated elite, Sand saw the need to make Molière a poet of the people, a vital part of their living heritage, rather than a dusty figurehead of morality. In this, she succeeded.

NOTES TO "AURORE DUPIN DUDEVANT AND JEAN-BAPTISTE POQUELIN: GEORGE SAND RECONSTRUCTS MOLIÈRE"

1. "Préface," *Théâtre complet de George Sand* (Paris: Michel Lévy Frères, 1877) 1:1. All translations from the French are mine.
2. Gay Manifold, *George Sand's Theatre Career* (Ann Arbor, MI: UMI Research Press, 1985), 155. Appendix A lists not only the premiere dates and titles, but also the names of the Parisian theaters at which Sand's plays were produced. This does not include the plays Sand wrote which were produced solely at Nohant, her country home.
3. Ralph Albanese, Jr., "The Molière Myth in Nineteenth-Century France," in *Pre-Text Text Context,* ed. Robert L. Mitchell (Columbus: Ohio State University Press, 1980), 241.
4. After 1667; before that, the troupe's official name was the Troupe de Monsieur, for Louis's brother Philippe d'Orléans.

5. Louis also moved the Troupe out of the space in 1673, only months after Molière's death, and forced it to merge with the actors from one failing theater and then another, forming the Comédie Française.

6. George Sand, "Préface" to Molière, in Théâtre complet de George Sand, 1 : 320.

7. George Sand, "Préface," Théâtre complet de George Sand, 1 : 3.

8. Albanese, 241. These virtues include, as Albanese puts it, a lack of originality, "prudence as a cardinal virtue," and the bondage of the golden mean. Sand has little interest in any of these for her character of Molière.

9. Manifold, 37. The date given in Sand's published manuscript was 9 April 1848; there is no explanation of the discrepancy.

10. Le Roi attend, in Théâtre complet de George Sand, 1 : 125. Manifold dates the play's premiere as 6 April (37).

11. In The French Stage in the Nineteenth Century (Metuchen: Scarecrow Press, 1972), Marvin Carlson notes that this renaming of the theaters drew upon names previously established by the 1789 Revolution and marked a return to revolutionary ideals (101).

12. Interestingly, according to Sand's script, only six of the shades speak to Molière: "Eschyle," "Sophocle," "Euripide," "Shakspeare," "Voltaire," and "Beaumarchais." In addition, "Voltaire" leads "Jean-Jacques Rousseau" by the hand, but "Rousseau"—one of Sand's heroes—is silent.

13. André Maurois, The Life of George Sand (New York: Penguin, 1978), 404 (italics added).

14. Naomi Schor, George Sand and Idealism (New York: Columbia University Press, 1993), 136. Schor's book does not discuss Sand's drama; instead, it concentrates on the novels and nonfiction.

15. F.W.J. Hemmings, Theatre and State in France, 1760–1905 (Cambridge: Cambridge University Press, 1994), xi.

16. At the time of this writing, two new biographies of Molière are being written.

17. Manifold, 75. Manifold derives this from Sand's correspondence, from a letter to Pierre Bocage of 1851 (vol. 10, 108–9).

18. Manifold, 78. Quoted from Sand's correspondence to Charles Poncy, 6 June 1851.

Venetian Mirrors: Barrett or Browning as the Artist?

ROSELLA MAMOLI ZORZI

Many authors have been fascinated by other writers to the point of turning them into characters in their works. But how many women writers are there who have similarly caught hold of an author's imagination, and who have been turned into characters? The most obvious explanation for this state of relative neglect would appear to be one of identity: the male author finds himself echoed, or finds a mirror, or a guide and exemplum, in another male writer, according to traditional patriarchal rules. But what about women authors? Could they not find echoes or mirrors or exempla in women authors? From a historical perspective, it might be expected that as women and women writers become more self-confident, more works in this parallel tradition of the woman author as character will be produced.

Against the background of this situation involving the choice of male and female authors as characters, the celebrated couple of the Brownings, Robert and Elizabeth Barrett, is a case in point. The Brownings are a famous couple not only for their poetry, but also for their romantic love story: the story of a young Victorian woman who chose to be an invalid, keeping to her own room, spending her time reading and writing poetry in order to escape the patriarchal imposition of social and familial rules until she was "saved" by a man. It was a romantic story, because, as is well known, Elizabeth eloped to Italy with Robert Browning in 1846, starting a new life. Although she continued to read and write, Elizabeth was no longer an invalid; her health even allowed her to experience motherhood.

In spite of the fact that both Brownings were famous poets, they have not been treated alike in later fictional accounts of their lives. The figure of Elizabeth, certainly the better known of the two poets at least during her lifetime, has rarely become a character *as a poet*. Where one finds her as a character, she is the protagonist of the famous elopement: evidently, it is the love story that makes her interesting, not her poetic genius.

The neglect of Elizabeth's status as a poet may be illustrated with reference to Carola Lenanton's *Miss Barrett's Elopement* (1929), and even to the famous play by Rudolf Besier, *The Barretts of Wimpole Street* (1930).[1] Both of these very different works can be seen as biographical fictions using authors as characters but concentrating solely on the love story. Moreover, in Besier's play, the portrait of an egocentric, cruel father is central, not the single female author as character. There is no lack of biographies of Elizabeth and Robert; but there are few if any actual stories, novels, or poems in which it is Elizabeth who becomes the central character in her capacity as an author.

With Elizabeth's husband Robert, in contrast, it is almost invariably his status as an artist that is stressed. Stories, poems, and novels about him are often set in Italy, and in particular in Venice, where he died. Venice, traditionally represented as the city of art and death, almost automatically evokes speculation about the relationship between poetry and (im)mortality.

A rare exception to the apparent rule is Elizabeth's portrayal as a writer in Virginia Woolf's *Flush* (1933). Ironically, of course, in Woolf's prose work, it is Elizabeth's spaniel, the eponymous Flush, who commands the main narrative focus. Elizabeth is there to allow the author to play out in the text the theme she is interested in—being the contrast between instinct and rationality, between animal expression and human expression, physical expression lacking words and verbal expression—but also the possible identity of animal instinct and what of animal instinct there is in the human being, as rational and controlled as the latter may be.

At the beginning of this imaginary biography, Flush and Elizabeth are shown facing each other:

> Each was surprised. Heavy curls hung down on either side of Miss Barrett's face; large bright eyes shone out; a large mouth smiled. Heavy ears hung down on either side of Flush's face; his eyes, too, were large and bright: his mouth was wide. There was a likeness between them. As they gazed at each other each felt: Here am I—and then each felt: But how different! Hers was the pale worn face of an invalid, cut off from air, light, freedom. His was the warm ruddy face of a young animal; instinct with health and energy. Broken asunder, yet made in the same mould, could it be that each completed what was dormant in the other? She might have been—all that; and he—But no. Between

them lay the widest gulf that can separate one being from another. She spoke. He was dumb. She was woman; he was dog.[2]

The chasm opening because of lack of words seems unbridgeable. However, when Elizabeth doubts the power of words ("do words say everything? Can words say anything?" 37), the gap between the rational and verbal being and the wordless animal is bridged, if only for an instant:

> She was lying, thinking; she had forgotten Flush altogether, and her thoughts were so sad that the tears fell upon the pillow. Then suddenly a hairy head was pressed against her; large bright eyes shone in hers; and she started. Was it Flush, or was it Pan? Was she no longer an invalid in Wimpole Street, but a Greek nymph in some dim grove in Arcady? And did the bearded god himself press his lips to hers? For a moment she was transformed; she was a nymph and Flush was Pan. (38)

Communication can exist on levels different from the rational and verbal ones, in a moment of sensual-sexual encounter. Words would, in fact, destroy communication. The passage continues: "But suppose Flush had been able to speak—would he not have said something sensible about the potato disease in Ireland?"

Of course, Woolf was interested in Elizabeth Barrett because she was a poet, the epitome of humans using words and language. But Barrett is *not* the main focus; as we have seen, what really interested Woolf in this novel was the relationship between the rational being and the instinctual being. Elizabeth, therefore, is in this context only the required counterpart to Flush, not the protagonist.

Robert Browning, in turn, is also a character in Woolf's novel. He is less important than Elizabeth, however, since the dog belongs to *Elizabeth*. Above all, Robert represents a rival for Flush, at least at the beginning of his relationship with Elizabeth. He is accepted by Flush only when Elizabeth's devotion to the spaniel causes her to make her own decisions, contrary to Robert's advice.[3] In spite of the literary quality of the novel, and of Woolf's feminist stand in many of her essays, ironically not even she chose the great poet Elizabeth Barrett as her main character in this work.

Part of *Flush* is set in Florence, where the Brownings lived permanently after their flight to Italy. Michael Didbin's novel entitled *A Rich Full Death* (1986) is completely set in Florence. Once again, Elizabeth is hardly a protagonist. She is recognized as the greater of the two poets by the narrator of the novel ("To be permitted to worship at the feet of the poetess of the age is a favor eagerly sought after by all who live in or pass through Florence"), but the figure who is central to this literary thriller is Robert.[4] Robert Browning is the main interest of the (most unreliable) male narrator, Mr. Booth, who is telling a story of multiple murders that look like accidents. Suspicion falls on the character named Robert Browning, who eventually is cleared of any guilt. The narrator of the novel, which takes the form of letters to a friend, finally presents himself as the murderer. Yet the reader is left in doubt: maybe Mr. Booth is only a compulsive writer and a creator of lies, vying with the creativity of the poet. Summarizing and explaining his murders, the narrator compares himself to Browning when he exclaims: "But how much more a poet, how much greater an artist, am I! The bold conception, the reach, the range—these are mine, and mine alone" (200–1).

What seems to interest the author of *A Rich Full Death* most is the contradictory personality of Robert Browning, a great poet who has an "accursed shopkeeper's fascination with petty facts and dreary details" (200). It is Browning's interest in "dreary details" that allows him to find out the (narrator's) truth about the murders. This double personality ascribed to Browning seems to make him an interesting character; his interest in the "dreary details" of life is linked to his interest and rendering of dreary details in poetry, as—according to the narrator—in *Porphyria's Lover* (96–97). The poet is interested in morbid subjects, but he leads a normal life. It is the same discrepancy between Browning's powerful and disquieting poetry and his apparently inexhaustible social life that had fascinated Henry James, who apparently based his short story, "The Private Life" (1892), on this dichotomy.[5]

Whereas most fictional accounts of Elizabeth Barrett's life take her romantic elopement as the central event of her life, with her husband Robert Browning it is his last days in Venice, where he died in 1889, that form the core of the myth that has been created around him. To illustrate this, I will now proceed with two contemporary works that focus on Browning's passing away in that most hackneyed, if poetic, of cities. They are Richard Howard's poem "Venetian Interior, 1889," and Jane Urquhart's short story, "The Death of Robert Browning."

The American poet Richard Howard wrote a collection of dramatic monologues that, in their very form, are a homage to Browning, the creator and practitioner of this form. As a setting for his poem, "Venetian Interior, 1889," Howard uses the huge, luxurious Palazzo Rezzonico, which the Brownings' son, Pen, a mediocre painter and sculptor, had bought with his wife Fannie's money. The scene of Howard's poem is the "Venetian interior" of the palace, where Pen is painting a Dryope, looking at a naked model partially draped in a silvery material and embraced by a python. Pen is shown making conversation with Fanny and Robert, who are playing at draughts:

> I had the Jew come by
> with this brocaded velvet yesterday—
> I bargained some old clothes against it, Fan,
> so you needn't ask how much it cost in dollars.[6]

After the description of the trio making conversation basically about money, while Pen is painting, and the description of the "sumptuous junk" collected by Pen in the Rezzonico, the poem soars off in a series of stanzas on death:

> *Dryope* followed Dryope underground,
> the girl carried off by a chill and buried
> at San Michele, the great daub interred
> in the cellars of the Metropolitan . . .
> "Dear dead women, with such hair, too,"
> we quote, and notice that hair is the first
> of ourselves to decay before—last after—death.
>
> In a year Robert Browning was dead, immortal . . . (65)

The destiny of the painting ("Dryope") to be buried in the subsoil of a great museum, of the young and beautiful model, buried in the Venice cemetery ("San Michele"), the quotation of the famous line from the last stanza of Browning's "A Toccata of Galuppi's," and finally the linking of that line to a most unpoetical observation on hair—all serve to introduce the theme of Browning's own death.[7]

The twin themes of decay and death had been announced in the third stanza of the poem apropos the great *palazzo:*

> the ripened fruit of centuries,
> rat- and roach-infested, peeling, rank,
> withers with each tide that rots the piles.
> ("Venetian Interior, 1889," 62)

The metaphor of the ripe, and possibly overripe, fruit for the *palazzo,* undermined at the very basis of its structure with the piles rotting, links the destiny of destruction and death of works of art, like the *palazzo* (built by the famous architects Longhena and Massari), or would-be art (Pen's painting is a "daub") and people (the girl, the women of the "Toccata," the poet) to one of the most persistent representations of Venice as the city of decay and death.

Presenting Venice as the city of decay and death, it may be argued, is stereotypical rather than original. Arguably, Thomas Mann's *Death in Venice* (1912) is the best-known novella of the present century linking the destiny of the artist to his death in the city of art. But one could also think of earlier works such as Maurice Barrès's *Amori et dolori sacrum: La mort de Venise* (1909), a key text of the Decadence, where the city of art becomes the ideal setting for the detailed description of corruption and decay, or of D'Annunzio's *Il fuoco* (1911). The representation of Venice as the city of decayed liberty (Byron), or of decay and madness (Shelley), adds multiple layers of new negative qualifications to the Venice of the Protestant tradition, the beautiful, alluring and dangerous city of love and sex.[8] Richard Howard's Browning poem follows this type of representation in toto, as the final lines of the poem indicate:

> Darkness slides over the waters—oil sludge
> spreading under, till even Venice dies,
> immortally immerded.
>
> ("Venetian Interior, 1889," 66)

One must not be led astray by the use of the modern "oil," or by the vulgar "immerded"; what prevails is the image of slimy death. Darkness and death are man's destiny but perhaps not the destiny of the poet: Browning was "dead" but at the same time "immortal," because, like every artist, he had expressed, through poetry, whatever "illumination"—in Howard's words—could come in the darkness that envelops the human being. "Dead" as a person but "immortal" as a poet: because of this immortality, the contemporary poet looks into the dark mirror of the Venice canals, symbols of the darkness of human life, but also of the city of art:

> We realize our task.
> It is to print earth so deep in memory
> that a meaning reaches the surface. Nothing but
> darkness abides, darkness demanding not
> illumination—not from the likes of us—
> but only that we yield. And we yield.
>
> ("Venetian Interior, 1889," 66)

Because of the "illumination" that poetry yields, the dark mirror becomes a shining one, where the present-day poet sees the figure of his predecessor, the poet Robert Browning.

A similar constellation involving the city of Venice and the poets Browning and Shelley underlies the structure of the story by the Canadian author, Jane Urquhart, entitled "The Death of Robert Browning" (1987). Again, the contemporary author, though herself a woman, has chosen Robert Browning and his last days in Venice as the central theme. The third-person prose narrative introduces this theme right from the beginning of the story: "In December of 1889, as he was returning by gondola from the general vicinity of Palazzo Manzoni, it occurred to Robert Browning that he was more than likely going to die soon."[9] It is not a question of age or illness: Browning sees his "health shining vigorously" even in the "dark mirror" of the canal waters (40). Rather, it is a question of symbols, carrying "personal messages" (40). After this initial premonition of death, the reader is offered Browning's musings after his return to the Rezzonico and during his random walk toward the northern part of the city, Fondamente Nuove, but, above all, Browning's obsessive memory of Shelley's poetry and death. The story ends with Browning's death.

After his return to the Rezzonico by gondola, the poet is presented in the luxurious setting of the *palazzo*. Lying on the "magnificently carved bed" in his room, he is haunted by the conventionality of his past life, opposed to the visions of romantic and tragic dealings of the characters in his poetry. By an association of ideas, he comes to think of copulation:

> Copulation. What sad dirge-like associations the word dredged up from the poet's unconscious. All those Italians: those minstrels, dukes, princes, artists, and questionable monks whose voices had droned through Browning's pen over the years. (43)

Urquhart interprets Browning's musings in the light of her knowledge of Browning's poetry and of his early love for Shelley's poetry, quoting fragments from this, as remembered by Browning.

The haunting presence of Shelley in Browning's musings is justified by the latter's poem, *Pauline, A Fragment of a Confession* (1832), the first poem he ever published. It is in this poem that the young poet apostrophized Shelley, the "Suntreader," asking him to be close to him, especially in the moment of death:

> Thou must be ever with me, most in gloom
> If such must come, but chiefly when I die,

> For I seem, dying, as one going in the dark
> To fight a giant.
>
> (Browning, *The Poems*, I, 33)

Jane Urquhart bases the plot of her story precisely on this invocation. The lines desultorily remembered by Browning are from Shelley's *Prometheus Unbound, Lines Written Among the Euganean Hills*, and *Julian and Maddalo*. The imagery of water—so important in the beginning of *Lines Written Among the Euganean Hills*—and the imagery of the city of decay (*Julian and Maddalo*) merge with the imagery of Shelley's death by water and with the actual setting of Browning's last days, the city of water, Venice. Browning's final vision of Shelley is that of the drowned poet drifting in water:

> In complete silence the young man swam through the rooms of Palazzo Manzoni, slipping up and down the staircase, gliding down halls, in and out of fireplaces: he appeared briefly in mirrors. He drifted past balconies . . . ("The Death of Robert Browning," 51)

Finally, the dismembered body disappears: "The drowned man's body separated into parts and moved slowly out of Browning's mind" (52). In this vision *au ralenti,* in perfect silence, Shelley seems to impose his drifting presence in the palace Browning wanted to own, Palazzo Manzoni, then disappears from Browning's vision only to let another water image surface, that of Browning's "last journey by water," to the island of the cemetery.

The story of Browning's musings and wanderings in the city includes an episode where he seems to get lost in the maze of the streets, that may be an oblique reference to *Death in Venice,* and to Henry James's *Aspern Papers,* if taken together with the reference to Verrocchio's equestrian monument to Colleoni. In Jane Urquhart's story, Colleoni's statue seems to be a favorite of Browning's.

What Browning's last meditations and random memories seem to suggest is the close kinship with the poet who preceded him, in an "anxiety of influence" that resulted in a constant effort to achieve the perfection of expression of Shelley's poetry. This is the challenge of the poet to the world, the same as Prometheus's, an impossible but fiery challenge against death, corruption, and oblivion.

Urquhart's choice of Venice allows her to superimpose images of water and death: Shelley's death by water off Lerici, the tradition of Venice as the city of decay and death:

> Sepulchres where human forms
> Like pollution nourished worms
> To the corpse of greatness cling
> Murdered and now mouldering . . .

These lines, taken from *Lines Written Among the Euganean Hills,* but isolated from the rest of the passage where freedom is invoked, only point to decay and corruption, and to the prevalent tradition in the representation of Venice.[10] Urquhart seems to continue this tradition:

> Statues appeared to leak and ooze damp soot, window-glass was fogged with moisture, steps that led him over canals were slippery, covered with an unhealthy slime . . . now even small roof gardens seemed to grow as if in stagnant water, winter chrysanthemums emitting a putrid odour, which spoke less of blossom than decay. ("Death of Robert Browning," 47)

To this tradition of the representation of Venice, the (real) death of Browning in the city added a further hue of death: but the city of death is also the city of art, the city of poetry, and the city of poets. Interestingly, the fictional Browning in Urquhart's short story recalls Shelley's "Ozymandias" ("Death of Robert Browning," 46). In this famous sonnet, the king of kings addresses the following command to posterity: "Look on my works, ye mighty and despair!" In fact, however, "Nothing beside remains" (Shelley, 303). Naturally, Shelley's poem, inspired by the (reported report of the) ravages of what was once a commanding statue, is heavily ironic. Life is short, Shelley suggests, and so is art. Still, somehow, Urquhart's "Death of Robert Browning" suggests that matters may well be different when the contemporary author evokes the ghosts of the poets who lived, in the medium fittest to celebrate once more the power of writing.

In fiction that features authors as characters, the fates of Elizabeth Barrett and Robert Browning are as different as they could be. Robert has ensured his immortality by dying in Venice, the city of death and art.

NOTES TO "VENETIAN MIRRORS: BARRETT OR BROWNING AS THE ARTIST?"

1. See Besier, *The Barretts of Wimpole Street,* in *Sixteen Famous British Plays,* compiled by Bennett A. Cerf and Van H. Cartmell (New York: Modern Library, 1942).

2. Woolf, *Flush: A Biography* (1933; repr. London: Hogarth Press, 1983), 23–24.

3. This concerns Elizabeth's decision (against Robert's advice) to go look for Flush, who has been stolen by thieves who want a ransom for the dog.

4. Didbin, *A Rich Full Death* (London: Faber & Faber, 1986), 14.

5. For "The Private Life," see *The Complete Tales of Henry James,* ed. Leon Edel (London: Rupert Hart-Davis, 1963). The name of the poet does not appear in the story, but on August 3, 1891, James wrote down the idea for this tale in his notebook as follows: "*The Private Life*—the idea of rolling into one story the little conceit of the private identity of a personage suggested by F. L., and that of a personage suggested by R. B." As explained in the note, "F. L." was the painter and president of the Royal Academy, Sir Frederic Leighton, while "R. B." was Robert Browning. See *The Complete Notebooks of Henry James,* ed. Leon Edel and Lyall H. Powers (Oxford: Oxford University Press, 1987), 60.

6. Howard, "Venetian Interior, 1889," in *Fellow Feelings* (New York: Atheneum, 1976), 63.

7. Robert Browning, *The Poems,* ed. John Pettigrew and Thomas J. Collins, 2 vols. (Harmondsworth: Penguin Books, 1981), 1, 552.

8. Venice is the city of decayed liberty in Lord Byron's *Ode on Venice* and the fourth canto of *Childe Harold's Pilgrimage.* Byron's mock-heroic *Beppo,* with its gently ironic eighteenth-century tone, was less popular. For Shelley and Venice, see his *Julian and Maddalo.*

9. Jane Urquhart, "The Death of Robert Browning," in *Storm Glass* (Erin, Ontario: Porcupine's Quill, 1987), 40. Palazzo Manzoni was the palace on the Grand Canal that Browning wanted to buy from Count Montecuccoli. The poet was advised not to buy it, and the preliminary agreement was interrupted. In the meantime Pen, Browning's son, bought the huge Palazzo Rezzonico.

10. Urquhart, "The Death of Robert Browning," 48. See also, P. B. Shelley, *The Poetical Works of Percy Bysshe Shelley* (London: Ward, Lock, & Melbourne, n.d.), 323.

Joyce the Postmodern: Shakespeare as Character in *Ulysses*

LOIS FEUER

Just as James Joyce reconfigured narrative expectations in *A Portrait of the Artist as a Young Man* by, for example, rendering on its first page not the more predictable adult character's account of his childhood memories but the fragmented memories themselves as present experience, so, in *Ulysses,* he expands our understanding of what constitutes a character in a novel in a variety of ways. He gives us such an array of narrative voices that the narrators themselves become several characters, shifting from section to section. Presented as well with two protagonists, half a dozen significant cast members, and scores of minor figures in walk-on parts, the reader resorts to indices and guides to keep them straight. Joyce takes the most radical step in *Finnegans Wake* as human figure morphs into river; in *Ulysses,* he foreshadows this move by having one of the novel's most significant figures, Shakespeare, appear in the flesh, as it were, for only a few seconds in the Circe chapter, where Shakespeare's features are momentarily superimposed on those of Bloom and Stephen as they gaze into Bella Cohen's mirror:

> *Stephen and Bloom gaze in the mirror. The face of William Shakespeare, beardless, appears there, rigid in facial paralysis, crowned by the reflection of the reindeer antlered hatrack in the hall.*[1]

What are we to make of a "character" who appears in only a few sentences of a 650-page novel: can we find a vocabulary that expresses the status of this figure without making nonsense of what we mean by "character"? I will argue that, if we are willing to grant

167

"character" status, however problematic, to the figure of Shakespeare in the novel, we are thereby enabled to talk about the ways
in which Joyce uses this figure as a means of traditional characterization, as an anticipation of twentieth-century literary theory, as
an emblematic figure for the author of the novel himself, and as a
means of addressing the relationship of life to art, one of *Ulysses'*
primary themes.

Readers of *Ulysses* have long been aware of the novel's extensive
use of Shakespeare; as William Schutte demonstrated in 1957, hundreds of allusions to Shakespeare's plays, and quotations, oblique
or otherwise, permeate the text.[2] Most obviously, in the library
scene where Stephen expounds his theory of *Hamlet,* but also on
virtually every page, Joyce creates an overpowering presence for
his literary predecessor. Beyond allusion, quotation, and echo, the
words of characters or narrator keep Shakespeare and his works
continually present to the reader. When, for example, Professor
MacHugh murmurs "The ghost walks" in anticipation of payday
at the *Evening Telegraph,* he is using theatrical slang, but not so
coincidentally, the phrase reminds us of the Ghost in *Hamlet* and
may even derive from actors' references to it.[3] One could argue
that there are more overt or oblique references to Shakespeare
and his works than to the *Odyssey,* long established as central to
the novel's theme and structure. Schutte finds, in the library scene
alone, Stephen using "no fewer than ninety direct quotations or
adaptations of quotations from Shakespeare's works" (66).

Of course, references alone, however plentiful, do not a character make. More to the point is Stephen's evocation of the figure of
Shakespeare in the library scene. As Stephen sets the scene for
his theory of the relation of life to art, of which *Hamlet* is his
example, he works in "local color" by describing Shakespeare in
the present tense:

> A player comes on under the shadow, made up in the castoff mail of a
> court buck, a wellset man with a bass voice. It is the ghost, the king,
> a king and no king, and the player is Shakespeare who has studied
> *Hamlet* all the years of his life. . . . He speaks the words to Burbage,
> the young player who stands before him beyond the rack of cere-
> cloth. . . . (9.164–69)

As Stephen summons Shakespeare before his auditors' eyes (and
ours), the playwright is conjured up as a character might be summoned in a script, understood to be represented on stage. This
forms a present-tense narrative *within* Joyce's present-tense narra-

tive of Stephen in the library, and has the same ontological status. Shakespeare, constantly evoked by Stephen, by Bloom, by other characters, and by the narrative voices, is as present in our imaginations as, say, May Dedalus, herself "appearing" only in the Circe episode but pervading the novel through Stephen's constant imagining of her, or as Blazes Boylan, seen only in intermittent glimpses but saturating Bloom's consciousness and ours.

Consider the analogy from *Hamlet* itself. There, we have characters who themselves play characters: the actor greeted warmly by Hamlet becomes the Player King (portraying a semblance of the elder Hamlet), and both were represented on stage by a "real" actor contemporary with the "real" author of the play. Has the Player King any more or any less claim to being a "character" in the play than, say, Osric? Stephen and his creation Shakespeare are both the fictive creations of James Joyce, as are the hundreds of others, historical and otherwise, who populate *Ulysses.* Joyce makes all of them—invented and historical, biographical, autobiographical and imagined—serve his artistic purposes.

Character as construct has become problematized in contemporary criticism; the nineteenth-century view of fictive characters as beings possessing psychological coherence and individuality has been replaced by, in Jonathan Culler's words, "nodes in the verbal structure of the work, whose identity is relatively precarious."[4] Joyce has it both ways: his characters possess the precariousness of the postmodern's self-conscious construct, "wholly constituted," as Roland Barthes has it, by their semantic features; as well as the robustness of the illusorily rounded figure with a past and a future extending beyond the novel's present.[5]

Joyce renders the constructed quality of character transparent by insisting on its multi-facetedness; like the living persons of our acquaintance, Joyce's characters are seen from a multitude of perspectives. This multiplicity of vision (represented in the novel by Bloom's musings on *parallax,* the viewing of an object from binocular perspectives) exists simultaneously with the novel's insistence that human beings have "mystery" at their hearts which the onlooker cannot pluck out: "The objective world and the soul of a character are for Joyce at once knowable from a thousand perspectives and eternally mysterious, noumenous."[6] Character in Joyce is indeterminate in two senses, ultimately unknowable as well as seen from multiple points of view. The many angles from which Shakespeare is seen in *Ulysses*—the many consciousnesses through which his presence is filtered—are part of his significance as a character, and that significance far outweighs the brevity of his actual "appearance" in the novel.

Let me review briefly the ways in which the figure of Shakespeare characterizes both Bloom and Stephen in *Ulysses*. The literal level of Stephen's theory, that *Hamlet* may be read as a parable of Shakespeare's life, with Shakespeare as the cuckolded King Hamlet, is, in the first instance, an authorial cross-reference to Stephen's fellow character Leopold Bloom, betrayed by his wife with Blazes Boylan a few hours after the library scene takes place in the novel. Stephen envisions an isolated Shakespeare, wounded in his soul by Anne Hathaway's seduction and betrayal of him, with obvious affinities to the lonely Bloom, figure of scorn, painfully aware all day of Molly's appointment with Boylan. The references to Shakespeare characterize Bloom, universalizing his predicament while undercutting its significance: Bloom's comic and pathetic dodging of encounters with Boylan, for instance, contrasts strongly with the more elevated spirit of melancholy that Stephen attributes to Shakespeare.

The theory also characterizes Stephen. To begin with, his myriad allusions to Shakespeare's works, as well as the citations from dozens of other authors, demonstrating a detailed knowledge of the state of Shakespeare scholarship in 1904, give independent "evidence" of Stephen's qualifications as a scholar.

In addition, Stephen has created a Shakespeare with strong affinities to his vision of himself as isolated artist: "As Stephen [sic] read his Lee or his Brandes, it must have occurred to him that Shakespeare had used the three weapons which he himself set down as proper to the arsenal of the artist: silence, cunning and exile."[7] The theory further characterizes Stephen in its very extravagance. Joyce has him distort his evidence, instructing himself: "don't tell them he was nine years old when it [the firedrake he describes Shakespeare as seeing as he walked home from seeing Anne Hathaway] was quenched" (9.936). Stephen does not tell his auditors either that Shakespeare's brothers Richard and Edmund, his supposed cuckolders, were ten and sixteen years younger than Shakespeare and thus not likely to have been the older Anne's lovers. He instead piles up a welter of allusions to Shakespeare, his plays, his contemporaries and critics, "overwhelm[ing] his listeners with the quantity of material he lavishes on them and with the virtuosity of the performance itself so that they will have no time to weigh the merits of what he is saying" (Schutte, 59).

These auditors, too, are characterized by their responses to Stephen and his theory. They interrupt like Eglinton, leave abruptly

as AE does, make irrelevant objections as does Best, and largely
miss the point, in often hilarious parody-by-anticipation of the response of Joyce's Irish readers to *his* work. Stephen's Shakespeare
is as doomed to misunderstanding as Joyce's Stephen.

Thematically functional as well, the theory itself, focusing on
sonship and paternity, parallels the web of relationships so central
to *Ulysses*. Stephen presents us with a Shakespeare re-creating his
dead son in the living Prince of Denmark. On the narrative level
of the novel, the fatherless and sonless Bloom paternally protects
a Stephen alienated from his own wastrel father, saving his money
in the brothel and pulling him away from a fight with the British
soldiers, taking him home for cocoa and offering him a bed for the
night. On a more metaphorical level, "father" and "son" can be
understood as "phases of the self," in Maddox's phrase, different
stages of growth in the same man (107). So the father is himself
his own son, creating himself out of the experiences of his life and
his response to them. "The father is he who has passed through
experience, whose beaver is up (*Ulysses,* 197), who is now out of
the fray. He can now turn round upon his experience, see it steadily
and whole as from a great height, and write the play of it."[8] And
"the play of it" is exactly what Stephen *does* write, summoning
up the historical character Shakespeare, acting in his own drama.
Stephen's evocation of Shakespeare as Hamlet *père* and *fils* is one
of Joyce's most significant renderings of this theme.

Joyce uses Stephen's construction of Shakespeare's life as a
commentary on the late-nineteenth-century taste for biographical
criticism. Of the critics referred to in the library scene, and those
employed most heavily by Stephen, many make the kind of facile
equation of life and art—far less nuanced than Stephen's offering—
memorably parodied by C. J. Sisson in *The Mythical Sorrows of
Shakespeare*.[9] In Dowden's rendering, for example, Shakespeare's
career is divided into periods, each controlled by a dominant emotion; thus he is "in the depths" when writing tragedy, or "on the
heights" when writing comedy.[10]

More striking is Joyce's anticipation, in Stephen's discussion, of
several of the directions literary theory was to take in the twentieth
century. Derrida puts this anticipation in characteristically para-
doxical fashion by claiming of Joyce: "He's read us all, and pillaged
us, that guy." Further, Derrida claims that Richard Ellmann "has
quoted many other writers who confess to the malaise of being
written in advance by Joyce's texts."[11] And no wonder: *Ulysses* is
a deconstructionist's dream, providing on every page ample evidence of its capacity for subverting its own characters, themes,

and prose. Other modern theory, too, is foreshadowed in the novel. Least surprising perhaps, is Joyce's anticipation of psychoanalytic criticism, the "new Viennese school" mentioned by Stephen in passing (9.780). Creation as therapy, the artist's production of art being a concomitant of his neuroses, is glanced at in Stephen's description of the retired Shakespeare returning to Stratford: "He goes back, weary of the creation he has piled up to hide him from himself" (9.474–75).

The variety of Shakespeares envisioned by the characters of *Ulysses* and the authors to whom they allude anticipate a deconstructionist universe in which not only character but authorship is indeterminate. "Bleibtreu believes Shakespeare was the Duke of Rutland, Father Butt holds he was a Catholic, Stephen 'proves' him a Jew, the Germans see him as 'the champion French polisher of Italian scandals,' Greene thought him a deathsman of the soul, Chettle felt he was upright in dealing, Goethe considered him a hesitating soul, and AE insists that it does not matter who or what he was. The man behind the plays is so elusive that, as Lyster says, 'everyone can find his own.'"[12]

This infinitely various, indeterminate Shakespeare—Will in overplus, as the sonnet has it—is matched in *Ulysses* by a text itself indeterminate in more than one way. The many reprintings, lists of errata, and the recent new edition of *Ulysses* point to the difficulties of locating a definitive, authoritative text. The vagaries of its printing history, and Joyce's continuous emendations of fair copy, typescripts, and page proofs have all contributed to the difficulty of knowing or reproducing its author's intentions, themselves changing over time.[13] Perhaps not entirely coincidentally, *Hamlet* and the *Odyssey* share with *Ulysses* the difficulty of establishing an authoritative text. They are, as Fritz Senn points out, texts that are *about* the difficulty of bringing order out of disorder. The novel is indeterminate in another sense: *Ulysses* changes under the experience of rereading, different elements surfacing more prominently, depending on the experience of the reader in the interim. This is, of course, true of all texts to some extent, as is the related point that things occurring later in the book explain, shed light on, earlier phrases and events; but, in *Ulysses,* this fact of the reader's experience is "not just described but integrated, acted out," with the reader actively engaged in seeking contextual meaning, with that context continually shifting (Senn, 109 and 115). Each chapter forces us to begin anew, insisting on its own narrative voice and stylistic epistemology. Like a New Historicist commentary, Joyce's versions of Shakespeare make us acutely aware of the impossibility of reconstructing the past, and of the subjectivity of the constructor.[14] The deadpan list of Molly's lovers in the Ithaca episode, twenty-five persons long and extending indefinitely into the future ("to nolast term") containing as it does the improbabilities of the Lord Mayor of Dublin and not one but two priests, makes clear the impossibility of determining even the most straightforward "facts" (17.2133–42).

Like a dutiful New Historicist document, Joyce's novel reveals its temporal and social contexts abundantly. Although its Irishness is often noted, in topics ranging from Celtic folklore to contemporary politics, perhaps its most audaciously Irish statement is its appropriation of the most English of cultural heroes for Irish literature.[15] Shakespeare and his works are subsumed into this Irish epic, the English author identified with the Irish Stephen, the Jewish-Irish Bloom and even more, the self-exiled Irishman Joyce himself. One Patrick W. Shakespeare is among the Irish heroes listed by the narrator in the Cyclops episode (12.190–91). Joyce has given this figure the first name and initial of Patrick W. Joyce, an Irish scholar who shared his own last name. Thus the mythical Shakespeare becomes as Irish as the name Patrick and the identification with Joyce can make him, in Joyce's appropriation of the quintessential Englishman to whom he is the literary heir.[16] The conflated naming of "Patrick W. Shakespeare" is emblematic of a larger significance, the use of the English dramatist as a figure of the author himself, the shaping hand behind the various narrative voices of the novel. Joyce uses the figure of Shakespeare to call our attention to the visible role of the author; the reflexive, metapoetic quality of *Ulysses,* that dimension whereby the novel is *about* literature itself, is enabled by this identification of the modern novelist with the Renaissance dramatist. As Shakespeare is identified with Hamlet father and son in Stephen's theory, so Stephen, Bloom, and Joyce himself are so equated. From its opening chapter, with its half-ironic echo of *Hamlet*'s first scene up on the battlements, with Mulligan as both Horatio and Claudius, "twitting Stephen on his black costume and delivering sententious wisdom on the inevitability of death" onward, Joyce invites us to see in Stephen—the artist as a young man—and in Bloom—the artist as middle-aged exile—figures of himself and of Shakespeare.[17] Stephen equates God with Shakespeare, and the artist with God, in an algebra familiar to readers of *A Portrait of the Artist as a Young Man.* In the library, Stephen mentions "the playwright who wrote the folio of this world" (9.1046–47), a role echoed by *Finnegans Wake*'s reference to "Great Shapesphere" (295.04).[18] Stephen's insistence in *A Portrait of the Artist* that the author's personality must be refined out of a work of art has been revised in *Ulysses* into a theory of the artist's transformation of his life experiences into art.[19] The novel itself exemplifies this theory, since in it Joyce has reshaped the experience and sensibilities of James Joyce into those of Stephen and Bloom. Thus, *Ulysses* reveals the story of its making, "the drama of its own conception" (Michaels, 176). The narrative of this process, whereby the book recapitulates its own history as well as that of its author, is sufficiently well known not to require a rehearsal of it here; we may let Ellmann's description stand for many. As he discusses the ways in which the Circe episode intertwines the ghosts of Shakespeare with those of the novel's characters, Ellmann says:

> If neither Bloom nor Stephen is more than a crude Shakespeare, they are none the less artists, mixing memory and desire to bear artistic issue. The living Shakespeare evokes himself as dead man and his dead son Hamnet as living one; Stephen evokes his mother as dead woman and Bloom his son Rudy as living. This is Joyce's principal equivalent to the play within a play (there are joking playlets as well in Stephen's consciousness in the library scene), that is, it is his model for the artistic process which is at work within the book as a whole.[20]

The figure of Shakespeare enables Joyce to call attention to the transformation of memory into art—distorting and refining, renewing and falsifying—both within and without the narrative texture. So intense is the presence of Joyce in his novel that critics often mistake his own biography for that of Stephen or Bloom, having the right stick but grasping it at the wrong end, aesthetically speaking. Joyce has invented for his authorial presence a figure more overt than persona, more oblique than a character:

> He is not the real Joyce, of course—the Joyce who was known to his friends and died in 1941; not a mere *persona* either; but Joyce the artistic or poetic personality whose voice has completely passed into his work. In *Ulysses* he lives in his characters, but beyond them.[21]

Joyce's symbol in *Ulysses* for this artistic personality is Shakespeare, and his omnipresence in the novel is represented by the pervasive figure of Shakespeare.

As the emblematic figure of Shakespeare enables Joyce to call attention to his own presence in the novel, so does the *Hamlet* theory Stephen expounds enable Joyce to foreground the relationship of an author's life to his work. As Stephen discusses, extravagantly, the relationship of Shakespeare's life to *his* art, we are led to reflect on Joyce's use of *his* biography in *this* work. For example, as Claudius is the false father, the seemer, of *Hamlet,* so Russell and his circle, rejecting Stephen by ignoring him, represent the false art Stephen's creator must overcome (Michaels, 180). Joyce, creating Stephen out of the transformed materials of his own life, mirrors this process in Stephen's creating Shakespeare as a character out of a pastiche of historical information, critical speculation, and Stephen's own obsessions. The ultimate model for this methodology is Shakespeare himself, using such historical figures as Henry V but creating them, transforming them to suit his own artistic ends.

Joyce as mature artist subsumes both Stephen and Bloom, shifting back and forth between them in the novel's equivalent of parallax. Joyce embeds this maturity in Bloom, whose achievement of forgiveness is one of the signal human accomplishments of the book. Like Prospero, who, Stephen would say, is an image of the mature Shakespeare forgiving *his* brother ("Where there is a reconciliation, Stephen said, there must have been first a sundering," 9.334–35), Bloom comes to terms with his own responsibility for Molly's behavior ("my fault perhaps") and sees his own acceptance as part of his own mortality: "Hate. Love. Those are names. Rudy. Soon I am old" (11.1069). By the novel's end, Stephen approximates this acceptance as closely as his own relative immaturity will allow; quoting Blake, he understands the fashion in which he must conquer his enemies: "*(he taps his brow)* But in here it is I must kill the priest and king" (15.4436–37). According to Goldberg, this process of acceptance is represented for Stephen by *Hamlet:*

> In the very writing of *Hamlet* Shakespeare won a self-understanding that is itself the gift he transfers. The knowledge the play provides is not simply of guilt and betrayal, an ineluctable pattern forever to be repeated, but of the nightmare of history from which Shakespeare the man partly awoke as Shakespeare the artist understood the causes and their pattern. (Goldberg, 83)

The conflation of Bloom and Stephen in the novel, of both with Shakespeare and of each and all with Joyce, is represented metaphorically by the novel's interest in metempsychosis, the transmigration of souls, first introduced as a theme when Molly asks Bloom the word's meaning early in the novel.[22] The transmigration of a soul through many forms is depicted more literally by the equation of one character to another: the Jewish Bloom, the Greek-named Stephen, and Shakespeare himself are conjoined in "jew-greek is greekjew" (15.2097–98), with Mulligan's joking reference to Bloom as Greeker than the Greeks (9.614–15), Stephen's acceptance of Eglinton's challenge to "prove he [Shakespeare] was a jew" (9.763), Bloom's being cast in the role of the Ghost played by Shakespeare (in Circe, J. J. O'Molloy says of Bloom, echoing the Ghost's words to Hamlet, that "he could a tale unfold" 15.951–52), and Stephen's later conflation of himself, Bloom and Shakespeare: Bloom, pointing to a scar of his, now twenty-two years old, provokes in Stephen this reflection:

> See? Moves to one great goal. I am twentytwo. Sixteen years ago he was twentytwo too. Sixteen years ago I twentytwo tumbled [as Shakespeare was "tumbled" in the cornfield by Anne Hathaway]. Twentytwo years ago he sixteen fell off his hobbyhorse. (15.3718–20)

Bloom and Stephen echo each other in ways only author and reader can know. Stephen's tipsy "Long live life!" (15.4474) echoes Bloom's earlier affirmation of "warm fullblooded life" (6.1005). Stephen's words from the Scylla and Charybdis chapter, "Do and do. Thing done. In a rosery of Fetter Lane of Gerard, herbalist, he walks, greyedauburn. An azured harebell like her veins. Lids of Juno's eyes, violets. He walks. One life is all. One body. Do. But do" (9.651–53) intrude almost verbatim into Bloom's thoughts in Sirens:

> Quotations every day in the year. To be or not to be. Wisdom while you wait. In Gerard's rosery of Fetter lane he walks, greyed-auburn. One life is all. One body. Do. But do.[23]

Bloom and Stephen's thoughts thus "bleed" into each other's in an unobtrusive but unmistakable literalizing of their equation. This "psychological seepage" increasingly occurs in Circe, with one of them echoing a thought or words the other had earlier. Stephen's vision of his mother, "I pray for you in my other world" (15.4202), recalls Bloom's memory of Martha's "I do not like that other world" (6.1002), as his "raw head and bloody bones!" (15.4213–14) duplicates Bloom's "rawhead and bloody bones" evocation of the butcher shop in Lestrygonians (8.726).

Such a seepage from one character to another highlights the hand of the artist at work, insisting as it does that we turn back to trace the echo, forcing us to compare the characters, to make judgments about their relative maturity, to read as allegorizers and resisters of allegory at the same time. Not surprisingly, the book contains its own internal reference to such equations: Mulligan's assertion that Stephen "proves by algebra that Hamlet's grandson is Shakespeare's grandfather and that he himself is the ghost of his own father" (1.555–57) makes the point that, as in the algebraic axiom, things equal to the same thing are equal to each other, and thus Joyce and Bloom, Joyce and Stephen, Shakespeare and Joyce, Bloom and Stephen are all momentarily merged into the "complete all-round man" Joyce envisions Odysseus as being and the artist whose presence in his work is so insistent.[24]

The moment of this merging is the instant when Bloom and Stephen, gazing into Bella Cohen's mirror, see reflected not their own faces but Shakespeare's. Shakespeare's face is superimposed on theirs as emblem of their linkage, as Shakespeare, with the humanity of Bloom and the intellect of Stephen, joins the two characters in his one. Joyce has prepared us for this mirroring, literal and figurative, in a variety of ways. In the Oxen of the Sun chapter, we have Bloom looking at a younger version of himself:

A score of years are blown away. He is young Leopold. There, as in a retrospective arrangement, a mirror within a mirror (hey, presto!) he beholdeth himself. . . . But, hey, presto, the mirror is breathed on and the young knighterrant recedes, shrivels, dwindles to a tiny speck within the mist. Now he is himself paternal and those about him might be his own sons. (14.1041–62)

More immediately beforehand, Stephen reformulates the words first said in the National Library ("We walk through ourselves, meeting robbers, ghosts, giants, old men, young men, wives, widows, brothers-in-love. But always meeting ourselves" [9.1044–46]), into an expanded version which brings together the theme of the artist as God, with the equation of Shakespeare and Bloom ("commercial traveller"): "What went forth to the ends of the world to traverse not itself, God, the sun, Shakespeare, a commercial traveller, having itself traversed in reality itself becomes that self" (15.2117–19). Bloom has, earlier, given us his own version of them: "Think you're escaping and run into yourself" (13.1110). And Stephen: "His image, wandering, he met. I mine" (9.580).

The self in the mirror is *another,* differing self, as Joyce has made clear from the beginning of this book of mirrors. Mulligan's shaving mirror is for Stephen a metaphor for the distortions of Irish art, the "cracked lookingglass of a servant" (1.146). Schutte takes the unstable image of Shakespeare in the brothel mirror (it morphs into Martin Cunningham's face and babbles) as evidence of the sterility of modern life (144), but in fact this mirroring repeats itself, when Stephen and Bloom bid farewell later that night, "Silent, each contemplating the other in both mirrors of the reciprocal flesh of theirhisnothis faces" (17:1183–84). Here, clearly, the suggestion is one of communion and fellowfeeling ("reciprocal flesh") amid the recognition of the other ("theirhisnothis") as other. Like Shakespeare when he wrote *Hamlet,* Bloom is both fatherless and sonless, but he is momentarily father to Stephen as the two together merge in the minds of artist and reader into the image of the Shakespeare Joyce calls "mirrorminded" in *Finnegans Wake.*[25]

In the Circe mirroring, Bloom sees a beardless Shakespeare, a younger self whose antlers evoke their common cuckoldry. The words Shakespeare babbles, "Iagogo! How my Oldfellow chokit his Thursdaymornun," elusive as they are even in Circe's elusive context, pull us out of the narrative frame by their very lack of sense (15.3828–29). Perhaps the line refers to Joyce, the Oldfellow creating the story, as well as to Shakespeare's Iago, "creator" of the jealousy-mad Othello. Earlier in the book "old fellow" is simply "father" (9.614), paternity and creation (of the novel, of the self) here joined.[26] Joyce has a character refer to him at least one other time in the novel, when Molly calls on him by name in her soliloquy: "O Jamesy let me up out of this" (18.1128–29).

Joyce has, in fact, left his signature on every page. He anticipates his own practice: in a 1903 review of three novels by A.E.W. Mason, Joyce comments on the stamp affixed by the artist as a rendering of his self-portrait: "Leonardo, exploring the dark recesses of consciousness in the interests of some semi-pantheistic psychology, has noted the tendency of the mind to impress its own likeness upon that which it creates. It is because of this tendency, he says, that many painters have cast as it were a reflection of themselves over the portraits of others."[27] Foreshadowed here is the visual equivalent of *Ulysses'* insistence on the presence of its author, a presence Stephen sees in Shakespeare's plays as well:

> He has hidden his own name, a fair name, William, in the plays, a super here, a clown there, as a painter of old Italy set his face in a dark corner of his canvas.[28]

Joyce has left trace images of his authorial presence on every page of his book. His most significant means for doing so is the figure of Shakespeare: predecessor, quintessential artist, character.

NOTES TO "JOYCE THE POSTMODERN: SHAKESPEARE AS
CHARACTER IN *ULYSSES*"

This essay was written with the assistance of a grant from the California State
University, Dominguez Hills, Sally Casanova Memorial Awards Program, and I
am grateful for this support, as well as for the keen editorial eyes and encouraging
spirits of Marilyn Garber, Tom Giannotti, and Bryan Feuer.

1. *Ulysses* (1922). The Corrected Text, ed. Hans Walter Gabler with Wolfhard
Steppe and Claus Melchior (New York: Random House, 1986), 5.3821–24. Subsequent references are to this edition, in the now customary form of chapter and
line numbers.

2. Schutte, *Joyce and Shakespeare: A Study in the Meaning of* Ulysses (New
Haven: Yale University Press, 1957). Schutte's interest in Joyce's use of Shakespeare is anticipated by William Peery in "The Hamlet of Stephen Dedalus,"
University of Texas Studies in English 31 (1952): 108–19. Schutte himself credits
previous lists of allusions by B. J. Morse, *Englische Studien* 65 (1930–31): 367–81;
and Arthur Heine, *Shakespeare Association Bulletin* 24 (1949): 56–70.

3. For a gloss on this phrase, see Don Gifford with Robert J. Seidman, *Notes
for Joyce: An Annotation of James Joyce's* Ulysses (New York: Dutton, 1974).

4. Culler, *Structuralist Poetics: Structuralism, Linguistics, and the Study of
Literature* (Ithaca, N.Y.: Cornell University Press, 1975), 231. Culler goes on to
remark that each of these views has a valid point, but that neither is sufficient
in itself.

5. Roland Barthes, *S/Z* (Paris: Seuil, 1970), is quoted by Culler, 237.

6. James H. Maddox, Jr., *Joyce's* Ulysses *and the Assault upon Character*
(New Brunswick, N.J.: Rutgers University Press, 1978), 12.

7. Schutte, 89. So persuaded of the reality of Stephen as character is Schutte
that in the quoted passage he has Stephen, rather than Joyce, researching the
topic in contemporary Shakespeare critics.

8. James Michaels, "'Scylla and Charybdis': Revenge in James Joyce's *Ulysses*," in *James Joyce Quarterly* 20:2 (Winter 1983): 177.

9. Sisson, *Mythical Sorrows of Shakespeare*, British Academy Annual Shakespeare Lecture (London, 1934). For a thorough discussion of Joyce's borrowings
from Shakespeare scholars of the time, see Schutte, Appendix A, in "The Sources
of Stephen's Shakespeare Theory."

10. Edward Dowden is perhaps the best known today of these biographical
critics; see his *Shakspere* (1877). Dowden, an Irishman, is cited directly by Mulligan, who quotes him on the subject of Shakespeare's putative homosexuality
(9.731–33).

11. Derrida is quoted by Maud Ellmann, "The Ghosts of *Ulysses*," in *James
Joyce: The Artist and the Labyrinth*, ed. Augustine Martin (London: Ryan, 1990),
195. The second Derrida quotation is Ellmann's rendering of his point.

12. The summary is Schutte's, 88. I have omitted his page references to *Ulysses* as confusing here.

13. See the afterword to the Gabler Edition. The point about the indeterminacy
of the text of *Ulysses* is made by Fritz Senn, in "Righting *Ulysses*," in *Modern
Critical Interpretations: James Joyce's* Ulysses, ed. Harold Bloom (New York:
Chelsea House, 1987), 99–121.

14. For this point, I am indebted to Vincent Cheng, *Shakespeare and Joyce:
A Study of* Finnegans Wake (University Park: Pennsylvania State University
Press, 1984), 24. Of course, literature has been playing versions of this game for

some time. As a reader of this paper has reminded me, *Tristram Shandy* has a good claim to being the first postmodern novel. On that topic, see Robert Alter, *Partial Magic: The Novel as a Self-Conscious Genre* (Berkeley and Los Angeles: University of California Press, 1975).

15. On Joyce's Irishness, see Seamus Deane, "Joyce the Irishman," in *The Cambridge Companion to James Joyce,* ed. Derek Attridge (Cambridge: Cambridge University Press, 1990), 31–53; and Frederick K. Lang, *Ulysses and the Irish God* (Lewisburg: Bucknell University Press, 1993).

16. Cheng, *Shakespeare and Joyce: A Study of* Finnegans Wake (1), has noted the naming of Patrick W. Shakespeare in the beginning of his discussion of Shakespeare's influence on the *Wake.* P. W. Joyce authored books on Irish history and legend used by James Joyce in writing *Ulysses.* Harold Bloom sees the presence of *Hamlet* in *Ulysses* as an example of the anxiety of influence: "Joyce's obsession with *Hamlet* is crucial in *Ulysses.* His famous reading of Hamlet, as expounded by Stephen, can be regarded as a subtle coming-to-terms with Shakespeare as his most imposing literary father in the English language." Introduction, in *Modern Critical Interpretations,* 5. But see Richard Ellmann: "He exhibits none of that anxiety of influence which Harold Bloom has recently attributed to modern writers." In *The Consciousness of Joyce* (New York: Oxford University Press, 1977), 47–48. Let Nora Joyce have the last word here: "Ah, there's only one man he's got to get the better of now, and that's that Shakespeare!" (quoted in Cheng, 1).

17. Schutte, 17–18, is quoting Hugh Kenner, *Dublin's Joyce* (London: Chatto & Windus, 1955), 194.

18. *Finnegans Wake* (New York: Viking Press, 1959).

19. Schutte (10n) assumes that Stephen's theory is Joyce's own—erroneously, I think, and certainly ignoring the distance Joyce so carefully creates between himself and his character. It may be that Joyce once held the view of the artist disappearing from the work, refining himself out of existence (Schutte cites an early version of it in 1903), but I would argue that by the time he wrote *Ulysses,* Joyce saw this "refining" as a process of transforming one's biography rather than dissolving it.

20. Richard Ellmann, *Consciousness,* 71.

21. S. L. Goldberg, *The Classical Temper: A Study of James Joyce's* Ulysses (New York: Barnes and Noble, 1961), 35.

22. I find that I am anticipated in this, as in many other points, by James Maddox, who cites metempsychosis, parallax, and Proteus as metaphors of the relation of surface to substance (though not of the figures named to each other), 12.

23. *Ulysses,* 11.907–8. Maddox (74–75), cites these passages for a parallel but not identical point. The phrase "psychological seepage" in the next sentence derives from Maddox, 137.

24. Budgen, *James Joyce and the Making of* Ulysses (Bloomington: Indiana University Press, 1960), 15–16.

25. Quoted in Cheng, 8. For mirrors in *Ulysses,* see Michael H. Begnal, "Art and History: Stephen's Mirror and Parnell's Silk Hat," in *Joyce's* Ulysses: *The Larger Perspective,* ed. Robert D. Newman and Weldon Thornton (Newark: University of Delaware Press, 1987), 233–43.

26. For a discussion of this line, see Marilyn French, *The Book as World: James Joyce's* Ulysses (Cambridge, MA: Harvard University Press, 1976), 193.

27. *The Critical Writings of James Joyce,* ed. Ellsworth Mason and Richard Ellmann (New York: Viking Press, 1959), 130. The headnote to this review points out its relationship to Stephen's words in Scylla and Charybdis.

28. *Ulysses,* 9.921–23. See Maddox, 95–96n.

One Author in Search of a Character: Ezra Pound's "Homage to Sextus Propertius"

MARTINE L. DE VOS

Many a student of Pound is bound, at one point or other, to wonder if the poet could not write in plain English. The student tends to be flabbergasted by the foreign gibberish and the quotations which, at first glance, hardly seem to serve any purpose. Pound's poetry is difficult to read and raises questions about the status of literature. In addition to the text, multiple guide books are needed to make sense of it. Pound evokes cries of frustration, and these are relevant. Not just undergraduates are bound to articulate them; many a scholar is daunted by the work of this modernist poet, frequently unwilling to perform the excavation necessary to discover the meaning of Pound's poetry. Others find him a jewel thief, an overrated juggler of other people's work, a pretentious man of letters. Several classical scholars, meanwhile, have discovered in Pound's work an "ignorance" of Latin with no due respect for the classics.[1]

This latter criticism was leveled against Pound especially when his "Homage to Sextus Propertius" was published in 1919. In fact, controversy over this poem raged for a long time, with scholars hurling epithets back and forth. Those who attacked the poem variously called it a bad imitation of a classic, a desecration, an ignorant mistranslation, a distortion, a perversion. The poem's defenders, however, termed it a brilliant reinterpretation of a classic poem, a tribute, a fine piece of criticism, a masterpiece of parodic translatorese, a per-version (the hyphen key), while the speaker was dubbed one of Pound's major personae.[2]

The characterizations of "Homage to Sextus Propertius" formulated in either camp are important, for they shed light on the multiple meanings of the poem. The classicists, for instance, were correct in pointing out that the poem was no translation but a distortion. For Pound, however, this abuse proved one of his points, namely that contemporary scholarship had blinded itself to

181

life; in the process of chasing accuracy, it had become sterile, abstract, meaningless. In that sense, the poem's champions had seen accurately that, at one level, the poem pokes fun at an entire class of translators.

The poem operates at more levels, however. It not only criticizes the business of translation and scholarship, but an entire cultural apparatus aimed at the mechanization and regimentation of life. This force was not unconnected for Pound at the time in which he wrote it—during World War I—to business and military forces, especially as they were perceived to cooperate closely in the Western imperialist effort. In that sense, the poem functions as a piece of political criticism as well.

The poem is also a work of literary criticism in its widest sense: a work not only of interpreting literature but also of criticizing the literary business, the entire culture industry. For all these reasons, Pound's choice of Sextus Propertius as the poem's main character is key. For, in 1917, Pound closely identified with this Roman poet who lived and worked in the first century A.D. The historical figure of Propertius, therefore, became one of Pound's major personae (necessitating the "gibberish" and quotations), not only because he was regarded as a major poet worthy of tribute, but also because the increasingly marginal poet in wartime London, anxious to justify himself and his politico-artistic project, believed that they shared views on politics, art, the culture industry, as well as love and sexuality. This made Propertius a perfect character for Pound's purposes.

In order fully to understand Pound's choice of Propertius as the focus of his poem, Pound's development in wartime London needs to be traced. A good starting point is June 1914, when Ezra Pound, Wyndham Lewis, Henri Gaudier-Brzeska, and other Vorticists published their first issue of *Blast,* a magazine that "blasted" England for matters ranging from its "effeminate lout within," its aesthetes and "feminine snobs," to its "professionals," "amateurs," and "art-pimps."[3] In addition to outrageous manifestos which, among other things, linked the feminine with "bad" art, the magazine also contained poems by Pound.[4] Many of these predominantly aggressive and angry poems address the contemporary British artistic climate. In "Fratres Minores," for example, Pound pokes fun at the many "minor" poets popular with readers whose work, according to him, consists of complaints "in delicate and exhausted metres" about insignificant and well-known facts.[5]

Pound's contempt and anger in these poems are, however, not confined to his colleagues. He also voices his loathing for those he ultimately finds responsible for a climate in which "minor" poets flourish and "major" ones are marginalized to magazines like *Blast*. In "Salutation the Third," he abuses everyone he believes to be complicit in a system in which literature is commodified: the "gagged reviewers," the "pandars and jobber[s]," and those "who pat the big-bellies for profit." What all these people have in common is that, in rendering art a commercial undertaking, they have been guilty of rewarding the clichéd, the hackneyed, and of discouraging art intended to "make it new." For that reason, they are "slut-bellied obstructionist[s] [and] sworn foe[s] to free speech and good letters."[6] The result is not only stale and conventional art, but also the marginalization of what Pound called the "serious" artist.[7]

Pound's contribution to *Blast* did not alleviate his own marginalization in the world of letters. Never welcome in the pages of England's mainstream press, in part because his work was said to lack "beauty," after 1914, Pound was also less welcome in smaller magazines. The editor of the *Quarterly Review,* for one, was upset by *Blast* and Pound's association with it. Consequently, the editor informed him: "I do not think I can open the columns of the *Q. R.*—at any rate, at present—to any one associated publicly with such a publication as *Blast*. It stamps a man too disadvantageously."[8]

Pound's marginal position was exacerbated when, in August, England declared war on the Central Powers. This declaration had almost immediate ramifications in the world of letters. Virginia Woolf pointed to one change when she observed: "The war, people said, had revived their interest in poetry."[9] It was, however, a very specific kind of poetry in which interest was rekindled: patriotic verse. As Richard Aldington explained, the war did not spell an increased interest in poets like himself or Pound: "Literary papers disappeared, literary articles were not wanted, poems had to be patriotic."[10] One result was that Pound's income, already low before 1914, dwindled significantly during the first year of the Great War and continued to remain low for years to come.[11]

In contrast, patriotic poets did quite well, both critically and economically. Henry Newbolt, for instance, republished a collection of his poems, which almost immediately sold 70,000 copies.[12] Other less well-established poets joined the effort to supply "recruiting verses." For example, John Oxenham published a collection entitled *All's Well! Some Helpful Verses for the Dark Days of War*. The title poem invoked a rhetoric already familiar to readers of such popular poets as Henry Newbolt, Rudyard Kipling, and Alfred Noyes:

He died as few men get the chance to die,—
Fighting to save a world's morality.
He died the noblest death a man can die,
Fighting for God, and Right, and Liberty;—
And such a death is Immortality.[13]

These emotionally loaded appeals to morality, nobility, God, Right, Liberty, and Immortality obscured the horrible nature of the war being fought on the Continent.

Moreover, as Paul Fussell, among others, has shown, this language was typical not only of many literary texts produced at this time but also of official government and military communications.[14] Both relied on abstract language, cliché, and euphemism to render the character of the war both "impenetrable" and heroically grandiose (Fussell, 175).

Many men who fought in World War I eventually rebelled against the dishonest and euphemistic way in which the war was represented. Many of the war poets, including Siegfried Sassoon, Robert Graves, and Wilfred Owen, attempted in their works to offer the public a more realistic picture of the dramatic events unfolding across the Channel. In doing so, they sought to undercut both the themes and the rhetoric of patriotic verse.

Pound wished to aid this effort, feeling contempt for most of the patriotic poems filling the newspapers (Longenbach, 112). For one, he believed that many of these poems were not telling the truth about the war. He insisted, moreover, that a poet could not write war verse without first-hand experience. Lacking it, the poet could only write poetry that would be "facile and opportunistic, the emotion literary and false" (Longenbach, 115).

Pound's impatience with the war verse that sold so well increased radically in the spring of 1915 when he began to receive letters written in the trenches from his fellow-Vorticist, the sculptor Henri Gaudier-Brzeska. These letters gave Pound a more accurate insight into the brutal events faced by the combatants. The ultimate futility of the war, however, was brought home to him in June when the sculptor was killed on the battlefield. Gaudier-Brzeska, whom Pound later described as "the most complete case of Genius" he had ever known, became after his death "a symbolic figure who had been sacrificed in a conflict that would prove nothing."[15]

As a result of the deaths of Gaudier-Brzeska and a number of other "serious" artists, Pound concluded that "the war destroyed not only individuals, but the possibility of culture."[16] A viable cul-

ture was impossible when the war killed those in the artistic community who were capable of creating and sustaining it. More important, however, not only did the war dash any possibility of a
viable culture; it also, Pound increasingly believed, had been
caused by an impoverished, commercial culture. At the outbreak
of World War I, he had voiced his suspicion that "This war is
possibly a conflict between two forces almost equally detestable.
Atavism and the loathsome spirit of mediocrity cloaked in graft."[17]
This mediocrity was evidenced in the dominant literature which,
through its lack of "perfectly bald statements," prevented the public from "look[ing] *anything*—animal, mineral, vegetable, political,
social, international, religious, philosophical, or ANYTHING
else—in the face" (*Selected Letters*, 138). In later years, Pound
reiterated this opinion when he said, "Europe went blind into that
war . . . because all general knowledge had been split up into useless or incompetent fragments. Because literature no longer bothered about the language 'of law and of the state' [,] because the
state and plutocracy cared less than a damn about letters."[18]

While the war continued, he received one confirmation after
another of his perception that his "plutocratic" culture did not care
about serious literature. Serious art failed, after all, to have eager
purchasers, even among alternative publishers. For a nine-month
period, for instance, Pound quarreled with Harriet Monroe, who
did not want to publish T. S. Eliot's poems in *Poetry*.[19] Similarly,
he searched for nearly two years for publishers for James Joyce
and Wyndham Lewis, while he persisted in having to struggle to
see his own verse in print.[20] These difficulties formed for Pound a
type of censorship which, combined with other events, proved to
him that the culture at large—especially in wartime—curtailed the
circulation of quality art.

Pound's suspicion that the plutocracy conspired, through direct
or indirect censorship, to marginalize serious, revolutionary art,
was confirmed when Joyce faced opposition to the serialization of
Ulysses on account of obscenity charges. In fact, Pound moved
quickly to link the *Ulysses* scandal to matters beyond the purely
literary. In a letter, he admitted that the issue "was something
larger than the question of whether Joyce writes with a certain
odeur-de-muskrat." Both the outrage over the book and the raging
world war were expressive of the same thing, namely "the English
and American habit of keeping their ostrich heads carefully down
their little silk-lined sand-holes" (*Selected Letters*, 138).

The war was thus partly a direct result of ignorance, caused by
the limited use Anglo-Saxon capitalist culture made of its serious

artists. As long as full circulation and appreciation of their work was curtailed, the population's knowledge and mental capacities would be limited—rendering them an easy prey for crafty politicians—and war would remain inevitable.

This point Pound made explicitly in his essay "Provincialism the Enemy"—of crucial importance to an understanding of "Homage to Sextus Propertius," and likewise written in 1917. In this essay he quotes, ironically, Kipling as saying, "Transportation is civilisation." Pound asserts the truth of this statement, explaining that communication between people—a direct result of "transportation"—can lead, "if not toward a perpetual peace, at least toward a greater peace probability." Since this has been limited in England and America, these nations have become "dust-heap[s] of bigotry," the result being a bloody war. For Pound, then, the ultimate cause of World War I is "precisely [the] stoppage of circulation."[21]

A lack of extensive circulation of quality art results in "isolation" which, adds Pound, is the desire of all possessed by "the ever damned spirit of provincialism." Importantly, only the diminishing of one's isolation and broadening one's horizons can ensure civilization and peace (Selected Prose, 201). This, in turn, requires an increased level of communication between people, facilitated by the increased dissemination of texts by "serious" writers. This enlarged circulation is effected for Pound in several ways, in part through the incorporation in one's own work of bits and pieces from other quality artists—poets such as Sextus Propertius, whom Pound admired especially for his irony and his Laforgue-like use of language (Selected Letters, 178), or logopoeia.[22] It is crucial to note in this respect that, with the poem "Homage to Sextus Propertius," he never intended to provide a translation of the Roman's work but rather, in his own words, "to bring a dead man to life, to present a living figure" (Selected Letters, 149). By offering twentieth-century readers not only a revision of the work of a first-century poet but also an interpretation of the character of that very poet, Pound tried to ensure the continuing "distribution of poetic currency." In other words, the poem in this instance "encourage[s] the commerce of the living and the dead,"[23] between two "serious" artists and the public.

By the time he wrote "Provincialism the Enemy," however, Pound's primary concern was no longer art. That is, by 1917, he was not convinced that the war was due solely to a culture of mediocrity that did not appreciate its serious intellectuals. Instead, he was by this time of the opinion that it had been instigated quite intentionally by a particular group of people for its own benefit; it had been planned by "a belly-fat commerce" experiencing a "lust for imperial spoils," particularly in Asia and Africa.[24] Its roots were thus economic, and those who ultimately were behind the millions who were killed or maimed consisted of the plutocrats—the "usurers" Pound would soon start investigating.

He knew, of course, that the soldiers had not been mobilized by naked force; the war effort had been supported not only by governmental propaganda but also by less official cultural expressions such as patriotic verse, whose aim had been the recruitment of combatants. All these had served to whip up support for the imperialists.

This visible support in the realm of culture was echoed by a less obvious, more permanent cultural effort; and by 1917 Pound's focus was moving to this latter form. For him, this consisted of capitalist culture's denial of people's individuality, its disparagement of original thinking and, in general, its mechanization of life (*Selected Prose*, 196)—a state of affairs that victimized not only the "serious" artist but all people outside plutocratic circles.

Pound explains this more totalizing line of thought in "Provincialism the Enemy," where he links not only the publishing machinery's drive to marginalize "serious" art but, more generally, the ongoing imperialist war with an entire cultural apparatus that fosters mechanized thinking and living. This machinery consists primarily of a system of education (the "Germanic ideal of scholarship") which inhibits original thought and transforms students into automatons.

More specifically, this educational apparatus encourages and rewards passivity, as well as the accumulation of useless pieces of information:

> The student has become accustomed first to *receiving* his main ideas without question; then to being indifferent to them . . . [partly because] the mind [is] switched off all general considerations of the values of life, and switched on to some minute, unvital detail.[25]

Education, then, had become a passive and sterile process, undertaken not, as it should be, to enrich the life of the individual and community but, writes Pound, "for some exterior reason, a reason hidden in vague and cloudy words such as 'monuments of scholarship,' 'exactness,' 'soundness,' etc., 'service to scholarship'" (*Selected Prose*, 197). Thus, students were urged to undertake their studies not for themselves but to serve something they were taught in the process to believe is greater—scholarship. These "larger" reasons, however, ultimately prove to be meaningless abstractions, fostering an education and a line of thinking that is sterile exactly because it underscores a dissociated sensibility.

It is precisely Pound's above statement, however, that sheds light on the poem "Homage to Sextus Propertius." While his statement pokes unambiguous fun at the things scholars themselves tradition-ally have prized so highly—exactness, soundness, service to and monuments of scholarship—the poem does so more surrepti-tiously. It *is* no "exact" translation of Propertius's *Elegies*. Pound's work is *not* a monument of scholarship as it had been practiced. Instead, his radical reinterpretation was meant precisely to redeem the Roman poet "from scholarly bondage," to take the poet from the scholars and give him to the people.[26] If, in so doing, the poet's language was rendered modern, "translated" into twentieth-century speech, then that was exactly the point: it enhanced the possibility of true communication between Propertius and readers of Pound's work. Communication (transportation) equals civiliza-tion—a point made formally by the poem and one the outraged classicists and other scholars so tellingly missed.

In his critique of the "Germanic ideal of scholarship," however, Pound's aim was also explicitly political. He firmly believed that education in the name of vague abstractions was not only dehu-manizing but, finally, politically insidious. Such an education, after all, is little concerned with individuality; in the process, it negates both education and individuality (*Selected Prose,* 194). For con-temporary higher education is "habituating men to consider them-selves as bits of mechanism for one use or another" (*Selected Prose,* 195). Given this process, it is no great step, according to Pound, to "the idea that man is the slave of the State, the 'unit,' the piece of the machine" (*Selected Prose,* 192). As a result, it facilitates the state's mobilization of men to become part of the war machine and, if necessary, to die en masse.

People's vision of themselves as units is exacerbated by the edu-cational system exactly through the promotion of itself through abstractions. For Pound, once a student is encouraged to study for a reason exterior to himself—to serve "scholarship"—a process is begun of preparing "his mind for all sorts of acts to be undertaken for exterior reasons . . . without regard to their merit" (*Selected Prose,* 197). Abstractions beget abstractions; the current educa-tional system has fostered a "state [in which the student] has ac-cepted the Deutschland über Alles idea, in this state he has accepted the idea that he is an ant, not a human being. He has become impotent, and quite pliable" (*Selected Prose,* 192). Education, then, is part of a huge machinery enabling the manipulation of people, with the disastrous result that people die in the trenches for abstract reasons—for "glory" or "to make the world safe for democracy"—without an examination of the war's merit or its "human value" (*Selected Prose*, 197). For that reason, Pound insists, it is imperative that the educational system and the culture at large be made "*safe for the individual.*"[27]

The radical individuality for which Pound had called in art a few years earlier is thus, by 1917, extended to every arena of life, for a denial of the value of individuality fuels everything abominable to him at this juncture: provincialism, imperialism, war. To the American poet, everything was becoming interconnected: mediocre art, the provincial spirit, abstract language, the Germanic ideal of scholarship—all were perceived as expressing and fostering an environment where originality and critical analyses of issues were the exception, and where standardization and an uncritical acceptance of platitudes were the rule. In the end, this environment was interpreted as supportive of the interests of the plutocracy and discouraging of peaceful, unique, and nonconforming individuals.

It is exactly for this reason that Pound chose Sextus Propertius as the persona of his "Homage." Composing it in the year in which he was perhaps in his most profound anti–imperialist mood,[28] Pound wished to express "certain emotions as vital to [him] in 1917, faced with the infinite and ineffable imbecility of the British Empire, as they were to Propertius some centuries earlier, when faced with the infinite and ineffable imbecility of the Roman Empire" (*Selected Letters*, 231). The poem thus builds on a repetition in history—a concept around which Pound's *Cantos* would also be constructed.

Sextus Propertius, importantly, was perceived as sharing one of Pound's primary concerns, namely the way in which "the empire is maintained."[29] For the poem's Propertius is keenly aware that imperialism is not only a military effort but also a cultural one. He recognizes that patriotic writers function, in their own way, as the imperialists' "chief of police."[30] By rehearsing platitudes about war, or "Martian generalities" (*Personae*, 207), they serve the "Imperial order" (*Personae*, 229). Propertius, however, refuses to fall in with his patriotic colleagues. Unlike the popular versifiers of war—of imperial Rome or, implicitly, of imperial England (the "'Prolific Noyes' with output undefeatable"[31])—Propertius refuses to write verse for either "the mid-crowd" (*Personae*, 210) or the recruitment of soldiers. He tells his patron, "if . . . I were able to lead heroes into armour, I would not" (*Personae*, 217). Instead, he undercuts his culture's imperialist exploits by versifying its true nature:

> Caesar plots against India,
> Tigris and Euphrates shall, from now on, flow at his bidding,
> Tibet shall be full of Roman policemen,
> The Parthians shall get used to our statuary and acquire a Roman
>   religion.
>
> <div align="right">(<i>Personae</i>, 219)</div>

Imperialism is thus shown to be based on hubris, impossible expectations as to the extent of control (the rivers shall "flow at his bidding"), force and coercion—a far cry from the numerous idealized pictures presented elsewhere.

Moreover, Propertius undercuts imperialism's rhetoric when he maintains that "It is noble to die of love, and honourable to remain uncuckolded for a season" (*Personae*, 218), thereby implicitly condemning the "old men's lies" which insist on the "honor" and "glory" involved in military action.[32] As Pound wrote elsewhere, "War blew up a lot of clichés," and this lesson of World War I is shared by the Roman poet.[33] Both he and Propertius, writes Pound, hate "rhetoric and [are] undeceived by imperial hog-wash" (*Selected Letters*, 150).

Both struggle to resist pressures to write propaganda and, instead, fight to maintain their own artistic integrity, feeling acutely their duty as "serious" artists to tell the truth to a reading public whose eyes had been trained not to see fundamental relations, or "anything . . . of importance" (*Personae*, 228). Despite pressures to write popular but mediocre verse, Propertius is determined to compose poetry filled with "beauty" in a form that is not hackneyed but "strange," thereby expressing his "genius" and making it new (*Personae*, 208–9). Contemptuous of war verse and following his own heart, Propertius "turn[s] aside from battles" (*Personae*, 218). He will not write patriotic poetry for his patron Maecenas, despite its profitability, but rather remains firm in his intention to versify love. After all, he is "the slave of one passion" (*Personae*, 219) refusing, as all "serious" artists must, to be the slave of either pecuniary motives or the (Roman) imperial state.

In his determination to versify his intense love for Cynthia, Propertius also voices a belief held by Pound by 1917, that there exists an intricate connection between sexual experience and "serious" artistic production. Between 1910 and 1920, Pound read and developed theories on the connection between male sexuality, visionary experience, and creativity.[34] Importantly, he viewed Sextus Propertius as having shared these, adding another incentive to focus on the Roman poet in his "Homage." Propertius, after all, concentrates on Cynthia, the woman who plays a crucial role in his poetic production. For it is she who is the source of his inspiration, the cause of his visionary experience: "And Cynthia was alone in her bed. / I was stupefied" (*Personae*, 225). The Roman is aware that a poet's "genius is no more than a girl"[35] with whom he shares love and sex:

> If she goes in a gleam of Cos, in a slither of dyed stuff,
> There is a volume in the matter; if her eyelids sink into sleep,
> There are new jobs for the author;
> And if she plays with me with her shirt off,
>   We shall construct many Iliads.
>
> (*Personae*, 217)

Cynthia provides the poet with "visionary reality" necessary for the composition of "serious" art.[36]

Propertius's awareness of the importance of this source of creativity for the (male) poet was an important reason for Pound's "Homage." But, as we have seen, there were others. The Roman poet's struggle to retain his artistic integrity in a war-mad culture; his critique of Roman imperialism; his faith in the importance of "serious" art—all these determined Pound's choice of Propertius as a major persona in his poem. Through the figure of Propertius, Pound was able to express his own criticism of British imperialism, his abhorrence of the products of the culture industry, as well as his own vision of the nature and function of "serious" art. The Roman poet, moreover, provided him with support, aiding him in justifying his position and ideas in a world in which he felt increasingly isolated and marginal.

At the same time, the poem critiqued an entire cultural apparatus aimed at the regimentation and dehumanization of life—an apparatus perceived as functioning in the interest of the plutocracy, or the usurers. It was exactly this group to which he would shift his focus at the end of World War I. Unlike Propertius, Pound, by 1918, felt the need to leave love songs behind (Longenbach, 127), and to throw all his weight behind the task of educating the public about the war-mad usurers: "Nothing 'matters' till some fool starts resorting to force. To prevent this initial insanity is the goal, and always has been, of intelligent political effort" (*Selected Prose*, 193).

Therefore, when the war ended, Pound did not retreat into the realm of the aesthetic. Instead, as he later admitted, "I began an investigation of causes of war, to oppose same" (as quoted in Tytell, 146). This decision to concern himself with the political did not constitute as sudden and radical a change of direction as some critics maintain (Tytell, 146), for he had been steering this course throughout the war. His own wartime poverty and that of other "serious" artists (including James Joyce and T. S. Eliot); their difficulty in being published; the deaths of men such as T. E. Hulme and Gaudier-Brzeska; the atrocities of the war itself; the hysteria in wartime London—all these events had shattered Pound's world (Tytell, 251) and convinced him of the urgent need to conduct an in-depth investigation of what seemed to him one of the primary causes, namely "an uncaring state, a greedy financial structure" (Zinnes, 54). In the process he hoped to prevent a repeat in history. By 1918, therefore, he was ready to concern himself more directly with politics and economics, spelling a decisive turn on a path leading to Pound's later embrace of Italian fascism.

NOTES TO "ONE AUTHOR IN SEARCH OF A CHARACTER: EZRA POUND'S 'HOMAGE TO SEXTUS PROPERTIUS'"

1. See, for example, the commentary of William Gardner Hale in the April 1919 issue of *Poetry.*
2. For a good description of this controversy, see Christine Froula, *A Guide to Ezra Pound's* Selected Poems (New York: New Directions, 1983), 105–11.
3. "Manifesto," in *Blast: Review of the Great English Vortex,* ed. Wyndham Lewis (London: John Lane, June 1914; repr. Santa Rosa, CA: Black Sparrow, 1989), 11 and 15–16. Subsequent page references are to this reprint edition.
4. Harriet Zinnes has aptly described *Blast* as "not far from a hate manual." See "Nature and Design: 'Burying Euclid Deep in the Living Flesh,'" in *Ezra Pound: The Legacy of Kulchur,* ed. Marcel Smith and William A. Ulmer (Tuscaloosa: University of Alabama Press, 1988), 53.
5. Pound, "Fratres Minores," in his *Personae: The Collected Shorter Poems of Ezra Pound* (New York: New Directions, 1971), 148.
6. Pound, "Salutation the Third," in his *Personae,* 145.
7. Pound, "The Serious Artist," in his *Literary Essays of Ezra Pound,* ed. T. S. Eliot (New York: New Directions, 1968), 41–57.
8. Quoted in Noel Stock, *The Life of Ezra Pound,* expanded edition (San Francisco: North Point Press, 1982), 162.
9. Quoted in James Longenbach, *Stone Cottage: Pound, Yeats, and Modernism* (Oxford: Oxford University Press, 1988), 112.
10. Quoted in John Tytell, *Ezra Pound: The Solitary Volcano* (New York: Anchor, 1987), 121.
11. Pound's income for the period from November 1914 to October 1915 amounted to 42 pounds (Stock, 187). Because of his poverty throughout the war,

he repeatedly wrote his father: "Dear Dad, Can you send me five dollars?" (Pound, as quoted in James Laughlin, "Pound's Economics," in *Ezra Pound: The Legacy of Kulchur,* 70).

12. C. K. Stead, *The New Poetic: Yeats to Eliot* (New York: Harper & Row, 1964), 89.

13. C. K. Stead, *The New Poetic,* 90. Although Hardy and Yeats were also writing at this time, these men were among the most popular poets in England in the period 1900–1916, forming what Ford Madox Ford called "the physical force school." Their immense popularity was illustrated in 1913, when the *Journal of Education* conducted a poll to discover the identities of the most popular living poets (Swinburne and Meredith both having died in 1909). These proved to be, in descending order, Kipling, William Watson, Robert Bridges, and Noyes (Stead, 53, 62).

14. See Fussell's *The Great War and Modern Memory* (Oxford: Oxford University Press, 1975). Of course, students of Pound's work are well aware of the fact that, in practice, "the people" find his poetry too esoteric and burdensome to read.

15. Respectively, Ezra Pound, "D'Artagnan Twenty Years After," in *Selected Prose: 1909–1965,* ed. William Cookson (New York: New Directions, 1973), 459; and Tytell, 119.

16. Longenbach, 131. T. E. Hulme, for instance, also died in the trenches, while Pound attributed the comparatively peaceful deaths of Henry James and Rémy de Gourmont to the war as well (see his "Rémy de Gourmont" in *Selected Prose,* 420; Longenbach, 130).

17. Pound, *The Selected Letters of Ezra Pound, 1907–1941,* ed. D. D. Paige (New York: New Directions, 1971), 46.

18. Pound, "The Jefferson-Adams Letters," in his *Selected Prose,* 153.

19. See, for example, Stock, 180; and *Selected Letters,* 40–61.

20. Harriet Monroe, for instance, rejected his poem "Moeurs Contemporaines," whereas the otherwise supportive Elkin Mathews was horrified by a number of poems Pound wished to include in his volume *Lustra,* finding them violent and indecent. Consequently, *Lustra* was first published as a private edition with the four offending poems removed (Stock, 194–95).

21. Pound, "Provincialism the Enemy," in his *Selected Prose,* 199–200.

22. See Pound's "How to Read," in *Literary Essays of Ezra Pound* (New York: Directions, 1968). In this essay, Pound also states that "*Logopoeia* does not translate" (25).

23. Maud Ellmann, *The Poetics of Impersonality: T. S. Eliot and Ezra Pound* (Brighton: Harvester Press, 1987), 147.

24. See Tytell, 146. The economic essence of World War I was also argued by Lenin, whom Pound read and quoted in his own work. See V. I. Lenin, *Imperialism, the Highest Stage of Capitalism: A Popular Outline* (New York: International Publishers, 1939); and Ezra Pound, "What Is Money For?" in his *Selected Prose,* 298–99.

25. *Selected Prose,* 192. Pound can thus be interpreted as criticizing what bell hooks has called "the banking system of education." See hooks, *Teaching to Transgress: Education as the Practice of Freedom* (New York: Routledge, 1994).

26. K. K. Ruthven, *A Guide to Ezra Pound's* Personae *(1926)* (Berkeley: University of California Press, 1969), 85.

27. Ezra Pound, "Economic Democracy," in his *Selected Prose,* 210 (emphasis is Pound's).

194	MARTINE L. DE VOS

28. See also Frank Lentricchia, "Lyric in the Culture of Capitalism," *American Literary History* 1 (Spring 1989): 77.

29. Pound, "Moeurs Contemporaines," in his *Personae,* 178.

30. Pound, "Homage to Sextus Propertius," in his *Personae,* 228.

31. Pound, "L'Homme Moyen Sensuel," in his *Personae,* 240.

32. Pound, "Hugh Selwyn Mauberley," in his *Personae,* 190; the "old men's lies" refer to Horace's "dulce et decorum est pro patria mori"; Pound states that the soldiers' experience was "non 'dulce' non 'et decor.'"

33. Pound, "Jean Cocteau Sociologist," in his *Selected Prose,* 433.

34. For more detail, see my "The 'Serious' Poet and the Phallus: The Gender Politics of Ezra Pound," *Frame: Tijdschrift voor Literatuurwetenschap* [Utrecht], 10:2 (1995): 19–27.

35. Propertius, as quoted in Ezra Pound, "Postscript to *The Natural Philosophy of Love* by Rémy de Gourmont," in his *Pavannes and Divagations* (New York: New Directions, 1958), 214. This line is repeated in the poem (*Personae,* 217).

36. Kevin Oderman, *Ezra Pound and the Erotic Medium* (Durham, NC: Duke University Press, 1986), 19.

Displacing Goethe: Tribute and Exorcism in Thomas Mann's *The Beloved Returns*

GAMIN BARTLE

In 1939, Thomas Mann published his "Goethe novel," *Lotte in Weimar,* which was translated into English as *The Beloved Returns.* The novel is based on Charlotte Buff Kestner's visit to Weimar in 1816. Charlotte, known as the model for the character Lotte in Goethe's early novel, *The Sorrows of Young Werther* (1774), becomes a fictional character once again in Mann's novel. Although Charlotte—or, rather, Lotte—is the eponymous character in the German original of Mann's masterpiece, the novel resonates with the presence of Johann Wolfgang von Goethe. It is Goethe, rather than Charlotte, whom one is tempted to call the main character in *The Beloved Returns.* Through the use of his great predecessor as a character, and, more specifically, by writing an inner monologue from the perspective of the versatile man in Weimar, Mann allows himself—at least, on a fictional level—to walk in the great writer's shoes. In so doing, Mann articulates his feelings for and against the individual who stands out as Germany's greatest author. This essay explores the complex relationship of Mann to his celebrated predecessor, a relationship that spanned Mann's entire career. Mann's attitude toward Goethe changed dramatically over the years, and through writing *The Beloved Returns,* he effectively "displaced" his eminent precursor.

Mann was both drawn to and intimidated by Goethe; herein lies the foundation of his ambivalence. This idea encompasses the notions of tribute, which Mann felt he owed to Goethe, and of exorcism, which he decided he owed to himself in order to affirm his own identity in German literature as distinct from a predecessor like Goethe. Mann's path to Goethe was most certainly not an easy one. It led him through and beyond Schiller, as well as the famous triad of intellectual authorities Mann himself often named: Schopenhauer, Wagner, and Nietzsche. Approaching Goethe meant

moving away from these earlier influences. Terence Reed dates
Mann's conscious affiliation with Goethe as follows:

> From his middle years, Mann began to link himself with the greatest
> figure in German literary culture, Goethe, and eventually celebrated a
> "mystical union" with him in the novel *Lotte in Weimar*, where quota-
> tion and allusion, from being a favoured technique, become the continu-
> ous substance.[1]

In some ways, Thomas Mann consciously followed in the tradition
of Goethe, whom he also sought to emulate. Just as Goethe's fame
rests in part on his *Bildungsroman*—namely, *Wilhelm Meisters
Lehrjahre* (1795/96) and its sequel, *Wilhelm Meisters Wanderjahre*
(1821)—so Mann wrote *Der Zauberberg* (1924). Intriguingly, Mann
also produced *Die Bekenntnisse des Hochstaplers Felix Krull*
(1954), best described as an *anti-Bildungsroman*. Just as Goethe
wrote his literary contribution to the Faust myth in the form of
two plays—*Faust I* (1808) and *Faust II* (1832)—Mann added his
novel, *Doktor Faustus* (1947), to the store of German literature. By
writing on themes Goethe had also explored, Mann continually
compared himself to the nineteenth-century master. To a considerable degree, Mann modeled his writing career on Goethe's. But
Goethe's thematic influence over Mann changed radically with the
latter's decision to present the Weimar giant as a character in *The
Beloved Returns.*

Of the four recent Mann biographers, Ronald Hayman, Donald
Prater, Klaus Harprecht, and Anthony Heilbut, Heilbut paints the
most literary portrait of Mann, and the novelist's complex relationship to Goethe is analyzed in remarkable detail.[2] Just as Mann
compared himself to Goethe on many occasions, both implicitly
and explicitly, Heilbut compares the two authors throughout his
biography. These comparisons usually are quite explicit, and they
almost always have to do with Mann's interpretation of the great
friendship between Schiller and Goethe as a homosexual relationship, especially from Schiller's perspective. Heilbut writes: "When
considering literary history, he [Mann] enjoyed couples, charging
the marriage of true minds with a physical Eros. Thus Schiller's
courtship of Goethe. . . ." (Heilbut, 43). This argument, culled
mainly from Mann's nonfiction about Goethe and Schiller, is intriguing; it is also well argued in its place: Heilbut's book.

In this essay, however, I wish to concentrate on the purely literary relationship between Mann and Goethe. Here, Heilbut gives
pointers as well. According to him, by 1929, "comparison to

Goethe had become habitual" (Heilbut, 10). Moreover, as Mann's fame increased, he "frequently cited Goethe's egomaniacal remark, 'Do we live if others live?'" (Heilbut, 360). With this kind of remark, Mann displayed Goethe's and his own egotistical world view. In addition, the world saw him as a Goethe-figure as well: "The boy who barely escaped Gymnasium was now the apparent successor to great Goethe himself" (Heilbut, 355). Heilbut points to many instances of Mann's stature as being comparable to Goethe's. Apparently, Roosevelt even considered appointing Mann as the postwar head of Germany. This idea, while not acted upon or taken that seriously, might well have pleased Mann, especially with regard to Goethe. The great man in Weimar had been a government official, but being named head of Germany would have allowed Mann to eclipse his eminent predecessor in the political realm. This was not to be. But Mann was able to transcend Goethe in another area: literature.

While Mann modeled his literary career after Goethe's, there was also an element of derision. As Heilbut points out:

> [T]he two attempted similar projects. Goethe wrote a youthful epic about Joseph, the subject of Mann's immense tetralogy. Both, amidst their other achievements, kept returning to a single, evidently irresistible subject. Goethe began *Faust* as a youth and completed it in his old age. Mann began *The Confessions of Felix Krull* in his mid-thirties and completed it forty years later. But this Goethean ambition mocked itself. *Felix Krull* is a deliberate parody of Goethe, the world-grasping Faust demoted to the status of a middle-class hustler.
>
> (Heilbut, 41)

Heilbut also writes that Mann's Joseph project was actually something planned by Goethe: "he now planned a novella about Joseph as an expansion of the Bible story, a project once contemplated by Goethe" (Heilbut, 536).

On the whole, Heilbut's intriguing erotic biography of Mann concentrates on the biographer's interpretation of Mann's statements on German history and intellectual history as a series of homosexual relationships, or "couples." The scope of the biography reaches only to Mann's late fifties, covering the later years in a postscript which unfortunately does not fully elaborate on Mann's literary triumph over Goethe in *The Beloved Returns*. Priority is given to Mann's nonfiction writing about Goethe, especially his essay on Goethe and Tolstoy. Here, too, there is a hint of iconoclasm: "Despite his well-known identification with Goethe, he combines an erotic sympathy with an unfailing sense of his master's limitations"

(Heilbut, 367). Mann knows that his great predecessor had imperfections. He shows them in nonfiction and, as we shall see, the fiction of *The Beloved Returns.*

Of course *The Beloved Returns* is not the only work in Thomas Mann's oeuvre that incorporates an author or other artist as character. Such works span his career, from "A Weary Hour" (1905), which fictionalizes Friedrich von Schiller, via *Death in Venice* (1912), in which Gustav von Aschenbach embodies several artists from Richard Wagner to Gustav Mahler, to *Doktor Faustus* whose eponymous character mirrored mainly Friedrich Nietzsche, Alban Berg, and Arnold Schoenberg. It is *The Beloved Returns,* however, which features Mann's most intimidating German precursor as a character. In this novel, Mann invokes Goethe in order to break free from him. This may seem odd after years of imitation, but it is for the same reason understandable as Mann's means of distinguishing himself.

In the early short story "A Weary Hour," Thomas Mann invokes the image of Goethe through the image of another great German author, Goethe's eminent contemporary, rival and friend, Friedrich von Schiller. The nameless character, obviously modeled after Schiller, spends a difficult hour fighting against both illness and his writer's block while trying to complete his tragedy of *Don Carlos* (1787). Schiller's ambition and his belief that physical and mental suffering must lead to greatness keep him awake at night:

> *Und dies war seine Eifersucht: daß niemand größer werde als er, der nicht auch tiefer als er um dieses Hohe gelitten.*[3]

And this was his ambition: that no one should be greater than he who had not also suffered more for the sake of this high ideal.[4]

The inner monologue of Schiller continues to invoke the idea, if not the name, of one author who was—or could be—considered greater than himself. This author's greatness was at the same time inspiring and upsetting, enough in the course of the weary hour depicted in the short story, to rid Schiller of his writer's block, and to complete *Don Carlos* successfully:

> *Niemand! . . . Aber er fühlte schon den Stachel dieses unvermeidlichen Gedankens in seinem Herzen, des Gedankens an ihn, den anderen . . . an den dort, in Weimar, den er mit einer sehnsüchtigen Feindschaft liebte . . . Und wieder, wie stets, . . . fühlte er die Arbeit in sich beginnen, die diesem Gedanken folgte: das eigene Wesen und Künstlertum gegen das des anderen zu behaupten und abzugrenzen . . .* (377)

No one. . . . For already the inevitable thought had stabbed him: the
thought of that other man . . . that man over there in Weimar, whom
he loved and hated. And once more, as always . . . there began working
within him the inevitable sequence of his thoughts: he must assert and
define his own nature, his own art, against that other's. (294)

Schiller's thought of "that man . . . in Weimar" obviously refers
to Goethe, the "other" author with whom all contemporary as well
as subsequent German authors were forced to compete. Schiller
most certainly was affected by the overshadowing presence of
Goethe in the literary world, as was Mann years later. Could these
lines from "A Weary Hour" not refer also to Mann's own attitudes
about Goethe? On the one hand, "that man" in Weimar inspired
imitation by his greatness. On the other hand, that same greatness
angered and frustrated writers who demanded to be heard by the
literary world. How could any German author after Goethe, in this
case Thomas Mann, confront the great predecessor if not with both
love and hate?

Before creating Goethe as a literary character, Mann retained a
certain distance not only by writing about Goethe through the
image held by his fictional Schiller, but also as a literary critic.
Mann wrote an essay on Goethe's *Elective Affinities* in 1925, and
two major Goethe essays in 1932. In "Goethes *Werther*" (1941), an
essay about Goethe's early novel *The Sorrows of Young Werther,*
Mann writes of the novel's swift canonization and the immediate
classification by society of Werther and Lotte as a couple on the
same high literary level as Shakespeare's Romeo and Juliet in the
tragedy that carries both their names. Mann's essay argues that
Werther and Lotte were not of the same calibre; Werther, falling
in love with a woman engaged to be married, is simply too foolish
and selfish to sacrifice his love for her sake. He commits suicide,
and leaves Lotte upset and embarrassed for having sanctioned or
encouraged Werther's love for her in the first place. It is generally
known, Mann continues, that there was a situation in Goethe's own
life at about the time he wrote *Werther,* quite similar to that between the epistolary novel's hero and Lotte. Mann comments that
much of *Werther* is taken word for word from Goethe's diaries and
letters, and he makes the fairly common interpretative claim that
Goethe wrote *Werther* in order to exorcise a potentially traumatic
experience. Those who were assumed to have followed Werther
and actually killed themselves as a result of unrequited love, instead of following Goethe by moving past the experience, had sim-

ply misunderstood the novel and Goethe's purpose in writing it.
Mann stated:

> *Während nun aber er [Goethe] sich erleichtert und aufgeklärt hatte,*
> *indem er die Wirklichkeit in Poesie verwandelte, wurden andere junge*
> *Leute dadurch verwirrt und glaubten, man müsse die Poesie in Wirk-*
> *lichkeit verwandeln, den Roman nachspielen und sich allenfalls*
> *selbst erschießen.*[5]

> While Goethe felt relieved and enlightened since he had transformed
> reality into poetry, other young people became confused and believed
> that they must convert poetry into reality, imitate the novel and possi-
> bly shoot themselves. (My translation)

Interestingly, as Mann was coming to terms with the Werther myth
in critical prose, he was nevertheless being a ventriloquist to the
historical Goethe. Mann's words are taken almost directly from
Goethe's autobiographical *Dichtung und Wahrheit,* where the latter wrote:

> *Wie ich mich nun aber dadurch erleichtert und aufgeklärt fühlte, die*
> *Wirklichkeit in Poesie verwandelt zu haben, so verwirrten sich meine*
> *Freunde daran, indem sie glaubten, man müsse die Poesie in Wirklich-*
> *keit verwandeln, einen solchen Roman nachspielen und sich allenfalls*
> *selbst erschießen.*[6]

> But whereas I felt relieved and serene for having transformed reality
> into poetry, my friends were misled into thinking that poetry must be
> transformed into reality, that they must reenact the novel, and possibly
> shoot themselves.[7]

Even if the events described in *Werther* were similar to events in
Goethe's life, it is obvious that Goethe did not advocate suicide as
a solution to romantic woes. The problem with the public reception
of *Werther* was due to a misunderstanding, a confusion between
reality and poetry. Mann assumes that readers of *Werther* were too
quick to equate reality and poetry. Although he was trying to come
to terms with an unhappy love—it was Mann's assumption—the
young Goethe who wrote *Werther* consciously meant to preserve
the distinction between reality and poetry, and *Werther* belonged
to the latter field of experience. Thomas Mann carried out a comparable maneuver in the writing of *The Beloved Returns,* mastering
his relationship with his greatest predecessor in German literature
and demonstrating the consequences of reading too literally.

Precisely how the world read and misread Goethe's novel *The Sorrows of Young Werther* is reflected in one of the strategies that Thomas Mann adopted in the writing of *The Beloved Returns*. Mann did not write a historically accurate account of the meeting between Charlotte and Goethe in Weimar in 1816. Like Goethe in *Werther,* he combined historical elements with his own artistic imagination to create a novel, a fictional text. Mann substantiated the historical meeting of Charlotte and Goethe, and projected onto it his own twentieth-century interpretation.

At the beginning of the novel, Charlotte Kestner arrives in Weimar, ostensibly to visit relatives. Mann pokes fun at the townspeople by having them crowd around Charlotte's hotel hoping to catch a glimpse of Werther's Lotte. These people—whose behavior is modeled on the response of the historical *Werther* readers— plainly and mistakenly identify Charlotte with Werther's Lotte. Even Mann's Charlotte confuses her own identity with that of her fictional namesake cum counterpart in *Werther.* She has misread the book and its intended function, which was to combine a number of the author's personal and other experiences primarily to create a fictional work. Mann's Charlotte has attempted to read the novel literally, as fact. Her naive assumption that *Werther* should be "her" story, as well as the public's similar conjecture, constitute for Mann a misunderstanding, if not a misuse of literature. Even if Goethe had used her as a model for his character, this does not warrant an equation between Werther's feelings for Lotte, on the one hand, and Goethe's for Charlotte, on the other. This is the lesson the fictional Charlotte learns in Mann's *The Beloved Returns.*

In a sense, Mann's writing career is analogous to Charlotte's pilgrimage to Goethe in the novel. Mann often referred to Goethe, wrote about him and his works, chose themes for his own work comparable to Goethe's, and finally invoked Goethe as a fictional character. He thus moved closer and closer to Goethe throughout his career. Charlotte in the Mann novel, too, moves closer to Goethe, first physically in her trip to Weimar, then socially as she meets with various citizens of Weimar. In *The Beloved Returns* both Mann and Charlotte, each for reasons of their own, made their way toward Goethe together.

The structure of *The Beloved Returns,* with each chapter introducing a character who has an increasingly closer association with Goethe, lends itself to Mann's use of the novel as a vehicle of expression for his contradictory attitudes about Goethe. As Charlotte is visited at her hotel by various citizens of Weimar, of course the topic of discussion is recurrently Goethe. Each conversation increases Charlotte's expectations of a meeting with the man himself. It is to be a meeting for which she has even brought along a dress similar to that worn by Lotte in *Werther.*

Seen against this background, Jürgen Seidel's article "Die Position des Helden im Roman" justly contends that even though Goethe has not yet appeared at this point in the text, he is present throughout the novel. In this context, Seidel calls Goethe's position in *The Beloved Returns "perizentral"*: while Goethe is practically everywhere in the novel, his presence is limited by mediation. Herein lies the distance for Seidel:

> As a topic of conversation Goethe indirectly centers action around himself, functioning at the same time as a decentralizing factor on the other figures—as a speaker he appears as a bright light that shows him in dramatic profile with centralizing power. This power pulls itself apart at its own center, thus dousing the light.[8]

Goethe serves as a common subject of conversation for the different characters in the novel, but not necessarily as a binding force. He is portrayed from many different perspectives through the first six chapters of *The Beloved Returns*. In the next chapter, Goethe himself finally appears.

Although each chapter introduces Goethe's friends, acquaintances, and colleagues in a rather regular fashion, the chapter that introduces the author himself as a character represents a break. In contrast to all the other chapters in the novel—headed *"Erstes Kapitel," "Zweites Kapitel,"* "Chapter 1," "Chapter 2," and so on—the Goethe chapter eschews the expected heading of *"Siebentes Kapitel"* (or, "Chapter 7"), opting instead for the foregrounding alternative phrase, *"Das siebente Kapitel,"* or "The seventh chapter." The seventh chapter marks a significant break in the narrative time of the novel. In this seminal section, the novelist turns the clock back to earlier that same morning, to the point where Goethe wakes up. As Charlotte is mentally preparing for the almost inevitable encounter with Goethe, the great man himself is distracted by other matters. As the reader moves into the inner monologue around which the material of the seventh chapter is structured, Mann as a writer of fiction takes the place which he had allotted to Schiller in "A Weary Hour." In "A Weary Hour," Mann had maintained a certain distance between himself and Goethe first by opting for Schiller, and subsequently by having this author as character refer to Goethe as a writer residing at a symbolic distance—"that man over there in Weimar." Moving inside the great man's mind via an extended inner monologue enabled Mann to express—albeit still to a certain extent implicitly—both his admiration and his disdain for Goethe.

It is in this chapter that Mann most effectively displays his conflicting attitudes about Goethe. Mann's "hateful love" and "loving hate" for Goethe inform this chapter. His portrayal of Goethe is both flattering and disparaging. Here he depicts Goethe as a highly intelligent, but self-centered, man who considers himself superior to all others. To invoke Goethe as a character must necessarily be to pay tribute to him; to parody the author as a character is to exorcise him.

In the seventh chapter, Mann shows his admiration and respect for Goethe by highlighting his active mind, and suggesting his many interests. Goethe awakens on this fictional morning with many questions and ideas on topics ranging from poetry and natural science to whether there is enough of a certain type of pastry on hand. The significant and the trivial are interwoven in Goethe's complex mind. Mann pays tribute to Goethe by portraying him as lively and interested in the world. Goethe's motto is:

"Was gab es also, was fordert der Tag?"[9]

"Well, and what does the day demand of me?"[10]

Goethe even takes time, albeit begrudgingly, to help one of his servants with a problem before going on with some dictation.

This favorable image is only half the picture of Goethe created by Mann in the seventh chapter. The other side of Goethe's personality is marked and marred by arrogance and an immense sense of self-importance. The character Goethe seems to praise Schiller by paying him a compliment in the following claim:

Er, er wäre imstande gewesen, starb ich vor ihm, den "Faust" zu vollenden. (619)

He, if I had died first, would have been up to finishing the *Faust*. (284)

By praising Schiller in this manner, however, Goethe actually is praising himself and his own *Faust,* establishing the play as a standard by which all literature ought to be judged. By extension, with Schiller dead, there is no one left for Goethe to communicate with, no one left to read and judge his writing. Goethe mourns the passing of Schiller not for Schiller's sake but for his own.

According to Mann's Goethe, the common people were not capable of judging his writing, nor should they have been allowed to
do so. He complains:

*"Daß sie urteilen dürfen! Daß jeder urteilen darf. Sollte verboten
sein."* (624–25)

"That they dare to judge! That anybody may judge! It ought to be
forbidden." (290)

Goethe has become his only critic. Not everything he writes is
acceptable. When he does find something good, Goethe remarks:

*"Das ist gut, das läßt sich hören, das ist von mir, das mag den ganzen
Quark tragen."* (623)

"That's good, reads well, has my mark, can carry the polite rubbish
the rest of it has to be." (289)

It is as if other things he might write were not good enough to bear
his mark. He implies, however, that no reader since Schiller's death
would notice the difference. The German people had already institutionalized Goethe as a literary icon. Instead of being pleased
with his reputation as one might expect, Goethe is depicted as a
cynic vis-à-vis his reading audience. Therefore, on hearing that
all of Weimar wants to see Charlotte as Werther's Lotte, Goethe
comments: *"Närrisches Volk!"* (694)—"What a silly lot!" (371).
   The German people in the Mann novel misunderstand Goethe
and his writings. They equally misunderstand Germany as a nation.
The fictional Goethe laments the situation, and cannot miss this
opportunity to glorify himself:

*Ich habe mein Deutschtum für mich—mag sie mitsamt der boshafter
Philisterei, die sie so nennen, der Teufel holen. Sie meinen, sie sind
Deutschland, aber ich bins, und gings zugrunde mit Stumpf und Stiel,
es dauerte in mir. . . . denn Deutschtum ist Freiheit, Bildung, Allseitig-
keit und Liebe,—daß sies nicht wissen ändert nichts daran.* (658)

What I have of Germany I will keep—and may the devil fly away with
them and the philistine spite they think is German! They think they
are Germany—but I am. Let the rest perish root and branch, it will
survive in me. . . . for that sort of Germany is freedom, is culture,
universality, love. All this is no less true because as yet they do not
know it. (331)

Mann is no longer blindly paying tribute to Goethe. Rather, he would seem to delight in exhibiting his predecessor's questionable sense of self-importance.

Despite his opinion of the general reading audience, Goethe continues to provide them with poetry. Later in the seventh chapter, a servant recommends a poem to Goethe for use in a ladies' calendar:

> *"Dies hier vielleicht, Excellenz: 'Sagt es niemand, nur den Weisen'—*
> *Es ist so geheimnisvoll."* (674)

> "Perhaps this one, Your Excellence: 'Tell It Only to the Wise Ones'—
> it is so pregnant." (349)

Goethe replies:

> *"Nein, das nicht. Ist mir zu schade. . . . Ist ja ein Damenkalender."*
> (674)

> "No, not that one. I could not bear it. . . . And this album is for la-
> dies." (349)

Mann's Goethe callously implies that this poem is too good for women because they would not be able to understand it. This is a backhanded tribute to Goethe, indeed. Mann shows Goethe's great intellect and poetic understanding but at the same time emphasizes the disdain Goethe had for readers who were incapable of understanding his work.

To augment the unfavorable aspect of the portrayal, Mann depicts Goethe in such a state of self-absorption that he barely notices his son August coming to talk with him. He also ignores the calling card Charlotte sends him, as well as his son's inquiry about a reply. Only much later in their conversation does Goethe allow August to return to the topic. Incapable of imagining the significance a meeting might have for Charlotte, he invites her to dinner. Goethe sees no importance in their encounter. By way of a reply to her note, he instructs August to send her

> *die übliche an distinguierte Weimar-Pilger: Eine Einladung zum Mit-*
> *tagessen.* (693)

> the usual thing to distinguished pilgrims to Weimar: an invitation to
> dinner. (370)

Charlotte, by contrast, takes the meeting very seriously. For the occasion, she wears the white dress of "Werther's Lotte," calling

attention to her view of herself in Goethe's early fiction and to
her misunderstanding of *Werther.* Goethe ignores her. From his
behavior at dinner, it is evident that the master of Weimar does
not sense the need, nor experience any wish to concern himself
with Charlotte. He is, and must remain, the focus of attention. The
insinuation here is that, unlike the people of Weimar and Charlotte
herself, it is still Goethe himself who knows and upholds the divi-
sion between poetry and reality, between *Dichtung* and *Wahrheit.*
Goethe and Charlotte shared the experience of their abortive summer love together. Goethe, in addition, had the experience of writing *Werther,* an experience tantamount to putting the folly of the
affair behind him. Charlotte, however, did not share in the experience of writing a novel and, instead, has had to be content with
reading—and misreading—his version. Consequently, over a period of forty-four years she has failed to master the events. This
also explains why she expected something significant from a new
meeting with Goethe, as well as why, when nothing happens, she
leaves, a disappointed woman. The implicit suggestion in the meeting between Charlotte and Goethe is that writing is a liberating
act, a means of mastering past experience. Writing the meeting
between Goethe and Charlotte in *The Beloved Returns,* Mann was,
in a comparable manner, attempting to free himself from the persistent memory of his distinguished precursor, Goethe.

For this reason, too, the second and final meeting between Charlotte and Goethe, paradoxically, has more significance for Thomas
Mann than for either fictional character. We must not lose sight of
the fact that it is Mann who orchestrated this fictional meeting
between Charlotte and Goethe. Mann leaves it open to interpretation whether Charlotte and Goethe actually converse, or whether
Charlotte only imagines him in the carriage across from her. Obviously, Mann has written the scripts of both speakers in this dialogue, or imagined dialogue. The words of Charlotte and of Goethe
came from Mann's pen. Mann can be read as both the pilgrim who
seeks the great artist and the great artist himself. Throughout the
novel, Mann can be closely identified with Charlotte because of the
similarity between their pilgrimages to Goethe. This identification
cannot, however, preclude an identification between Mann and his
famous predecessor. Although Mann does, indeed, identify with
Charlotte, it must be assumed that he used her character as a
convenient vehicle on the road to Weimar, and to Goethe.

In his article "*Lotte in Weimar:* Un Roman d'amour," Han Verhoeff reads the meeting in the carriage as the reunion of two old
lovers. He does not see *The Beloved Returns* as a literary treatise

or an essay, but simply the end of a love story. He places Charlotte in the central role, citing her trip to Weimar as the impetus for the novel's plot. In the end, Verhoeff claims that the meeting between Charlotte and Goethe is a rekindling of their old love: "His serious and sincere justification brings about their reconciliation, which is crowned by Lotte's closing remark: 'Peace to your old age.' This is a moment of love."[11] Moreover, this moment is the end of the "war" between Charlotte and Goethe. Verhoeff writes: "With this remark, Lotte introduces the peace which concludes this war between them, between Goethe and the woman now reconciled by an old and new union" (189). I see the outcome of this war in a different light.

The subject of Charlotte and Goethe's discussion is Goethe's poetic process and, more specifically, Mann's explanation of it. Here, author and character, Mann and Goethe, join to speak with one voice. They, or Mann through Goethe, admit using (and thereby sacrificing) real people in their fiction. Goethe apologizes to Charlotte for using her. Many of Mann's characters—including Goethe—are based, however loosely, on real people. Here, Mann places himself on Goethe's undisputed, eminent level by suggesting parallels; but, also, he simultaneously overshadows his prominent predecessor by practicing the same kind of presumptuous misuse on him, for which Mann does not apologize. In the course of the novel, the metaphor of Goethe's poem "Tell It Only to the Wise Ones" becomes a metaphor for writing:

> Sagt es niemand, nur den Weisen,
> Weil die Menge gleicht verhöhnet,
> Das Lebendge will ich preisen,
> Das nach Flammentod sich sehnet.
>
> [. . .]
>
> Keine Ferne macht dich schwierig,
> Kommst geflogen und gebannt,
> Und zuletzt, des Lichts begierig,
> Bist du, Schmetterling, verbrannt.[12]

Tell it to no one, tell it only to the wise, for the mob will only mock: I would praise the living thing that longs for death by fire. . . . No distance can weigh you down, you come flying, fascinated, and at last, lusting for the light, poor moth, you perish in the flame.[13]

The butterfly in this poem is attracted to the flame and then burned by it. This is, for Goethe, the only respectable way to live and to write. A writer must be attracted to the flame of his muse, so attracted that he does not notice the danger of being burned. If he is consumed by the flame, a true author can rise again to a new life and work. Goethe likens himself to the flame, the candle, and, finally, to the butterfly:

> *Willst du denn, daß ich diese sei, worein sich der Falter begierig stürzt, bin ich im Wandel und Austausch der Dinge die brennende Kerze doch auch, die ihren Leib opfert, damit das Licht leuchte, bin ich auch wieder der trunkene Schmetterling, der Flamme verfällt,—Gleichnis alles Opfers von Leben und Leib zu geistiger Wandlung. Alte Seele, liebe, kindliche, ich zuerst und zuletzt bin ein Opfer—und bin der, der es bringt. Einst verbrannte ich dir und verbrenne dir allezeit zu Geist und Licht.* (763)

> Say, if you will, that I am the flame, and into me the poor moth flings itself. Yet in the chance and change of things I am the candle too, giving my body that the light may burn. And finally, I am the drunken butterfly that falls to the flame—figure of the eternal sacrifice, body transmuted into soul, and life to spirit. Dear soul, dear child, dear childlike old soul, I, first and last, am the sacrifice, and he that offers it. Once I burned you, ever I burn you, into spirit and light. (451)

Whereas the fictional Goethe seems to revel in his self-inflicted martyrdom to his poetic flame, he feels no guilt for burning others like Charlotte in the process. He admits hurting Charlotte by using her as a character in a novel and then discarding her. Mann continues the cycle by using Goethe as a character in his novel. Mann illuminates Goethe by paying tribute to him, then consumes him as a fictional character. Just as Charlotte had no control over how she was portrayed in *Werther,* or indeed in *The Beloved Returns,* Goethe has no power over the image of himself created by Mann in *The Beloved Returns.*

Mann's exorcism of Goethe takes place in the final discussion between Charlotte and Goethe. He has sent his carriage to take her to the theater. When she emerges after the performance, Goethe seems to be inside, and they have their final conversation. It is intentionally left unclear whether Goethe is "really" in the carriage with her or whether she imagines him being there. With this technique, Mann demonstrates that it matters little whether Goethe is present or not. Whether Charlotte imagines or hears the words is irrelevant, since she is either "hearing" or "thinking" through Goethe, more specifically through Mann's image of Goethe. The thoughts, in effect, are not her own; they are Mann's.

As I have suggested, Mann can be identified with both Charlotte and Goethe, especially in this passage. Regardless of whether the conversation takes place between these two characters or is imagined by one of them, it is clear that Mann's sympathies are divided between them. Just as Goethe describes himself as the candle, the flame, and the moth of the poetic process, Mann could be asking the reader to see him as both Charlotte and Goethe. If, as I suggest, it was Mann's goal to displace Goethe, then it is reached through this maneuver of putting these words in the fictionalized Goethe's mouth. Goethe's actual presence in the carriage has become extraneous because Mann is writing the dialogue, or perhaps the monologue.

Mann allows himself to speak as Goethe. But it is not Goethe who has the last word in *The Beloved Returns*. Instead, it is the ironic side of Mann, or misunderstanding personified in Mager who closes the novel.

> *Guter Himmel, Frau Hofrätin, ich muß es sagen: Werthers Lotte aus Goethes Wagen zu helfen, das ist ein Erlebnis—wie soll ich es nennen? Es ist buchenswert.* (765)

> Good heavens, Frau Councillor, I cannot refrain—I really must say: to help Werther's Lotte out of Goethe's carriage, that is an experience that—what shall I call it? It ought to be put down. (453)

The implications of such an ending refer back to the genesis of the story. Readers will continue to mistake poetry for reality, unless they come to understand the difference as Charlotte does. As a result of the conversation in the carriage, real or imagined, Charlotte has been indoctrinated into the realm of those who understand literature. She realizes that *Werther* is not her story, but Goethe's. Mager, symbolically helping her out of the carriage where Goethe and Mann's understanding of Goethe linger, remains in blissful ignorance, unaware of his grave and dangerous misunderstanding of literature. Goethe has been honored, but also cast out, when he is left behind in the carriage.

Leaving Goethe in the carriage completes the analogy between Charlotte's path to Goethe in the novel and Mann's path to Goethe in his career. Charlotte had received guests in her hotel room, and with each chapter she met someone with a closer relationship to Goethe. Her last visitor, Goethe's son August, had facilitated her reunion with Goethe. Their meeting can hardly be called a reunion; Goethe's harsh treatment of Charlotte, at least from her perspective, is the beginning of her freedom from the belief that *Werther* was her story. It must be read as Goethe's story, and not as the historical person Goethe, but rather the author. This is a hard lesson for Charlotte, but we can almost see a smile of satisfaction on her face as Mager calls her "Werther's Lotte." She knows better; she has traveled to and beyond Goethe.

Charlotte Kestner does not travel this path to and beyond Goethe alone. Neither does Thomas Mann. Germany and the Germans have also done so, or at least attempted to do so, sometimes in a more political way. When Egon Günther filmed *The Beloved Returns* in the mid-1970s, for example, he combined film and politics through the use of Mann's novel and his own political situation. The film was produced for the international celebration of Mann's 100th birthday. It took Mann's dream of letting Goethe live again one step further, putting the actor's body behind the words in the novel. As Dennis Mahoney points out, the Goethe in the film is not exactly the one Mann depicted when he wrote *The Beloved Returns*. The film Goethe, according to Mahoney, reflects a wider interpretation of Goethe that was emerging in the mid-seventies in the German Democratic Republic. To Mahoney it is clear that the film's focus is "on Goethe the person, not Goethe the artist."[14] The monologue of Mann's seventh chapter is all but left out; only the petty side of Goethe and his self-centeredness are on display here. Mann certainly presented an ambivalent picture of Goethe for his readers, but in the film that ambivalence became a solely unfavorable depiction. It is here that Günther missed the point of the novel; it is also where he laid the groundwork for a new idea of Goethe as was current in the GDR at the time, as Mahoney suggests: "By demystifying Goethe so utterly, then, Günther is in effect preparing the viewer for a fresh perspective on the writer and his works" (110). Mahoney goes on to place the film version of *The Beloved Returns* in a wider cultural context: "[T]he film *Lotte in Weimar* becomes part of a widespread effort to take Goethe off his pedestal and conduct a critical evaluation of his person and his surroundings" (112). Goethe has been attacked from all sides. Mahoney sees Günther's film as a widening of Thomas Mann's very personal battle with Goethe to one of pan-German proportions. Before the film, it must be remembered, came Mann's novel. It is his personal battle with Goethe that has been the focus of the present study.

Like that of his fictional Charlotte Kestner, Thomas Mann's path to Goethe can be seen as a series of concentric circles. As mentioned above, Mann wrote distantly about Goethe at first, invoking him through the character of Schiller. He wrote nonfictional essays about Goethe and his works and used Goethean themes in his own fiction. He then used Goethe as a fictional character in his novel. When Mann finally got so close that he allowed himself to enter a fictional representation of Goethe's mind, he had almost reached his destination. Once he had put words into Goethe's mouth, Mann had become strong enough to cast aside his prominent literary forefather. What is left unsaid at the end of the novel is that Mager shuts the carriage door after helping Charlotte out. For Mann, this means locking Goethe inside. He has freed himself of Goethe and his influence. Mann risked much by taking up such a tradition-laden topic. He reached back over time to a discourse from the past, one which he himself ran the risk of misunderstanding. It is only through such expression and exposition that Mann was able to assert and define his own literary identity. He placed Goethe in Charlotte's position. For even though Goethe can be read as the main character in *The Beloved Returns,* it is, after all, only a Goethe in a Thomas Mann story.

Notes to "Displacing Goethe: Tribute and Exorcism in Thomas Mann's *The Beloved Returns*"

1. Terence J. Reed, *Thomas Mann: The Uses of Tradition* (Oxford: Clarendon Press, 1974), 1.

2. See Heilbut, *Thomas Mann: Eros and Literature* (New York: Alfred Knopf, 1995).

3. Mann, "Schwere Stunde," *Gesammelte Werke in dreizehn Bänden* (Frankfurt am Main: Fischer Verlag, 1974), vol. 8, *Erzählungen,* 377. Subsequent quotations from "Schwere Stunde" are from this edition and are quoted in the text.

4. Mann, "A Weary Hour," in *Stories of Three Decades,* trans. H. T. Lowe-Porter (New York: Alfred A. Knopf, 1976), 294. Subsequent quotations from "A Weary Hour" are from this edition and are quoted in the text.

5. Mann, "Goethes *Werther,*" in *Gesammelte Werke in dreizehn Bänden* (Frankfurt am Main: Fischer Verlag, 1974), vol. 9, *Reden und Aufsätze 1,* 643.

6. Johann Wolfgang Goethe, *Sämtliche Werke,* ed. Karl Richter (Munich: Carl Hanser Verlag, 1985), vol. 16, *Aus meinem Leben. Dichtung und Wahrheit,* ed. Peter Sprengel, 621–22.

7. Goethe, *From My Life: Poetry and Truth, Parts One to Three,* trans. Robert R. Heitner (New York: Suhrkamp Publishers, 1987), 432.

8. Seidel, "Die Position des 'Helden' im Roman: Zur Figuralstruktur in Thomas Manns *Lotte in Weimar,*" *Goethe Jahrbuch* (Weimar), 103 (1986): 207–34 (p. 233). Translations from the German are my own.

9. Mann, *Gesammelte Werke in dreizehn Bänden* (Frankfurt am Main: Fischer Verlag, 1974), vol. 2, *Königliche Hoheit / Lotte in Weimar,* 623. All quotations from *Lotte in Weimar* are taken from this edition and are noted in the text.

10. Mann, *The Beloved Returns,* trans. H. T. Lowe-Porter (Berkeley and Los Angeles: University of California Press, 1990), 289. All quotations from *The Beloved Returns* are taken from this edition and are noted in the text.

11. Verhoeff, "*Lotte in Weimar:* Un roman d'amour," in *Fathers and Mothers in Literature,* ed. Henk Hillenaar and Walter Schönau (Amsterdam and Atlanta: Rodopi, 1994), 183–97 (p. 185). Translations from the French are my own.

12. Goethe, "Selige Sehnsucht," in *Goethes Werke: Hamburger Ausgabe in 14 Bänden* (Munich: C. H. Beck, 1974), vol. 2, *Gedichte und Epen II,* ed. Erich Trunz, 18–19.

13. Goethe, "*Selige Sehnsucht,*" in *Goethe,* trans. David Luke (Baltimore: Penguin Books, 1964), 240.

14. Mahoney, "Goethe Seen anew: Egon Günther's Film *Lotte in Weimar,*" *Goethe Yearbook* (Columbia), 2 (1984): 105–16 (p. 107).

Hermann Broch and Virgil

JATTIE ENKLAAR

The commemoration of Virgil's 2000th birthday in 1930 initiated a reassessment of the cultural history of Western civilization. Theodor Haecker's *Vergil: Vater des Abendlandes* viewed Virgil as an intermediary between classical antiquity and Christianity, and turned the poet into a symbol of the dialectics of poetic craftsmanship and myth.[1] The interest in Virgil rekindled a similar interest in Dante's *Divine Comedy* (featuring Virgil as a character), as a topos of the old and new, the *antico* and *nuovo*.[2] In choosing Virgil as the protagonist of his novel *Der Tod des Vergil* (1945), translated into English as *The Death of Virgil*, Hermann Broch managed to span nearly three millennia of historical continuity.[3] There was a straight line from Homer's epics, absorbed into Virgil's *Aeneid,* via the medieval conception of Virgil and the Renaissance view—with Virgil given a leading role in Dante's *Divine Comedy*—to Broch's own twentieth-century vision in *The Death of Virgil.*

Broch's novel captures the last eighteen hours of the poet's life as described from the perspective of the dying man. Broch turns Virgil into a key figure, the link between the beginning and ending of a cultural era, where oppositions within art, life, religion, and politics usher in new ethical standards. Broch's Virgil, presented both as a poet laureate and as a countryman, becomes the prophet of new values beyond Reason.[4] In fact (and here the Latin poet shakes hands with his Austrian novelist-biographer), Virgil becomes the exponent of an ideal that directs twentieth-century Western civilization to its final destiny.

If Homer had been the "sweet master" for Western civilization, Virgil for Dante was the "sweetest father" (*dolcissimo padre*). Virgil, whose "embodied" soul guides Dante—"Midway this way of life"[5]—like a shadow on his journey to Paradise, supports the process of awakening consciousness which the "I" undergoes as it approaches the concept of God within the forlornness of the world. Virgil's guided tour in the *Divine Comedy* achieves a sublime metamorphosis: from the world of classical antiquity, in which the Platonic idea had led the way, Virgil, the master, directs his "precious son" Dante to "eternal goodness," predicting the peace of everlasting love.

Like Dante, Broch saw the midway point on the path of life as a crucial moment for reflection. Another, perhaps more significant bond between the two writers was that Broch began working on his great Virgil project when he was fifty-one, the age at which Virgil died. Broch presents the dying Virgil at a time of prospective decay within the Roman empire, whose savior, Octavianus Augustus, was able to defer apocalyptic disaster only once more. By the time Broch came to write his work, in 1936, the shadow of the Third Reich loomed, instilling in Broch a sense of imminent decay, in both personal and cultural terms. This mood inspired works such as "Erwägungen zum Problem des Kulturtodes" ("Reflections on the Problem of the Death of Civilization," 1936), and "Die Kunst am Ende einer Kultur" ("Art at the End of Civilization," 1933). In both critical prose works, death is portrayed as the unconditional state in the impenetrability of the future in a way that foreshadows *The Death of Virgil*.

The biographical foundation on which *The Death of Virgil* rests had also been Dante's point of departure:

> No man, although I once was man;
> My parents' native land was Lombardy
> And both by citizenship were Mantuan.
> *Sub Julio* born, though late in time, was I,
> And lived at Rome in good Augustus' days,
> When the false gods were worshipped ignorantly.
>
> Poet was I, and tuned my verse to praise. (73)

Implicit in the last line is the question concerning the value of language in the face of death. This issue is also broached in Broch's novel, when Lysanias, acting as the angel of death, predicts to the ailing Virgil on his way to Brundisium: "Your path is poetry, your goal is beyond that of poetry" (*Death of Virgil*, 60). According to Broch, the object of literature lies in its "self-dissolution." In this respect, Virgil is his "experimental subject," who in his hour of death is tormented by doubt:

> Nothing availed the poet, he could right no wrongs; he is heeded only if he extols the world, never if he portrays it as it is. Only falsehood wins renown, not understanding.
>
> (*Death of Virgil*, 15)

Disgusted by the masses and by fame, Broch's Virgil begins to question his poetic calling with trepidation:

> Down there they did not understand him and paid no attention to him, these up here maintained that they revered him, yes, they even believed it; but, be that as it may, whether they presumed to cherish his work by falsely pretending to be connoisseurs, or whether, no less falsely, they paid homage to him as Caesar's friend, it was of no moment, he Publius Vergilius Maro had nothing in common with them . . .
>
> (*Death of Virgil*, 16)

At the hour of death, the bond between people and poet disintegrates:

> Yes and this was the people, the Roman people, whose spirit and honor he, Publius Vergilius Maro, he a real farmer's son from Andes near Mantua, had not so much described as tried to glorify! To glorify and not describe, that had been the mistake, oh, and this represented the Italy of the *Aeneid*!
>
> (*Death of Virgil*, 22)

Broch sees Virgil's ascent into the crystalline sphere as the end.

There is a considerable degree of resemblance between Broch's self-image and his conception of Virgil. A brief biographical sketch illuminates the novel. Hermann Broch, born in Vienna on 1 November 1886, lived in a period of profound changes. After retiring as head of his father's textile factory in 1927, he devoted himself to the study of mathematics, philosophy, and psychology. His urge to acquire insight and knowledge through scientific methods is recorded in his *Philosophische Schriften* ("Philosophical Writings") and *Theorie des Massenwahns* ("Theory of the Illusion of the Masses").[6] His desire in fiction to revive the dying Virgil must be seen against this background:

> [D]er Tod war uns, die wir nun gewissermaßen am Rande des Konzentrationslagers lebten, plötzlich so handgreiflich nahegerückt, daß die metaphysische Auseinandersetzung mit ihm schlechterdings nicht mehr aufschiebbar war. Und so begann ich 1937, beinahe gegen meinen eigenen Willen, sozusagen als Privatangelegenheit des eigenen Seelenheiles, mit einem strikt esoterischen Buche, dem "Vergil."
>
> (*Gesammelte Werke*, 9:51)

To us, who were now living at the edge of the concentration camp, so to speak, death had suddenly become so palpably close that a metaphysical confrontation with it simply could not be put off any longer.

And so, in 1937, almost against my own will, as a sort of private matter
concerning my own salvation, I started working on a strictly esoteric
book, *Virgil.*

In 1938, after his arrest by the Gestapo in Alt-Aussee and his
three-week imprisonment, Broch left Austria for America. There,
Virgil and the psychology of the masses formed the focus of his
interest, and *The Death of Virgil*—which was meant to demonstrate how the poet who had started out in the textile business
could convert the fundamental conflict within his philosophy into
literary material—was to be the crowning achievement of his life.
Broch wrote five versions of *The Death of Virgil* between 1936 and
1945.[7] Even so, he felt that the last version had been published
much too soon. Shortly before a trip back to Europe, on 30 May
1951, Broch died.

Like Thomas Mann and Giuseppe Antonio Borgese, also one-
time exiles in the United States, Broch desired to find a new theoretical foundation for Europe as a world democracy. This desire
led Broch to make strongly-worded statements about fighting the
global plague, *"die Bekämpfung der Weltseuche."* He was afraid of
German influence, even in America, and hoped to set his theoretical humanism against this threat. His fear of the "perverted" and
"kitschy" romanticism of Hitler and Nazi Germany is aptly captured in *Adolf Hitler's Farewell Address*, which appeared in the
Saturday Review of Literature (1944). Broch's Hitler makes a fictional suicide speech. It is the "self-revelation of a madman," of
a "surrogate savior," who, as the direct descendant of German
expansionist romanticism, represents the end of romantic idealism,
spouting the clichés of heroic language in order to exonerate himself from any personal responsibility.[8] For Broch, this "final outbreak of megalomania—*Hitler's Farewell Address*"[9] had the
purpose "of educating his readers to their latent susceptibility to
the insidious appeal of mass hysteria."[10] Broch believed that this
was a better way of calling the attention of the audience at large
to the danger of demonic demagogy than through his theoretical
writings about mass psychology. Interestingly for our understanding of *The Death of Virgil,* Broch turns both Hitler and Virgil into
characters within his literary fiction, secluded from the world and
trapped within their own monologues. Both served his purpose of
elucidating the truth of human responsibility, be it in a direct address to the world (Hitler), or in an interior monologue (Virgil).
In pleading historical inevitability, *Adolf Hitler's Farewell Address*
constitutes Broch's farewell to the "Old World"; in Hitler's down-

fall as "master of human moods," he provides a personally felt reading of the Holocaust. Virgil as a character is Hitler's opposite: Virgil's farewell to art gives a new vision of the earthly absolute, realized "in loving perception" (*Death of Virgil,* 446). In Broch's Virgil, the Germanic culture of the Occident is presented with an example that is intended to have a purifying effect on the spirit of the age.

For Broch, this Virgilian view of man is also a political landmark; only by reference to the concept of Virgilian man will Europe be able to rise from its ashes after 1945. The cultural consciousness propagated as "German culture" by the hysterical Hitler character in his downfall is contrasted with Virgil's favorable "helplessness" at Brundisium where Broch depicts his pseudo-ego thus: "So he lay there, he the poet of the *Aeneid,* he Publius Vergilius Maro, he lay there with ebbing consciousness, almost ashamed of his helplessness."[11] Virgil represents the intimation of a different totality, a totality based on the autonomy of the consciousness which Broch had defined in his *Theorie des Massenwahns* as *"die Erkenntnis, in der die Welt immer wieder zum ersten Mal ersteht"* ("the understanding, in which the world comes into being for the first time over and over again").[12]

The author Broch leads his fictional Virgil to the edge of Truth by poetic means, by a language of unprecedented force, which indissolubly fuses the rational and the irrational. In one long breath, the modern epic moves through more than 500 pages, like a composition consisting of a motif with infinite variations. In one of his own commentaries, Broch writes:

> *Obwohl in der dritten Person dargestellt, ist es ein innerer Monolog des Dichters. Es ist daher vor allem eine Auseinandersetzung mit seinem eigenen Leben, mit der moralischen Richtigkeit oder Unrichtigkeit dieses Lebens, mit der Berechtigung und Nicht-Berechtigung der dichterischen Arbeit, der dieses Leben geweiht war—Vergil wollte sein gesamtes Werk vernichtet haben—, doch da jedes Leben in die Epoche seines Daseins eingebunden ist, umfaßt die Auseinandersetzung die Ganzheit der geistigen und vielfach mystischen Strömungen, von denen das Römische Reich in diesem letzten vorchristlichen Jahrhundert durchpulst gewesen ist, und die Vergil zu einem Vorahner des Christentums gemacht haben.*
>
> (*Gesammelte Werke,* 6:265)

Although it is written in the third person, it is an interior monologue of the poet. It is therefore above all a confrontation with his own life, with the moral rightness or wrongness of that life, with the justifiability

or unjustifiability of the literary work to which this life had been dedicated—Virgil wanted his complete works to be destroyed—but as every
life is inextricably tied up with the era of its existence, this confrontation comprises the whole of the spiritual and often mystical movements
that abounded in the Roman empire in this last century before Christianity, and that gave Virgil precognition of Christianity.

In an intertextual genesis, Broch captures the images of two
worlds, those of Virgil Maro and Hermann Broch. Broch's text,
interspersed with quotations from Virgil, unites dream and reality
in a lyrical continuo, culminating in a feverish ecstasy. The translation of "reality" and "dream" into Broch's terminology raises the
issue of the "rational" and "irrational" and their interdependence.
Reason, which has dominated thought since the eighteenth century,
surrenders to the eternal at the borderline of life and death, where
the irrational becomes tangible. This transition seems to develop
almost naturally within the lyrical language of the text. After all,
only the metaphysical demands totality. This totality takes shape
in the "*Denkschauen*," the gnostic revelation granted to the dying
poet, as a complete identification with the world of objects. Dying
is a combined experience of the remembrance of things past and
a consciousness of the end, an area in which the confrontation
with the ineffable almost becomes a utopia of security. Dying leads
life away from the strictly personal to the all-encompassing, frees
it from the biographical, which includes both life and art. Virgil's
dying is the representation of the ultimate form of expression.

The representation of Virgil as the protagonist of the novel is based
on two traditions about his life, known as the "Virgiliana" (Lützeler, 297). The first is the so-called prophecy of Christ in the
Fourth Eclogue, which Virgil addressed to consul Pollio when in
46 B.C. he became the father of a son. Here, Virgil pays tribute to
the coming generations. He depicts a blissful future, as had been
predicted in the prophecies of the Cumaean sibyl. Through Pollio's
son, in whom other yet unborn sons are represented and in whose
image the victory of Octavian is symbolized as a blessing for the
Roman empire, Virgil allegorically conjures up a great Messianic
vision of the future. As it says in the last line of the Fourth Eclogue:
"*Aspice, venturo laetentur ut omnia saeclo!*" ("See how all things
rejoice at the approach of the happy age"). Virgil's life looks forward to a new millennium, just like in 1945, after the horrors of
the Third Reich, the second millennium of Western civilization
seemed to be coming to an end. In the midst of this decline, Broch

reaches out to Virgil, so that the rise and fall of civilization take place under the star of Bethlehem. What to the ancient poet is the mythical prophecy of salvation is, to Broch, the simultaneous downfall of culture and art.

As to the second of the "Virgiliana" on which the representation of Virgil in the novel is based, the following may be noted. The dying poet Virgil had specifically requested that the unfinished manuscript of the *Aeneid* be burned. This request is an indication of a "new spirit amongst the gods" and announces the beginning of a new era. Virgil's pursuit of the truth implies doubt about art,

> *an der Schönheit als solcher . . . Und so führten diese Zweifel auch dazu, daß er sich nicht länger imstande sah, die Aeneis zu vollenden. In seinem fünfzigsten Lebensjahr beschloß er . . . sein restliches Leben ausschließlich der Erkenntnissuche zu widmen. Tödlich erkrankt schon bei seiner Ankunft in Athen, vermochte der Augustus, der sich gerade damals zufällig in Griechenland befand, Vergil zur Rückkunft nach Italien . . . zu bewegen. Vergil starb kurz nach seiner Ankunft in Brundisium. Vermutlich dank des Einspruches des Augustus wurde die Aeneis vor der Vernichtung bewahrt.*[13]

> about beauty as such. . . . And so these doubts also made him feel incapable of completing the *Aeneid*. In his fiftieth year, he decided . . . to dedicate the remainder of his life exclusively to contemplation. He was already terminally ill when he arrived in Athens, and Augustus, who just happened to be in Greece at the time, managed to persuade Virgil to return to Italy. Virgil died shortly after his arrival in Brundisium. It is probably due to the interference of Augustus that the *Aeneid* was saved from destruction.

This historical fact provided Broch with the starting point for his novel, partly because the pursuit of *Erkenntnistiefe*, or depth of understanding, as well as the rejection of beauty as an aim in itself were two of Broch's own preoccupations. One wonders if it is Broch or Virgil one hears when the Latin poet in the novel announces: "What I have written must be consumed by the fire of reality" (*Death of Virgil*, 245). Virgil falters, trying to express to Augustus his feelings on the meaning of incompleteness and imperfection:

> Caesar did not comprehend, no one grasped the truth, no one knew that the divinity of beauty was only a sham-divinity, the shadow cast by the coming of the gods. "There is no need of poetry, oh, Caesar, to understand life . . ."
>
> (*Death of Virgil*, 320–21)

The gulf between art and understanding dissolves in "the understanding of death," which alone can lead the way: "'The understanding of death.'—It was like a re-found, a re-recognized, a
homecoming enlightenment" (*Death of Virgil*, 321). To Broch's Virgil, the *Aeneid* as a work of art stands in the way of understanding:
"The poem . . . I must attain perception . . . the poem stands there
like an obstruction to perception; it is in my way" (*Death of Virgil*,
332). Dying, however, broadens the understanding: one leaves the
realm of art behind to proceed into the realm of death. It comes
as little of a surprise, therefore, that the *Aeneid* as the symbol
of an empire in the novel acquires widely different meanings for
Augustus and Virgil. Hence their confusion:

> "Aye, Augustus, you simply do not want to see, you do not want it to
> be true, that the poetical task no longer exists."
> "No longer exists? No longer? You sound as though we were standing
> at the end of something . . ."
> "Perhaps it would be better to say, not yet! for we may assume that a
> time for artistic tasks will dawn again."
> "No longer and not yet,"—Caesar, much dismayed, was weighing these
> words—"and between them yawns an empty space."
>
> (*Death of Virgil*, 335)

The answer to Augustus's attempt to comprehend is emphatic: "No
longer and not yet." "*Sein zum Tode*," or living for death, is the
mode of participation in the transcendental. Within the dying man
the ineffable truth takes shape, in which it is no longer the downfall
of an empire that is of central importance, but Augustus who reap-
pears in the imagination of the poet as a stinking old man:

> Come Virgil, come with me, lie there with me on my couch, for we
> must go back; we must keep on going back, we must reach beyond the
> first forefathers; we must return into the mass that sustained us, we
> must go back into the humus of the beginning.
>
> (*Death of Virgil*, 420)

At this point, worldly concerns have been left behind. And at the
point when Virgil dedicates the poem to Octavian—"Octavian . . .
the poem is yours"—something has taken place within Virgil that
reaches beyond the prophecy of the downfall of the Roman empire.

In the person of the dying Virgil, the rise and fall of a culture
coincide. What to Broch's Virgil is a moment of complete consciousness, actually is a portrayal of the doubts that plagued Broch
in confronting the issues of his own time.[14] *Der Tod des Vergil* is

not a historical novel, nor a belated necrology, but a twentieth-century epic of world history. The "I" to whom the combined eschatological and utopian view of the future is granted, is not so much "I" as the writer, or "I" as Virgil, but "I" as man in general.

The epistemological doubt, so typical of modernism in the postwar situation, develops in Broch's case into a need to invoke a "Platonically unknowable reality," thanks to and in spite of doubts about language and expression.[15] This is what the leitmotif of *"nicht mehr und noch nicht"* refers to, also echoed in the novel's last sentence as "it was the word beyond speech" (*Death of Virgil*, 482). Through the vehicle of language, the biographical core recedes in favor of the universal character and applicability of the work. The plot is no more than the sum of a number of moments, moments which were not individual per se, but what Broch calls *"Geschichtsaugenblicke,"* or moments of history.[16]

The basic opposition within the novel, in which Broch identifies with his fictionalized Virgil, leads to a state of utopian expectation. In the twilight zone of night, which coincides with that of the dying man, the boundaries of space disintegrate. This is the empty space, the yawning abyss that is not comprehended by the emperor and general, Augustus. The extreme individuality of the dying "I" unveils a glimpse of the paradisiacal beauty of humanity.

The cosmic dimension becomes a symbol of the memory of all human origin. Fading into death is seen as the closing of a circle, which symbolizes past and future beyond the dimension of time, and thereby man's participation in the collective unconscious, the mythical archetype:

Gewiß, des Menschen Paradiesessehnsucht ist nicht bloß Frucht der Kulturkatastrophen, die ihn ereilt haben, ist nicht bloß Frucht seines Erschreckens. . . . er fühlt es, selbst wenn er von göttlicher Vollbewußtheit und tierischer Nichtbewußtheit, den beiden Bewußtseinspolen, zwischen denen sein dämmerndes Absinken vonstatten geht, nicht das geringste weiß, und eben weil er beides, Anfang wie Ende des Absinkens, ahnend fühlt, steigen Traumbilder in ihm auf, wunscherfüllt hoffende . . . Vielleicht sogar von Erinnerungsbildern an eine ferne Menschheitsvergangenheit umdämmert, erhob sich für ihn nicht nur die Frage nach dem Anfangsstadium . . . sondern er verlangte auch noch außerdem, daß der ganze Vorgang des Absinkens sich darin als gefahrlos dartue. M.a.W., Anfangs- und Endzustand des Absinkens sollen zusammenfallen, damit dieses zu einem glücklichen Kreislauf sich schließe, in dem der dämmernde Hang zum Tierischen sich unverbindlich-harmlos befriedigen läßt. Es wurde zum paradiesischen Sehnsuchtsbilde . . . in dem Mensch und Tier in innerlicher Einheit

ineinander, nebeneinander leben, sie beide in friedlich-weisem Dahin-
dämmern, sie beide ich-begabt . . . sie beide weise eingefügt in das
Gottesgebot.

(*Gesammelte Werke,* 9:281)

Surely, man's longing for paradise is not merely a fruit of the cultural catastrophes that have befallen him; it is not merely the fruit of his fear . . . he feels it, even when he knows nothing of divine all-consciousness and animal unconsciousness, the two extremes of consciousness between which his drowsy sinking into death takes place, and precisely because he intuitively feels both the beginning and the approaching end of his dying process, dream images arise in him, hoping for the fulfillment of his wishes. . . . Perhaps even vaguely conscious of memories of the distant past of humanity, not only the question of the beginning arose for him . . . but he also demanded that the entire process of dying should appear without danger. In other words, beginning and end of the dying process should coincide, so that it should close in a happy cycle, in which the slumbering desires of man's animal nature can be satisfied in a non-committal, harmless manner. It became an image of paradisiacal longing, in which man and animal live within each other and next to each other in internal unity, both in a peaceful and wise slumber, both ego-talented . . . both sagely reconciled to God's commandment.

If, perceived from this perspective, the work of art is a reverse creation, and if Virgil's dying emblematically shows death as the greatest creator of human enlightenment, the question remains as to the deeper meaning underlying Broch's last literary work. What cultural pessimism motivated the author describing Virgil's dying hours to let the ancient poet struggle through a psychological abyss, through plebeian misery and vanity, to arrive at last on the higher plane of a cosmic order? Once he beholds the landscape of eternity, it no longer matters whether or not the manuscript is burned: the *Aeneid* is allowed to remain as a witness of the hope and the human struggle for deliverance.

Thus, Broch leads his alter ego from the twilight of the impending night through the valley of soul-searching questions into the spheres of deliverance. The purification of Broch's Virgil is achieved by the cosmos within the scope of language. This is why Broch saw this work as a last deed of expression, in which dying man pours out his soul in language hoping to reach beyond language, in a trial of his utmost abilities. Paradise draws nearer as language approaches its limits. Broch not only succeeds in forging a link between himself and the dying poet through the medium of language, but he also is able to investigate the essentials of the biography of Virgil, the poet and man. Virgil, who has been led from the slums of Brundisium into the nameless Nothingness, is at last like Moses placed on a mountain top, and granted a vision of the landscape of the future (Götz Wienold, 265). Between "So he lay there, he the poet of the *Aeneid*," "He lay and listened," and "He lay, he rested, he was allowed to rest on," Virgil has gone through his phase of remorse, in which he decided to burn the *Aeneid*.[17]

To the dying Virgil, the re-creation that takes place between beginning and end is a reality also reflected in the landscape. As the twilight gathers over Brundisium, the loneliness of the sea presents itself to the dying man as a promise—"mother-of-pearl spread over the open shell of heaven" (*Death of Virgil*, 11)—which finds its fulfillment in another infinity in the last chapter, "Air-The homecoming." In perceiving the union of past and future, the poet is filled with awe, "for the ring of time had closed and the end was the beginning" (*Death of Virgil*, 481). Thus, Broch leads his poet to the beginning of "loving perception" (480), drowsing in paradisiacal forgetfulness, where the divine Logos as a principle of order is joined to the dumbness of the animal and orphic worlds.

Through Virgil, Broch demonstrates how the human capacity for insight, disconnected from art, develops into intuition and secret communion with the divine Nothingness. In such a tour de force, in which lyricism suggests connections beyond the grasp of Reason, poetry outstrips language. Broch saw the concentration of images within poetic reality as the last possible act of language. In this vision, the gnostic revelation granted to his Virgil as the first poet of Western civilization becomes a symbol for the last poets of the Occident, whose only prospect is destruction. To Broch this was not an escape into irrational metaphysical expectations, nor the hope of a new Messiah; the position assigned to the first poet of Western civilization implies a kind of completion. Who could be a better spokesman for Broch than Virgil, the poet, and the countryman descended from a lineage of Roman farmers?

Fast durchaus auf das Diesseitige beschränkt, auf Acker und Wachstum . . . akzeptiert der Bauer auch den Tod als etwas Diesseitiges, und der Blick ins Ewige gilt nicht so sehr dem Jenseitigen als einem irdischen Fortbestand der gestorbenen Persönlichkeit, gilt dem doppelten Einst der Vergangenheit und Zukunft . . .
(Gesammelte Werke, 9:275)

Being almost entirely limited to the this-worldly, to his fields and the growth of his crops . . . the farmer also accepts death as something this-worldly; and when he looks to eternity, it is not the other-worldly he is looking for, but an earthly continuation of the personality that has died, blending the "once" of the past with the "once" of the future.

In his Virgil, Broch creates a man who is not shackled by history, but who independently and instinctively recaptures life through the stage of semi-conscious slumbering. A lowering of the level of consciousness is associated with the continuity of civilization as progress, which, on the one hand, is constantly threatened by animal instinct, and fed by animal warmth and earthiness, on the other. The Promethean aspects of man are continually impeded by the subconscious; on each occasion, however, it also creates a point of repose, each time followed by a renewed evolutionary leap. This vision makes Virgil the representative of Broch's theories about civilization, history, and politics. The great Roman surpasses Prometheus, when in his state of slumber he succeeds in shifting the boundaries between man and beast, and breaks through to Truth beyond language, beyond the concerns of civilization. Broch thus retraces civilization to its original state. Dante's "I once was man—Poet was I" enters into the modern era, which—according to Broch—can only evolve into a new millennium by returning to the secret of Creation, bound to the triad of the farmer or country-man, in which the natural, the moral, and the sinless are identical. It is the utopia of an increasing humanism, growing because of the insight in the earthly logic of inner and outer reality.

Broch's utopia embraces two mutually balancing ideals. On the one hand, there is the awakening of the individual consciousness, of which Virgil is his model; on the other, there is a constant analysis of demonic forces which, in times of mass hysteria, tend collectively to break down personal consciousness. Here, *Adolf Hitler's Farewell Address* functions as a literary model that sounds a warning. Any consciousness-raising process, even democracy, may engender a hazardous belief in the "mystical infallibility of the majority of the people." For Broch, such processes are cyclical and innate to man's psyche, *"gesetzpsychische Zyklen."*[18] Man's potential addiction should be countered by moral exempla, *"Wert-modelle,"* or value-models. Seen from this perspective, the death of Virgil is an exemplum in which the character leads the way to the victory of the higher rational forces, which transcend politics, economics, even art, in order to take us back to the origins, the inner experience as the central value that, for Broch, takes precedence in every social structure.

At the end of Broch's portrait of Virgil, there is a self-portrait, written in the crystalline sphere of the wordless. The dying Virgil, as a man of the Occident, holds the promise of freedom. Philosophically this means humanitarian enlightenment, politically it means democracy, and in religious terms it entails the abolition of the antinomy in Promethean man.[19]

> *Im Vergleich mit dem biblischen Paradies . . . wird hier, sozusagen durch eine Hintertür, ein Stückchen Erkenntnis und ein Tröpfchen Arbeitsschweiß in die seligen Gefilde eingeschmuggelt, und daß ein derartiger idyllisch-bukolischer Halb-Antiprometheismus keine geeignete Rezeptur zur Lösung einer Antinomie sein könne, daß zum Aufbau eines neuen Paradieses, auch wenn es ein bäuerliches sein sollte, es vorher einer radikal gründlichen Aufräumarbeit bedürfte, das konnte der Denkehrlichkeit Vergils auf die Dauer nicht verborgen bleiben, umsoweniger als der prometheische Gehalt seines frommen Gehorsams bereits alle Ansätze zu endgültiger Radikalisierung in sich getragen hatte: offenbar nach schwersten inneren Kämpfen radikal antiprometheisch geworden, verfügte Vergil am Ende seines Lebens, daß alles, was in diesem prometheisch gewesen war, also sein eignes Werk . . . vernichtet werden möge, und dieser Entschluß war im Letzten nichts anderes als der Durchbruch all seiner christlichen Vorausahnungen.*

> (*Gesammelte Werke*, 9:283ff)

Compared to the biblical Paradise . . . here a bit of understanding and a drop of honest sweat is smuggled into the happy fields, through the back door, so to speak. Virgil was too honest in his thinking not to realize, finally, that such an idyllic-bucolic semi-anti-prometheanism could not be a suitable recipe to resolve an antinomy; that in order to build a new paradise, even if it was only to be a bucolic one, a radical and thorough-going clean-up would be required first; the more so, as the Promethean quality of his pious obedience had already contained the seeds of a definitive radicalization. Having become radically anti-Promethean, apparently after great inner struggles, at the end of his life Virgil commanded that everything in his life that had been Promethean, so his own work . . . should be destroyed; and this decision was, in the final analysis, nothing but the breakthrough of all his Christian premonitions.

The Western world will have to act. The thoroughgoing clean-up Broch envisioned in 1945 no longer meant the spiritual asceticism he postulated for his Virgil. Instead, it was concerned with the individual in the process of resurrection from apocalyptic destruction. This signified a concrete utopia of humanity. This basic humanistic principle can be achieved only by bridging the gap between the "masses" and the "I," by guiding Prometheus, present in every human being, who in his ultimate shape is Mephisto. Bridging the gap remains an ideal and as such it is doomed to founder, just like the ideals of all Broch's predecessors, which collapsed due to their anti-prometheanism. Broch's portrait of Virgil renounces every form of revolutionary conservatism and every call to turn back to the historical past. Instead, Broch appeals to future man to recapture his humanity by self-examination, as long as he is not thwarted by complete destruction.

NOTES TO "HERMANN BROCH AND VIRGIL"

Translated from the Dutch by Paul Franssen and Evelyne Tax.

1. Rudolf Borchardt, "Vergil," in his *Reden* (Stuttgart: Klett, [1955]), 254–72; Ernst Robert Curtius, *European Literature and the Latin Middle Ages,* trans. Willard R. Trask (1953; repr. Princeton: Princeton University Press, 1990); T. S. Eliot, "Virgil and the Christian World" (1951), in *On Poetry and Poets* (London: Faber and Faber, 1957), 121–32; Theodor Haecker, *Vergil, Vater des Abendlandes* (Leipzig: Hegner, 1931). Richard Heinze, *Die Augustische Kultur* (Leipzig: Teubner, 1930), contains an important chapter on Virgil, introducing the *Aeneid* as the Bible of religious nationalism. See also Rudi van der Paardt, *De goddelijke Mantuaan,* Leidse opstellen, 5 (Leiden: Dimensie, 1987).

2. Allen Mandelbaum, "Taken from Brindisi: Vergil in an Other's World," in *Vergil at 2000,* ed. John D. Bernard (New York: AMS Press, 1986), 225–41.

3. Broch, *Der Tod des Vergil,* in *Gesammelte Werke,* 10 vols. (Zurich: Rhein-Verlag, 1958), vol. 3. Further references to Broch's works in the original German will be to this edition. For the English translation of Broch's novel, see *The Death of Virgil,* translated by Jean Starr Untermeyer (New York: Vintage International, 1995). Further references to this translation of the novel will be given after quotations in the text. For an excellent analysis of the connection between historical reality and fiction within the novel, see Otto Tost, *Die Antike als Motiv und Thema in Hermann Brochs Roman* Der Tod des Vergil, Innsbrucker Beiträge zur Kulturwissenschaft, Germanistische Reihe, 53 (Innsbruck: Institut für Germanistik, 1996).

4. Jattie Enklaar, "*Der Tod des Vergil*—ein Gedicht über den Tod?" in *Duitse kroniek* 36:3–4 (1986): 63–91; and "Kunst aan het einde van millennia: Hermann Broch en *De dood van Vergilius,*" in *Nexus* 9 (1994): 50–81.

5. *Divine Comedy I. Hell,* trans. Dorothy L. Sayers (1949; repr. Harmondsworth: Penguin Books, 1983), 71, line 1.

6. P. M. Lützeler, *Hermann Broch: Eine Biographie* (Frankfurt am Main: Suhrkamp, 1985). During Broch's life, not only *Der Tod des Vergil* was published, but also the following literary prose works: *Die Schlafwandler* (1931–32), *Die unbekannte Größe* (1933), and *Die Schuldlosen* (1949). Even before Broch's death, several fragments of his work were released, although they were not to be published until after his death. *Theorie des Massenwahns* was published in the United States in 1959, eight years after Broch's death.

7. These versions were, respectively: (1) "Die Heimkehr des Vergil" (1936); (2) Untitled (1937); (3) "Erzählung vom Tode" (1938); (4) "Die Heimkehr des

Vergil" (1938–40); (5) (Definitive version): *Der Tod des Vergil* (1940–45). See also *Hermann Broch, Der Tod des Vergil: Kommentierte Werkausgabe,* ed. P. M. Lützeler, 17 vols. (Frankfurt am Main: Suhrkamp, 1976–81), 4:457–58. The first edition appeared in New York (Pantheon, 1945). The Zurich edition appeared only two years later (Rhein, 1947).

8. Broch, *Kommentierte Werksausgabe,* 11:61.

9. Broch, *Kommentierte Werksausgabe,* 6:333–43. The German original was not published during Broch's lifetime.

10. Roderick H. Watt, "Hermann Broch's *Adolf Hitler's Farewell Address* and George Steiner's *The Portage to San Christobal of A. H.,*" in *Hermann Broch, Modernismus, Kulturkrise und Hitlerzeit: Londoner Symposium 1991,* ed. Adrian Stevens, Fred Wagner, and Sigurd Paul Scheichl, Innsbrucker Beiträge zur Kulturwissenschaft, Germanistische Reihe, 50 (Innsbruck: Institut für Germanistik, 1994), 183.

11. *Death of Virgil,* 12. In "Broch's *Death of Virgil:* Program Notes," Hermann Weigand draws attention to the similarities between the work of Dante and Broch. See *PMLA* 62 (1947): 525–54. These similarities, however, are rejected by Broch. Broch always stressed the fact that *The Death of Virgil* had not been inspired by literature *("daß der* Tod des Vergil *nicht von der Literatur inspiriert worden war").* See Manfred Durzak, *Hermann Broch* (Reinbek: Rowohlt, 1966), 134. See also Broch's letter to Weigand of 12 February 1946, in Broch, *Gesammelte Werke,* 8: 243.

12. Broch, *Kommentierte Werksausgabe,* 12: 461.

13. Broch, "Vergils Persönlichkeit und seine Probleme," in *Hermann Broch. Kommentierte Werksausgabe,* 4:467–68. See D. Meinert, *Die Darstellung der Dimensionen menschlicher Existenz in Broch's* Tod des Vergil (Bern and Munich: Francke, 1962).

14. See Götz Wienold, "Die Organisation eines Romans: *Der Tod des Vergil,*" in: *Materialien zu H. Brochs* Der Tod des Vergil, ed. P. M. Lützeler (Frankfurt am Main: Suhrkamp, 1976), 252.

15. See Peter Altink, "Eenheid door herhaling en continuïteit in *Der Tod des Vergil,* of: in hoeverre kan H. Broch modernistisch genoemd worden?" unpublished paper (Utrecht University, 1997).

16. See Broch, *Gesammelte Werke,* 9:279.

17. *Death of Virgil,* 12, 75, 222, and 161–62, respectively.

18. Broch, *Kommentierte Werksausgabe,* 12:309 and 311.

19. *Gesammelte Werke,* 9:278. See also, Hermann Broch, "Gibt es noch Demokratie?" in *Gesammelte Werke,* 9:313–61. On Broch's critical analysis of Modernism, the cultural crisis, and the politics of the Third Reich, see also *Hermann Broch, Modernismus, Kulturkrise und Hitlerzeit* (1994).

Camões: A Portuguese Renaissance Poet in Brazilian Popular Literature

RIA LEMAIRE

Like many other European countries, Portugal has its great Renaissance poet: Luís de Camões, the author of the national epic *Os Lusíadas,* or *The Lusiads,* which celebrates the heroic enterprise of the discovery of the maritime itinerary to India (1498) and, in doing so, glorifies the Golden Age of Portuguese history, the period of the discoveries. Camões's life, like that of many other national icons, has been constructed in various often antithetical ways, to serve different interests. This essay focuses on two contrasting images of Camões: the national hero sanctioned by official culture within Portugal itself, and the far less respectable vagrant poet appropriated by the oral tradition of one of Portugal's former colonies, Brazil.

Very few historical documents tell us about Camões's life; we do not know when or where he was born, nor where and how he acquired the vast knowledge, erudition, and wisdom that confronts the reader of *The Lusiads* in its 10 cantos and 1,122 stanzas, composed in ottava rima. Scholars generally suppose that Camões was born in 1524 or 1525. His parents belonged to the poor, lower nobility. As a young man, he lived at the court in Lisbon for some time and was sent to Africa, where he fought against the Moors and lost his right eye. Back in Lisbon, he lived the turbulent life of a bohemian for some years, which landed him in prison. An official letter from the king of Portugal released him, saying that the prisoner "is a young man without fortune who is going to serve me in India."[1] For seventeen years Camões led a life full of adventures and misfortunes in the Orient. He was in Canton and suffered a shipwreck along the coast of Cochinchina in 1561; he stayed in Goa for some time, where he was imprisoned once again; he traveled through the Persian Gulf, the Red Sea, to China and Macau. In 1567, debt-ridden, he decided to return to Portugal. Unable to pay at once the entire voyage to Lisbon, he had to stay in Mozambique for some time, where the Portuguese writer Diogo do Couto met him, living on the charity of generous friends. When he arrived in Lisbon in 1569, he offered the manuscript of *The Lusiads* to the king. It was published in 1572 and gained him a royal pension, which, after his death on 10 June 1580, was transferred to his mother.[2]

Born in the period in which Portugal had reached the summit of its power and wealth, Camões died at the moment of the "death" of the nation, caused by Spanish occupation (1580–1640). This affected him profoundly, as we know from a letter he wrote to a friend some days before his death: "Finally, my life is coming to an end and everybody will discover that I have loved my country so much, that I will not content myself with dying in my country, but that I will die with my country."[3]

The year 1580 marks the moment of Camões's physical death and, at the same time, his symbolic rebirth. In the period of profound national despair caused by the Spanish occupation, the author of the national epic became the hero and symbol of the Portuguese nation. His life was considered more or less paradigmatic of the life of the country, of its grandeur and misfortunes. More than ten editions of the epic were published in these unfortunate sixty years. Later on, classicism and the Enlightenment were also to discover the lyric poetry, and to place the figure of Camões in the gallery of the great poets of humanity.

In the year 1825, the romantic writer Baptista Leitao de Garrett published a long, narrative poem on his life. The book, entitled *Camões,* attributed to the already symbolic, national figure of Camões some typically romantic features. The verses sing of his many colorful adventures and his always unhappy loves for princesses; they create a myth of the banishment, exile, and persecution, of the poverty and solitude of a misunderstood genius.

Within the political context of growing nationalism everywhere in Europe, the national appropriation of the mythical hero reached a new climax in 1880, when, on 10 June, Portugal commemorated the death—three hundred years earlier—of its national hero. The king of Portugal ordered the supposed bones of the poet removed from the cemetery (from where they had already disappeared during the earthquake of 1755) to a monumental tomb in the Mosteiro dos Jerônimos: Camões was given a magnificent and sumptuous second funeral. Ceremonies, celebrations, feasts, three new editions of *The Lusiads,* and a complete popular edition of 30,000 copies, distributed gratis, marked the third centenary.

Thus, Camões, already the national hero within the erudite tradition of the Portuguese elite, also became a popular hero, the source of inspiration of the nationalist feelings that the Portuguese elite wanted to inculcate in the lower strata of the population. Nowadays, Camões is omnipresent in the popular imagination: his name or portrait is to be found on monuments, squares, associations, institutions, wines and cookies, bands of cigars, stamps, and ceramics. And no one can forget him on the national holiday.

As to the history of his works, some parallels can be drawn with his life. Very few historical documents can prove his authorship of the works which have been ascribed to him; the process of symbolic and mythical construction of the national hero is paralleled by a slow and progressive elaboration of a corpus of texts attributed to the national author. We are not even certain about the origins of *The Lusiads*. Official historiography asserts that the manuscript was written by Camões in the Orient. Generations of students and scholars have repeated the intriguing story of the shipwreck along the coast of Cochinchina, which made the lover Camões lose his beloved Chinese companion who died in the waves but at the same time permitted the poet to rescue the heavy manuscript of the epic by swimming in the hostile sea. Did Camões really write down the poem that early? Or did he still, like epic poets all over the world, compose and memorize it orally? Did he, perhaps, dictate or write it down later and use the shipwreck-intrigue, which transforms his "oral" epic into a written one, to confer more prestige and authority to the text? Or, did he bring from the Orient a manuscript written by someone else and use the shipwreck-intrigue to hide other realities? We will probably never know, but it is fascinating to ask these questions at the end of the millennium we are living in and in which so many well-established forms of authorship have been put into question and seen more and more, not as biographical realities, but as results of processes and strategies of what Michel Foucault has called "the making of an author," this typical form of myth-making, characteristic of Western, bourgeois scholarship since the seventeenth century.

During Camões's lifetime, only *Os Lusíadas* and three lyric poems were published. All the other lyrics were found after his death in manuscripts and song-books, gathered by people who loved songs and wrote them down or copied them from other collections and who ascribed these poems—rightly or wrongly—to Camões. The original preface to the first edition of his lyrics (1595), based on a manuscript composed by the poet himself, refers explicitly to the problem of authorship and gives a significant example:

of 175 poems attributed to Camões in this edition, two had been discovered in the *Cancioneiro Geral* published in 1516, before Camões was born. After the first edition, we witness the slow and progressive construction of the corpus: 63 new poems in the second edition (1598), 34 in the third (1616); every new edition was to bring new texts. Roger Bismuth, who produced the most recent French translation of *The Lusiads,* concludes that at the end of the nineteenth century, 618 poems had been gathered in the corpus of lyric poetry ascribed to Camões. In the meantime, mainly on the basis of this corpus of lyric poetry, the romantic myth of the poet of genius Camões had been elaborated. At the end of the nineteenth century, this myth was used by political nationalism to transform him into the most complete and pure expression of the Portuguese soul and heroism.

At the moment when the poet arrived at the zenith of his glory, the myth also reached the turning point in its history. Two German scholars, Wilhelm Storck and Carolina Michaëlis de Vasconcellos, initiated the long and painful way back to reality. First of all, these scholars discovered the huge abyss which existed between the extreme scarcity of reliable documentary evidence proving facts of his life and the profusion of biographical studies built on it. Secondly, they discovered more and more false attributions, which were to motivate generations of scholars to pursue the quest for the real Camões. In 1967, finally, Emmanuel Perreira Filho established an "irreducible lyric corpus" of 133 compositions that he proposed should be ascribed definitely to Camões; a corpus which, since then, has been questioned again and again. Recent publications discuss parts of individual poems, stating that they are corrections, errors or additions made by transcribers, who mutilated the original compositions by Camões. We cannot know at this moment when or how this disenchanting, but fascinating process of deconstruction of the mythical poet Camões will end.

In the year 1500, the Portuguese discovered the part of the South American continent now called Brazil. During the colonial period, neither industry nor typography was permitted in the colony. Schools were rare and all books were imported directly from Portugal. Only an extremely small, generally white elite could read and write and, thus, had access to the great Portuguese writers of the erudite tradition and to the popular literature, called *literatura de cordel,* divulged in broadsheets and chapbooks. Over the centuries, the huge mass of Brazilian illiterates developed an immense treasure of oral traditions, from very simple to extremely sophisti-

cated or complicated genres. Illiterates also had access, sometimes, to written literature, erudite as well as popular, by means
of literates or semi-literates who would read aloud the few books
available in the community and recite them again and again in front
of an audience.

After independence in 1822, typography spread throughout Brazil and arrived, in the second part of the nineteenth century, in the
Nordeste—the Brazilian Northeast—a region which is at the same
time the most deprived and underdeveloped from an economic
point of view, and the richest and most varied in cultural terms.
There, at the end of the century, a cultural process began which
we know so well from early modern times in Europe: popular,
mainly (but not always) illiterate poets dictated the compositions
they had been chanting traditionally in marketplaces and feasts to
the owners of the first printing presses. They were printed on cheap
paper, folded twice and thus transformed into small booklets,
which the popular poets would sell during their performances in
fairs, festivals, and poetic tournaments, called *cantoria* (derived
from *cantar* = to sing).

To this pamphlet literature, the people of the Northeast have
given the name *folheto,* derived from *folha,* sheet of paper. It always has the same dimensions: 4 by 6.5 inches (that means: one
sheet, doubled twice) and a characteristic number of pages: 8 (one
sheet), or 16 (two sheets) and so on, up to sixty-four pages. Scholars, later on, began to use the Portuguese term, *literatura de cordel*
(literature on a cord or string), alluding to the characteristic way
in which these booklets are often sold: hanging from cords or
strings in the marketplaces.[4] At the same time, this term stresses
an important fact, namely that the *literatura de cordel* really is
literature in the authentic sense of the word: it is poetry, each
generation has its famous artists, it possesses a rich variety of
genres, each of them with its specific rules of composition, its
rhetoric and stylistics, its classifications and laws, that is, its *ars
poetica.*

Although, today, many poets are literate, and many now *write*
their *folhetos,* and though many more people in the Northeast are
now able to read them themselves, this literature is still deeply
rooted in orality and repeats, or reproduces many of the traditional
forms, schemes, and contents which, one century ago, constituted
the basis of Northeastern oral traditions. In marketplaces, one still
sometimes finds *folheto* writers, chanting or reading aloud the texts
of their booklets that they want to sell and others who also are
professional singers, called *repentistas* (poet-improvisers), like so

many of the famous Northeastern poets of the past have been. And some of the famous "authors" will confess that they still compose their stories entirely in their heads, before writing them down.

The use of the term *literature* for *folhetos* might produce some ambiguities, if we are not aware of its very specific character and history. Originally it belonged to the world of orality, which means that its production, performance, and conservation were based on mechanisms and strategies radically different from those of written literature.[5] To begin with production: the two basic and most appreciated processes of poetic composition were (and still are in the context of Northeastern *cantoria*) improvisation and memorization/repetition in the context of a poetic performance realized in front of an audience. Unlike the reader of written literature, who appreciates originality and individuality, the audience of the Brazilian poet-improviser will appreciate and prefer the repetition of traditional forms and themes. If the message is radically new, as was, for instance, the suicide of the Brazilian president Getúlio Vargas in 1954, the audience will only accept the message if it is molded into the forms and contents of a preexisting genre; in this case: the subgenre dedicated to the death of great heroes.

Improvisation as a central technique of poetic, oral composition is situated exactly at this meeting point of tradition and novelty: it is the art of expressing the—surprising—novelty, integrating it, with endless variants and variations, into the same traditional "grammar" of forms, techniques and literary/poetic styles, into the treasure of knowledge and values that all the members of the community possess and will be pleased to recognize in the new performance. This means that each individual performance can vary, that it can be "original" within the limits of the audience's horizon of expectation.

In this poetic context, a poet-*repentista* can develop specific aspects of a theme, hero, or event, while, at the same time, omitting other aspects that might seem essential to readers of written literature. Such aspects can remain unsaid because, implicitly, they are present as well in the collective memory of the audience, in its "imagination," where the evocation of one characteristic aspect of a theme will function as a "trigger" for the implicit reproduction of the complete theme. Thus, if we want to study, for instance, the presence and function of the Portuguese poet Camões as a character in a *folheto,* we cannot limit ourselves to analyzing exhaustively one specific story. It will, of course, mention some facts, some characteristics, but these elements cannot be fully understood, or will even be misunderstood, if we are not able to bring to mind all the other elements that exist in the poet's and audience's imagination. We have to possess that underlying "competence," or "grammar" of forms and themes which is at the basis of the individual performance and enables performer and audience to reactualize, with the help of just a few characteristic elements, the implicit imaginary world that generates them.[6]

As to the pseudo-biographical use of the real-life author Camões, the Brazilian *folhetos* offer a fascinating range of reworkings of elements of the biography of the real-life author Camões, as well as of the mythical poet Portuguese elites have constructed in the centuries after his death.[7] Titles with his name in them tend to belong to three types, or subgenres, of this pamphlet literature: rogue or astuteness stories, the riddle contest, and the marvelous tale.[8] All can be classified within the genre of the adventure story. They also have in common that they belong to the type of the *folhetos de encontros* (contests or duels) and that Camões is the winner of all the conflicts told by the *folhetos* in which he appears.

The *folheto de astúcia* (astuteness, trick) in a joking tone tells of the tricks that its protagonists, who are, or have been poor vagabonds, play on each other and, alone or together, on the people that they meet during their wanderings. In doing so, the stories belonging to this subgenre show the exceptional intelligence of these popular heroes. Deceit, lies, betrayal, swindling, and robbery belong to their daily repertory, but the Northeasterners approve of and admire most of their feats. For this type of story, they often use a name which is indicative of its main function: *folheto de gracejo* (jest, joke):

> *O povo sorria tanto*
> *Que a barriga doía*
> *quem ouvia Camões*
> *Contando também sorria.*

> People laughed so much
> That their stomach ached
> And when someone listened to Camões
> Telling stories, he would laugh also.

Within a socioeconomic context of extreme injustice and inequality, the stories are seen as a challenge to the established order, and as a form of revenge taken by the have-nots against the rich.

O Encontro de Camões com Cancão de Fogo depicts the adventures of Camões during his wanderings with the famous *quengo* or *malandro* (rogue or trickster) of Northeastern popular tradition,

Cancão de Fogo. Camões is depicted as more intelligent than the Northeastern champion of astuteness, Cancão, who is the loser of all the deceitful tricks he tries to play on the companion of his wanderings. This type of *folheto* stresses, first of all, his superior intelligence and sense of humor, even when the popular poets do not forget his talents as a poet:

> *Camões foi poeta de*
> *indiscutível valor*
> *coluna mestre das letras*
> *mas destes verses o autor*
> *pretende mostrar ao mundo*
> *Camões o gênio do humor.*
>
> Camões was a poet of
> indisputable worth
> the main pillar of letters
> but the author of these verses
> intends to show to the world
> Camões the genius of humor.

The second subgenre in which Camões occurs as a hero is called the *adivinhacões* or *adivinhas* (divination and riddle-solving). They are the Brazilian version of a widespread genre in oral cultures all over the world: the riddle contest. Like proverbs, myths, and fables, the riddle belongs to the main strategies of organized/formulated knowledge and wisdom in oral traditions, where it has been associated with divination and invested with magical, enchanting powers, as early written literature and its protagonists (for instance, Homer, Oedipus, Samson, Solomon, and the Queen of Sheba) still teach us.

The Brazilian riddle contest is often a sort of tournament or duel confronting a poor, powerless poet with a powerful man, usually a king. In a certain sense, its happy ending reverses the social and political orders. Camões, the poor but clever guy, will be the winner and sometimes, thanks to his intelligence, superior knowledge and wisdom, he obtains high social position. As in many other parts of the world, "class-consciousness is quietly but effectively preached in a riddle story in which the intelligent underdog outwits the powerful king."[9] The first question of *O Grande Debate de Camões com o Sábio,* the debate of Camões with the sage, shows that social inequality is a main theme of the riddle contest:

> *Responda por que existe*
> *Gente pobre e gente rica*

Se filhas do mesmo Deus
Por que uma sobe e outra fica?

Answer me why do exist
Poor and rich people
If all are daughters of the same God
Why does one rise and the other stay behind?

Although Northeasterners find amusement in these stories, they are much more serious, and are generally listened to with a deep, solemn respect. Riddles have a magic, sacred function; in many cases, they will be a question of life or death, as the king in *As Perguntas do Rei e as Respostas de Camões* (The Questions of the King and the Answers of Camões) announces:

> *Eu tenho trinta perguntas*
> *para você responder*
> *se falhar uma das tais*
> *sem recurso vai morrer.*

> I have thirty questions
> for you to answer
> if you miss one of them
> you will die without appeal.

The characters pitted against each other in these contests are famous, first of all, for their intelligence:

> *Camões, amigos leitores*
> *Poeta por excelência*
> *Guardava dentro do crânio*
> *Uma rara inteligência.*

> Camões, dear readers and friends,
> The poet above all others
> Possessed in his skull
> A rare intelligence.

The protagonists are no less renowned for their knowledge and wisdom:

> *O rei D. Luiz Segundo*
> *era muito encapetado*
> *hospedou Camões uns dias*
> *na corte do seu reinado*

Camões de tudo sabia
a sua sabedoria
deixava o rei espantado.

King Louis the Second
was a very crafty man
received Camões for some days
at the court of his kingdom
Camões knew everything
his wisdom
left the king astounded.

Camões is also a *sábio,* a sage or wise man, another characteristic hero in Northeastern popular imagination. He seems to synthesize all the elements of the archaic, archetypal figure of the wandering poet-sage-soothsayer of oral traditions, who is received as a guest at the court of the powerful and stays there for some time, amusing, teaching, healing, predicting the future, or giving advice in difficult situations.

In *O Grande Debate* the reader also witnesses another archetypal conflict, one caused by the confrontation of orality and literacy. The words of the wise man, who has been invited by the king for a contest with the poet Camões, echo the invectives of Plato against the poets and the wisdom they possess[10]:

Terra onde poeta vence
Sábio, meu rei, reconheça
É lugar onde homem veste
As calças pela cabeça.

A country in which the poet defeats
The wise man, my king, please agree,
Is a place where people put on
Trousers passing them over their heads.

They also reveal the weakness of bookish wisdom in a world of oral, sacred knowledge, when the *sábio* has to confirm that he does not know the answer to one of Camões's questions:

Nenhum livro tem escrito
essa secreta ciência.

No book has written down
your secret science.

Camões, the winner of the riddle contests, will be decorated, become the king's adviser, and stay with him forever, or marry the king's daughter.

Before entering into the world of the marvelous tale, we have to consider a group of *folhetos* that intermingle the two subgenres discussed so far. They reveal important elements of the structure of the adventure stories and the figure of Camões. *As Perguntas do Rei e as Respostas de Camões* adds to the portrait of the hero a talent which is often ascribed to wandering poets and sages—namely, clearsightedness and divination:

> *Com sete anos Camões*
> *Começou a viajar*
> *Pelo mundo abertamente*
> *Profetizando o futuro*
> *O passado e o presente.*

> When he was seven, Camões
> Began to wander
> Through the world openly
> Prophesying the future
> The past and the present.

But, whatever his attributes, people love Camões most of all for his sense of humor. After solving thirty riddles and playing some deceitful tricks on the jealous king:

> *Camões desertou dali*
> *I não quis mais brincadeira*
> *Reinou tristeza na corte.*

> Camões left that place
> And did not want jests anymore;
> Sadness reigned in the court.

As Astúcias de Camões shows how a poor but intelligent man will survive and become famous. The first part of the *folheto* narrates how Camões takes his revenge on the king who deceives him several times and, finally, leaves him as poor as he was before. The second part presents him as a lawyer, an advocate of victims of injustice, before bringing him back, in the third part, to the king's court, in defense of his brother condemned to death. By giving the right answers to the three enigmatic questions of the king, he saves his brother and becomes a famous *sábio,* wise man:

A História prova que
resolvendo essas questões
Luís de Camões viveu
Instruindo os sabichões
Notabilizou-se em leis
Deixando a todos os reis
O dom das suas lições.

History proves that
By solving these riddles
Luis de Camões lived
Teaching the great sages
Laws he made, made him famous
Giving to all the kings
The gift of his lessons.

As Palhaçadas de Camões, finally, presents him as a Portuguese, a poet, and a philosopher. As to the poet, he is depicted in two different ways: he is a very popular and humorous storyteller and a famous *repentista,* a poet-improviser. After a series of very amusing *palhaçadas,* burlesque adventures that enable him to seduce the queen and the king's three daughters, he solves all the riddles proposed by the king and thus deserves the final reconciliation with the king.

The third subgenre in which we meet Camões is the marvelous tale. It combines three main themes of *cordel* literature: magic, love, and heroism. In *Camões e o Rei Mágico,* the poet is presented as the astute, intelligent son of a poor family who has been received by the king at his court and given an excellent education; he has become the *"príncipe dos poetas,"* the prince, the best, the first of all poets. Once again, Camões becomes the rival of the king, but this time the story is not about astuteness and intelligence, but about magic and authentic heroism. The queen falls in love with Camões, who becomes her lover. A terrible jealousy makes the king decide to kill Camões. The marvelous adventures of Camões consist of three trials, which provide the tale with mythological and magical dimensions. The king-magician metamorphoses himself successively into three mythical animals, a snake, a bull, and a lion. Camões survives the first two trials—with the snake and the bull—by touching the talisman and crying the magical formula given to him by the queen. The third trial transforms him into an authentic hero in his own right, when, courageously, he attacks the lion-king and hurts him so badly that he dies. The new—adult—hero thus deserves to marry his beloved queen.

Now that we have arrived at the conventional happy ending of
Camões's adventure stories as they are told in the *folhetos* belonging to the Fonds Raymond Cantel, a first conclusion might be that
the real-life Renaissance author Camões is still, nowadays, really
present and alive in Brazilian popular literature. The fact that three
subgenres of the adventure story feature the poet as their protagonist calls to mind his life full of adventures and misfortunes in the
Orient. The heroes of the *folhetos* are vagabonds, as Camões himself was for so many years. They are poor and wander from one
place to another, always trying to earn some money to survive.
They do not even have a birth certificate, and that is exactly what
is also missing in Camões's biography.

At the same time, these adventure stories continuously call to
mind his reputation as a poet. In Portugal, as well as in the Brazilian *folhetos*, he is the *"príncipe dos poetas,"* the best of all poets.
The *folhetos* repeat in endless variations the characteristics that
the reader of *The Lusiads* will also discover in its verses: his superior intelligence, knowledge, and wisdom.

The relationship with the romantic myth is more complicated.
Love for princesses and queens is a common theme in the Portuguese myth and in the *folhetos*, but unlike Portuguese tradition,
which created the tragedy of his always unhappy, impossible loves
for inaccessible ladies, the Brazilian Camões is an amusing, successful, and happy lover, in secret love affairs with queens and
princesses as well as in open rivalry with powerful kings. Unlike
the Portuguese Camões, he is not a loser but a winner. This is
also the main difference between the Portuguese poet-adventurer-
wanderer-vagabond who lived and died in poverty and his Brazilian
counterpart who will, finally, be decorated, rich, a lawyer or a
judge, the husband of a princess or a queen.

Unlike the Portuguese Camões, whose epic celebrates the heroic
adventure of the discovery and conquest of the world by the Portuguese and, in doing so, legitimizes the politics which the Portuguese elite had imposed, the Brazilian Camões undermines the
views of those in power; he challenges the established order and
all the values on which it is based. Paradoxically, the solidarity
shown by sixteenth-century Camões with his nation and its elite
makes him a loser; he is a poor man his entire life. In contrast, the
Brazilian Camões teaches his people that nonconformism, humor,
tricks, intelligence, and wisdom can serve as powerful strategies
against injustice.

In this sense, the relationship the two poets have with the powerful elites and the people is significant. In the case of the Brazilian

Camões, we wonder about the familiarity of his contacts with the powerful: the poet discussing and joking with kings, living at the court or receiving them in his house, abusing their absence to sleep with the queen or their daughters. The contacts of the Portuguese Camões with the powerful whose deeds, feats, and ideology he celebrated, seem much more distant, rare, and authoritarian. He dies poor and in solitude, whereas his Brazilian counterpart will live on, cherished and surrounded by the Northeastern people who admire him.

Who is, all things considered, the Brazilian Camões as he is revealed by the three subgenres? He is, first of all, a popular hero, cherished for his jests, jokes, and tricks, his sense of humor, intelligence, and astuteness. He is a wise man, respected for his sometimes sacred and secret knowledge and wisdom. He is a poet-improviser, a famous storyteller, a seer, visionary, and magician. In other words, he is the archetypal poet of the oral tradition to whom Northeasterners had been listening for centuries before the arrival of the printing press.

This is what makes him differ radically from the Portuguese Camões, who, through successive appropriations by early nationalism, by the humanistic, scriptocentric tradition of Renaissance studies, by romantic and nationalist movements of the nineteenth century, has been presented as one of humanity's great poet-*writers* of genius.

But, was the real-life poet Camões really the type of poet traditional scholarship wants us to admire? Or do the Brazilian popular poets, who once again appropriated the figure of Camões to make him fit into the imaginary world of their oral traditions, offer us new ways and insights that will help us transform the painful process of the deconstruction of Portugal's national hero into a new and fascinating vision of a puzzling author, of a world to which traditional scholarship has blocked the entry?

Notes to "Camões: A Portuguese Renaissance Poet in Brazilian Popular Literature"

1. *Vierhonderdste verjaring van "Os Lusíadas" van Camões, 1572–1972* (Brussels: Koninklijke Bibliotheek Albert I, 1972), 16.

2. *Os Lusíadas*, 1st ed. (Lisbon, 1572). The first translation in Spanish appeared in 1580; in English in 1655, in Italian in 1658, in French in 1735, in Dutch in 1777. An excellent French translation is Roger Bismut's *Les Lusíadas de Luís de Camões* (Lisbon: Fondation Calouste Gulbenkian, 1961). A new bilingual (Portuguese-French) edition is Luís de Camões, *Os Lusíadas—Les Lusiades*, trans. Roger Bismut (Paris: Laffont, 1996). A useful English translation is William

Atkinson's prose rendering in the Penguin Classics series (Harmondsworth, 1952). For biographical information and a survey of the criticism, see *Lusiads*, ed. Frank Pierce (Oxford: Oxford University Press, 1973).

3. José Anastácio da Cunha, *Notícias Literárias de Portugal* (1780; repr. Lisbon: Seara Nova, 1971), 44 (translation is my own).

4. See Candace Slater, *Stories on a String: the Brazilian "Literatura de Cordel"* (Berkeley: University of California Press, 1982).

5. See Walter Ong, *Orality and Literacy: The Technologizing of the Word* (London, Methuen, 1982); and Paul Zumthor, *Introduction à la poésie orale* (Paris: Seuil, 1983).

6. See John Miles Foley, *The Singer of Tales in Performance* (Bloomington: Indiana University Press, 1995).

7. The *folhetos* which will be cited belong to the Fonds Raymond Cantel. Raymond Cantel was the founder of the Center for Latin-American Studies of the University of Poitiers, France. He created his famous collection of Brazilian *literatura de cordel* between 1960 and 1980 and in the same period initiated the academic study of cordel literature, in Brazil, as well as in France. See *Raymond Cantel: La Littérature populaire brésilienne*, ed. Jean-Pierre Clement and Ria Lemaire (Poitiers: CRLA, 1993).

8. The *folhetos* which have been analyzed are the following:
—*As Astúcias de Camões*, by A. Pinto de Souza, 32 pp.
—*As Palhaçadas de Camões botando chifre no Rei*, by J. Costa Leite, 14 pp.
—*As Perguntas do Rei e as Respostas de Camões*, by S. G. de Oliveira, 16 pp.
—*Camões e o Rei Mágico*, by José Cavalcanti and Ferreira Dila, 8 pp.
—*Camões e o Rei Mágico*, by Ferreira Dila, a 16-page version.
—*O Casamento de Camões com a Filha do Rei*, by José Costa Leite, 16 pp.
—*O Encontro de Camões com Cancão de Fogo*, by José Soares, 16 pp.
—*O Filho de Camões*, by José Soares, 16 pp.
—*O Gênio Camões*, by G. Ferreira da Silva, 8 pp.
—*O Grande Debate de Camões com um Sábio*, by A. Pinto de Souza, 32 pp.

9. See "Riddles," in *Funk & Wagnalls, Standard Dictionary of Folklore, Mythology and Legend*, ed. Maria Leach (San Francisco: Harper & Row, 1972), 938–44.

10. See Eric Havelock, *Preface to Plato* (Cambridge, MA: Harvard University Press, 1963).

The Gender of Mourning: A. S. Byatt's "The Conjugial Angel" and Alfred Lord Tennyson's *In Memoriam*

CHRISTIEN FRANKEN

INTRODUCTION

At the age of nineteen you are engaged to be married to a man who is considered the bright light of his generation. He is a man of letters and a scholar. The people who matter speak highly of his philosophical mind and generous nature. He also happens to be your brother's closest friend. One day fate intervenes: while abroad, your fiancé dies unexpectedly at the age of twenty-two. Your brother receives the news in a letter, and when he tells you, you faint. It takes four months to ship the body back home. You are seriously ill for a year. Your brother is, like you, inconsolable, both of you having lost a man you love. When eight years later you marry, society at large expresses its disapproval, and your former fiancé's family thoroughly dislikes your new husband.

Your brother, it seems, fares better. He secures his fame as a poet with an elegy, written in commemoration of your fiancé. He calls himself a widower and takes the death as the starting point for a poetical and autobiographical investigation into the nature of grief, religion, and love. Seventeen years after the fateful event, the long poem is published to great acclaim, there to be scrutinized for years to come.

In 1992, a century and a half later, the English novelist A. S. Byatt used these events as inspiration for her short story, "The Conjugial Angel." In this story she is the first to imagine what it must have been like to be Emily Tennyson: bride to be of Arthur Henry Hallam, who died in Venice in 1833; wife of Captain Jesse, whom she married in 1842; and, of course, sister of the poet Alfred Lord Tennyson, Hallam's closest friend and the author of *In Memoriam: A. H. H.*

The story of "The Conjugial Angel" is set in 1875, twenty-five years after the publication of *In Memoriam* and more than forty years after Hallam's death. Emily Tennyson is in her sixties and lives in Margate with her husband Captain Jesse. She is a member of a group of spiritualists and has an avid interest in seances. These seances give a typically Victorian atmosphere to Byatt's story. According to Esther Schor, the Victorians celebrated "the cult of death and mourning" and used the seance as a manner of making visible the "interpenetration between the worlds of the living and the dead: intuitions of the beyond, visitations by the dead."[1] In "The Conjugial Angel" the seances are organized by two women—Sophy Sheekhy and Lilias Papagay—which also is typical of the time, as Alex Owen has shown.[2] Sophy Sheekhy acts as a medium through which the dead are called on to speak, among them Emily's fiancé Hallam. The main story focuses on Emily Tennyson and her thoughts about her past, her brother, Hallam, and her husband Captain Jesse. In an embedded story, Byatt has Lord Tennyson interpret *In Memoriam* and explain his friendship with Hallam.

There were reviewers who had their doubts about Byatt's use of these historical figures in her fiction:

> Byatt makes the familiar point about the status of historical record as literary text, fit to be unravelled and made anew. Others will have difficulties with the idea of taking real people and inventing things about them. Hallam, always a shadowy figure, has now, for good or ill, become the Hallam of A. S. Byatt.[3]

It is not Byatt's appropriation of Hallam, however, that makes "The Conjugial Angel" a remarkable story; it is her use of Tennyson as a character and the appropriation of Emily's perspective, which have a number of fascinating effects. The brother and sister are shown to react differently to Hallam's death, with the narrator implying that this difference is determined partly by gender. That is, "The Conjugial Angel" suggests that, as a Victorian woman who was economically dependent upon her family and expected to find a husband, Emily Tennyson was simply not in the position to mourn Hallam as long and in the same way as her brother did.

What is more, Byatt's story is critical of the nature of Alfred Tennyson's prolonged grief over Hallam and, hence, of *In Memoriam*. I will use Freud's distinction between mourning and melancholy to argue that Byatt's Emily Tennyson does not suffer from the "melancholy narcissism" that determines *In Memoriam* to such a large extent.[4] For "The Conjugial Angel" contains an unconventional reading of *In Memoriam*. According to Jerome McGann, nearly all Tennyson commentators read *In Memoriam* as a poem of synthesis and resolution. As a critic, A. S. Byatt has, indeed, talked of *In Memoriam* in these terms. She admires Tennyson's elegy for its coherence and has described it as "a search for integrity and meaning, a re-creation of energy, in which reason and passion, sensuality and humanity may be fused."[5] McGann finds that the emphasis on synthesis reduces Tennyson's elegy:

> Because human experience in its historical passage is at all points marked by struggles, by blindness and self-deception, by contradictions . . . poetry inevitably reproduces the conflicts and contradictions which it is itself seeking to deal with.[6]

He argues that contradictions "are precisely the source of Tennyson's poetical strengths" (177). Unlike Byatt-the-critic, the novelist reads *In Memoriam* in ways that reflect the approach advocated by McGann. Through the juxtaposition of the two different perspectives—the brother's and the sister's—Byatt *does* pay attention to the tensions and contradictions typical of the mourning process and of Tennyson's poem.

MOURNING AND THE BROTHER'S PERSPECTIVE

Alfred Tennyson spent a lifetime mourning Arthur Henry Hallam. They were both members of the Apostles, a debating society at Trinity College, Cambridge, founded in 1820. Hallam became extremely important to Tennyson as a friend, an advocate of his poetry and a future brother-in-law. They studied and traveled together, and shared a room when Hallam visited Tennyson's parental home. Generally, Tennyson felt physically and mentally better when he was in Hallam's company.[7] Hallam's unexpected death had long-term effects on Tennyson. Robert Martin gives numerous examples of the ways in which the memory of Hallam influenced the most important events of Tennyson's life. His fame as a poet rested on *In Memoriam A. H. H.,* which he was unable to read aloud because it was too painful: "It breaks me down. . . . I cannot" (*Unquiet Heart,* 421). He used *In Memoriam* to woo his wife Emily Sellwood, and their first child was named after Hallam. According to Martin, Tennyson assumed until the end of his life that he was "the true guardian of the memory of Hallam" (*Unquiet Heart,* 547).

Critics have reacted in various ways to the intensity of Tenny-son's love for and grief over Hallam, ranging from discomfort over any homosexual implications to admiration for his consistency in mourning. Alan Sinfield accuses critics of being blatantly one-sided in their interpretations of *In Memoriam:*

> In the case of *In Memoriam,* criticism has made much of science and religious doubt, which are no longer issues for most educated people, but a subversion of mainstream constructions of sexuality is either explained away or, even more firmly, not discussed at all.[8]

One can, indeed, see this phenomenon at work in Robert Martin's standard biography of Tennyson. Although he devotes three sepa-rate chapters to the Hallam-Tennyson friendship, Martin is ada-mant that it was a "normal" one, that is, a friendship which was not homosexual. The subject is obviously a dangerous one, given Martin's extreme caution in discussing the mere possibility that there was a sexual aspect to the friendship: "Perhaps all relations have at least a slight element of sexual awareness, and it is probable that Tennyson's regard for Hallam had more of that than he would have wanted to admit, even to himself" (*Unquiet Heart,* 94). Mar-tin accuses "post-Freudian" critics of being "unsubtle" in attaching homosexual labels: "Love is described as either homosexual or heterosexual with little awareness that it may consist of a good deal that defies those categories" (*Unquiet Heart,* 94). It is quite inconsistent, then, that he should describe Hallam as "deeply heterosexual."

In "The Conjugial Angel," Byatt is outspoken about the possibil-ity that Tennyson was aware that his feelings for Hallam were partly sexual. Byatt's Tennyson is not the sexually innocent man critics have taken him for: "he knew more than he said . . . he was a child of an altogether less innocent time."[9] Byatt describes his friendship with Hallam as partly determined by sexual tension and as more fulfilling than his marriage. Thus, although A. S. Byatt has been uncharacteristically scathing in criticizing Alan Sinfield's *Alfred Tennyson* for its "intellectual bullying," in "The Conjugial Angel" she shares Sinfield's emphasis on the homosexual nature of the love between Tennyson and Hallam.[10]

The second type of critical reception of *In Memoriam*—an admi-ration for Tennyson's consistency in mourning—is also absent from Byatt's fictional portrait of Tennyson. On the contrary, "The Conjugial Angel" is quite critical in this respect. Byatt describes Tennyson as a poet who, even at an old age, remains obsessively preoccupied with Hallam, the nature of their friendship, and *In Memoriam*. Byatt's perspective is a critical one, in that she questions Tennyson's motives for holding on to Hallam in the long-term way he did:

> [H]e had had all sorts of worries and wicked thoughts about his poem. Perhaps he was using it to keep alive a memory and a love it would have been stronger and more manly to let lie. Perhaps he was in some wrong way *using* his beloved to subserve his own gain, his own fame, or more subtly, making something fantastically beautiful out of the horror of Arthur's dissolution, which it would have been wiser, more honest, to stare at in dumb and truthful uncomprehending pain, until its hurtful brightness either faded like a fire eaten away, or caused him to drop his own eyes.
>
> ("Conjugial Angel," 268)

Here, Tennyson distrusts his own motives for writing *In Memoriam,* making Byatt's analysis similar to Marion Shaw's interpretation of the poem.[11] Shaw suggests that, in a Freudian sense, Tennyson's elegy is more an expression of melancholy than of mourning. Whereas mourning is a process of healing, a necessary step in coming to terms with loss, melancholy cannot let go of the beloved object and is accompanied by feelings of "self-abasement" and "nihilism" (Shaw, 145). Melancholy is "a sickness, a condition restraining the ego within a state of depressive narcissism" (Shaw, 148). Indeed, Byatt's Tennyson can think of nothing but Hallam, his own loss, and the motives that informed *In Memoriam*. He is imprisoned in melancholy.

Moreover, he seems to be melancholic more than mournful, in that he does not feel the tensions so typical of and necessary to mourning. Gill Plain describes these tensions as a combination of love, pain, and resentment. Mourning, she argues, contains "an element of resentment":

> The love object is hated and resented for the crime of abandonment at the same time as it is cherished and mourned. . . . The work of mourning is a burden, its painfulness evident in the tension between the desire to remember and the instinct to survive that demands that we forget.[12]

Byatt's Tennyson is imprisoned in remembrance, and his thoughts about *In Memoriam* circle around death, decay, and terror. Even forty years after Hallam's death he is unable to let go and does not feel the necessary resentment described above.

There is a second way in which Byatt's portrait of Tennyson does not follow conventional interpretations of *In Memoriam* and the nature of Tennyson's grief. Although *In Memoriam* is presented as a beautiful work of art, it also is seen as an expression of male bonding which excludes women, notably Emily Tennyson. In her fiction and criticism, Byatt has shown herself susceptible to the gendered implications of this kind of exclusionary friendship between men. In *Imagining Characters* she notices, first, that, in American literature, "the major bonded pairs are always almost two men" and, second, that women are described as "peripheral, dangerous and frightening."[13] The idea unmistakably resurfaces in "The Conjugial Angel." Although Alfred Tennyson stood by his sister when she mourned Hallam, he did not mention her in *In Memoriam,* appropriating Hallam for himself. As Victoria Glendinning succinctly puts it: "When Hallam died, Tennyson immortalized the male emotional bond by writing *In Memoriam,* thus stealing Emily's lover from her, replacing her with himself."[14]

Byatt revises this process by giving Emily Tennyson a voice of her own.[15] She describes Emily's grief and mourning as different from her brother's. In doing so, she pays attention to the different social positions both had at the time of Hallam's death—one a well-known poet, the other an unmarried middle-class woman—and the effect this had on their mourning.

MOURNING AND THE SISTER'S PERSPECTIVE

In describing Emily's past, Byatt follows the biographical facts: Emily's meeting with Hallam and the subsequent engagement, Hallam's death, her illness and grief, her marriage to Captain Jesse, which was abhorred by the Hallam family—all these facts can also be gathered from the scant information Robert Martin has managed to collect about the real Emily Tennyson Jesse. Byatt imagines these events from Emily's perspective, a perspective that gradually changes over the course of the story. At the beginning of "The Conjugial Angel," Mrs. Papagay, who is a participant in the seances, tells the reader that Emily Tennyson is "the heroine of a tragic story," tragic because she was engaged to a man who died. Byatt's descriptions of the seances that take place in Margate further reinforce the connection between Emily Tennyson and unremitting mourning. According to Mrs. Papagay, Emily Tennyson participates in the seances because "she desired to see and hear [Hallam], he was alive to her, though gone for forty-two years, almost twice the length of his stay on earth."[16] In an essay written before "The Conjugial Angel," Byatt already mentions that Emily

Tennyson raised the spirit of Hallam at a seance. In "The Conjugial Angel," Emily visits the seances because she wants to have the feeling she is in the presence of Hallam. According to Murray Parkes and Plain, this is one of the ways people have of coping with grief after the death of a loved one.[17]

Thus, it seems that there is no difference between the description of Tennyson's strong melancholy over Hallam's death and Emily Tennyson's reasons for participating in the seances organized by Mrs. Papagay. Both the brother and the sister seem caught in the memory of Hallam and the inability to let go of him and finish the process of mourning. As "The Conjugial Angel" progresses, however, it becomes clear that Emily Tennyson's memory of Hallam is different from Tennyson's. Judging from Martin's biography of Tennyson, the engagement between Emily Tennyson and Arthur Hallam was fraught with difficulties. Their families quarreled about the financial arrangements. They were unable to meet often and grew frustrated at the delay of three years, Emily complaining of illness and Arthur writing to her from London about the women he had met (*Unquiet Heart,* 157 and 158). Although Byatt portrays Emily as loving both Hallam and Tennyson, Emily also feels a resentment through which they and *In Memoriam* stand accused. Some critics recognized this aspect of "The Conjugial Angel." Paul Taylor wrote: "As well as offering a bracing, felt perspective on the poem, Emily's imagined thoughts give us an intricate understanding of the position of a bereaved Victorian woman, trapped by the disapproval of others, her love upstaged by male friendships."[18] And Marilyn Butler noted that "this is a version of Victorianism that cuts incisively into Victorian sentiment about the family."[19]

It is through Emily's perspective that "The Conjugial Angel" criticizes the exclusionary male sexual bonding between the two men:

Alfred had taken Arthur and bound him to himself, blood to blood and bone to bone, leaving no room for her. (234)

[S]he could never be wholly easy about the way in which Alfred's mourning had overtaken her own. Had not only overtaken it, she told herself in moments of bleak truthfulness, had undone and denied it. (229)

If she was wholly truthful with herself, she remembered the sight of those two male backs . . . going up to the attic with the white beds, with the sensations of one excluded from Paradise. (226–27)

As mentioned, the combination of love and resentment is typical of the mourning process. Whereas Byatt presents Tennyson as imprisoned in melancholy, Emily goes through the different stages of mourning and comes out healed at the end, because she refuses to be a prisoner of the glorified memory of Hallam.

As a middle-class Victorian woman, she has few alternatives but to marry. The scene in which she accepts Captain Jesse's marriage proposal is comic, recalling Scarlet O'Hara's grudging agreement to a marriage with Rhett Butler in *Gone with the Wind*. Both Emily Tennyson and Scarlet O'Hara are presented as women who are not used to sexual attraction and cannot resist it when it crosses their paths, even though this means they have to marry apparently unsuitable men. Captain Jesse is Hallam's opposite, but, against the expectations of her family and friends, Emily's marriage is a reasonably happy one, both in a sexual and an emotional way. It also puts an end to her mourning: "she had married Richard in 1842 and closed her mourning" ("The Conjugial Angel," 232). Here, "The Conjugial Angel" follows Robert Martin, who writes that the real Emily Tennyson seemed

> never to have marred [her] marriage by repining over Hallam's death.
> . . . Emily's forgetfulness was a more healthy reaction than Alfred's remembrance of every detail of his friendship with Arthur. (*Unquiet Heart*, 258–59)

Martin also provides the anecdote that allows Byatt to give a positive ending to Emily's story (259). When Emily is promised a permanent reunion with Hallam after her death, she flatly refuses—"I consider that an extremely unfair arrangement, and shall have nothing to do with it"—and tells her husband: "We have been through bad times in this world, and I consider it only decent to share our good times, presuming we have them, in the next" (283).

CONCLUSION

According to Jerome McGann, poetry written in another historical period than our own assumes a reader who will "enter the poet's world from a distance, at a point of difference which encourages both sympathy and judgment" (McGann, 181). It is this sympathy and judgment on the writer's part that makes "The Conjugial Angel" such a convincing story. Byatt's fictional interpretation of *In Memoriam* contains insights into the nature of mourning and melancholy that I believe are relevant to contemporary readers. She refuses to read *In Memoriam* as a unified whole leading to a resolution. Instead, "The Conjugial Angel" investigates the tensions and ambivalences so typical of the mourning process. In this context, I would also like to suggest that "The Conjugial Angel" is of great interest because it forces the reader to think about the relation between art and morality. I would argue that, in this sense, the story is exemplary of A. S. Byatt's lifelong interest in the rewards and disadvantages of art. For "The Conjugial Angel" does not subscribe to the classical view that art is a product of a totally free imagination, unrestricted by ethics, love, gender, personal histories, and family identities. The story makes us aware that, even though, as an elegy, *In Memoriam* is a beautiful work of art, it has its darker sides when looked at from the imagined perspective of Emily Tennyson.

NOTES TO "THE GENDER OF MOURNING: A. S. BYATT'S 'THE CONJUGIAL ANGEL' AND ALFRED LORD TENNYSON'S *IN MEMORIAM*"

1. Schor, *Bearing the Dead: The British Culture of Mourning from the Enlightenment to Victoria* (Princeton: Princeton University Press, 1994), 234.

2. Owen, *The Darkened Room: Women, Power and Spiritualism in Late Victorian England* (London: Virago, 1989). A. S. Byatt wrote a sympathetic review of Owen's study. Here, one may already witness a strong interest in Victorian spirituality and the gender aspects of the seances. See Byatt, "Chosen Vessels of a Fraud," *Times Literary Supplement,* 2–8 June 1989.

3. Kathryn Hughes, "Repossession," in *New Statesman & Society,* 6 November 1992.

4. For the "melancholy narcissism" of Tennyson's poem, see Peter M. Sacks, "Tennyson: *In Memoriam,*" in *The English Elegy: Studies in the Genre from Spenser to Yeats* (Baltimore: Johns Hopkins University Press, 1985), 166–203 (195).

5. Byatt, "Distrusting the Intellect," in *New Statesman,* 19 May 1967, 689–90.

6. McGann, "Tennyson and the Histories of Criticism," in *The Beauty of Inflections: Literary Investigations in Historical Method and Theory* (Oxford: Clarendon Press, 1985), 182.

7. Martin, *Tennyson: The Unquiet Heart* (Oxford: Clarendon Press, 1980), 147.

8. Sinfield, *Alfred Tennyson* (London: Blackwell, 1986), 128–29.

9. A. S. Byatt, "The Conjugial Angel," in *Angels and Insects* (London: Chatto & Windus, 1992), 259.

10. Byatt, "Insights ad Nauseam," in *Times Literary Supplement,* 14 November 1986, 1274. In her criticism, Byatt has more difficulty making up her mind about the subject. In an essay in *Passions of the Mind* she first denies any homosexual implications—"Tennyson's intense desire, in *In Memoriam,* to touch and grasp his lost friend, is not the excessive sensuality of a homosexual memory, as is now

often argued, but part of the climate of the time." However, she also quotes the lines "I loved thee, Spirit, and love, nor can / The soul of Shakespeare love thee more," and says they "could be used as evidence for both kinds of feeling." See Byatt, *Passions of the Mind* (London: Chatto & Windus, 1992), 62. For an extensive discussion of the creative tensions between Byatt's critical work and her fiction when it comes to questions of gender and writing, see my *A. S. Byatt: Art, Authorship and Creativity* (London: Macmillan, forthcoming).

11. Shaw, *Alfred Lord Tennyson* (London: Harvester, 1988), 141–65. In "Remembering the Victorians in the Nineties," Shaw reads "The Conjugal Angel" in ways that are similar to mine. See *(W)righting the Nineties* (Ghent: English Department, University of Ghent, 1995), 63–74.

12. Plain, "'Great Expectations': Rehabilitating the Recalcitrant War Poets," *Feminist Review* 51 (1995): 41–65 (57 and 49).

13. Byatt, *Imagining Characters* (London: Chatto & Windus, 1995), 206–7.

14. Glendinning, "Angels and Ministers of Graciousness," *The [London] Times,* 7 November 1992.

15. For a comparable type of gender inversion, see Christine Brückner, *Wenn du geredet hättest, Desdemona. Ungehaltene Reden ungehaltener Frauen. Mit Zeichnungen von Horst Janssen* (1983; repr. Frankfurt am Main and Berlin: Verlag Ullstein, 1986). Brückner acts as a ventriloquist for a.o. Desdemona, Katharina Luther, Sappho, Effi Briest, Donna Laura, Mary, and Clytemnestra.

16. "The Conjugial Angel," 177. The other women participating in the seances also do so for reasons associated with grief and mourning. Mrs. Hearnshaw, for instance, has lost her fifth child in seven years. The narrator makes a clear distinction between her grief and her husband's, and subtly emphasizes the power difference between them. Mr Hearnshaw "allowed his wife to come to the séances because otherwise he found the rich violence of her grief intolerable and embarrassing. It was his nature and his profession to repress displays of excessive emotion" (168). Mrs. Papagay's husband, a sailor, has disappeared: "She had attended her first séance really in order to find out whether she was or was not a widow, and had been answered, as is so often the case, ambiguously" (168).

17. Parkes, *Bereavement: Studies of Grief in Adult Life* (London: Tavistock, 1972); and Plain, 54.

18. Taylor, "A Mixed Benison from Tennyson," *Independent on Sunday,* 25 October 1992.

19. Butler, "The Moth and the Medium," in *Times Literary Supplement,* 16 October 1992.

Tennessee Williams "Outs" Scott and Ernest
PETER L. HAYS

In both his own and other people's fiction, Ernest Hemingway seems a range of characters united by only a name, four wives, three sons, and some common traits. In his own work, he is sometimes a sensitive, starving artist or the quintessential white hunter; in others' works, he is sometimes the patron demon of all male chauvinist pigs.[1] Even biographers have appropriated Hemingway to illustrate their own theses.[2] Tennessee Williams in *Clothes for a Summer Hotel* has Scott Fitzgerald say to Hemingway, "You are fortunate in having such an inexhaustibly interesting and complex nature, Hem, that regardless of how often you portray yourself in a book—."[3] The sentence is not completed, but presumably Scott would conclude that there were various selves for Hemingway to choose from.

Williams's *Clothes for a Summer Hotel* (1980), his last Broadway play, is a study of Scott and Zelda Fitzgerald. In it, Williams uses a Fitzgerald and Hemingway somewhat based on biographical facts, but of his own construction and for his own intentions. Those purposes, though manifold, would include, I suggest, the following. Williams makes Fitzgerald and Hemingway homosexuals like himself, thereby forming a bond with two of America's canonical writers, bolstering his own image as a writer in the process. Williams also implies that Fitzgerald's and Hemingway's art gained by their homosexuality: it made them, like himself, more sensitive, especially to women. The latter is a claim that Hemingway's feminist detractors, like Judith Fetterley or Nina Baym, would deny.

Like *The Glass Menagerie*, *Clothes* is a memory play, but with complications. Rather than simply looking back from the perspective of one character, as *Menagerie* does, *Clothes* combines Scott's fictitious last visit to Zelda (at Highland Hospital in Asheville, North Carolina), with Sara and Gerald Murphy's 1926 party (at Antibes) at which the Fitzgeralds and the Hemingways were present, and welds these into a Sartrean hell of other people.[4] The play, which is subtitled "A Ghost Play," is much like a Japanese *noh*

253

play.[5] Like *noh, Clothes* is plotless, and it is divided into two parts. Like *noh,* it features elaborate dance, is haunted by ghosts, and, like many *noh* dramas, specifically by the ghost of a madwoman. In *Clothes,* all the characters are dead, yet they act in the present with foreknowledge of the future, mixing past and present. This is confusing to viewers who do not know the biographies of Fitzgerald and Hemingway well, which may have contributed to the play's short run. (It lost $400,000 after just 14 days, despite starring Geraldine Page and Kenneth Haigh and being directed by José Quintero.[6]) *Clothes for a Summer Hotel* also lacks dramatic tension. It is a rambling mood piece, designed, as is much of Williams's work, to generate compassion and "deep feeling" (*Clothes,* 1).

Given Williams's compassion for abused or oppressed women, the main thrust of the play is sympathy for Zelda, mad in large part because Scott has stifled her natural talent for writing—her psychiatrist tells Scott that Zelda's writing is the superior of the two—and because she refuses to live only as "Mrs.–Eminent Author" (*Clothes,* 59). Williams has used Nancy Milford's *Zelda* and Hemingway's *A Moveable Feast;* he has done research—not always accurately—blaming Scott for Zelda's mental illness. Besides, Williams has projected himself liberally, both in his sympathy for the insane—"the visits by Scott to Zelda Fitzgerald in the mental asylum are representations of the visits by Tom to [his sister] Rose Williams"[7]—and in seeing his own homosexuality in the two other authors.[8]

Since the focus is on the Fitzgeralds, Hemingway is an incidental character, appearing in only a part of the play. Whenever Hemingway appears, his coarseness, ruthlessness, and overt machismo are contrasted with Scott's femininity. Where others have seen Scott's envy of Ernest's talent, energy, and active life, Williams sees a reciprocated current of sexual energy.

From Rolf Hochhuth's *The Deputy* to E. L. Doctorow's *Ragtime,* to name just a few examples of the past fifty years, authors have used the technique of actual figures in their art to broaden the scope of their work or to ask important historical questions. But others do so in a literary equivalent of name-dropping, being cute in a way that cheapens their work with evanescent topicality or by portraying the real figure in a less-than-flattering light, often to make themselves look good. Hemingway is guilty of this in his memoir *A Moveable Feast,* particularly in his portraits of Gertrude Stein, Ford Madox Ford, and Fitzgerald. Williams does something similar to Fitzgerald and Hemingway in *Clothes for a Summer Hotel.* Williams's Hemingway is crude and boorish. Hemingway frequently was so, but not at the ostensible setting, a party at Sara and Gerald Murphy's villa in 1926. That summer, Hemingway's son Bumby had whooping cough and was banned from the company of the Fitzgerald and Murphy children, which caused tension among the families, but no reported explosions from Hemingway. In contrast, the historical Fitzgerald was drunk, rude to guests, and threw ashtrays, as at another party he had smashed Sara's fine Venetian crystal, as alluded to in the play.[9] Disregarding fact for the sake of a contrast that will make Fitzgerald appear as the more sensitive of the two authors, Williams's stage direction portrays Hemingway thus: "*Hemingway laughs loudly, coarsely drunk*" (59). Hemingway then encourages Scott to provoke an effete black singer, who promptly knocks Fitzgerald down, thereby showing Scott's lack of macho masculinity. Host Sara Murphy proclaims, "Whenever [Scott] approaches Ernest I alert the waiters to prepare for a disturbance" (61). While much later, a heavily drinking, paranoid Hemingway disrupted some parties—at his birthday in 1959, for instance—the Hemingway of the 1920s was more in control, whereas Fitzgerald was frequently drunk and disorderly, even arrested for being so in Rome. Of course, Williams telescopes time here, for all the characters: Scott, throughout, takes nitroglycerin for his angina, foreshadowing his death by heart failure and implying a contrast with the equally stricken but large-hearted, generous Kilroy of *Camino Real*.

In order to ensure that wife-dominating, career-stifling, but more sensitive because more feminine Fitzgerald does not appear at a disadvantage beside the foil that Williams has set for him in Hemingway, we have the following interchange:

HEMINGWAY: My work will be hard and disciplined till it stops. Then— quit by choice—and rich . . . but—
HADLEY: Will I still be your girl?
HEMINGWAY: Be good.
HADLEY: You mean devoutly devoted to you, even when discarded for the next?

(57; internal ellipsis is Williams's)

Thus, both Hadley and Zelda join Williams's other abused women: Laura, Blanche, Catherine Holly, and the others.

Williams does not allow us merely to intuit the writers' feelings about the relation of gender identification and writerly ability, for much of Scott's and Ernest's conversation touches on writers' sensibilities, and their own. Hemingway tells Fitzgerald, with an implicit attack on Scott's masculinity, "It's often been observed that duality of gender can serve some writers well," this after accusing Scott of trying to appropriate Zelda's identity (thereby echoing and strengthening her own complaint of Scott's use of their lives in his fiction) and nearly appropriating her gender (64). Thus Williams's Hemingway boosts his own ego and his own sense of masculinity. Scott responds to Ernest: "We do have multiple selves as well as what you call dual genders" (65), a statement paralleling Michel Foucault's about homosexuals, "a kind of interior androgyny, a hermaphrodism of the soul."[10] Fitzgerald's claim also iterates Virginia Woolf's insight that the most comprehensive creativity came from androgynous minds.[11] In having Fitzgerald and Hemingway discuss the artistic benefits of androgyny, Tennessee Williams would seem to be paying a compliment to himself, insisting that it was his homosexuality, his ability to respond to the feelings of both men and women that made him the artist that he was, and conversely, denying artistry to writers who lacked such androgyny.[12]

In the play, Zelda herself wonders why Scott has worked so hard at promoting Ernest:

> Is it the attraction of Ernest's invulnerable, virile nature? Isn't that the implication, that Scott is magnetized, infatuated with Ernest's somewhat too carefully cultivated aura of the prizefight and the bullring and the man-to-man attitude acquired from Gertrude Stein?
>
> (57)

A bitchy, though also rather funny, comment on Zelda's part, both in implying that Fitzgerald's admiration for Hemingway was based on homosexual attraction and in suggesting that Hemingway's he-man pose was in imitation of Gertrude Stein. Earlier in the play, when Zelda calls Scott "pretty," he responds:

> SCOTT [with an edge]: Don't keep on with that, Zelda, that's insulting.
> ZELDA [approaching him, touching his throat]: I don't understand why you should find it so objectionable.
> SCOTT: The adjective "pretty" is for girls, or pretty boys—of ambiguous gender . . .
>
> (30, Williams's ellipsis)

When Scott Fitzgerald denounces homosexuals as "fairies," Zelda says, "You're too hard on them, Scott. I don't know why. Do they keep chasing you because you're so pretty they think you must be a secret one of them?" (31). Williams's implication, through Zelda's comment, is that Fitzgerald is overreacting defensively, protesting too much the truth of the accusation. Williams even has Hemingway say to Fitzgerald, "Don't be a bitch" (64).

Williams is interested in his characters' sexual identities, and thus has Fitzgerald discuss with Hemingway two of the latter's short stories that deal with homosexuality, "A Simple Enquiry" and "A Sea Change." In the first, he mistakenly reports that the orderly escapes the major's attentions by announcing himself as married, an error the play's Hemingway does not correct. Williams then has Hemingway confuse his own "Sea Change," with its overt lesbianism, with the scene in *Death in the Afternoon* (180–82) where a young man is approached sexually by a slightly older but wealthier man, leaves, is retrieved, screams at what sounds like rape, but then succumbs and acquiesces to the relationship to such an extent that he is later seen in his lover's company with his hair hennaed.[13] Hemingway, of course, would not have forgotten into which of his texts he had placed the story. Whereas critics have noticed that Hemingway has dealt with homosexuality of both genders frequently in his writing, Comley and Scholes point out Hemingway's even-handed treatment: sometimes critical, in line with popular prejudices of his day, and sometimes sympathetic. Williams, however, treats *only* these two episodes, and merely alludes briefly to Hemingway's other works: *The Sun Also Rises, A Farewell to Arms*, and *Across the River and Into the Trees*. Williams is interested primarily in those texts that support his point that Hemingway is interested in male homosexuality.

Finally, Williams develops Zelda's intimation of Scott's homosexuality, including a statement by Scott to Zelda that sexual passion "was never the really important thing between us, beautiful, yes, but less important" (11). Borrowing from Hemingway's description in *A Moveable Feast* of both Fitzgerald and the journey the two men made together to retrieve the Fitzgeralds' car in Lyon, Williams has the following dialogue:

> SCOTT: Ernest, you've always been able to be kind as well as cruel. Why that night I was so sick in Lyon—. . . You cared for me with the tenderness of—
> HEMINGWAY [*breaking in quickly*]: The night?—Scott? You had the skin of a girl, mouth of a girl, the soft eyes of a girl, you—you solicited attention. I gave it, yes, touchingly vulnerable.
> SCOTT: These attributes, if I did have them—. . . And they were— repellent to you?
> HEMINGWAY: They were disturbing to me.

258   PETER L. HAYS

The passage shows little attempt to mimic Hemingway's frequently documented speech patterns, and it ignores the exasperation Hemingway reported in *A Moveable Feast* in dealing with Fitzgerald's hypochondria and juvenile inability to act responsibly: missing a train, constantly delaying their journey unnecessarily, falling drunkenly asleep into his dinner, and so on. Instead, Williams creates a homoerotically charged scene, as this stage direction insists: "*He approaches Scott. For a moment we see their true depth of pure feeling for each other. Hemingway is frightened of it, however*" (64). Hemingway leaves the stage, the Fitzgeralds have an awkward goodbye, Zelda returning to the sanitarium in which she will burn to death, leaving Scott with "his haunted eyes [that] ask a silent question which he knows cannot be answered" (77).

Williams has asked questions in this play about how authors use people's lives, their own, and those of loved ones. Zelda, accusing Scott, tells him, "*What was important to [him] was to absorb and devour*" (11, Williams's emphasis); later she denounces him "as a husband who appropriates [his] life as material for his writing" (12). Such denunciations have a reflexive ring to them, coming from the playwright of *The Glass Menagerie,* particularly if Donald Spoto is right that institutionalized Zelda represents to Williams his own institutionalized sister, Rose.

As often in his plays, Williams tries to generate our understanding and compassion for the maimed and repressed, the outsider, often a female character, in this play, Zelda. In addition to projecting his own pain and guilt onto the characters of the play, he has also projected his own homosexuality onto Scott and Ernest. It is true that the play's Fitzgerald utters a truism in his discussion with Hemingway: "We do have multiple selves as well as what you call dual genders" (65), what in Foucault's terms would be "psychic hermaphrodism" (101), and what Virginia Woolf calls "androgynous minds" (148). Also, Fitzgerald in drag "makes a very seductive girl," as the picture of him in costume for the Triangle Club production of *Girl* reveals. And Hemingway's description of him in *A Moveable Feast*, indeed, captures those feminine qualities:

He had very fair wavy hair, a high forehead, excited and friendly eyes and a delicate long-lipped Irish mouth that, on a girl, would have been the mouth of a beauty. His chin was well built and he had good ears and a handsome, almost beautiful, unmarked nose. This should not have added up to a very pretty face, but that came from the coloring, the very fair hair and the mouth.[14]

But, beyond Fitzgerald's attempts to think like a woman for his fiction, and put himself in a woman's role, there is no evidence— despite the real Zelda's accusation designed to hurt him—that Scott ever acted out homosexual impulses. The same, regardless of the sexual games he played with his wife Mary, is true of Ernest. For example, Mary records in her diary a mock interview with a reporter that Hemingway contrived:

REPORTER: Mr. Hemingway, is it true your wife is a lesbian?
PAPA: Of course not. Mrs. Hemingway is a boy.
REPORTER: What are your favorite sports, sir?
PAPA: Shooting, fishing, reading and sodomy.
REPORTER: Does Mrs. Hemingway participate in these sports?
PAPA: She participates in all of them.

And on the next page of the diary, Ernest writes that Mary

has always wanted to be a boy and thinks as a boy without ever losing any femininity. . . . She loves me to be her girls, which I love to be. . . . In return she makes me awards and at night we do every sort of thing which pleases her and which pleases me. . . . Mary has never had one lesbian impulse but has always wanted to be a boy.[15]

This is the Hemingway who had dyed his own hair red and had written to Mary saying that he would dye her hair if she were unable to have it done satisfactorily in Chicago, a hair fetishist clearly, as his novels also indicate.[16] It is also a Hemingway that Williams seeks to deny: an author self-conscious of his sexuality and willing to explore it in his fiction, from the emasculated protagonist of *The Sun Also Rises* to the menage à trois of *The Garden of Eden* with its strange sexual experiments. But, as Jeffrey Meyers says, "Despite all the theorizing, there is not one shred of real evidence to suggest that Hemingway ever had any covert homosexual desires or overt homosexual relations."[17]

Williams's identification with the dissolute, struggling Fitzgerald is understandable: both were addicts, guilty in their own minds of betrayals of loved ones, now late in their careers with little recent commercial success. Williams's bond with Hemingway stems from a different source:

In the last years of his life, Tennessee developed a fixation about Hemingway . . . associating the writer's decline and his mental collapse

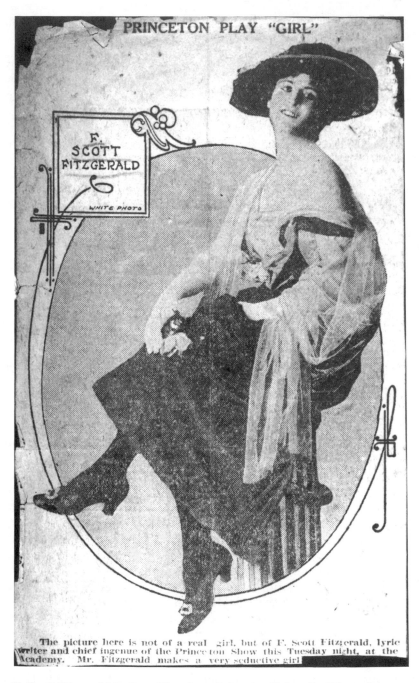

PRINCETON PLAY "GIRL"

F. SCOTT FITZGERALD

WHITE PHOTO

The picture here is not of a real girl, but of F. Scott Fitzgerald, lyric writer and chief ingenue of the Princeton Show this Tuesday night, at the Academy. Mr. Fitzgerald makes a very seductive girl.

F. Scott Fitzgerald in drag (Courtesy: Princeton University Library).

with his own fears of senility and nonproductivity. . . . And always, of course, there was the nagging suspicion that he might be going mad, like Hemingway, and not know it.[18]

In this play, then, Williams creates a bond between himself, Fitzgerald, and Hemingway: he points out their difficulties with alcohol, like his own; he points out how they, like he, used their own lives and those of people close to them in their works; he implies that to the extent each of the three successfully portrayed women it was because they had "androgynous minds." And of course, in both popular and academic critical estimation, Williams was the most successful of the three with his creation of sympathetic women. Finally, he claims that all three are homosexuals, but that only he, Tennessee Williams, is sufficiently self-confident to admit that truth. In conversation with Hemingway's granddaughter Margaux, Williams said, "I think both Hemingway and Fitzgerald had *elements* of homosexuality in them." Then, after summarizing Hemingway's description of Fitzgerald from *A Moveable Feast:* "I think he may have been in love with Fitzgerald, or at least sexually desired him. That was why he treated him so abominably in *A Moveable Feast*" (Rader 310–11, Williams's emphasis).

But Williams's portrayal of Hemingway in *Clothes for a Summer Hotel* provides us with a representation of Hemingway that both denies Hemingway's own insights and Williams's ability to create multi-dimensional characters. The Hemingway in Williams's play who answers Fitzgerald as to why "touching vulnerability" was disturbing to him with "I'd rather not examine the reason too closely" (66) is very much Williams's Hemingway, not the author of "A Sea Change," "A Simple Enquiry," "The Mother of a Queen," "A Lack of Passion," *For Whom the Bell Tolls*—all of which investigate varieties of homosexual experience—and certainly not the author of *The Garden of Eden,* where polymorphous sexuality is confronted boldly, and where the fictional, mad, bisexual Catherine has, ironically, more than a little of Zelda Fitzgerald in her. Fitzgerald, no doubt, would have protested Hemingway's portrayal of him in *A Moveable Feast,* as he had protested Hemingway's use of his name in "The Snows of Kilimanjaro." Thus, Williams was only doing what Hemingway had done before him, but with a pronounced sexual emphasis.

NOTES TO "TENNESSEE WILLIAMS 'OUTS' SCOTT AND ERNEST"

1. Judith Fetterley is his severest feminist critic in "*A Farewell to Arms:* Hemingway's Resentful Cryptogram," *The Resisting Reader* (Bloomington: Indi-

ana University Press, 1978), 46–71; another critical voice is Nina Baym's in "Actually, I Felt Sorry for the Lion," *New Critical Approaches to the Short Stories of Ernest Hemingway,* ed. Jackson J. Benson (Durham, NC: Duke University Press, 1990), 112–20.

2. James R. Mellow, in *Hemingway: A Life Without Consequences* (Boston: Houghton Mifflin, 1992), carefully marshals evidence to suggest strong latent homosexuality in Hemingway, both in his text and even in his choice of end papers for the volume, which feature photographs of Hemingway in all-male company: the front papers, of Hemingway's first wedding; the end papers, of a picnic without clothes on the Manzanares River in Spain.

3. Williams, *Clothes for a Summer Hotel* (New York: New Directions, 1983), 64.

4. Zelda entered Highland Hospital only in April 1936, and, while Scott lived in Asheville that summer, they only met half a dozen times, usually at the Grove Park Inn where Scott stayed, not at the hospital. The following June, Scott moved from North Carolina to Hollywood, visiting Zelda at Asheville in September and December of 1937, and having her join himself and their daughter in Virginia Beach in March 1938. In April 1939, he took Zelda to Cuba and did not see her for the rest of the year; he began *The Last Tycoon* in October 1939. Zelda was released from the hospital to return to her mother in Montgomery, Alabama, in April 1940, where she was when Scott died in December of that year. Thus there is no way he could have discussed *The Last Tycoon* with her at Highland Hospital, as he does in the play.

Zelda returned to Highlands in August 1943, went back to Montgomery in February 1944, then back to Highlands early in 1946 and died in a fire at the hospital in November 1947. See Nancy Milford, *Zelda* (New York: Harper and Row, 1970), 308ff.

5. Allean Hale makes the connection to *noh* drama, believing Williams to have been influenced by Yukio Mishima ("Tennessee's Long Trip," *Missouri Review* 7 [1984]: 201–12; and "The Secret Script of Tennessee Williams," *The Southern Review* 27 [Spring 1991]: 363–75, esp. 373).

The following analysis of *noh* is taken from Chifumi Shimazaki, *The Noh,* vol. 1 (Tokyo: Hinoki Shoten, 1972): *Noh* is plotless: "Unlike other forms of drama, there is hardly any drama or plot" (15). The play frequently opens with a traveler who, after introducing himself, sings a travel song followed by an arrival speech. In *Clothes,* Scott has just arrived in Asheville to see Zelda, inappropriately dressed, hence the play's title. In Williams's play, *noh*'s Buddhist monks are transmogrified into nuns, guarding the gates of Zelda's asylum. *Noh* plays are in two parts, as is *Clothes.* In the first part, the protagonist, or *shite,* is a ghost usually disguised for his or her earthly appearance. In the break between parts, the visitor (*waki*) is told of the *shite*'s troubled soul and sings a waiting song, determined to wait for the *shite*'s return (16), as Scott must wait for Zelda both at *Clothes*' opening, and as he had to do in real life. In *noh*'s second part, the *shite* returns undisguised, "telling who he is, or how he feels on coming back to the scene so familiar in his life time" (17). Unlike the elaborate costumes of *noh,* in *Clothes,* Zelda wears a ballet tutu, an overcoat, a beach robe, a dress, and in one scene she is "nude except for whatever conventions of stage propriety may be in order" (Williams 41). Scott's attire never changes.

Noh incorporates elaborate dances, and *Clothes* features both a *pas de deux* from ballet and a tango. Finally, a characteristic *noh* drama is the *Kyoran-mono* or mad piece, often featuring a mad woman (24). And where Zelda of *Clothes* is concerned with Scott's absorbing her identity and gender, in *noh,* all parts are played by males.

6. Otis L. Guernsey, Jr., *Curtain Times: The New York Theater: 1965–1987* (New York: Applause Theatre Books, 1987), 418, for cost of production; Maria St. Just, *Five O'Clock Angel: Letters of Tennessee Williams to Maria St. Just* (Boston: Little, Brown, 1985), 377, for length of run.

7. Donald Spoto, *The Kindness of Strangers: The Life of Tennessee Williams* (Boston: Little, Brown, 1985), 339. Donald Adler makes the same connection; see his "When Ghosts Supplant Memories: Tennessee Williams' *Clothes for a Summer Hotel,*" *Southern Literary Journal* 19 (Spring 1987): 6.

8. "[That] Scott and Zelda Fitzgerald [. . .] are hardly disguised projections of the author's own self-pity is obvious from the unsubtle ways Williams betrays his identification, repeatedly and pointlessly questioning Scott's heterosexuality." See Gerald M. Berkowitz, *American Drama of the Twentieth Century* (London: Longman, 1992), 163.

9. Williams, 52. See also, Carlos Baker, *Ernest Hemingway: A Life Story* (New York: Scribners, 1969), 170; Matthew J. Bruccoli, *Some Sort of Epic Grandeur: The Life of F. Scott Fitzgerald* (New York: Harcourt Brace Jovanovitch, 1981), 253.

10. Foucault, *The History of Sexuality,* vol. 1, trans. Robert Hurley (New York: Pantheon Books, 1978), 43.

11. Woolf, *A Room of One's Own* (1929; repr. London: Hogarth Press, 1953), 148.

12. Hilton Anderson makes the same point in "Tennessee Williams' *Clothes for a Summer Hotel:* Feminine Sensibilities and the Artist," *Publications of the Mississippi Philological Association* (1988): 1–9 (p. 4).

13. The scene in *Death in the Afternoon* was recently discussed by Nancy R. Comley and Robert Scholes in their *Hemingway's Genders: Rereading the Hemingway Text* (New Haven, CT: Yale University Press, 1994). George Monteiro had already noted Williams's error in his false identification of the Hemingway stories. See his "Tennessee Williams Misremembers Hemingway," *Hemingway Review* 10 (1990): 71.

14. Hemingway, *A Moveable Feast* (New York: Scribners, 1964), 149.

15. Mary Hemingway, *How It Was* (New York: Knopf, 1976), 425–26.

16. Baker, 461. Baker is wrong, however, that Hemingway dyed his hair accidentally, as the letter to Mary Hemingway makes clear (unpublished letter of 2 May 1947, in the Hemingway Collection of the John F. Kennedy Library).

17. Meyers, *Hemingway* (New York: Harper & Row, 1985), 202.

18. Dotson Rader, *Tennessee, Cry of the Heart* (Garden City, N.Y.: Doubleday, 1985), 309. The playwright's brother, Dakin, had Tennessee committed to a mental institution in the fall of 1969 (Rader, 3).

The Truthful Fiction of the Death and Life of the Author: Cervantes and Marlowe

HARM DEN BOER

To the best of my knowledge, *The Death and Life of Miguel de Cervantes* by Stephen Marlowe is the first novel in which the master of Spanish literature appears as the protagonist.[1] This may seem somewhat strange, for the great number of biographies written about Cervantes shows that the author's life is not lacking in interest, that it constantly invites romanticization, and is interpreted in very different ways.[2] There are some short fictionalized evocations of the author, of which those by Azorín deserve to be mentioned.[3] Both provide an explanation for the limited fictional exploitation of the writer: he is constantly compared to his greatest creation, the spirited Knight of La Mancha. Yet Cervantes's life would make a fertile subject for many a novel, even without *Don Quixote*.

Cervantes belonged to a complicated family, which constantly found itself in economic trouble and was constantly on the move. In the Spanish climate of his lifetime, poisoned by notions of "purity of blood," he was thought to be descended from recent converts. Intriguingly, this issue is still a topic for discussion, as when attempts are made to find an explanation for Cervantes's "tolerant," mildly ironical view of reality.

Through his exploits both in literature and on the battlefield, Cervantes embodied the ideal of the Renaissance man. Before acquiring fame as a writer, he had distinguished himself by his heroism as a soldier in the Battle of Lepanto (1571), the finest hour of Philip II's Spain. Having spent five years in the service of the Spanish empire, he spent another five as a captive of the Barbary pirates in Algiers, where he earned the admiration of his fellow prisoners for his exemplary attitude in the face of so much adversity, and because of his three, albeit unsuccessful, attempts to escape. However, there was also a completely unheroic side to his life; on his return to Spain, Cervantes was forced by lack of money to accept an obscure, frustrating job as a commissary and tax

264

collector in Andalusia, a personal humiliation that coincided with the Armada disaster, the symbolic nadir of the reign of Philip II. This was followed by renewed imprisonment, this time on account of debt, in the course of which he began his history of the hidalgo of La Mancha, the novel which met with enormous success as soon as it was published but brought its author little profit. While this oversimplified summary may give the impression of a richly documented life, it is remarkable how little is known about Cervantes, who himself was both reticent and selective as far as information about his life was concerned. There are gaps in his biography—including one of nearly four years—which are as intriguing as the well-known, spectacular episodes.

As an *author,* Cervantes, with his remarkably wide range of work, is an elusive, fascinating figure, someone with great potential as a literary character. His debut as a dramatist was not promising, although in the end he was to make a reputation for himself with a number of *entremeses,* or interludes, including the magisterial *El retablo de las maravillas.* He repeatedly tried writing poetry but never managed to distinguish himself in that field. What is striking in his brilliant mastery of prose is that, alongside the modernity of *Don Quixote,* he kept supporting the more traditional notions of fiction in his novel *Los trabajos de Persiles,* as well as in the *Novelas ejemplares.*

The American Stephen Marlowe, after exploring the potential of the pseudo-autobiographical form in his Columbus novel, was well placed to take up the challenge of fictionalizing the discoverer of that other New World, that of fiction.[4] The very title, *The Death and Life of Miguel de Cervantes,* suggests that this is no conventional biography. The subtitle, "A novel by Stephen Marlowe," the cover embellished with jolly "quixotic" figures, and the blurb quoting a review as saying, "Ride in triumph through remarkable Renaissance byways with this other Marlowe," leave no doubt about the book's fictional nature. Marlowe's Miguel de Cervantes begins recounting his "life" in spectacular novelistic fashion with a prologue in medias res, in which he describes his imminent execution. He finds himself in Algiers, on the scaffold of the Plaza of Atrocities, and preparatory to his hanging, the noose is placed around his neck. The reader may not be alarmed by such an opening, which might, after all, be followed by a long series of flashbacks, but he might be disconcerted by his historical knowledge: for, from this moment onwards, what is going to happen to Cervantes, who still has 36 years of his life and nearly his entire literary production ahead of him after Algiers?

The Death of History

The prologue announces an ingenious plot, which completely exhausts its possibilities and intentionally undermines the verisimilitude of the story. At the end of the first part—*The Death of Miguel de Cervantes*—the writer is actually hanged, but that is not the end of the story:

> It is what, on the scaffold, I feel now. (Although, with a noose throttling me, a frightening inability to breathe is perhaps not so strange.)
> Another thing reminds me of The Naval. Rather unmiraculously (or so it seems), I rise out of my body and from a height of a few feet look down at it. This I realize must be a part of dying, at least my way of dying.
> I hover for a moment, then float above the unremarkable-looking executioner and off the stage. . . .
> Off to one side Gabriel Múñoz the taverner, still at liberty and apparently back at his old job, is briefing a prisoner obviously just out of his first softening-up in solitary. As I swoop in, I get the shock of my life (or death). The new prisoner is *me*, Miguel de Cervantes—but a me with a normal left hand and a maimed right hand. (227–28)

From this moment on, it is clear to the reader that the "historical" Cervantes has been discarded; for, in contrast to the "old" one, the "new" one has a maimed *right* hand, so he is a double. In the second part this Cervantes again meets himself (or another self) in a duel with a "Knight of the Mirrors."[5] *The Death and Life of Miguel de Cervantes* is full of all sorts of unexpected events, sudden turns, and impossibilities. The reader is told by Cervantes–Marlowe not to be too amazed at these, even to anticipate them, although the author still wants to remain one step ahead of the reader. It is a game that lays bare its devices, yet wants to remain a game.

In this way the story explicitly points to the death of the "historical" Cervantes and to his new life as a literary character, or to the Death of History and the Life of the Imagination. This lands us in familiar territory: Marlowe seems to side with those postmodern writers who constantly and in various ways play with representations, in order to point at the limitations to an objective rendering of historical reality. History is demythologized, attacked, made fun of, by way of parody, irony, or gross exaggeration.[6]

Marlowe repeatedly puts statements in his character's mouth on the limitations of history, and therefore of the "official" biography of an author:

> So in historical time Andrea could not have been in Alcalá when Don Carlos fell downstairs. But in fictional time she *was* there. I know this for a fact because I was there too. (30)

> "But," I began to object, "but history is the —"
> "Truth?" Cide Hamete supplied. "Because it is documented? But why should the ledger be truer than the legend? The merely measurable truer than the truly memorable?" (30)

> At a certain point in time (it is always a point in time for historians, never a moment in space, we shall return to this strange prejudice), the afternoon of 15 September 1569 to be exact, historians do agree that Sigura and I fought: there is documentation. But about the princess Eboli they are mute. Was the Princess there? Of course she was. I saw her. (62)

The history that has been passed down is no more than a selection, after all, and one that always falls far short when it comes to providing a (psychological) explanation for a person's life.

In Marlowe's novel, the gaps in the author's life are filled in a way that is typical of the postmodern attitude: a generally accepted rendering is denied and replaced by an interpretation that undermines its own credibility. Cervantes mocks those critics who have postulated that he underwent traumatic sexual experiences as a consequence of his captivity in Algiers, but he does let on that the course of his life was to a large extent determined by the love he had conceived for his sister, Andrea.[7] That love, with its constant threat of incest, motivates the hero's travels, now in pursuit of his desire, then fleeing it. It also leads to years of impotence in his marriage with Catalina. When a solution presents itself—the discovery that Andrea is not Miguel's "real" sister—it is too late. The hero also admits to having had recourse to self-abuse in difficult moments, he turns out to be a stammerer, and his feats, including his conduct in the Battle of Lepanto (Cervantes is also known as "the hero of Lepanto") come about by accident, almost as if he has no control over them.

The writer is not the only distorted or grotesque reflection of reality as it has been handed down to us. The novel's universe is full of imposters, whores, sorceresses, spies, esoterics, and sadists. The seemingly unremarkable Catalina, Cervantes's wife, turns out to be one of the most original characters. Having been raised like a Sancho Panza in village simplicity, she regards sex as something completely natural, which she likes to discuss in all openness, and which she likes to engage in as often as she can, whenever and wherever possible. At the same time, however, she has an unwavering sense of morality, so that it never even occurs to her to seek her pleasure elsewhere when her husband becomes impotent, and so she enters a convent rather than give in to her desires. Finally, she sublimates her longing by devoting herself to the care of animals, a comic allusion on Marlowe's part to a one-time French sex symbol of recent cinema history, and maybe also to the slightly less complicated relations with animals typical of Spaniards in and around the bull ring.

Constant allusions in many forms are a typical way of undermining history. Characters and events are denied ontological status in "reality" by deliberate breaks with the conventions of realist fiction. There are absurdities on numerous levels. The narrator steps out of the fiction in a hilarious way by having his father say: "I didn't kill nobody," and adding that "the double negative, I ought to say, is no indication of a deficient education—my father was speaking Spanish, after all" (6). There are constant anachronisms: The Supreme and General Council of the Inquisition turns out to have an Investment Branch (155), and all the stops are pulled out when Cervantes speaks of a secret Nameless Organization, which runs the top-secret archives of the "so-called R&R Centre (more properly Base Iberia)" in the south of Spain, and which is preparing for an operation called "Weltschmerz," employing agents under the code names Mnemosyne, Quillpusher, and Von Nacht zu Nebel (287–94).

Many characters owe their existence to literature. The sleazy, plea-bargaining lawyer Picapleitos is reminiscent of Quevedo's satires (quite apart from a possible relatedness with his modern-day colleagues in the United States). Cide Hamete Benengeli, who serves as the friend-in-need/adviser to Marlowe's Cervantes, is not only the chronicler of *Don Quixote*, but also Faust's Mephistopheles and Candide's Pangloss. He is probably also the Dickensian "certain mutual friend" who has a hand in many events befalling the young Cervantes. Christopher Marlowe, dramatist and spy for a secret network, can be read as private-eye Philip Marlowe and probably also alludes to the author Stephen Marlowe. Lope de Vega is Cervantes's grotesque opposite: in the novel, he is depicted as a vain, superficial writer, who neglects his literary calling in favor of easy successes. Literature also demands, in despite of historical probability, that Cervantes should encounter Torquato Tasso, Christopher Marlowe, and Shakespeare. All of these meetings give rise to amusing dialogues and more or less profound exchanges about being an author.

From the preceding examples it may have emerged that the events in *The Death and Life of Miguel de Cervantes* bear little relation to the historical facts that are known to us concerning the author's life. As is the case with the characters, however, reality is indispensable in an ancillary role:

> If this were only fiction, I could write here that they were married on April 23rd. But this is the story of my death and life, in which fiction and that lesser truth, history, from time to time form a seamless whole. And truth constrains me to say the wedding took place on a blustery day earlier in the month. (323)

Some references to historical reality are necessary, then, if only because in this historical genre it is to be undermined and stood on its head. Stephen Marlowe does this with great skill and humor by adding an enormous number of stories and subplots, with so many turns and impossibilities all at once (disguises, changes of identity, disappearances, magic) that in the end Cervantes's "real life" completely disappears from view. It is the narrator himself who comes to this realization during his imprisonment in Sevilla, where he has decided to record his life:

> I thought about the family's Columbus connection and its converso origins. I thought about my father in debtors' prison, and the death of the Patriarch, and the first twinges of an illicit attachment to my sister Andrea who wasn't my sister. I thought about Picapleitos a/k/a Señor Zum, and about Luis the black slave, later Luis Blackslave, now Goldfang. I remembered rescuing Juan-O, who wasn't Juan-O yet, from the gypsies in Triana. I remembered the birth of postmature little Constanza, and my duel with Nicolas de Ovando's hulking stand-in Sigura, and my flight to Italy, and Cousin Gaspar and poor crazy-brilliant Tasso and his sister Cornelia ("e bella, bella!"). I remembered my brother Rodrigo pursuing glory like the Holy Grail, and I relived The Naval and our capture by Barbary pirates, met again Cide Hamete Benengeli on his deathmat and Zoraida the trance dancer and her uncle Suleiman Sa'adah Sometimes (how Erroneously Called the Wise) and Michele-Micaela of the classic callipygean curve (are you still playing your dangerous games, Micaela?). And I remember Shakashik-Who-Sings-His-Own-Songs and what he sang about me, and how could I forget

my own death in the Plaza of Atrocities? I remembered my poor dwindled father off the old road for ever, defending himself at the Bench of If-Only with an ancient rusty sword. I remembered Catalina as a bride, and Andrea. I remembered Gabriel Múñoz and Pierre Papin, and the Sands of Terminal Despair and the Fuggerman Hasko von Nacht zu Nebel and Kit Marlowe a/k/a Quillpusher and the brigand Aurelio Ollero whom I never met, and all the people and places that had gone by but also into me, and I looked at that stack of paper and that full inkhorn and those quill-pens. (397–98)

This is a magisterial and absurd summary of his life, an anagnorisis of the "I," and a key passage in the novel, for Cervantes decides on a definitive settling of accounts and a new beginning:

> I wrote about none of that. . . . I started on a fresh page.
> El ingenioso
> hidalgo
> Don Quixote
> de la Mancha. (398)

THE LIFE OF FICTION

Marlowe surveys Cervantes's life and decides that the only authentic way for him to approach this life is by way of fiction. This is the serious side to the playful provocateur, Marlowe.

> Write about what you know? It's not just bad advice, it's backwards. A writer *must go beyond* what he knows. And when he does, if he does it in the right way, a strange and wonderful thing happens. When he does, if he does it in the right way, the things he's not writing about, the things he knows firsthand, nevertheless by some inexplicable alchemy are there lending their truth to what he does write. (398)

In the last instance, the story of Cervantes–Marlowe looks like the poetics of a believer. It is no coincidence that the novel takes the creeds of two authors as its epigraphs: "The delusions of history and the illusions of art both require a suspension of disbelief" (Arthur Koestler) and "Art gives life to what history killed" (Carlos Fuentes). All narrative strategies that infringe upon reality in a grotesque, comic, and playful way at the same time create a world of independent validity. In that sense, the double meanings and pitfalls of the novel cause only limited damage. Accordingly, the text lends itself to a comparison—and actually invites such a comparison itself—with *Don Quixote,* which, apart from parodying chivalric romances, of course, also creates an autonomous world.

If the novel is read as pure fiction, we see that the character of Cervantes gives way to the author of *Don Quixote.* The destructive strategies which the writer applies when discrediting history, at the same time create an imaginary universe and form a tribute to the Cervantes of literature.

This is easy to see in the constant transformations, disappearances, and doubles. The best example is undoubtedly Michele/Micaela. During Cervantes's captivity in Algiers, we meet a fellow prisoner, an adolescent, who is continually provoking the Arab hostage takers sexually, but in reality turns out to be a young lady. She later becomes a secret agent, operating under the code name of Mnemosyne, which takes her to, among other places, Andalusia, Amsterdam, and London, where Cervantes unexpectedly recognizes her every time (the element of surprise ultimately disappears entirely, because there are constantly lots of transformations, disappearances, and sudden appearances). To these, add the doubles—Cervantes, Pedro (the Killer) Pacheco Portocarrero, Pedro (the Choirboy) Pacheco Portocarrero—, characters that are easy to mix up because of specific qualities (the brown and blue-eyed Constanza, Cide Hamete Benengeli . . .)—known as "mappings" in the criticism of postmodern fiction (McHale, 78–80)—and few characters remain with stable identities. Their lives, however, are firmly rooted in literature, for instance in *Don Quixote* and the narrative art of Cervantes. Girls/women disguised as boys/men like Michele/Micaela are a favorite motif in the prose and drama of the Spanish Golden Age. The presence of Micaela in England, where she is driven around the city in a coach by the queen, is a tribute to Cervantes's short story *La española inglesa,* just like Andrea's decision to live among the gypsies alludes to *La gitanilla.*[8]

In the narrator, too, a double, undermining and constructive force can be discerned. On the one hand, we can speak of the progressive erosion of his ontological status. The autobiographical "I," whose transfer from the dead Cervantes to a living double has already been described, is remarkable as a witness-narrator, because he moves freely through his past, his present, and his future. He talks about his youth as if he were in the middle of it, while at the same time he is able to elaborate on the historians and critics who have established and interpreted this or that moment of his life. And, although it becomes clear why Cervantes is telling his story, up to the end of the text, it remains unclear when he sickbed or imagining that he would have told his *Death and Life* to Micaela—the last remaining passion of his life—if he had succeeded in getting into the coach with her instead of falling and consequently ending up in his sickbed.

In addition, the limited perspective of Cervantes sometimes unexpectedly gives way to an omniscient narrator, who recounts what is happening to the other characters in his absence. The writer, of course, is aware of these breaches of narrative convention and puts forward a justification for this which takes away any illusion of verisimilitude: every author has to admit that characters in a story start to lead a life of their own and do not cease to exist when the writer is not telling you about them; so he regards his life as a story and the people in it as characters. Even the text exists by virtue of the fiction: in the middle of the autobiography we find an erratum, inserted by the printer, which informs us that several pages are missing; a bit further on in the book, Cervantes explains to us that a character had just walked in through a wall and inserted this misleading text in his story (356).

Although reality and representation are constantly intermingled in this way, the story can be fully explained by accepting that the master of storytellers, Cervantes, has invented and directed his own text/life. After all, is not the text also a tribute to *El ingenioso hidalgo Don Quixote de la Mancha,* which also features an omniscient narrator, who occasionally addresses the reader directly, attributes the beginning of his story to the Arab chronicler Cide Hamete Benengeli, in which characters from real life appear—Ginés de Pasamonte—who have read the work and in which Don Quixote and Sancho Panza, at the beginning of the second volume, discuss the readers of the first volume?

Marlowe's novel, too, has two parts. It is no coincidence that these are entitled *Part the First* and *Part the Second;* it has chapters with titles like "In Which I Am Excommunicated And Declared Anathema, And in Which Worse Things Happen." All these constitute unmistakable references to the author of *Don Quixote,* while Miguel de Cervantes perishes in his own life. Together, the carefully documented "history" and the unlikely series of events inspired by *Don Quixote* (or by Literature) that supplement it, reduce the man Miguel de Cervantes to a passive character in a huge theater of the world, a dedicated storyteller, perhaps, but someone who does not get round to a genuine reflection on his own life.

What I learned about writing, mostly, was this. The first thing writers of fiction have to do is willingly—and not just willingly but joyfully—

suspend *their own* disbelief. Then everything else follows. It's harder, of course, if you're a writer who worries a lot, telling yourself that even if what happens in imagination is as intense as the real world, still, you could be doing everything wrong; that writing about a hero who tries to impose on the world an impossible reality, a hero who must forever fail, is all a mistake, hopeless, irremediable. What if, pretty soon, you do more worrying than writing? There's a solution. I found it by accident when writing *Don Quixote,* and I'll pass it along. If you want to stop worrying, you must make so much go wrong for your hapless hero that there's no time left to agonize over your hapless self. (455)

That is the ineluctable corollary of Marlowe's professed belief in the epistemological superiority of fiction to reality: for an explanation of his person, his Cervantes ingeniously refers us back to his work. *The Death and Life of Miguel de Cervantes* is, above all, a paraphrase of other novels, with extremely amusing, but never convincing characters. In this respect, the author cannot, in the end, bear comparison with the Man from la Mancha.

CONCLUSION

In dealing with the author of the most famous of all fictions, *The Death and Life of Miguel de Cervantes* by Stephen Marlowe reflects both the possibilities and the limitations of using an author as character. Exploiting the rich and agitated life of Cervantes, Marlowe creates an elaborate narration full of witty and hilarious games with History and Literature. He turns upside down the known facts about Cervantes's biography, and gives way to a provocative, heterodox interpretation of the canonized writer. Literature enables Marlowe to create a fictional universe inhabited by a colorful range of characters, picked up from contemporary Spanish authors, Cervantes, world literature, and even modern cinema; Cervantes's undisputed art of storytelling inspires him to spin a dazzling narrative full of subplots, sudden turns, and intrigue.

At a first glance, *The Death and Life of Miguel de Cervantes* seems to land us on the familiar ground of postmodern fiction, in which the limitations of representing reality are continually challenged. Hence, the doubles, parallel versions of a "historical truth," constant quotes and paraphrases, the narrator's stepping into and out of fiction, a narrator who himself tells us that historical truth is not really to be found. The "death" of Miguel de Cervantes is thus his historical death. But in confessing that fiction is the only realm of meaning, the "living Cervantes," that is the character created by Marlowe, willingly submits whatever was left of his autonomous existence to Don Quixote, the character he had given life to. Thereby, the novel illustrates one of the pitfalls of this kind of fiction: at best *The Death and Life of Miguel de Cervantes* is a supreme parody on history and literature, but it does not appear to go beyond that. Depriving reality of any sense by confessing an absolute belief in fiction, Marlowe appears to have ignored the most important and enduring contribution of cervantine fiction, its essential, fascinating dialogue with History.

NOTES TO "THE TRUTHFUL FICTION OF THE DEATH AND LIFE OF THE AUTHOR: CERVANTES AND MARLOWE"

Translated from the Dutch by Paul Franssen.

1. Marlowe, *The Death and Life of Miguel de Cervantes* (London: Bloomsbury, 1987).

2. Including Luis Astrana Martín, *Vida ejemplar y heroica de Miguel de Cervantes Saavedra,* 7 vols. (Madrid: Reus, 1948–57). A well-documented, penetrating and captivating biography is that by Jean Canavaggio, *Cervantes* (Paris: Mazarine, 1986).

3. Azorín (a.k.a. Jose Martinez Ruiz, 1873–1967) felt particularly attracted to the person and work of Miguel de Cervantes. The work in this case nearly always means: *Don Quixote.* He wrote several short pieces about Cervantes and *Don Quixote,* some of them essays, some impressionistic fictional sketches. As far as the figure of Cervantes is concerned, the following are worth mentioning: "Genesis del Quijote" (1905), published in the collection *Al voleo* (1905–53); "Cervantes," one of the "portraits" in *Lecturas Españolas* (1912); and "Aventuras de Miguel de Cervantes," in *Pensando in España* (1940). Several impressions of scenes from Cervantes's life were included in *Con Cervantes* (1947) and *Con permiso de los cervantistas* (1948). Also of interest is his play *Cervantes, o la casa encantada* (1931), which depicts the penniless author in his last few years. See also Anthony Burgess, "A Meeting in Valladolid," in *The Devil's Mode* (London: Hutchinson, 1989), 5–21, which, like Stephen Marlowe's novel, features a meeting between Cervantes and Shakespeare; Jorge Luis Borges's short poem on Cervantes in *The Book of Sand,* with a translation by Alastair Reid (Harmondsworth: Penguin, 1979), 157; and, more recently, Federico Jeanmaire, *Miguel: Phantasmata Speculari* (Barcelona: Anagrama, 1991).

4. *The Memoirs of Christopher Columbus* (London: Bloomsbury, 1987).

5. See chapter 34, with the meaningful title "The Fateful Adventure of the Flying Horse Clavileño And Other Impossibilities," 440–44.

6. For a lucid account of postmodern fiction, see Brian McHale, *Constructing Postmodernism* (London and New York: Routledge, 1992).

7. Marlowe may have had in mind Rossi Rosa's *Ascoltare Cervantes: Saggio biografico* (Roma: Editori Riuniti, 1987), in which the author is able to "establish," with the help of psychoanalytical methods, that Cervantes's family were *conversos*—converted Jews—and that Miguel was a homosexual.

8. Both short stories may be found in Cervantes's *Novelas ejemplares.*

Hella S. Haasse's *In a Dark Wood Wandering:* Charles d'Orléans in an "Existentialist" *Bildungsroman*

MARTIJN RUS

In her novel entitled *In a Dark Wood Wandering* (1949), the Dutch author Hella S. Haasse depicts the life of the late-medieval French statesman and poet, Charles d'Orléans.[1] On the grounds of its style recalling the politico-literary chronicle tradition of the Middle Ages, *In a Dark Wood Wandering* may well be defined as a novel that is historical. The events that mark the life of Charles d'Orléans are presented in chronological order, forming a straight line from the cradle to the grave. These events may often be traced to various historical sources; and, on occasion, the novel even explicitly adopts authentic documents as a means of supporting its allegations about the man portrayed. Also the context within which the events of Charles d'Orléans's life take place is historically authorized. *In a Dark Wood Wandering* is a novel about the Hundred Years War, about the decline of the French nobility which masterfully manages to keep up appearances. This novel, with its immensely faithful depiction of the period's manners and morals, has the appearance of an authentic fifteenth-century document. Authenticity would seem also to be the word to apply to the portrait of the poet Charles d'Orléans painted by Hella Haasse. Here is a Charles d'Orléans as we know him from our literary histories, the aristocrat forced to write poetry by circumstances, as it were, courtly and ceremonious, fashionable (as the integrated ballads and rondels reveal), a host at Blois of numerous rhymers and poets— including François Villon, an author who was equally predestined to become a literary legend.

Yet, Haasse's *Dark Wood* is not only historical, it is also a novel. Many elements are fictional, invented by the author, like the thoughts and feelings of her characters, their dialogues, and their interior monologues. Indeed, Haasse never, as she herself says, aimed for "the illusion of historical accuracy." Rather, she con-

sciously decided to appropriate the historical past. She chose
Charles d'Orléans as her main character because, in the course of
writing his life story, she could address her own problems, portray
her own insecurities and fears, and, at the same time, sublimate
them.[2] Indeed, time and again, she emphasizes that this book, despite its historical guise, reflects her own reality, her inner world
during the period from approximately 1935 to 1945.[3] The knightly
codes of the Middle Ages, the courtly values of a world in which
everything had its fixed place and meaning in the hierarchy of
things, as well as the horror and the gloom, Haasse realized, "provided the ideal material for daydreams to someone who has not
yet got round to establishing contact with a reality in which one
is expected to be mature and responsible" (*Persoonsbewijs,* 58).
Elsewhere she discusses the novel in the context of her "transition
from solitary reveries to a more conscious concern with people
and society" (*Persoonsbewijs,* 60), during a "period of maturation,
from a passive to a conscious life."[4] In short, *In a Dark Wood
Wandering* is the image of the inner world of a writer on the verge
of maturity, on the threshold between the "ivory tower" of her
youth and the "school" of life, torn between the desire to flee the
chaos inherent in the reality around her by means of colorful and
flamboyant fantasies, and the growing need to order that chaos, to
assign meaning to it.[5]

In this essay I wish to study *In a Dark Wood Wandering* as a
novel, but not as a projection of any so-called personal problem
on the part of the novelist. Rather, I wish to assess how Haasse,
from the perspective of her own historical period, and from her
ideas and convictions as a woman of her time, stages Charles d'Orléans, the poet as human being, the human being as poet.

Important for an appreciation of this novel, which first appeared
in 1949, is that the original plan was devised in the years immediately following the Second World War, a period during which the
perplexing difficulties of human existence were central to the current philosophy and writing. This was the heyday of existentialism,
which permeated all areas of life. No writer in the fullest sense of
the term could remain unaffected or unconcerned. The act of writing itself was a means of taking a stand, of whichever kind, with
regard to the issues and questions of the day.

Haasse, too, adopted a position. This position, as I hope to demonstrate, was basically that of godless existentialism but interpreted in her own fashion. She embraced the sundry material
handed her by the masters of French existentialism to construct a
version of existentialism quite her own, and *In a Dark Wood Wan-*

dering is an apt illustration of the Haasse variant. Charles d'Orléans may be seen as an "existentialist" hero-to-be but in fifteenth-century garb. In this process of becoming, one can discern three phases. The first is the phase of *recognition*. Charles d'Orléans passively undergoes reality, which, like Sisyphus, he experiences as a burden. His is a world in which he, against his wishes, always has to be something, always has to be someone. Conditioned by circumstances, he does not have the courage to take his fate into his own hands, to free himself from the stifling straitjacket of duties and responsibilities. Slowly, very slowly, following much pain and many doubts, he arrives at the conviction that the life he is leading is basically meaningless and that it is up to him to give meaning to it. He thinks he may achieve this by withdrawing from reality. This leads to the second phase: *escape to Blois*. Charles d'Orléans retires to his castle at Blois, his "ivory tower," to indulge his love of poetry; but this proves to be no solution. Plagued by feelings of unrest, he ultimately comes to see that his escape was meaningless, as meaningless as the life he once led. Like the protagonists in the later works of Camus, he comes to the realization that he can truly be himself only in the encounter with the other, where he will be both one and all (*Zelfportret*, 115), that he has to "strive for the state of the self from which one can get nearest to other human beings, where the *sum-pathein* becomes a living and life-giving experience" (*Zelfportret*, 192). This state, the third phase, is perhaps best referred to as the *state of conscious being*.

RECOGNITION

Charles d'Orléans's attempt to understand his position and duties in life dates from an early age. As he himself puts it in the novel: "When I was young, I often asked myself bitterly why so heavy a burden had been laid precisely on my shoulders, why I had to carry out a task which was too much for my strength."[6] From Charles's confession it becomes clear that he has been conditioned by his high birth: he is a prey to fate, destined to become a leading figure of the House of Orléans in a world torn by feudal conflict. From his earliest years he finds himself in a straitjacket of duties and responsibilities from which, for aristocratic cum ideological reasons, he cannot escape. After all, a nobleman, it was felt, could do little else except realize his fate, that is, meet his duties. He was expected to perform the greatest of deeds in the public interest, deeds which, as we know, have been recorded in all kinds of literary and historiographic texts, epic poetry and chronicles, all commissioned by the nobility in an attempt to justify and perpetuate its privileged status.

Charles d'Orléans accepts his fate, though not wholeheartedly.[7] He knows that he is unfit for the task that rests on his shoulders. Although he has many opportunities to choose for himself, or to act on his own authority, his skepticism, his incompetence at making decisions, or, when necessary, to act, turn him into a pawn moved to and fro across the political chessboard by relatives and opponents alike (237–358). In spite of his awareness of his own shortcomings, he does not rebel. Nor does he evade his duties. He makes the best of a bad job, aware that he allows his life to be dictated by others. In fact, nothing or no one is capable of preventing him from fulfilling his predestined duty, which he considers sacred. Not even love can deter him, although he has developed an intense affection for his second wife, Bonne d'Armagnac, whom he originally married against his will, because it was his duty, the marriage having been arranged. In fact, he has come to love Bonne so intensely that "in her honor he had ordered the sleeve of his tunic [to be] embroidered with the opening words of a love song . . . Madame, I am overjoyed. My wife, never have I been happy as I am now" (336).

In the novelist's view, Charles is unacquainted with the classical conflict between love and duty, the controversy that was to fuel the plots of an endless series of novels and plays well beyond the Middle Ages. In fact, when duty, as he takes it, calls him to the field of Agincourt to defend the French cause against the English, he makes love, personified by Bonne, subservient to it in a near fatalistic manner. He does not choose for himself (love), he does not decide to take his fate into his own hands, and the consequences are dire indeed. Significantly and symbolically, he gets stuck in the mud at Agincourt. He "managed to stay on his feet, up to his ankles in a mash of mud . . . Then he fell in the mud beside his dead horse" (350).

Thus, Charles collapses under the weight he had to carry: he is a Sisyphus who persists in "unconscious being," meaning in his "un-happiness." This "un-happiness" is represented in aptly concrete terms here: he succumbs to the tenacity of the fate which, as he still believes, is his, due to time and circumstances, the fate which he has not (yet) claimed as his own. He is the prototype of the human being who does not realize himself because he refuses to be "free."[8] And indeed, no less fittingly, Charles is taken prisoner and carried away to England where, in the prime of his life, he is forced into inactivity for twenty-five years (363–467).

During his imprisonment in England he comes to write poetry, but even this is not the result of any free choice. The circumstances of life, as it were, force him finally to give way to a deep, inner urge that is of long standing, an urge that he had suppressed with a feeling of shame before because he believed that for a man of his social status it was not appropriate to dabble in rhyming: "Secretly he [had been] ashamed of this urge. He had never heard that a man thought about such things" (210). In England, Charles starts to write poetry out of boredom. It is a way to pass the time, as he himself openly acknowledges, but also a means of warding off a depression that is lying in wait to take possession of him: "Charles, who lapsed into melancholy when he had nothing to distract his thoughts, began to compose commendably intricate couplets" (364). And after a while, he has no alternative, particularly since he is no longer permitted to correspond with his wife: "These ballads are substitutes for the letters he is not allowed to write" (399).

Following his release, it is against his will but without complaining that he resumes his role as the political leader of the House of Orléans. In this capacity a new duty awaits him, a duty which, once again, is imposed in despite of himself. On behalf of England and of Burgundy, he begins to operate as a traveling ambassador for peace, trying to bring the warring parties that are destroying France closer together (471–515). His ambition is great, believing as he does that this is his duty, but he nevertheless remains a kind of robot, acting on the promptings of others. In brief, he sets out to improve the world, but against his will. He continues to believe that, due to his high birth, he is predestined to serve his people and his country, but he is only too aware that he lacks the competence to do so successfully. More than anything, he wants to retire to the peace and quiet of his study at the castle of Blois.

Charles's dull resignation to his sacred duty, precluding any choice and robbing him of any opportunity to take Fate into his own hands, comes to an end after his visit (still as a political assignment) to René d'Anjou. This meeting is to prove the turning point in the development of Charles's character (515–20), the beginning of the realization that life, as he had lived it up to that point, was meaningless, and that it is up to him to give meaning to it himself. In short, a milestone on the way to "conscious being," the milestone of comprehension.[9] Symbolically, René lures him into a kind of courtyard of oblivion—"Charles felt remarkably carefree, as though he had partaken of the nectar of oblivion" (516)—where he is made to see that the world which he is still serving with such impotent ambition is merely a world of appearances: "What do you call the world? Conferences, affairs of state, war, diplomatic maneuvering, money worries, obligations to all the world and his wife? . . . All things . . . are only dreams and illusions, lighter than smoke" (518). Next, René d'Anjou points out to him another world, allegedly the "real" world, the world of art:

> he pointed at the paintings: holy pictures, scenes from mythology, emblematic figures. "That is the world; there is the world for *me*," he said, his voice filled with affection. "During the hours I spent on that, I felt a completely fulfilled man."
>
> (*Dark Wood*, 518)

Charles d'Orléans can do little else but acknowledge the truth of René's views:

> "I have often thought almost the same thing . . . But I was never able to express the idea so clearly as you, Monseigneur. I have never dared to suppose that poetry could constitute the meaning and the purpose of my life. I thought I had . . . and have . . . many other responsibilities to perform."
>
> (*Dark Wood*, 518)

Finally, King René d'Anjou manages to get him to swear that from now on he shall choose for himself, meaning choose for poetry:

> "Swear that you will not disavow the deepest desires of your heart, that you will no longer resist the muse who is our truest friend and mistress."
>
> (*Dark Wood*, 519)

Charles d'Orléans complies and swears the oath: "Charles raised his right hand in a gesture of avowal. It seemed to him that he had never made a more significant promise" (519–20).

THE ESCAPE

After long hesitation, fully in accordance with his character, Charles d'Orléans enacts the vow made to René d'Anjou in the "fairy garden." Finally, as he is already nearing the age of sixty, he chooses for himself, for the vocation of a poet. He finally retires from the "world" where he always had to do something or be someone. Put differently, even though he has comprehended and become conscious, he flees from "conscious being." Of course, he chooses, he cannot do anything other, but he makes the wrong choice (*Zelfportret,* 79–80); his choice is as erroneous as that of the suicide, Camus would argue, or of the believer, who puts his or her faith in the transcendental, in God, or in an ideology.[10] Eventually, with his third wife, Marie de Cleves, Charles retires to his castle at Blois where he fully devotes himself to poetry:

> *Demourer en repos je veuil,*
> *Et en paix faire mon recueil,*
> *Sans guerre avoir aucunement.*

I want to be to myself, and in peace I want to collect my poems, far from all strife.[11]

In her *Zelfportret* (or, Self-Portrait), Haasse devotes attention to the final decision of Charles d'Orléans, a decision so difficult to reach and realize. Charles d'Orléans's life story, Haasse argues, "insofar as it may be reconstructed from the chronicles and from his own poetry, seems to me a striking example of the interaction between talent and circumstances, one long chain reaction, which ultimately leads the subject to an insight into his own failure as a 'man of action'" (68). The interaction between circumstances and talent, from Charles's earliest childhood on, features prominently in the early part of the novel, depicting the acceptance phase. Charles d'Orléans seems to have inherited his poetic genius from his father Louis. Louis d'Orléans was highly interested in poetry and, amid a vast group of artists, would act as host to the most famous poets of his day, including Eustache Deschamps and Christine de Pisan. Occasionally, too, Louis d'Orléans would himself write poetry. He could, as the novel has it, "write a really melodious verse when the mood was on him" (364). It is curious indeed that one of these poems—"En la forest de longue attente," attributed to Louis d'Orléans by the novelist—should have helped Haasse to the novel's title.

Charles d'Orléans's talent for poetry manifests itself in accordance with the typically romantic notion of the budding poet. Charles is a quiet, introverted boy with remarkable skills of perception. He does not play much, and certainly plays no wild games with his brothers. He prefers the library to his playing ground. There he rummages through books, innocently and ignorantly awaiting the moment when he will be taught to read: "He thought that there could be no pleasure greater than to be able to decipher the rows of beautiful characters in the books" (160). Once he can read, however, there are no holds barred:

> When lessons were over, Charles usually lingered in the room filled with books and writing implements . . . He was continually overcome by amazement that a world filled with adventure and beauty could rise from behind the black letters; that within a single page, a life could unfold, that death and heroism could be enclosed in a few strokes on the paper . . . Reading in the study, Charles lost all track of time. . . . In the summer he did not hear the wood crackling on the hearth.
>
> (*In a Dark Wood Wandering*, 162)

Charles soon discovers that he has a need to put a pen to paper, and to write of life around him.[12] However, before he can, with a carefree disposition, and without any feelings of shame or pangs of conscience, devote himself to the art of poetry, he will need to distance himself from his acknowledged duty. In other words, he must flee.

In his Blois castle he lives far from the world of duty. He lives in an ivory tower, which, as Haasse puts it in her autobiographical writings, had always been his secret longing, since in that case "he would not need to fight against his fear of reality, which was very likely a basic character trait of Charles" (*Zelfportret,* 69). And, as the novel has it:

> The outside world no longer mattered to him; he did not even want to know what was happening in the cities and territories through which he had once traveled, filled with desire to serve King and Kingdom . . . He felt himself comfortably hidden, securely stowed away in the silence of Nonchaloir.
>
> (*In a Dark Wood Wandering*, 549)

His entire existence in this "carefree, sunny domestic Blois" is dedicated to the art of poetry. He reads and writes much, mainly rondels which had just become fashionable.[13] In his carefree existence, "[t]he only disturbance he had to endure was the restlessness which poetic inspiration brought with it" (549). Charles also enjoys organizing *concours poétiques:*

> poetry contests are the order of the day. . . . Nothing pleases him more than to gather guests, officials and servants around after the evening meal when work is done, and propose a theme to them which they must then work into the form of a ballad or a rondel.

(*Dark Wood*, 537)

He loves to discuss his craft with fellow poets who are always welcome, like François Villon, who enjoys "the privilege of coming and going as he pleased in the ducal residence" (*Dark Wood*, 560).

All conditions for a carefree life in peace thus seem to be fulfilled. Nevertheless he must eventually recognize—he is ten years older then—that his escape inward, to the ivory tower of poetry, has not really made him happy (550). The problem occupies him daily, and he fails to find an explanation. Charles d'Orléans remains still "in a dark wood wandering," unhappy because the path he has chosen turns out to be a dead end: he was expecting to find himself, but ultimately does not since he still fails to realize that he cannot discover himself without discovering the other, that the other is essential for his existence (Sartre, 41), or, as Haasse herself has put it: it is because he stubbornly continues to resist the notion of "we," because he is not prepared for the relationship with the other, not "committed" (*Zelfportret*, 179–80). Again, it takes someone else—his wife, Marie de Cleves, on this occasion—to help him out of his predicament. This time, however, Charles is shown the only right way. During a nocturnal conversation with Marie—which is a parallel to the exchange between Charles and René d'Anjou—Charles learns that if he really wants to become happy, he will need to give up the facile and self-centered motto that has for years been inextricably associated with his comfortable retreat, "Nonchaloir":

> "[W]hoever is self-centered and accepts love without giving it, feels depressed by day and lies awake at night, tormented by bitter thoughts. You are benevolent and friendly to everyone, but that is not praiseworthy because it costs you no effort. You do not really love the world or people, Monseigneur. You meditate only on yourself and live hidden in your own thoughts. And whoever beats at your door to gain entrance to your heart is not admitted."
>
> (*Dark Wood*, 551)

Orléans will have to choose once again, not for himself this time, but for the Other. Only if he fully opens himself up to that Other, will he achieve full "conscious being," which Haasse elsewhere defines as "the state of the self from which one can get nearest to other human beings, where the *sum-pathein* becomes a living and life-giving experience" (*Zelfportret*, 192).

THE STATE OF CONSCIOUS BEING

In the final section of the novel (552–74), Charles d'Orléans indeed opts for the Other: he comes to the realization that he cannot disavow the Other and act as though he were alone, that he is both one and all, and that as a result he must allow his own self, his own individual reality, to merge with the reality of the Other, to merge with a collective reality, which Haasse also calls an assertion of "human dignity," which is easily identified as Camus's "human nature." From then on, Charles passionately chooses sides with "human beings," always and everywhere, investing his entire, free personality for the benefit of others, for the others as a whole (*Zelfportret,* 118). He becomes a "humanist" in the sense of the term used by Camus. He establishes a closer relationship with his wife, and their relationship gains in intimacy. They have children, and if Charles had never even shown an interest in the daughter born of his first marriage, to Isabelle of France, he now shows genuine concern:

> He competed with Marie in expressing his affection for the little girl. How profoundly interesting everything was which concerned her. . . . The breaking through of a little tooth, the first step, the first word, provided Charles the opportunity to make his child the center of domestic festivities.
>
> (*Dark Wood,* 553)

He is happy now, and wants to share his happiness with others: "Charles had three golden écus divided among the stableboys and kitchen servants . . . with the request that they drink to her health" (553). After the birth of his son he "distributed rich presents to everyone who came to congratulate him and entreated each one to pray for the child's well-being" (562–63). Moreover, at his own initiative, Charles develops a number of activities obviously in the interest of his progeny: "he wanted to act in his children's interest; he reproached himself bitterly for having wasted so many years in pleasant tranquillity. For his son's sake he had to enter into important relationships, to conclude alliances" (565). Driven by this interest, he fights to maintain his Italian property at Asta, all for the sake of his son. "[H]e was even prepared to go so far as to join the ranks of the rebel princes" (565) who tried to crush the ever growing power of the king. But in his concern for his son, he does not forget his other relatives. He decides to defend his son-in-law, the Duke d'Alençon (the widower to his daughter Isabelle), when he is accused of high treason. Charles feels no sympathy for the Duke d'Alençon, but assists him nevertheless since it secures the future of the duke's children and grandchildren. Something similar occurs in the case of his young nephew François of Brittany. The King of France expresses "his lack of confidence in the good faith of François of Brittany who was on such a friendly footing with the envoys of England and Burgundy." Charles, in response, determines "to see the King and attempt to cleanse his name of all suspicion" (567).

In brief, Charles d'Orléans becomes a committed hero, even though his engagement is accompanied by suffering and pain— "The pain caused by breaking open oneself."[14] Charles's suffering is serious. His eyesight fades, he is quickly tired, and often feels dizzy and faint. Also his heart is giving way—"his heart had been troubling him again for some time" (567). Charles, however, persists, and it will ultimately mean his death.

A comparable kind of engagement or commitment may be observed in the poetry that the historical Charles continued to write.[15] But on this score, Haasse remains silent. Instead, she notes that "Charles read or wrote in the quiet library" (559). As Jacques Charpier notes in his biography of Charles d'Orléans, the egotism that characterized the ballads written in England makes way for a more elevated view of mankind.

> Orléans continues to place himself at the center, but more to function as an example (to the Other), in order to illustrate how much man may suffer. The time that passes is no longer the time which prolongs his imprisonment or that delays his ultimate release from prison; it has become the time that passes for everyone, and which removes us ever further from all our beautiful experiences of the past, without offering us anything in return. Love, which caused him such sweet pain before, is now no more than a game that he had rather others played, with the warning that there was little to be gained from it.[16]

The poetry of the historical Charles d'Orléans, then, testifies to the same slow process of developing self-awareness, and the discovery of the Other, which, as Haasse has remarked on numerous occasions, is the essence of writing. Writing ought to be considered as a process of developing awareness (*Zelfportret*, 75), as a means of discovering "a greater reality and another sense of freedom" (*Persoonsbewijs*, 60), "to express that which is more important than the writing itself: conscious living" (*Zelfportret*, 192), regardless of the pain it causes.[17]

In a Dark Wood Wandering traces the development of Charles d'Orléans into an "existentialist" hero. The term "existentialist" is best used in inverted commas here since, as I noted earlier, we are dealing with a free interpretation of the existentialist heritage, the so-called "Haasse variant," which is essentially an amalgam of statements formulated by Sartre on the one hand, and, on the other, mainly by Camus. Thus Charles may be seen as the embodiment of the Sartrean adage: Man is what he makes of himself. A human being, at first afraid to choose, a coward, reclining in deedlessness: sinking into the mud of Agincourt, pining away during his twenty-five years of captivity in England; only once he has conquered the fear to choose, only once he has dared condemn himself to "liberty" (a mode of liberty that is unthinkable without the Other), does he become a true human being. Equally, and perhaps more appropriately, one may see Charles as a fifteenth-century avatar of Camus's Sisyphus, who very gradually comes to see the meaninglessness of existence. It is a process of developing consciousness which first erroneously leads him to escape into the illusory oblivion of poetry, but which ultimately leads him to the conscious being of the *homme révolté*: he discovers the Other, with whom he wants to live in blissful union, in "sympathy" ("sumpathein," in Haasse's view, as "a feeling of solidarity, mildness, and tolerance").[18] Indeed he establishes a bond of solidarity with the Other, in deeds and in words committed to the page, "in continually new situations which call for a re-orientation of the self, and new self-scrutiny," in the "unchanging awareness that the individual is called upon each minute to form a new judgment, to make new decisions, to act" (*Persoonsbewijs*, 105). As the numerous parallels between Haasse's novel and her contemporary prose suggest, *In a Dark Wood Wandering* was the budding Dutch novelist's orientation of the self in sympathy with that multiple Other in historical, national, and gender terms, her predecessor Charles d'Orléans.

NOTES TO "HELLA S. HAASSE'S *IN A DARK WOOD WANDERING:* CHARLES D'ORLÉANS IN AN 'EXISTENTIALIST' *BILDUNGSROMAN*"

Translated from the Dutch by Ton Hoenselaars.

1. Hella S. Haasse is a popular Dutch novelist and critic. She was born in the Dutch Indies (Batavia, 1918), and left for the Netherlands in 1938 to study in Amsterdam. Since that time she has been active as a writer. After writing poetry and cabaret sketches, she opted for narrative prose. Her novels include *Het woud*

der verwachting (1949; trans. into English as *In a Dark Wood Wandering,* 1989), *De scharlaken stad* (1952), *De ingewijden* (1957), *Cider voor arme mensen* (1960), *Een nieuwer testament* (1966), *Huurders en onderhuurders* (1971), *Mevrouw Bentinck of onverenigbaarheid van karakter: een ware geschiedenis* (1978), *De wegen der verbeelding* (1983), *Berichten van het blauwe huis* (1986), and *Heren van de thee* (1992). She is also the author of short stories (like *Oeroeg,* 1948), essays, and autobiographical prose including *Zelfportret als legkaart* (1954) and *Persoonsbewijs* (1967).

Charles d'Orléans (1394–1465) was the son of Valentine Visconti and Louis, Duke of Orléans (brother to the mentally deranged King Charles VI). After the death of his father, murdered in 1407 by followers of John the Bold, Charles d'Orléans became the leader of the Armagnacs, one of the two noble families competing for the rule over France. At the Battle of Agincourt (1415), Charles d'Orléans was taken prisoner by the English and spent twenty-five years in an English prison. Back in France, he resumed his interest in politics, but in 1448 he retired to his castle at Blois a disappointed man. He was productive as a poet during his periods of political inactivity: his years in England, and his retirement. He wrote mainly ballads, songs, and rondels, which are characterized by a melancholy tone, and an introspective glance. Occasionally, however, they are also lighthearted. The poet himself is always the central figure.

2. Haasse, *Zelfportret als legkaart* (Amsterdam: De Bezige Bij, 1961), 69.

3. Haasse, *Persoonsbewijs* (Bruges and Utrecht: Desclée de Brouwer, 1967), 60.

4. Haasse, *Zelfportret als legkaart,* 81.

5. The years between 1935 and 1945 represent a period of drastic change for Haasse: she finishes secondary school in Batavia, and, by herself, leaves for the Netherlands to study Scandinavian language and literature at the University of Amsterdam (1938). She discontinued these studies in 1941. Next she trained at the Amsterdam Drama School until 1943. She got married in 1944, and had her first child at the end of that same year.

6. Haasse, *In a Dark Wood Wandering,* trans. Edith Kaplan, Kalman Kaplan, and Anita Miller (London: Arrow Books, 1989), 570. Further references to the novel will be to this edition.

7. One might profitably compare Charles d'Orléans and Albert Camus's Sisyphus before he knew the "happiness" of "conscious being": he is blind to anything but his reality, which is the task allotted to him, and with the execution of which he fills all his days without any prospects of change. As Haasse has put it in a different context, he carries his own reality with him, wherever he goes, whatever he does (*Zelfportret,* 15).

8. On the existentialist notion of freedom, see Jean-Paul Sartre, *L'Existentialisme est un humanisme,* Collection Pensées (Paris: Les Éditions Nagel, 1965), 47.

9. The way to "conscious being" is still a long one. To speak with Camus, Charles does not rebel.

10. See also, Haasse, *Zelfportret:* "our only hope lies in fighting, again and again, the supremacy of whichever dogma" (19).

11. Charles d'Orléans, *Poésies,* ed. P. Champion, 2 vols. (Paris: Champion, 1956), 2: 501.

12. *In a Dark Wood Wandering,* 210. The historical Charles d'Orléans wrote his first poem at the age of ten (*Le Livre contre tout péché*): a series of rhymed moral lessons, assigned to him by his private teacher. See *Poésies,* 2: 545–50.

13. Charles d'Orléans's poetry is written in the artificial and allegorical style of his time. It is courtly in a traditional sense, and conventional, despite its lyrical elegance. Just as in reality, in his poetry, too, Charles d'Orléans was thoroughly conditioned by his environment, Haasse assumes: even as a poet, he did not succeed in breaking free from the tight rules. See also *Persoonsbewijs*, 60.

14. *Zelfportret*, 181. One may recall the *Myth of Sisyphus*, in which Camus demonstrates how crushing a task it may be for the individual to maintain the state of conscious being. See also, Albert Camus, *L'Homme révolté* (Paris: Gallimard, 1951).

15. In 1460, Charles d'Orléans stopped writing poetry altogether. At that time he was suffering from gout, and his eyes were bad. See Champion, 1: vii.

16. Jacques Charpier, *Charles d'Orléans* (Paris: Seghers, 1958), 75.

17. I.e. "The pain caused by breaking open oneself" (*Zelfportret*, 181).

18. Haasse, *Zelfportret*, 79.

Notes on contributors

GAMIN G. BARTLE teaches in the Department of Germanic Languages and Literatures at the University of Virginia in Charlottesville. She is currently completing a dissertation on *The Women in Mann*.

HARM DEN BOER is Assistant Professor of Spanish at the University of Amsterdam. His research focuses on Iberian literature and culture of the sixteenth and seventeenth centuries. He wrote his Ph.D. on the literature in Spanish and Portuguese of the Sephardic Jews in Amsterdam. His major publications include *La literatura sefardí de Amsterdam* (1995); and "La Biblia de Ferrara y otras traducciones españoles de la Biblia entre los Sefardíes de Europa occidental," in *Introducción a la Biblia de Ferrara,* ed. I. Hassán (1994).

PHYLLIS RUGG BROWN is Associate Professor of English at Santa Clara University and specializes in comparative medieval and early modern literature, especially poetry and literature by women. Her publications range from "Beccel and the Theme of Death in *Guthlac B*" in *Mediævalia* (1996), to "Penance and Pilgrimage in *The Divine Comedy* and *The Song of Roland*" in *SMART* (1993), and "Louise Labé and Semiramis: A Feminist Reading" for *Women in French Studies*. Brown is currently working on two books, a study of myth in the writings of Louise Labé and, with William P. Mahrt, a study of Guillaume de Machaut's virelais.

JATTIE ENKLAAR teaches modern German literature at Utrecht University. She is the author of *Adalbert Stifter: Landschaft und Raum* (1984) and co-editor of a number of volumes including *Albert Vigoleis Thelen* (1988); *Brandenburg-Preußen und die Niederlande: zur Dynamik einer Nachbarschaft* (1988); *Hermann Broch, 1886–1986* (1987); *Ungenaue Grenze: Deutsch-Niederländische Beziehungen in Vergangenheit und Gegenwart* (1994); and *Wechseltausch: Übersetzen als Kulturvermittlung: Deutschland und die Niederlande* (1995).

LOIS FEUER teaches in the departments of English and Humanities at California State University, Dominguez Hills. She holds a doctoral degree from the University of California, Irvine. She has written primarily on Shakespeare and on modern fiction. She held an appointment as a Fellow of the American Council of Learned Societies in 1993–94. Having recently ended a term as Associate Dean of the College of Arts and Sciences of her university, her current project is a book-length study of the author as providential figure.

ALEID FOKKEMA teaches in the English Department of Utrecht University. She has published various articles on postmodern fiction and postcolonial poetry, and is the author of *Postmodern Characters: A Study of Characterization in British and American Postmodern Fiction* (1991). Her current research is concerned with the relations between postmodernism and postcolonialism.

CHRISTIEN FRANKEN is a Lecturer in the English Department of the Free University in Amsterdam. She has held teaching and research posts in the Department of Women's Studies and the English Department at Utrecht University. She has also worked as an art critic, as editor of the Dutch *Journal of Women's Studies,* and has contributed to several journals on contemporary feminist and literary subjects. She is the author of *A. S. Byatt: Art, Authorship and Creativity* (London: Macmillan, forthcoming).

PAUL FRANSSEN teaches in the English Department of Utrecht University. He has published various articles on English literature, mainly of the early modern period. He is currently working on a full-length study of appropriations of Shakespeare as a literary character. He is editor of *Folio,* the journal of the Shakespeare Society of the Low Countries.

ROBERT HAYNES, a former M. L. Brittain Fellow in Writing at Georgia Institute of Technology, is an Associate Professor of English at Texas A&M International University in Laredo, Texas. He has published a number of reviews and reference articles. His essay "Thomas Lupset's *A Treatise of Charitie:* Dialogue as Charity in Action" appeared in the 1990 volume of *Renaissance Papers.*

PETER HAYS is Professor of English at the University of California, Davis. He is the author of *The Limping Hero in Literature* (1971), *Ernest Hemingway* (1990), and *A Concordance to Hemingway's In*

Our Time (1990). He has also published on F. Scott Fitzgerald and Tennessee Williams.

TON HOENSELAARS is Associate Professor in the English Department of Utrecht University. He is the author of *Images of Englishmen and Foreigners in the Drama of Shakespeare and His Contemporaries* (1992). He has edited, alone or with others, *Shakespeare's Italy* (1993, revised edition 1997); *Denken over Dichten* (1993); *Reclamations of Shakespeare* (1994); *The Italian World of English Renaissance Drama* (1998); *Vreemd Volk* (1998); and *Jeanne d'Arc entre les nations* (1998). He has also written on Emily Brontë, James Joyce, T. E. Lawrence and Joseph Conrad. He is the founding Chairman of the Shakespeare Society of the Low Countries, and the managing editor of its journal, *Folio*.

FREDERICK M. KEENER is Professor of English at Hofstra University, New York. His publications include *English Dialogues of the Dead* (1973), *An Essay on Pope* (1974), and *The Chain of Becoming: The Philosophical Tale, the Novel, and a Neglected Realism of the Enlightenment: Swift, Montesquieu, Voltaire, Johnson, and Austen* (1983); *Eighteenth-Century Women and the Arts*, co-edited with Susan E. Lorsch (1988); the *Penguin Classics* edition of *Virgil's* Aeneid, *Translated by John Dryden* (1997); and essays toward a history of the comprehension of literature.

CHRISTOPHER KLEINHENZ is Professor of Italian and Chair of the Medieval Studies Program at the University of Wisconsin-Madison. He received his Ph.D. from Indiana University and has held fellowships from the Fulbright Commission, the Institute for Research in the Humanities, and the Newberry Library. He has directed major curriculum development and research tools grants from the National Endowment for the Humanities. In addition to serving as editor of *Dante Studies*, he has published widely in medieval Italian literature, including a book on *The Early Italian Sonnet* and collections of essays on *Medieval Manuscripts and Textual Criticism, Medieval Studies in North America*, and *Saint Augustine, the Bishop*. He is currently vice-president of the American Association of Teachers of Italian and past president of the American Boccaccio Association and of the Medieval Association of the Midwest. He also serves as chair of the CARA committee of the Medieval Academy of America. His teaching and research interests center on Italian literature of the Duecento and Trecento, manuscript studies, and art and literature in medieval Italy.

JELLE KOOPMANS teaches medieval French literature at the University of Amsterdam, The Netherlands. His main research interests are the subculture of parisian worldly dramatists in the Middle Ages, and the culture of ambiguity in *Rhétoriqueur*-poetry. He has published several critical editions of forgotten or unknown texts (*Receuil de sermons joyeux*, 1988; and *Receuil des repues franches de maistre François Villon*, 1995). His recent study *Le Théâtre des exclus au Moyen age* (1997) establishes a link between medieval drama and exclusion rites like *charivaris*, witch trials, and popular heresy.

RIA LEMAIRE-MERTENS is Professor of Portuguese and Brazilian literature at the University of Poitiers in France, and head of the Brazilian research group of its Center for Latin-American Studies, which possesses a rich collection of Brazilian popular literature, called *literatura de cordel*. She also coordinates the interdisciplinary and international research-program called "Comparative Studies in Oral Traditions and their Relationships with Written Culture."

Her main passion as a researcher is comparative studies in medieval literature, with a special interest in nineteenth and twentieth-century literature in Brazil, including the interrelations between gender, race, and the definition of national identity, as related to a systematic theoretical and epistemological questioning of the traditional dichotomy which opposes History to Literature. She presently coordinates a French-Brazilian interdisciplinary research project in this field.

ROSELLA MAMOLI ZORZI is Professor of Anglo-American literature at the University Ca'Foscari of Venice. She has published full-length studies on William Faulkner and the Utopian Novel, and a large number of essays on Henry James, Gertrude Stein, and others. She has also published widely on the representation of Venice in American Literature and on the relationship between writers and artists.

MARTIJN RUS teaches medieval and early modern French literature at Utrecht University. He is the author of *De la conception à l'au-delà: Textes et documents français d'un siècle qui n'en est pas un (1450–1550)* (1995).

GRETCHEN ELIZABETH SMITH received her Ph.D. in Theater from Indiana University, Bloomington, Indiana, in 1996. She is Assistant Professor and Head of Playwriting and Critical Studies at the Meadows School of Arts at Southwestern Methodist University in Dallas, Texas. The major focus of her scholarship has been in the area of Renaissance and Baroque festival performance.

MATTHEW STEGGLE holds a Ph.D. from the University of Oxford where he is currently engaged in freelance teaching and research. His recent publications include: "'The Memorandum,' Sacraments and Ewelme Church" in *"The Muses Females Are": Martha Moulsworth and Other Women Writers of the English Renaissance*, ed. Robert C. Evans and Anne C. Little (1995); "Rhetorical Ordering in Moulsworth's 'Memorandum,'" in *Critical Matrix: The Princeton Journal of Women, Gender, and Culture* (1996); and "A New Marprelate Allusion," in *Notes and Queries* (1997). He is a contributing editor to the forthcoming *Ben Jonson Encyclopedia*, and his current research project is on the Renaissance reception of Ancient Greek Literature.

MARTINE L. DE VOS is a Lecturer in Utrecht University's English Department and American Studies Program. She is also Coordinator of Graduate Studies at the university's Research Institute for History and Culture. She received a Ph.D. in English at Duke University (U.S.), writing a dissertation under the supervision of professor Frank Lentricchia entitled, *The "Imperative Duty" of the "Serious" Artist: The Literary Politics of William Dean Howells and Ezra Pound* (1995).

Index

This index lists personal names and titles only. Given the phenomenon—unique to this essay collection—that certain authors, composers, or painters may also be fictional characters in the works of other authors, composers, painters, or movie directors, we have adopted a special method to avoid possible misunderstanding. We have listed all personal names as is done in regular indexes. In addition, in those instances where an author, composer, or painter as character is concerned, we have included an additional cross-reference (*See also*) to the work or works in which the artist occurs as a character

312 INDEX

Verlaine, Paul, 15, 78. See also *Verlaine* (Arthur van Schendel)
Verlaine (Arthur van Schendel), 15
Vermeer, Johannes, 26. See also *Johannes Vermeer* (Cocky van Bokhoven)
"Verses on the Death of Dr Swift, D. S. P. D." (Jonathan Swift), 140
Vida ejemplar y heroica de Miguel de Cervantes Saavedra (Luis Astrana Martín), 274
Vidor, Charles, 32
vie imaginaire, 15–16, 77
vie romancée, 15, 16, 17, 19, 20, 21, 23, 26, 34
Vies imaginaires (Marcel Schwob), 15, 77
Vigny, Alfred de, 28–29
Villon, François [François de Moncorbier], 15, 17, 32, 68–79, 275, 283. Works: *Ballad of the Appeal*, 70; *Ballad of the Hanged*, 70; *Ballad of Villon to His Mistress*, 75; *Ballade pour Robert d'Estouteville*, 74; *Lais*, 69, 76; *Testament*, 69, 70, 73, 74, 76, 77, 78. See also *Baal* (Bertolt Brecht); *Beloved Rogue* (dir. Alan Crosland); *Brief Hour of François Villon* (John Erskine); *For Love of a Sinner* (Robert Gordon Anderson); *François Villon* (Karel E. Eykman); *François Villon* (A. A. Noelte); *François Villon* (André Zwoboda); *François Villon oder die Legende eines Rebellen* (Fritz Habeck); *The Free Meals of Master Villon and His Companions* (Anon.); *If I Were King* (dir. Frank Lloyd); *The Judgment of François Villon* (Herbert Edward Palmer); "A Lodging for the Night" (R. L. Stevenson); *Le Roman de François Villon* (Francis Carco); *Der Scholar vom linken Galgen* (Fritz Habeck); *Le Testament de François Villon* (Ezra Pound); *The Vagabond King* (Michael Curtiz); *Villon: Comédie-héroï–comique* (Jean Alphonse Azals); *Villon, den ganz Paris gekannt* (Johanna Hoffmann); *Villon és a többiek* (Kardos G. György); *Villon the Vagabond* (Otis Skinner)

Villon: Comédie-héroï–comique (Jean Alphonse Azals), 72
Villon, den ganz Paris gekannt (Johanna Hoffmann), 74
Villon és a többiek (Kardos G. György), 17, 68
Villon, sa vie et son temps (Pierre Champion), 69
Villon the Vagabond (Otis Skinner), 68
Vindication (Frances Sherwood), 26
Virgil (Publius Vergilius Maro), 12, 16, 21, 23, 52–67, 118, 119, 120, 122, 124–25, 126, 128, 131, 213–27. Works: *Aeneid*, 12, 53, 55, 61, 63, 124, 213, 215, 217, 219–20, 222–23; *Eclogues*, 12, 54, 55, 61, 218; *Georgics*, 55, 63. See also *The Death of Virgil* (Hermann Broch); *Divine Comedy* (Dante Alighieri); *Poetaster* (Ben Jonson)
Vita nuova (Dante Alighieri), 67
Vita Virgili (Suetonius), 66
Vivaldi, Antonio, 34
Vogler, Georg Joseph, 34. See also "Abt Vogler" (Robert Browning)
Volcano Lover, The (Susan Sontag), 21
Voltaire [François Marie Arouet], 14, 21, 23, 144, 145, 268. See also *Le Roi attend* (George Sand)
Von ewiger Liebe: Ein Schumann-Brahms-Roman (Hermann Richter), 34
Vonnegut, Jr., Kurt, 17. See also *Back to School* (dir. Alan Metter)

Wagner, Richard, 17, 27, 32, 195, 198. Works: *Lohengrin*, 32; *Die Meistersinger von Nürnberg*, 17; *Parsifal*, 32; *Tannhäuser*, 32; *Tristan und Isolde*, 32. See also *On Mozart* (Anthony Burgess)
Waiting for the Moon (dir. Jill Godmilow), 32
Walker, Joan, 15
War of the Theaters, 12, 118–30
Watson, William, 193
"Weary Hour, A" (Thomas Mann), 198–99, 202
Webbe, George, 120
Weigand, Hermann, 227
Weiss, David, 34